GW00818547

Existentialist Engagement in
Wallace, Eggers and Foer

Existentialist Engagement in Wallace, Eggers and Foer

A Philosophical Analysis of Contemporary American Literature

Allard den Dulk

Bloomsbury Academic
An imprint of Bloomsbury Publishing Inc

B L O O M S B U R Y
NEW YORK · LONDON · NEW DELHI · SYDNEY

Bloomsbury Academic

An imprint of Bloomsbury Publishing Inc

1385 Broadway
New York
NY 10018
USA

50 Bedford Square
London
WC1B 3DP
UK

www.bloomsbury.com

BLOOMSBURY and the Diana logo are trademarks of Bloomsbury Publishing Plc

First published 2015

© Allard den Dulk, 2015

All rights reserved. No part of this publication may be reproduced or
transmitted in any form or by any means, electronic or mechanical,
including photocopying, recording, or any information storage or retrieval
system, without prior permission in writing from the publishers.

No responsibility for loss caused to any individual or organization acting
on or refraining from action as a result of the material in this publication
can be accepted by Bloomsbury or the author.

Infinite Jest by David Foster Wallace. Copyright © 1996 by David Foster Wallace.
By permission of Little, Brown and Company. All rights reserved.

Significant parts of Chapter 2, 5 and 6 have appeared in, respectively:
Studies in the Novel 44.3 (2012), 325–345; *Philosophy and Literature and
the Crisis of Metaphysics*, edited by Sébastian Hüsch (Würzburg: Verlag Königshausen
& Neumann, 2011), 343–358; and *Gesturing Toward Reality: David Foster Wallace and
Philosophy*, edited by Robert K. Bolger and Scott Korb (New York: Bloomsbury, 2014),
205–227. The author has made substantial changes and additions for this book.

Library of Congress Cataloging-in-Publication Data
Dulk, Allard den, 1978– author.
Existentialist engagement in Wallace, Eggers and Foer : a philosophical
analysis of contemporary American literature / Allard den Dulk.
pages cm
Summary: "A philosophical analysis of existentialist themes in the fiction of
Wallace, Eggers and Foer"— Provided by publisher.
Includes bibliographical references.
ISBN 978-1-62892-331-5 (hardback)
1. American fiction–21st century–History and criticism.   2. Wallace, David Foster–
Criticism and interpretation.   3. Eggers, Dave–Criticism and interpretation.
4. Foer, Jonathan Safran, 1977– Everything is illuminated.   5. Existentialism in
literature.   6. Literature–Philosophy.   7. Postmodernism (Literature)–United States.
8. Irony in literature.   I. Title.
PS374.E9D85 2014
813.009'384—dc23
2014021584

ISBN: HB: 978-1-6289-2331-5
ePub: 978-1-6289-2333-9
ePDF: 978-1-6289-2334-6

Typeset by Newgen Knowledge Works (P) Ltd., Chennai, India
Printed and bound in the United States of America

Contents

List of Abbreviations

(The overview below refers to the year in which the original text was first published; for further bibliographical details of the editions used, see 'Works Cited' section)

EUP	David Foster Wallace, 'E Unibus Pluram' (1993)
IJ	David Foster Wallace, *Infinite Jest* (1996)
AHWOSG	Dave Eggers, *A Heartbreaking Work of Staggering Genius* (2000)
YSKOV	Dave Eggers, *You Shall Know Our Velocity* (2002)
EII	Jonathan Safran Foer, *Everything Is Illuminated* (2002)
ELIC	Jonathan Safran Foer, *Extremely Loud & Incredibly Close* (2005)
LF	John Barth, *Lost in the Funhouse* (1968)
AP	Bret Easton Ellis, *American Psycho* (1991)
TE	Jean-Paul Sartre, *The Transcendence of the Ego* (1936)
BN	Jean-Paul Sartre, *Being and Nothingness* (1943)
CI	Søren Kierkegaard, *The Concept of Irony, with Continual Reference to Socrates* (1841)
EO	Søren Kierkegaard, *Either/Or*, Parts 1 and 2 (1843)
CUP	Søren Kierkegaard, *Concluding Unscientific Postscript to Philosophical Fragments*, Parts 1 and 2 (1846)
PI	Ludwig Wittgenstein, *Philosophical Investigations* (1953)
MS	Albert Camus, *The Myth of Sisyphus* (1942)
R	Albert Camus, *The Rebel* (1951)

Photograph by Allard den Dulk, 2006.

Foreword: 'Love Me till My Heart Stops'

'Love Me till My Heart Stops': the words were spray-painted on the pavement with the help of a stencil. I stumbled upon them while walking down Valencia Street, in San Francisco's Mission District. I had just come from the interview I did with the American writer Dave Eggers, at the start of my research project. It turned out that, throughout the neighbourhood, here and there, short phrases like this had been stencilled onto the sidewalk. I also found 'Your Existence Gives Me Hope', and 'You Make My Dreams Come True', and many others. Of course, such texts are easily exposed as affected, wall plate pseudo-profundities, as clichés that, even if they are seen to have some initial charm, will surely lose that spark of meaning in no time. But, somehow, 'Love Me till My Heart Stops' stuck with me. It seemed to express a desire akin to the portrayal of contemporary Western life in the literary works of the group of contemporary American writers (David Foster Wallace, Dave Eggers and Jonathan Safran Foer) that I wanted to analyse. Plus, I decided that the fact that someone had written 'Fuck off!' next to the text could be read as an indication that a naïve appeal like that of the stencil succeeded in making more cynical minds uncomfortable.

I inquired at McSweeney's and 826 Valencia (Eggers's publishing company and writing school, both situated on Valencia Street) whether they perhaps had anything to do with the stencils; I was told that, although they were quite fond of the sidewalk texts, they had not been involved in their creation. As for the phrase 'Love Me till My Heart Stops': it seemed to be taken from the Talking Heads' song 'This Must Be The Place (Naive Melody)'. Perhaps this made the words even more apt: derived from a song released in 1983 (more than a decade before the novels I am researching in this study, symbolizing the recurrence of my subject), by a band from the 1980s, the heyday of cynical vacuity (in which the qualification 'naïve' was of course highly suspect), who reportedly wanted to write a real love song, consisting of simple (one could perhaps say: clichéd) declarations.

Later, I found on the internet a somewhat longer note that had allegedly appeared simultaneously with the sidewalk texts. It read:

> WE CAN save each other. We see we are falling, but as we do we must just reach out and grab hold at the same time. We will surely fall. But as we fall together, there may be no bottom to break us apart. This is our chance. Do not wait, we are our own saviors, and now is the time. (AD)

The sender is unknown. The sign-off 'AD' could be someone's initials, but it might also be a pun on 'advertisement', as most street-art is partly a protest against the commercial vandalizing of public space. The message itself might, again, be read as affected and faux-sentimental. But when taken at face value, as a serious, sincere appeal, it directly calls to mind Albert Camus's description of the solidary community of individuals who all suffer from the same absurdity – from the uncertainty and meaninglessness – of human existence. It also resembles the desire, portrayed in Eggers's *A Heartbreaking Work of Staggering Genius*, to form a 'lattice', a mutually supportive framework, with as many other people as possible.[1] All in all, the street texts seemed to symbolize a desire similar to the subject matter of my research.

This holds, above all, for 'Love Me Till My Heart Stops': for the phrase can be seen to offer a condensed expression of the engagement that is formulated by the works of the above-mentioned fiction writers. First, 'Love Me till My Heart Stops' has the form of an appeal: it is a request to be loved. Such an appeal entails openness and vulnerability on the part of the person who formulates it. As such, it is an expression of what I will regard as *sincerity*, namely the person's desire to forge a stable connection with the world outside him. Secondly, the appeal contains an element of urgent *commitment* ('till my heart stops'), as the connection between speaker and addressee has to be established within the finite, uncertain *reality* of their existence. Finally, as an appeal, 'Love Me till My Heart Stops' is of course directed at someone else: the desired connection is the connection with another person. As such, it is an expression of the desire for *community* (which is what love is). These elements – the desire for sincerity, reality-commitment and community – constitute the engagement that will be analysed in this study.[2]

We will see that the engagement, formulated by these literary works, functions in response to the contemporary existential problems of 'hyperreflexivity' and 'endless irony': that is, in response to the constant self-awareness that over the past decades has made the Western individual so suspicious of, and eager to ridicule, all pretensions to sincere social commitment, to ideals and values. As such, this study itself can also be said to be partly an exercise against our (or, at least, *my*) own ironic reflexes and constant self-conscious distrust of such pretensions – of any appeal like 'Love Me till My Heart Stops'. This philosophical work is written with the conviction that to overcome this contemporary Western predicament some things have to be taken at face value. Some things have to be trusted if meaning and, consequently, meaningful existence, is to be acquired at all. Distrust must perhaps be recurrent, but cannot be constant: it should always be replaced by trust that, when prompted by certain signals, should be questioned again.

As to the relation of this study to the engaged portrayals offered by the works of Wallace, Eggers and Foer: they constitute a view that, as a result of the hermeneutic process of gaining and formulating a thorough understanding of it, I have come to share in many respects. Consequently, through the analysis offered in this study, I also hope to provide the view and its supporting arguments with further philosophical elaboration. I contend that it offers a promising and preferable view of overcoming the problems of contemporary existence and finding new sources of meaning.

---

[1] Cf. AHWOSG, 211.

[2] There seems to be no authoritative definition of 'engagement'. Also, in English, the use of the term in the denotation intended in this study (as, broadly speaking, 'existential commitment') is not as common and dominant as, for example, in Dutch (in which it is mainly employed in the mentioned, intended sense). In English, 'engagement' is used in a variety of competing meanings (including, of course, 'betrothal', but also as referring to 'brand loyalty' or to the 'absorption' of readers in texts or of students in their learning materials).

Introduction

1. Aims and method

From the first half of the 1990s onward a growing number of American writers of a younger generation (born, mainly, in the 1960s and 1970s) have started to express their discontent with the endless self-reflectivity and irony that during the preceding decades had come to pervade American culture (including American fiction). Moreover, their novels can also be seen to outline a response, a solution to the mentioned problems. David Foster Wallace (1962–2008) is generally regarded as the most important representative of this recent development in American fiction, and his 1079-page novel *Infinite Jest* (1996) – about addiction, irony, depression, freedom, and the general difficulties of contemporary human existence, of becoming a self – as its most important milestone. Dave Eggers (1971–) and Jonathan Safran Foer (1977–) are the two most pre-eminent examples of writers following in Wallace's footsteps, exploring similar paths in their own writing.[1]

The starting point of this study is the thesis that, in their portrayal of the situation of the contemporary Western individual, the novels of Wallace, Eggers and Foer share a certain philosophical dimension. In an interview, Wallace has stated:

> Fiction's about what it is to be a fucking *human being*. If you operate, which most of us do, from the premise that there are things about the contemporary U.S. that make it distinctly hard to be a real human being, then maybe half of fiction's job is to dramatize what makes it tough. The other half is to dramatize the fact that we still *are* human beings, now. Or can be.[2]

Accordingly, the shared philosophical dimension of these works can be said to have two sides. On the one hand, they describe the above-mentioned hyperreflexivity (that is, excessive, constant self-consciousness) and endless irony as two main problems of contemporary Western culture, that for many individuals lead to (self-)alienation and

---

[1] In my opinion, this development in fiction is mirrored by similar developments in independent cinema during the same period. Initially, I wanted to include the analysis of these related developments in the current study, but it quickly became clear that this would make the project too large and unwieldy. For the connection to film, see, e.g., my article on *Eternal Sunshine of the Spotless Mind* (Den Dulk, 'Een juweel op dun ijs').

[2] McCaffery, 'Interview', 131.

loss of meaning. On the other hand, the novels of Wallace, Eggers and Foer formulate an attempt to overcome these problems, through a desire for sincerity, reality-commitment and community, as the elements that make us human, that can make us into human selves – the elements of what I will describe as the engagement portrayed in these novels.

To further explicate, describe and analyse the philosophical dimension of the work of Wallace, Eggers and Foer, I will employ relevant aspects of the philosophy of different thinkers as heuristic perspectives. These perspectives are drawn from philosophies that can all be characterized as 'existentialist', in the broad sense of the term: namely, the thought of Søren Kierkegaard, Jean-Paul Sartre, Albert Camus, and also the later Wittgenstein (I will elaborate this further on). It is my contention that the resulting analyses will offer an illuminating description of some of the problems of contemporary Western life, and also of possible ways to overcome these problems.

Together, the above-mentioned problems – hyperreflexivity, endless irony – and elements of engagement – sincerity, reality-commitment and community – form the shared philosophical dimension of the fictional works in question. They are the hermeneutic keys used in this study to disclose the meaning and significance of these works. From a methodological perspective, it is important to note that these disclosive principles are derived from the works themselves: they are clearly present (in some cases even explicitly discussed by characters) in the story-worlds of these novels, and as such form the starting point of my analysis. This is one of the reasons why the insights of several philosophers are employed as heuristic perspectives: my aim is not to impose one philosophical view on a group of novels, and use these novels to illustrate a certain philosophical position; my aim, as mentioned above, is to bring out the philosophical views implied in these novels.

I regard the shared philosophical dimension of the novels as a set of 'family resemblances' between different 'language-games'; each novel represents its own language-game, that nevertheless displays certain kinships with the other novels (what I have called their shared philosophical dimension) – kinships that justify bringing the novels together under one view (perhaps more so than automatically taking together different works by the same author). The Wittgensteinian notions of language-games and family resemblances emphasize both the kinship and the particularity of the literary works in question; the studied novels are not regarded as exchangeable products of a monolithic philosophical system of unequivocal values and ideas.[3]

It is this shared semantic field of the novels, their explicit exploration of the above-mentioned existentially laden issues (which amounts to their engagement) in the main story lines and most important characters, that in my opinion connects these novels, and forms what we could call their 'new aesthetic'. Although the term 'aesthetic' might call to mind mostly issues of style and form, here it is meant to refer, above all, to a

---

[3]   Alastair Fowler uses Wittgenstein's notion of family resemblances to explain how works within a certain genre are connected (Fowler, *Kinds of Literature*, 41; cf. Perkins, *Is Literary History Possible?*, 77).

shared *thematic* preoccupation. In fact, by far the most important formal aspect of these novels is their reaffirmation of the possibility of connecting fictional stories to the real world.

This is also what distinguishes these novels most fundamentally from certain preceding literary 'trends'. For, in addition to the critical portrayal of the above-mentioned problems of hyperreflexivity and endless irony on the (existential) level of their story-worlds, the works of Wallace, Eggers and Foer also imply a critique of these problems on a more 'theoretical' level. These literary texts inevitably embody a certain view of fiction, and as such can be seen to criticize the view of fiction underlying the preceding literary 'trends' of 'postmodernist metafiction', epitomized by the work of John Barth (1930–), and 'postmodernist minimalism', epitomized by the work of Bret Easton Ellis (1964–). Whereas the works of Barth and Ellis can be seen to deny, as a result of their excessive self-consciousness and endless irony, the possibility of forging a meaningful connection between fiction and the real world, the works of Wallace *cum suis* reaffirm exactly that possibility. Part of the critique of these two instances of escalated reflexive-ironic fiction has been formulated explicitly by Wallace, in his fiction, and in essays and interviews. Another part of the critique lies on a more implicit level, namely in Wallace's, Eggers's and Foer's literary works 'doing it differently' – both formally and thematically –, in their new direction that contrasts with those preceding literary trends. The analyses of these underlying views of fiction will be addressed separately from the existential portrayal of the mentioned problems and solutions in the story-worlds of the works of Wallace, Eggers and Foer.

I am aware that by placing the works of these writers together, and opposing them to other bodies of work in American fiction, I am not just making a philosophical claim about these works, but also a literary historical claim. This implies both an organization and an explanation of literary periodization. In my interpretation I am inevitably constructing certain contexts and then subsequently using those contexts to explain literary works (as shaping, 'causing' those works).[4] This process is always selective and can never be all-embracing. For instance, my decision to focus on the novels' thematic preoccupation with certain existential issues, means that some of the formal and stylistic aspects of these works will perhaps remain underexposed. The highest that any literary interpretation – including mine – can (and should) strive for is plausibility, which 'must ultimately mean plausibility for me and for whoever thinks as I do', writes David Perkins. He continues: 'This view of the matter does not in the least imply blithe tolerance of whatever opinion someone happens to maintain. The effort for plausibility is strenuous and self-corrective, if only because the criteria of credibility one happens to hold necessitate this.'[5]

We can distinguish between the 'descriptive' and 'referential' plausibility of an interpretation: the former refers to the more self-evident 'basic conventions of an interpretive argument' (among other things: having knowledge of interpretations of the

---

[4] Cf. Perkins, *Is Literary History Possible?*, 146; 'The distinction between event and context is not intrinsic, but conventional and practical, the event being the portion of the context that one foregrounds and tries to explain' (ibid., 147–8).

[5] Perkins, *Is Literary History Possible?*, 17.

same text or period – which I will of course explicate, at different points in this study); the latter refers to the argumentation for the employed framework of interpretation, of the factors Elrud Ibsch describes as 'responsible for the final comprehensive meaning of the text'.[6] The referential plausibility of the interpretations offered in this study is based on two different factors mentioned by Ibsch. First of all, my interpretations take into account the 'context' in which the texts in question have been 'communicated',[7] that is: they take into account the 'problem situation' to which the texts are intended to be an 'answer'. This also means that comments by the author about the aim of his work are deemed relevant – even though, in my opinion, they can never underpin an interpretation by themselves, they are also not to be completely ignored as a source of meaning.[8] At the same time, my interpretations are necessarily based on the 'interactive process' of the construction of meaning by myself, as a reader. In this study, my reading of the texts in question has led me to derive heuristic perspectives from existentialist philosophy. This is a specific and inevitably partial reading of the texts. However, this reading is prompted by the problems and solutions which these texts themselves explicitly address, and which are established existentialist themes. So, there is a constant reciprocity of the factors of interpretation – which is probably how it should be in all literary interpretations.[9]

To summarize: in this study, I will analyse the philosophical dimension of the novels of Wallace, Eggers and Foer, by viewing these literary works in light of heuristic perspectives derived from the philosophies of Kierkegaard, Sartre, Wittgenstein and Camus, in order to attain a better understanding of the novels' portrayal of the problems that characterize contemporary Western existence (hyperreflexivity and endless irony) as well as to better understand the way the novels suggest these problems can be overcome (through the virtues of sincerity, reality-commitment and community).

2. An 'aesthetic sea-change' in American literature

The new literary trend, embodied by the works of Wallace, Eggers and Foer, is increasingly recognized as an 'aesthetic sea change'[10] in American literature.[11] We should note that the self-reflectivity and irony they criticize are established hallmarks

---

[6] Ibsch, 'The Conventions of Interpretation', 114; Ibsch, 'Der Interpretation und kein Ende', 25.
[7] Ibsch speaks of 'authorial communicative context' (Ibsch, 'The Conventions of Interpretation', 114).
[8] Not least because, in a literary climate where a new book is promoted through author interviews, essays, et cetera, comments made by the real-life author about the background, motivations or aim of the book, are bound to influence the expectations of the reader and partly merge with the reader's perception of the communicative intention of the text; cf. Claassen, *The Author's Footprint in the Garden of Fiction*, 30.
[9] Cf. 'any sophisticated literary history must now draw on both immanent and contextual considerations' (Perkins, *Is Literary History Possible?*, 173).
[10] McLaughlin, 'Post-Postmodern Discontent: Contemporary Fiction and the Social World', 55.
[11] Throughout this study I will use 'fiction' and 'literature' as interchangeable terms to refer to the works of Wallace, Eggers and Foer. I am aware that these general terms denote different, partially

of postmodernism,[12] in both literature and philosophy; they are the favoured instruments of the postmodernist strategy to expose the contradictions and hypocrisies inherent in contemporary Western thought.[13] However, from the perspective of this new group of works in American fiction, postmodernism is regarded as a 'blind alley', as A.O. Scott writes.[14] In response to this perceived 'dead end of postmodernism' – in Robert McLaughlin's formulation –, the mentioned writers place new emphasis on the idea that communication and searching for new sources of meaning are the most important purposes of fiction.[15]

As mentioned above, Wallace is regarded as the most important, pioneering member of this new group of writers.[16] In Wallace's writing the engagement with the above-mentioned problems, and with the need to move beyond them, is constantly present.[17] An analysis of these problems and possible solutions can also be found in Wallace's *non-fictional* texts – above all, the 1993 essay 'E Unibus Pluram' –, elements of which can also be recognized in his fictional writings. In this essay, Wallace describes the possible direction of the change in American fiction as follows:

> The next real literary 'rebels' in this country might well emerge as some weird bunch of *anti*-rebels, born oglers who dare somehow to back away from ironic watching, who have the childish gall actually to endorse and instantiate single-entendre principles. Who treat of plain and old untrendy human troubles and emotions in U.S. life with reverence and conviction. Who eschew self-consciousness and hip fatigue. [. . .] The new rebels might be artists willing to risk the yawn, the rolled eyes, the cool smile, the nudged ribs, the parody of gifted ironists, the 'Oh

---

overlapping concepts. E.g. literature includes not just prose novels but poetry and non-fiction writing such as biographies and memoirs, while the term fiction can be used to refer to, for instance, cinematic works of fiction, not just writing. Also, the term literature implies the notion of 'high art', of 'fine writing', whereas the term 'fiction' can be regarded as referring primarily to the fictionality of (the fictitious, 'non-existent' nature of what is portrayed in) a text or artefact that might very well be considered 'low art' or not art at all (cf. the separate chapters on 'Literature' and 'Fiction' in: Lamarque, *The Philosophy of Literature*, 29–83 and 174–219). Therefore, I would like to specify that, in this study, my use of the terms fiction and literature refers specifically to the fictional prose novels of Wallace, Eggers and Foer.

[12] 'Postmodernism' and the possible relation of the studied novels to this notion do not form a central subject of this study, because the unclarity and disagreement surrounding the term prevent it from truly furthering our understanding of the matter at hand. However, as it has become part of 'standing' terminology (as in the mentioned literary trends of postmodernist metafiction and postmodernist minimalism), the term has to a certain extent become unavoidable.

[13] E.g. Hutcheon, *A Poetics of Postmodernism*, 27, 182–3.

[14] Scott, 'The Panic of Influence', 40.

[15] McLaughlin, 'Post-Postmodern Discontent: Contemporary Fiction and the Social World', 55; cf. Den Dulk, 'American Literature'; Grassian, *Hybrid Fictions*, 6–13.

[16] Cf. Annesley, 'Review Essay: David Foster Wallace', 132; Baskin, 'Death Is Not the End'; Burn, 'Some Weird Bunch of Anti-Rebels and Millennial Fictions'; Kirsch, 'The Importance of Being Earnest'; McLaughlin, 'Post-Postmodern Discontent', 55.

[17] Other writers, like Richard Powers and William Vollmann, have also been widely credited for their innovative fiction, which has often been compared to that of Wallace (cf. Leclair, 'The Prodigious Fiction of Richard Powers, William Vollmann and David Foster Wallace'). But in their writing the problems of postmodernist literature and culture are, in my opinion, less prominent and less clear than in Wallace's.

how *banal*. To risk accusations of sentimentality, melodrama. Of overcredulity, of softness.[18]

A.O. Scott and Sven Birkerts, respectively, describe Wallace's work as striving to 'forge ahead', as 'bent on taking the next step in fiction'.[19] Stephen Burn writes that: '[Wallace's fiction] circulates through the bloodstream of American fiction'. He adds that: '[*Infinite Jest*] represents a culmination of reading and theorizing about contemporary fiction, and many of the signposts along that journey seem to have been written into Wallace's work during the period'.[20] Adam Kirsch calls Wallace 'the voice of his generation, for better and for worse', implying an awareness of the inherent difficulty with such pronouncements.[21] Jon Baskin formulates this difficulty more explicitly, while still confirming the underlying undeniability of such a contention: 'It became a commonplace and then a cliché and then almost a taunt to call [Wallace] the greatest writer of his generation'.[22]

Wallace's example of a new direction in American literary fiction has inspired many other novelists. Elise Harris calls Wallace the 'tribal elder' who 'challenged young writers' to act as he had suggested in the above-quoted essay, namely to 'treat of plain old untrendy human troubles and emotions in U.S. life with reverence and conviction'.[23] Kirsch writes: 'In the fifteen years since Wallace published *Infinite Jest*, this sovereign sincerity, this earnest hostility to irony, has come to define the best younger writers, making them a distinctive literary generation'.[24] As was mentioned, Eggers and Foer are the two most prominent examples of this influence and kinship.[25] Their works clearly exhibit the influence of the new aesthetic that Wallace's work can be seen to propose.[26] Burn writes that the 'thumbprint of [*Infinite Jest*'s] influence' can be seen in

[18] EUP, 81–2.
[19] Scott, 'The Panic of Influence', 40; Birkerts, 'The Alchemist's Retort', 113.
[20] Burn in: Moore et al., 'In Memoriam David Foster Wallace', 12, 13.
[21] Kirsch, 'The Importance of Being Earnest'.
[22] Baskin, 'Death Is Not the End'.
[23] Harris, 'Infinite Jest', 46. Harris calls Wallace '*ironic* tribal elder' (emphasis added, AdD), a potentially confusing statement, as a critique of irony is an important aspect of this new direction in fiction; cf. Baskin, who writes: '"E Unibus Pluram" inspired an assortment of earnest millennial fiction' (Baskin, 'Death Is Not the End').
[24] Kirsch, 'The Importance of Being Earnest'; cf. Burn, who writes: 'The desire to adapt (rather than explicitly reject) the legacy of postmodernism and move towards a fiction that humanly engages is probably *Infinite Jest*'s most palpable contribution to contemporary fiction' (Burn, 'Some Weird Bunch of Anti-Rebels and Millennial Fictions').
[25] Other writers who are often mentioned in the quoted sources, are Jonathan Franzen and Zadie Smith. However, even though it might seem obvious to affiliate Franzen with Wallace, on account of their friendship and several declarations by Franzen of the similar intent of their fiction, Franzen's work often seems to propose fiction move 'back' in some way, to a more traditional mode of writing, whereas Wallace, and Eggers and Foer, seem to much more incorporate the 'lessons' of preceding, 'postmodernist' fiction and thought but overcoming its problems (cf. Franzen, 'Why Bother?', 91); as McLaughlin summarizes it: 'Unlike Franzen, [Wallace] doesn't write as if he's above it all' (McLaughlin, 'Post-Postmodern Discontent: Contemporary Fiction and the Social World', 63). While Smith is perhaps the most expressed admirer of Wallace's work, she is a British author, bringing with it an additional set of completely different influences that have to be taken into account. Plus, the mentioned central themes simply do not seem quite as prominent in her fiction as in that of Wallace, Eggers and Foer.
[26] cf. Annesley, 'Review Essay: David Foster Wallace', 132; Baskin, 'Death Is Not the End'; Boswell, *Understanding David Foster Wallace*, 19; Burn, 'The Believers'; Burn, *Infinite Jest. A Reader's*

'writers such as Dave Eggers [. . .] and Jonathan Safran Foer'.[27] When Kirsch speaks of 'the young novelists who followed in Wallace's wake', who 'have shared his righteous refusal of irony', and who 'believe that literature should be positive, constructive, civically engaged, a weapon against alienation', he names Foer and Eggers as 'the most prominent' of that group.[28]

The influence of Wallace and *Infinite Jest* on Eggers becomes clear in the foreword that Eggers wrote for the 2006 tenth anniversary edition of *Infinite Jest*, in which he describes the novel as 'something other', that came across as 'very different than virtually anything before it'. According to Eggers, *Infinite Jest* gives the 'sense' of a writer who 'wanted' to 'and arguably succeeds' at 'nailing the consciousness of an age': 'The themes here are big, and the emotions (guarded as they are) are very real, and the cumulative effect of the book is, you could say, seismic'.[29] In an 'In Memoriam' after Wallace's death, Eggers refers to the scene in the film *Dead Poets Society* where the students salute their teacher, 'in protest of his premature departure', with the words 'O Captain my captain', from the eponymous poem by Walt Whitman; in doing so, Eggers salutes Wallace in a similar way.[30] And in the interview I did with Eggers, he explicitly professed to the similarity of his and Wallace's views: 'I'm on the same page with [Wallace] in a lot of ways'.[31] Eggers's *A Heartbreaking Work of Staggering Genius* even subtly alludes to *Infinite Jest* through main character Dave's fear that his upbringing of his younger brother Toph will somehow lead to Toph later in life killing kittens by putting them in garbage bags and slamming these against walls – which is in fact the gruesome habit of *Infinite Jest* character Randy Lenz.[32]

James Annesley describes Foer's novels as a 'striking expression' of the 'kind of project mapped out by Wallace'.[33] In my interview with Foer, he did not speak of Wallace having an explicit influence on his own fiction, but did express an admiration for Wallace's 'love for writing': 'He really loves language, he really loves ideas. [. . .] I think he is a very brave writer, and a very, very good writer'.[34] Looking at Foer's works themselves, we could say that the mangled English of Alex, one of the main narrating characters from Foer's first novel *Everything Is Illuminated* (2002), calls to mind the

---

Guide, 76; Burn, 'Some Weird Bunch of Anti-Rebels and Millennial Fictions'; Grassian, *Hybrid Fictions*, 42–9; Harris, 'Infinite Jest', 46; Kakutani, 'Critic's Notebook: New Wave of Writers Reinvents Literature'; Kirsch, 'The Importance of Being Earnest'; Mattson, 'Is Dave Eggers a Genius?', 81; Myers, 'A Bag of Tired Tricks', 115; Timmer, '*Do You Feel It Too?*', 11; Weber, 'David Foster Wallace, Influential Writer, Dies at 46'.

[27] Burn, 'Some Weird Bunch of Anti-Rebels and Millennial Fictions'; Burn also mentions Franzen.
[28] Kirsch, 'The Importance of Being Earnest'; Kirsch also mentions Smith.
[29] Eggers, 'Foreword', xiii, xii, xiv.
[30] Eggers in: Moore et al., 'In Memoriam David Foster Wallace', 4.
[31] Interview with Dave Eggers by Allard den Dulk, dd. 23 May 2006.
[32] Eggers, *A Heartbreaking Work of Staggering Genius* [1st edition], 256; cf. Burn, *Infinite Jest. A Reader's Guide*, 76; IJ, 541–8. About *A Heartbreaking Work of Staggering Genius* Wallace wrote: 'I don't have a history that's as off-the-charts sad and rife with bathos-hazard as yours [. . .] I report here that I was almost as moved by your willingness to risk it as I was impressed by the high-wire skill with which you avoided it' (Eggers, *A Heartbreaking Work of Staggering Genius* [1st edition], dust jacket).
[33] Annesley, 'Review Essay: David Foster Wallace', 132.
[34] Interview with Jonathan Safran Foer by Allard den Dulk, dd. 26 June 2006.

'Frenchified' speech of the character Marathe from *Infinite Jest*. Even more so, the sincerity of precocious, 9-year-old Oskar, the main character from Foer's second novel *Extremely Loud & Incredibly Close* (2005), strongly resembles the character Mario from *Infinite Jest* (as I will elaborate further on in this study – see Chapter 6).

We should note that Eggers's and Foer's novels, because they build on the preliminary work done by Wallace, show a less conflicted struggle with, and therefore a perhaps lighter, less laborious portrayal of, the shared themes. We could say that they show us – for lack of a better word – an 'intuitive' adaptation of many of Wallace's ideas (whereas in Wallace's work we witness the more reflective labour to arrive at these ideas).[35] As Marshall Boswell writes, perhaps sounding more negative than intended (given his further remarks on writers like Eggers): 'Since *Infinite Jest*, a whole new group of emerging young writers has copied the elusive Wallace "tone"' (the term 'tone' should not be interpreted as referring solely to certain formal, stylistic aspects of writing, but to the overall view of what fiction 'should do', to use Wallace's formulation).[36] At the same time, the worldwide success of Eggers's and Foer's bestselling novels in a sense signifies the success of this new direction in American fiction, and has given Wallace's ideas a far wider exposure than they perhaps would have received solely through his own, more difficult fiction.[37] Including Eggers and Foer in this study also indicates that the analysed development does not just concern the literary work of one man, but a wider trend. Accordingly, the works of Wallace, Eggers and Foer are regarded in this study as the three most determinative instances of this trend.

However, because Wallace is in fact the pioneer and theorist of this new direction in fiction, and Eggers and Foer are regarded as taking on this project, as intuitively adopting it, Wallace's work will function throughout as the primary source of the identified themes, and the philosophical reading thereof. However, in some cases the works of Eggers and Foer might offer – for the sake of clarity – a better, more intuitive place to start the elaboration of these different themes. Similarly, the interpretative arguments based on what Ibsch calls the 'authorial communicative context' will be derived primarily from the context of Wallace's works, on account of being the originary source of the development.

The terms most frequently used to label the development in American literary fiction outlined above are 'post-postmodernism' and 'new sincerity'.[38] I am reluctant, though, to adopt these terms outright. Although, as was already announced above, a desire for sincerity (in response to the problems of hyperreflexivity and endless irony) is an important aspect of the works in question, sincerity is not their only theme. Furthermore, the form of sincerity portrayed amounts to a specific and complicated

---

[35] This is probably an important part of its esteemed literary quality, compared to the work of Eggers and Foer.

[36] Boswell, *Understanding David Foster Wallace*, 19.

[37] Cf. as just one example of a publication offering an overview of this 'success': Vaessens and Van Dijk (eds), *Reconsidering the Postmodern*.

[38] E.g. McLaughlin, 'Post-Postmodern Discontent'; Kelly, 'David Foster Wallace and the New Sincerity in American Fiction'; cf. Rutten, 'Russian Literature: Reviving Sincerity in the Post-Soviet World', 28, 30–3. In relation to Wallace, Marshall Boswell speaks of 'some still-unnamed (and perhaps unnameable) third wave of modernism' (Boswell, *Understanding David Foster Wallace*, 1).

notion (which will be examined in Chapter 6). It is not a simple form of naïveté which is readily achieved. The term 'new sincerity' (without a clear definition of what that sincerity amounts to) does not fully communicate this complexity. The term 'post-postmodernism', in turn, provides us with an ugly label that carries forth the (terminological) unclarity that already surrounds the definitions of 'modernism' and 'postmodernism'. Moreover, the prefix 'post-' suggests too strongly a state of already 'being beyond' or 'having left behind' something, whereas in the case of the novels studied it seems just as much a case of finding new ways of coping with the same thing, namely: contemporary Western existence.[39]

More important, however, than such terminological discussions is the task of mapping out, and thereby deepening our understanding of, the shared dimension of these works. The preceding has already offered a broad impression of the themes and desires that these novels are said to have in common. As the above-quoted sources indicate, a consensus seems to have arisen on the fact that these works are indeed connected and share an interest in certain themes. But these assessments function merely as the starting point for an analysis aimed at a better understanding of these themes and of the connection between the works that portray them.

The contribution of this study to the existing (and rapidly expanding) body of scholarly work on Wallace, Eggers and Foer lies in the elucidation of the philosophical themes that connect the novels in question and of the literary development that these novels embody. Although some of their connections as well as the possible affinities with existentialist philosophy have already been remarked upon in a number of publications on this new group of fiction writers,[40] an extensive, systematic philosophical analysis of the mentioned themes has not yet been undertaken.

As my interpretation of these works is based on a philosophically framed reading of the main story lines and most important characters from the novels, below I will begin by providing a general overview of the works of Wallace, Eggers and Foer that this study will focus on.

3. Outline of primary literary works

3.1. David Foster Wallace

Wallace's most important work, the expansive, vastly rich novel *Infinite Jest* (1996) will form the main literary focal point of this study. The novel has a number of important characters (and countless additional ones), but the two main protagonists are Hal Incandenza and Don Gately. Hal is a hyperintelligent adolescent, an academic and tennis prodigy, enrolled at the Enfield Tennis Academy; Hal is also a marijuana addict. Gately is a former drug addicted criminal, who works as a resident staff

---

[39] Cf. note 12.
[40] E.g. Boswell, *Understanding David Foster Wallace*, 137–40, 143–4.

member at Ennet House, a halfway facility for recovering drug addicts, and is an active member of 'Addicts Anonymous' (AA). *Infinite Jest* traces the development of these two characters from an initial situation of addiction – symbolizing a certain attitude towards existence –, to a different life-view, which I will call sincerity. Addiction, of all kinds (to alcohol, drugs and entertainment), is a central motif – almost everybody in the novel is addicted to something – and is directly connected to the problems of hyperreflexivity and endless irony thematized in the novel. In *Infinite Jest*, addiction and the connected philosophical problems are shown to lead, ultimately, to depression; so, in addition to being addicted, most of the novel's characters are also shown to be depressed.

The portrayal of Gately starts at the moment that he has been clean for just over a year, and his old life as an addict and criminal is portrayed through a series of memories and dreams; in Gately's story line, the guidelines of AA are shown to lead him to a new and meaningful life. In the case of Hal, *Infinite Jest* portrays the peak of his marijuana addiction, his subsequent decision to quit drugs, and the first changes in his behaviour. The novel then leaves a gap in Hal's story line. The next descriptions show him a year later, in a scene that forms the opening of the novel, but chronologically is the last episode of the entire story line; these descriptions are ambiguous as to Hal's current state, leaving it up to the reader to interpret this, as well as to fill in what might have happened in the meantime.

These two story lines take place in a story-world, situated slightly in the future (in relation to the novel's publication date), in which years are no longer referred to as successive numbers but are subsidized, taking their name from a commercial product or brand (for example, 'Year of the Whopper'). Also the United States has absorbed Mexico and Canada, to become the Organization of North American Nations (ONAN), and the president of the country is a former Las Vegas night club 'crooner'. This already grotesque story-world forms the background for a larger plot in which separatist Quebecois wheelchair terrorists and ONAN intelligence services both want to retrieve the master copy of the lethal film 'Infinite Jest', which is so entertaining that it makes its viewers slip into a catatonic state, ignoring even the primary necessities of life, and therefore leads, ultimately, to their death. The film was directed by Hal's father, James Incandenza, who has committed suicide and, as a wraith, visits Gately while the latter is in the hospital.

Other important characters, relevant to this study, are: Remy Marathe, a Quebecois wheelchair terrorist, whose conversation with secret agent Hugh Steeply about the American focus on negative freedom (freedom-from) and the connected inability to choose meaningfully, forms a recurring narrative thread, spread out over the novel, which thereby obtains added significance for the interpretation of the novel; Joelle van Dyne, a recovering drug addict who arrives at Ennet House, becomes a member of AA, and there befriends Gately (her experiences with addiction and getting clean, complement those of Gately, and offer an additional impression of AA, as an alternative to addiction and depression); and Mario Incandenza, Hal's physically deformed older brother, who is about the only character in the novel who is neither addicted nor depressed, but instead friendly, empathetic and happy.

Before *Infinite Jest*, Wallace published two other literary works: the novel *The Broom of the System* (1987) and the story collection *Girl with Curious Hair* (1989). These works should be regarded as 'formative',[41] as uneven attempts that express the desire for a new direction in fiction but do not succeed in realizing it. However, they provide an insight into Wallace's literary ambitions and philosophical affinities. *The Broom of the System* revolves around Lenore Beadsman's search for her grandmother, a former student of Ludwig Wittgenstein who has disappeared from her retirement home.[42] Wallace called the book 'a conversation between Wittgenstein and Derrida'.[43] *Girl with Curious Hair* contains the 150-page novella 'Westward the Course of Empire Takes Its Way', Wallace's (failed) attempt to 'explode' postmodernist metafiction (that is, the type of fiction written by John Barth) by means of its own methods.[44] In turn, the title story 'Girl with Curious Hair' is aimed at the other literary trend of which Wallace is critical, namely the postmodernist minimalism of Bret Easton Ellis.[45] In the story collections *Brief Interviews with Hideous Men* (1999) and *Oblivion* (2004), Wallace addresses the same central themes as in *Infinite Jest*; for example, the story 'Octet' (from the former collection) offers an exploration of the dialogue between writer and reader, and of the need for openness and trust in order to make that relationship work. Finally, Wallace's unfinished, posthumously published novel *The Pale King* (2011), about employees of an IRS tax office, explores the importance of being able to endure boredom and to truly pay attention, to the world and others.

3.2. Dave Eggers

Eggers's debut, *A Heartbreaking Work of Staggering Genius* (2000), is an autobiographical novel. The book is a memoir (focusing on Eggers's life in his early twenties), but also explicitly reflects on the impossibility of writing a truly *non*-fictional memoir

---

[41] Boswell, *Understanding David Foster Wallace*, 116.

[42] The title of the novel refers to the later Wittgenstein's contention that the meaning of our words is determined by their use, via a scene in which Grandma Beadsman asks what part of the broom is 'more fundamental', 'the bristles or the handle', concluding that it depends on whether 'you want to *sweep* with the broom', for 'if what we wanted a broom for was to break windows, then the handle was clearly the fundamental essence of the broom' (Wallace, *The Broom of the System*, 149–50).

[43] Lipsky, *Although Of Course You End Up Becoming Yourself*, 35; cf. 'By the time Wallace started writing *Broom*, he had developed a serious interest in Wittgenstein's late philosophy. [. . .] at the simplest level, Lenore just *is* Wallace, and *The Broom of the System* is just a fictionalized retelling – a "little self-obsessed *bildungsroman*", Wallace called it – of the intellectual struggles he was then undergoing' (Ryerson, 'Introduction: A Head That Throbbed Heartlike', 20).

[44] 'I wanted to get the Armageddon-explosion, the goal metafiction's always been about, I wanted to get it over with, and then out of the rubble reaffirm the idea of art being a living transaction between humans', Wallace said. He added: 'maybe "Westward"'s only real value'll be showing the kind of pretentious loops you fall into now if you fuck around with recursion' (McCaffery, 'Interview', 142). Boswell calls the novella a 'piece of pretentious juvenilia' when taken on its own, but a fascinating 'declaration of intent' when seen in relation to *Infinite Jest* (Boswell, *Understanding David Foster Wallace*, 102).

[45] With sentences like 'Gimlet allowed me to burn her slightly and I felt that she was an outstanding person', 'Girl with Curious Hair' is a clear parody of Ellis's style and subject matter (Wallace, 'Girl with Curious Hair', *Girl with Curious Hair*, 63); Boswell writes: 'the story eerily forecasts Ellis's 1991 slasher novel *American Psycho*' (Boswell, *Understanding David Foster Wallace*, 79).

(an impossibility that in the book is connected with the problems of excessive self-consciousness and irony which are analysed in this study).[46] This hybridity of fiction and non-fiction makes the book neither purely a memoir nor purely a novel (hence, my term 'autobiographical novel').[47] In what follows, I will refer to the book's first-person narrator and main protagonist as 'Dave', and to the book's author as 'Eggers'. In *A Heartbreaking Work of Staggering Genius*, both of Dave's parents die of cancer within a period of three months, after which Dave becomes responsible for the upbringing of his younger brother Toph. The book offers a highly self-reflective portrayal of Dave's attempts to shape his existence, to balance his freedoms and responsibilities, which often amount to a struggle with his own self-reflectivity, his tendency to second-guess every step he takes. In this respect, an important element of the book is the portrayal of *Might*, the magazine that Dave starts, together with a couple of his friends, as these passages offer a critical description of the problems of endless irony.

You Shall Know Our Velocity (2002) is Eggers's second book. First-person narrator Will has received a large sum of money which he feels he does not deserve. He is also mourning the death of his friend Jack. Will decides to take a trip around the world, in only eight days, together with his other best friend, Hand. During the trip, Will wants to give his money away to people he feels are more deserving, more in need of it. Maybe even more so than Dave from *A Heartbreaking Work of Staggering Genius*, Will is plagued by a highly self-reflective mind, paralysed by his head having constant, overpowering discussions that he cannot control and wants to end. The novel thus portrays Will's search for a way 'out of his head'. This is also connected to Will's inability to choose a certain direction in his life; he has countless far-fetched dreams and ambitions, but has never undertaken anything to start realizing one of them. Willy-nilly, the trip proves to be a cathartic experience, leading Will to insight.

Eggers has subsequently published: the story collections *How We Are Hungry* (2004) and *Short Short Stories* (2005); the biographical non-fiction works *What Is the What: The Autobiography of Valentino Achak Deng* (2006) – about the experiences of a Sudanese refugee, on the run in Africa, and after he has received asylum in the United States – and *Zeitoun* (2009) – the story of a Syrian immigrant in New Orleans who, in the wake of hurricane Katrina, is unrightfully arrested and imprisoned, without

---

[46] The appendix added to later editions of *A Heartbreaking Work* explicitly reflects on some of the fictionalizations and compressions practiced throughout the book.

[47] This treatment of Eggers's *A Heartbreaking Work* as a hybrid, autobiographical novel and not a 'regular' memoir is in line with most of the existing scholarship on the book (cf. Timmer, 'Do You Feel It Too?', 186; Grassian, *Hybrid Fictions*, 42). Additionally, I would like to point out that all the works analysed in this study are characterized by a certain overlap of fiction and non-fiction: we know that Wallace's descriptions in *Infinite Jest* are based very directly (autobiographically) on his own encounters in AA and experiences with addiction and depression (cf. Max, *Every Ghost Story Is a Love Story*); Jonathan Safran Foer went on a search for his family's roots similar to that of his character 'Jonathan Safran Foer' in *Everything Is Illuminated*; and Dave Eggers made more or less the same trip around the world as his characters Will and Hand in his novel *You Shall Know Our Velocity*. Finally, as I will argue in the rest of this study (most explicitly in Chapter 5), fiction is not opposed to reality, but, on the contrary, is deeply invested with reality. Thus, my treatment of Eggers's book as an 'autobiographical novel' does not at all diminish the work's forceful expression of real-world problems.

being charged, for 23 days; and the novels *A Hologram for the King* (2012) – about a middle-aged, American businessman in Saudi Arabia, waiting to pitch an IT project, while struggling with the emptiness of his life – and *The Circle* (2013) – the story of a young woman who starts working for a powerful internet company, giving rise to questions of privacy and true community in the digital age. For reasons of limitation, I will leave these works largely undiscussed in my philosophical analysis. However, it is interesting to note that, with the above-mentioned biographies and continuing into the subsequent novels, Eggers's portrayal of the real world, of events and people, has become increasingly open, honest, realistic and less self-conscious. This is in line with the desire expressed in his two earliest works that will form the focal points of my analysis.

3.3. Jonathan Safran Foer

Foer's first novel, *Everything Is Illuminated* (2002), consists of two main plot elements: the story of the young American 'Jonathan Safran Foer' (to whom I will refer, in what follows, as 'Jonathan', while referring to the author as 'Foer'), who visits the Ukraine to search for traces of his Jewish ancestry. He is assisted by a young Ukrainian guide, Alexei Perchov, who also has to come to grips with his own family history, and who narrates this part of the story line in mangled English. The other part offers the reconstruction of Jonathan's heritage, of the Jewish village Trachimbrod, mainly of his 'great-great-great-great-great-grandmother' Brod and his grandfather Safran. Jonathan has had to make up this story almost completely, as his search in the Ukraine yielded very little information, resulting in a highly fantastic, magical rendering of the supposed past; the same reflective flight from reality is mirrored in the life-view of Jonathan's ancestors Brod and Safran. Whereas Jonathan chooses not to focus on the reality of what he and Alex actually did find and experience in the Ukraine, Alex does: their search has yielded an insight into Alex's grandfather's questionable actions during World War II, bringing Alex to the realization of what he feels are his responsibilities in life, which results in him kicking his alcoholic, abusive father out of the house, and taking on the care of his mother and little brother.

Foer's second novel, *Extremely Loud & Incredibly Close* (2005) is the story of 9-year-old Oskar Schell, whose father Thomas died in the 9/11 attacks on the World Trade Center. An important subplot is that of Oskar's grandparents (Thomas's parents). Oskar is precocious and eloquent, but at the same time appropriately naïve for his age, which makes him unabashedly open, kind and trusting. Initially his attempts to cope with the death of his father seem to contain an element of denial, because he interprets random things his father left behind as clues that Oskar now has to decipher, thereby keeping his father present in his life. But Oskar also sets out on a quest throughout New York, which brings him into contact with a host of different people, whose lives he affects with his uncommon straightforwardness and openness. Oskar's grandparents survive the Holocaust and meet again in the United States. The grandfather (also called Thomas) has gradually lost the power of speech, which seems to be connected to his compulsive, constant thinking, as a result of which words simply seem to become disconnected from their meaning, and therefore unutterable. The grandfather leaves the grandmother before their child (Thomas Jr) is born. After the death of their child in 2001, the grandfather returns, and Oskar strikes up a relationship with him, not knowing that he is his grandfather (to Oskar, the man is just the tenant in his grandmother's house). In the end, together they dig up the empty coffin of Oskar's father and fill it with letters that the grandfather wrote to his son but never sent.

Foer has published a number of short stories, including 'A Primer for the Punctuation of Heart Disease' (2002), also released as part of *The Unabridged Pocketbook of Lightning* (2005). In 2009 Foer published *Eating Animals*, an essay on the food industry and climate change, constituting a heartfelt and extensively argued plea for vegetarianism. Foer's *Tree of Codes* (2010) is a reworking of Bruno Schulz's *The Street of Crocodiles* (originally from 1934) from which most of the words have been literally 'cut out', resulting in a new story. However, these publications will not form an integral part of my analysis, which will focus on Foer's two novels.

3.4. John Barth

John Barth's *Lost in the Funhouse* (1968) is generally regarded as *the* classic example of postmodernist metafiction – one of the forms of fiction (im- and explicitly) criticized by the works of Wallace, Eggers and Foer.[48] Together with writers like Thomas Pynchon, William Gass and Donald Barthelme, Barth stands at the forefront of a new wave of self-conscious, experimental writing that arose in American fiction in the 1960s. The theoretical concerns of this literary trend – namely: the constructed nature of fiction and reality, as well as the relationship between the two – are connected to those of postmodernist philosophy and critical theory, which also emerged around the same time.[49] Metafiction can be defined as fiction that self-consciously exposes and discusses its own constituting, fictional structures. *Lost in the Funhouse* embodies the concerns and methods of postmodernist metafiction in a concise but dense work. The book consists of a series of short stories that, according to the 'Foreword', are nonetheless meant 'to be received "all at once"'.[50] The 'author' and sometimes explicit protagonist of the stories in *Lost in the Funhouse* is Ambrose Mensch (all the other protagonists are 'masks' of Ambrose), a cripplingly self-conscious writer.[51] More importantly, the connection between the stories lies in their shared metafictional intention, 'to acknowledge what I'm doing while I'm doing it is exactly the point', as it is summarized by the authorial voice in the story 'Title'.[52] As a result of this constant self-conscious undercutting, 'the idea that there is something to express, gets scrutinized and diminished by Barth', as Stan Fogel and Gordon Slethaug write.[53]

---

[48]   E.g. Worthington, 'Done with Mirrors', 118.
[49]   Harris, *Passionate Virtuosity*, x.
[50]   LF, xi.
[51]   Kiernan, 'John Barth's Artist in the Fun House', 373–4; cf. Harris, *Passionate Virtuosity*, 107.
[52]   LF, 111.
[53]   Fogel and Slethaug, *Understanding John Barth*, 13.

3.5. Bret Easton Ellis

Bret Easton Ellis is the most important representative of a wave of fiction that can, to a certain extent, be seen to follow postmodernist metafiction, namely the trend of minimalist fiction, portraying the bleak futureless present of a postmodern world in which self-conscious irony has unmasked every claim to meaning and value. Whereas postmodernist metafiction, by scrutinizing the workings of language and the relation between reality and fiction, is mainly aimed at *problematizing* the formulation of meaning and value, Ellis's postmodernist minimalism seems to have concluded that meaning and value are *impossible*, which results in the complete collapse of fiction as an instrument of expressing anything meaningful about reality. Julian Murphet writes: 'If we call Ellis a "postmodern" author, we probably mean this above all; this flattening and erasure of the texture of his world, manifest above all in the flatness and affectlessness of his prose style.'[54] Ellis's 1991 novel *American Psycho* offers the most extreme and consistent elaboration of this fixed style and subject matter.[55] The novel's first-person narrator, Patrick Bateman, is an investment banker, but also a bloodthirsty psychopath (whose acts of torture, rape and murder are described in great detail). Bateman does not accept responsibility for his actions, nor any limitations to them – *everything* should be possible. The violent acts he commits are the most obvious examples of this. The novel offers Bateman's perception of the world, narrated, almost without interruption, in the present tense. In a sense, these descriptions are more real or realistic than the ones offered in Barth's metafiction, as they are relatively unselfconscious; at the same time, they are much more unreal, as they do not attempt to truly constitute any meaning at all, only the impossibility thereof: they just offer endless lists of brand names, restaurant names, et cetera. Patrick Bateman's view of the world – and with that, the whole novel – is an extreme expression of the supposed futility of all attempts at formulating meaning and value.

4. Heuristic perspectives

The previous sections have already provided, in passing, a first impression of the centrality of the philosophical problems (hyperreflexivity, endless irony) and solutions (sincerity, reality-commitment and community) to the novels in question. They have also indicated some of the implicit and explicit philosophical interests and affinities that underlie these works. As previously mentioned, Wallace's work is regarded in this study as the primary source of the identified themes and the philosophical reading thereof. Below, I will offer a brief, first impression of the affinities between the existentialist heuristic perspectives employed in this study and Wallace's new aesthetic. First, I will point out the explicit connections between Wallace and the individual philosophers used in this study – Sartre, Kierkegaard, Camus and the later Wittgenstein. Then, I

---

[54] Murphet, *American Psycho. A Reader's Guide*, 20.
[55] Young, 'The Beast in the Jungle, the Figure in the Carpet', 93.

will make some very brief remarks on the connection between these philosophers themselves, as exponents of an existentialist line of thought.

In the existentialist view – the view that Kierkegaard, Sartre and Camus (and Wittgenstein also can be said to) share –, an individual is not automatically a self, but has to become one. A human being merely embodies the possibility of becoming a self. According to existentialism, there is no 'true core' that an individual always already 'is' or 'has', and which underlies selfhood. *Becoming* a self is the *task* of human life. A human being has to integrate his individual limitations and possibilities into a unified existence; this is the process of developing a self. If the individual does not assume himself in this way, he does not acquire a self; he is just an immediate, natural being, a thing among the things. Such a human being does not 'exist'; he just 'is'.[56] Throughout this study, we will recognize this view of the self in Wallace's writing.

Of the four philosophers I will examine in this study, Sartre is the only one Wallace makes no explicit reference to in either his fiction or in interviews and essays. However, Zadie Smith describes Sartre as a 'great favourite' of Wallace, and the former's dicta of being 'condemned to be free' and 'responsible for that freedom' as characterizing the predicament of Wallace's characters. The connection between Sartre and Wallace follows from their view of consciousness. According to both, consciousness should always be directed outward. It should transcend itself towards the world, to formulate it in Sartrean terms. Smith writes: 'If Wallace insists on awareness, his particular creed is – to use a Wallacerian word – *extrorse*', which means 'facing outward', 'awareness must move always in an outward direction'.[57]

Kierkegaard, however, is repeatedly mentioned by Wallace. In *Infinite Jest*, Kierkegaard is referred to in the following ways: in relation to Camus (Hal Incandenza states that Kierkegaard's influence on Camus is underestimated); in the filmography of James Incandenza, one of his movies is called a 'Kierkegaard/Lynch (?) parody' (referring to the filmmaker David Lynch, whom Wallace admired very much, thus suggesting an interesting connection between two possibly illuminating figures in the interpretation of Wallace's work); and, in the context of great love as inspiring choice and responsibility, Marathe mentions Kierkegaard and Regine (which is interesting, because Kierkegaard broke off his engagement with Regine Olsen, a choice that haunted him for the rest of his life, whereas Marathe, in the end, chooses his wife over everything, including his political ideals – 'Without the choice of her life there are no other choices').[58] The affinity between Kierkegaard and Wallace is strong and seems to encompass broad aspects of their views on human existence, and the different ways of evading or accepting responsibility for that existence.[59]

As was just mentioned, *Infinite Jest* refers to Camus in connection to Kierkegaard. The connection between Wallace and Camus, which remains largely implicit, seems to lie in their emphasis on the necessarily communal character of

---

[56] Cf. Taels, *Søren Kierkegaard als filosoof*, 96, 102.

[57] Smith, 'Brief Interviews with Hideous Men', 264, 268. This conception of consciousness will be elaborated in Chapter 1.

[58] IJ, 12, 992, 105; in the novel, Regine is spelled with an 'a' instead of an 'e' at the end.

[59] Wallace also compares Kafka's descriptions of the struggle of becoming a self with those of Kierkegaard (Wallace, 'Some Remarks on Kafka's Funniness', 64–5).

meaningful existence. Existentialism is often seen as a school of thought that directs all its attention to the individual, isolating him. This is a misconception, however, especially with regard to Camus, who emphasizes the importance of community as a means of bringing an end to loneliness and meaninglessness.[60] In *Infinite Jest* we can recognize this in AA's communal approach to beating addiction. This comparison is further cemented by a remark that Wallace made in an interview; following his statement 'that it is our job as responsible decent spiritual human beings to arrive at sets of principles to guide our conduct in order to keep us from hurting ourselves and other people', Wallace says: 'the remedy that I see for it is some very, very mild form of Camus – like existential engagement'.[61] The 'mildness' probably refers to the fact that Camus's notion of 'rebellion' is quite literal and overtly political, whereas Wallace's version of existential engagement seems to be aimed, above all, at urging individuals away from reflective confinement in the self, towards connection with others.

The relation between Wallace's fiction and Wittgenstein's later philosophy has already been mentioned above. This philosophical connection has been examined by several scholars, most notably and thoroughly by Boswell, who opposes the view shared by Wallace and Wittgenstein, to the postmodernist view connecting Barth and Derrida. He writes: 'Wallace uses Wittgenstein's elegant model to escape from what he regards as the dead end of postmodern self-reflexivity', by proposing 'a communal approach to communication'.[62] On the relation of his own thought to that of Wittgenstein, Wallace writes: 'I like to fancy myself a fan of the work of [Wittgenstein].' In the same article Wallace also contrasts this adherence with how he sees the works of Barth and Derrida: 'I personally have grown weary of most texts that are narrated self-consciously as *written*, as "textes" [. . .] [,] the Barthian/post-Derridean self-referential hosts.'[63] The connection between Wittgenstein and Wallace lies, to a large extent, in the fact that Wallace wants to free fiction from being turned in on itself, from the highly self-reflective view following from the postmodernist conception of language and literature. Wallace wants fiction to express the world we live in, 'to illuminate the possibilities for being alive and human in it'.[64] Again, this has to do with breaking with self-reflective tendencies that isolate the individual, and prevent him from expressing anything meaningful about the world (problems that Wallace sometimes refers to as solipsism and scepticism),[65] in this case resulting from a postmodernist view of language. Wittgenstein's thought helps Wallace realize this liberation.

Similar to the connection between the literary works of Wallace, Eggers and Foer, the philosophical existentialist works in question also share a number of family resemblances (which were already made apparent in the overview outlined above, of the connection between Wallace and the thinkers in question). As Gordon Marino

---

[60] Cf. Van Stralen, who also points out this common misperception of existentialist thought (Van Stralen, *Beschreven keuzes*, 21, 40).
[61] Karmodi, 'Interview'.
[62] Boswell, *Understanding David Foster Wallace*, 26, 22.
[63] Wallace, 'The Empty Plenum: David Markson's *Wittgenstein's Mistress*', 218, 221.
[64] McCaffery, 'Interview', 131.
[65] E.g. McCaffery, 'Interview', 142; Wallace, 'Joseph Frank's Dostoevsky', 272.

writes: 'the existentialists are linked by their commitment to the common themes of freedom, choice, authenticity, alienation, and rebellion' (these are also the themes that will dominate this study, with one slight addition, namely that I regard sincerity and not authenticity as the right label for the existentialist virtue par excellence). Marino adds: 'the existential movement is a response to the disenchantment of the world, that is, to the sense that the history and social structure of the world are not God sanctioned'.[66] In other words: we have to take up the task of becoming, of developing our selves. Grouping together Sartre, Kierkegaard and Camus as existentialist thinkers whose philosophies display multiple similarities, is a commonly accepted position.

The relation of the later Wittgenstein to these thinkers, however, does require some further explanation.[67] For the purposes of this study, the most significant point of contact between Wittgenstein and the existentialist philosophers is the similarity in the way they view the relation between consciousness and the world (and, in connection to this: the self and self-knowledge). This connection is strongest and clearest with Sartre: both Sartre and Wittgenstein regard consciousness, and what can properly be called *self*-consciousness, as inextricably tied in with the world outside consciousness, and the common idea of self-consciousness being aimed at something 'inside', as mistaken.[68] Of course, Sartre's argument rests on a phenomenological analysis and Wittgenstein's argument on descriptions of language use. But these methods of analysis might be more closely related than is often thought. Nicholas Gier concludes that 'there are significant parallels between Wittgenstein and the so-called "existentialist" phenomenologists' (Gier also uses these parallels to point out the differences between Wittgenstein and Derridean deconstructivism).[69] Indeed, Wittgenstein equated the term 'grammar' (that is, the structures of language use, which form the centre of all the 'linguistic analyses' Wittgenstein performs) with 'phenomenology': a chapter from the 'Big Typescript', from 1933, is entitled 'Phenomenology is Grammar'. He also remarked: 'You could say of my work that it is phenomenology'.[70]

5. Outline of the study

On the basis of the foregoing, this book breaks down into two parts: the first on the problematic issues described in the novels of Wallace, Eggers and Foer, and the

---

[66] Marino, 'Introduction', xiv.

[67] I do not want to pass over the differences that exist between their philosophies, although these differences seem to me to have been enhanced, thereby blotting out the interesting affinities, by the affiliation of Wittgenstein with Anglo-American, analytic philosophy, whereas existentialism is regarded as part of continental philosophy; cf. Wider, 'A Nothing About Which Something Can Be Said', 324.

[68] Both view the tendency to regard thoughts and feelings as objects that we somehow possess 'inside' ourselves, as a crucial mistake in our understanding of ourselves. Self-knowledge, for both Sartre and Wittgenstein, is not a result of consciousness looking at itself, as if it were an object, but of consciousness looking at its own relations to the world.

[69] Gier, 'Wittgenstein and Deconstruction', 174; cf. Gier, *Wittgenstein and Phenomenology*, 3.

[70] Wittgenstein to M. O'C. Drury (M. O'C. Drury, 'Conversations with Wittgenstein', 116; quoted in: Gier, 'Wittgenstein and Deconstruction', 174–5).

second on the solutions, the engagement portrayed therein. Both parts consist of, on the one hand, chapters dedicated to the existential level of the story-worlds of the mentioned novels, and on the other hand, chapters on the form that these problems and solutions take in different views of fiction.

Part 1 is dedicated to the explication and analysis of hyperreflexivity and endless irony. These are the two main problematic issues portrayed in the novels of Wallace, Eggers and Foer.

Chapter 1 focuses on the first issue: *hyperreflexivity*. Contemporary Western life is portrayed in the novels of Wallace, Eggers and Foer as requiring constant self-reflection, which is shown to easily take on an excessive form, leading to gradual estrangement from the self and its relations to the world and other people. To analyse the novels' portrayal of this process, I will employ the view of self-consciousness formulated in Sartre's early, phenomenological-existentialist philosophy. This chapter will offer insight into a misconception of self-becoming that will rear its head throughout this study, namely that the contemporary individual tends to regard his self as an object that he can find 'inside', through self-reflection. This tendency will be shown to cut off the individual from (meaningful connections to) the world and others.

In *Chapter 2* the second problematic issue will be addressed: *endless irony*. This problem can be said to follow from that of hyperreflexivity: a person who cannot stop thinking about himself and his possible actions, cannot or can only just come to conclusions and actions, let alone conclusions and actions to which he is fully committed. The attitude that will follow from this is irony. This ironic attitude, too, can take on an excessive, endless form. The portrayal of this attitude in the studied works implies a sharp irony critique. I will use Kierkegaard's analysis of irony and the related distinction between the aesthetic and the ethical life-view, as a heuristic perspective for the interpretation of the irony critique formulated in the novels.

In addition to the critical portrayal of the above-mentioned problems of hyperreflexivity and endless irony on the (existential) level of their story-worlds, the fictions of Wallace, Eggers and Foer also imply a critique of a similar escalation of self-reflection and irony on the level of the view of fiction underlying Barth's postmodernist metafictional works and Ellis's postmodernist minimalist works.

In *Chapter 3*, I will analyse *Barth's postmodernist metafiction* (specifically his influential work *Lost in the Funhouse*), by comparing it to the deconstructionist philosophy of Jacques Derrida. Whereas deconstruction is aimed at exposing the illusion of 'presence', which – according to Derrida – motivates the whole of Western thought (that our definitions of concepts connect to an underlying set of pure essences), metafiction is aimed at exposing the illusion of 'reality', which is regarded as an artificial construction, similar to fiction. Both deconstruction and metafiction are aimed, not at the destruction but at the endless 'exhaustion' of these illusions, which are deemed to be inevitable, necessary. This will be described as the (by definition) endless reflexive-ironic strategy of both deconstruction and metafiction. According to Wallace and several scholars, this leads to a non-committal introversion that is similar to the position analysed in Chapters 1 and 2 as a phenomenon in the story-worlds of the studied novels, but that in Chapter 3 is seen to be characteristic of a literary work itself.

In *Chapter 4*, we will see that, subsequently, this reflexive-ironic consideration of language and reality is, in a sense, taken even further in *Ellis's postmodernist minimalism*, which seems to express, above all, the impossibility of meaning (and of offering any meaningful description of reality): Ellis's novels portray postmodern reality as a grim, hopeless world, filled with shallow, egoistic characters, narrated in a blank, affectless tone. His 1991 novel *American Psycho* offers the most extreme and consistent elaboration of this fixed worldview. In this chapter, I will analyse the novel's first-person narrator, Patrick Bateman – whose perspective coincides completely with the perspective of the novel – as the embodiment of the form of irony criticized along Kierkegaardian lines in Chapter 2. I will show that *American Psycho* is not just a *portrayal* of extreme irony but also an *embodiment* of it; in Ellis's postmodernist minimalism it has become impossible to formulate any meaning or value, at all.

Part 2 of this study is dedicated to the explication and analysis of the portrayal, offered in the novels of Wallace, Eggers and Foer, of the solutions to – that is, the attempts to avoid, answer or overcome – the problems discussed in Part 1.

This requires, first of all, that an account is given of the *late-Wittgensteinian view of language and literature*, to which Wallace, as we have seen above, declares his adherence. As an alternative to the postmodernist view, the thought of the later Wittgenstein forms the basis of the ability of Wallace's works, and of Eggers's and Foer's works following in Wallace's footsteps, to speak meaningfully again about sincerity, reality-commitment and community. In *Chapter 5*, I will use Wittgenstein's descriptions to show that the supposed 'illusion' (crucial to deconstruction and metafiction) of the connection between language and reality, is actually irrelevant for the meaningful functioning of language. This will lead to the formulation of a late-Wittgensteinian view of literature, in which literature is understood as a form of 'grammatical' investigation: an investigation of our cultural semantic structures that forms an important foundation for our use of complex, moral concepts; that is, concepts that are tied in with what we regard as human virtue. Here, the term 'virtue' refers to what is needed to 'be' (to be human, a self), to live. Or as André Comte-Sponville writes: 'In the general sense, virtue is capacity; in the particular sense, it is human capacity, the power to be human.'[71]

This analysis of the (engaged) view of fiction underlying the works of Wallace, Eggers and Foer, paves the way for the analysis of the virtues – sincerity, reality-commitment and community – portrayed in the story-worlds of those works.

Chapter 6 will offer an analysis of the desire for *sincerity*. I regard sincerity as a basic attitude, forming a sincere, stable self (opposed to the empty fragmentation of hyperreflexive irony). To gain a better understanding of sincerity as such a basic attitude, as a virtue making all other virtues possible, I will again turn to Sartre. I will use the heuristic perspective of Sartre's view of consciousness to rehabilitate sincerity

---

[71] Comte-Sponville, *A Short Treatise on the Great Virtues*, 3; cf. Wallace's statement that he wants fiction 'to illuminate the possibilities for being alive and human in it' (McCaffery, 'Interview', 131).

as the basic existentialist virtue of the contemporary individual (thereby showing Sartre's critique of sincerity to be inconsistent with his own descriptions, and thus correcting and reconstructing the Sartrean view). Subsequently, I will analyse the novels in light of this concept of sincerity, via several case studies, which in turn will also serve to underpin this new understanding of sincerity.

In *Chapter 7*, I will further elaborate the desire for *reality-commitment*: the need for the individual to connect himself to the world, by making choices. In Kierkegaard's philosophy, 'choice' (as the alternative to endless irony, which implies not-choosing) marks the transition from the aesthetic to the ethical life-view. By means of additional Kierkegaardian notions (such as 'despair', 'passion', 'repetition', and the self as 'gift' and 'task'), I will analyse the novels' portrayal of how individuals come to realize, through the ethical action of choice, a commitment to reality. This will be shown to imply relying on something outside the self, something in the world, something that transcends the individual and that does not lie fully within the individual's control.

Chapter 8 will offer an analysis of the need for *community*. In my opinion, Sartre and Kierkegaard fail to sufficiently address the role of other human beings in meaningful self-becoming. Since this social element can be seen to play a very important role in the novels, the analysis offered in this final chapter will take its lead from Camus's descriptions of the rebellious, solidary community. First, Camus's two central notions of absurdity and rebellion will be connected to the other heuristic perspectives employed in the rest of the study. Subsequently, the importance of the other will be shown for Camus to flow from these observations, and the novels will be shown to offer a similar, if perhaps somewhat more tentative movement, through their emphasis on attention and trust. Finally, I will analyse, on the basis of the descriptions offered both in Camus and in the novels, wherein this importance of the other, of community lies.

Part One

Problems

1

Hyperreflexivity

Introduction

The novels of Wallace, Eggers and Foer are filled with characters whose self-consciousness has taken on an excessive form and has come to impede their attempts to live a meaningful life. Wallace's *Infinite Jest* describes such characters as identifying 'their whole selves with their head'. In the novel the problem of addiction is a metaphor for the problem of excessive self-consciousness (which is shown to be the essential characteristic of addiction). One of the slogans of 'Addicts Anonymous' (AA) is 'My Best Thinking Got Me Here'. *Infinite Jest* describes that 'most Substance-addicted people are also addicted to thinking', that almost all of their compulsive thinking is about themselves, and that the AA term for this addictive self-reflection is 'Analysis-Paralysis'.[1] In Foer's *Extremely Loud & Incredibly Close*, a similar dynamic of paralysing, alienating self-reflection is described by Thomas, Oskar's grandfather: '[T]he distance that wedged itself between me and my happiness wasn't the world, [it was me, my thinking]. I think and think and think, I've thought myself out of happiness one million times, but never once into it.'[2] In Eggers's *You Shall Know Our Velocity*, the main character Will is also plagued by the constant, self-reflective discussions in his head: 'It would be fun, I suppose, if it wasn't constant and so *loud*. [. . .] after many years of enjoying the debates, I wanted them to end. I wanted the voices silenced and I wanted less of my head generally.'[3]

Just to clarify: I will regard consciousness as the conscious experience of oneself and the world (for example, of pain, or of a tree); subsequently, in reflection consciousness turns back on that experience, making the experience as such the object of consciousness, reflecting on it (what does the pain feel like, what does the tree look like?); finally, in *self*-reflection (or: reflexivity) consciousness turns its attention towards itself, towards the consciousness that 'has' that experience and that performs the reflection upon it – so, it turns in on the consciousness feeling the

---

Unless otherwise indicated, translations are mine.
[1]   IJ, 272, 1026, 203.
[2]   ELIC, 17.
[3]   YSKOV, 27.

pain, seeing the tree. By excessive self-reflection is meant a form of consciousness that, because of its constant thinking about (distancing from, doubting) itself, estranges from that self, losing sight of (and contact with) its relations to the world and other people (leading to feelings of emptiness and even depression). To refer to this problematic form of self-consciousness, I will adopt the term 'hyperreflexivity', defined by phenomenological-psychologists Louis Sass and Josef Parnas as 'forms of exaggerated self-consciousness in which aspects of oneself are experienced as akin to external objects'. It is interesting to note that they regard hyperreflexivity as belonging to the 'prodromes' (early symptoms) of what they describe in general as 'self-disorders' (disturbances of the relation to or perception of the self).[4]

Whereas constant self-reflection is often regarded as a good thing, as the philosophical activity *par excellence*, precluding naïveté and forcing us to constantly re-evaluate our assumptions and judgements,[5] the novels of Wallace, Eggers and Foer portray it as also potentially *damaging* to the self. Such a portrayal does not imply a plea for mindlessness and is in fact a valid philosophical position. As Sass writes: 'According to one influential tradition, philosophical reflection is a sort of ultimate expression of the vitality of the human essence, but there is another tradition that has seen philosophy as something unnatural and "out-of-order", *contrary* to the health of the human condition.'[6] Watchfulness for such 'unhealthy' habits of thought has always been a central concern of Wallace. James Ryerson writes: '[Wallace] was perpetually on guard against the ways that abstract thinking (especially thinking about your own thinking) can draw you away from something more genuine and real.'[7]

This chapter will offer an analysis of the problem of hyperreflexivity, as portrayed in the novels of Wallace, Eggers and Foer, in light of Sartre's early, phenomenological-existentialist philosophy. But because these novels show constant self-reflection as a problem that has become exacerbated and widespread in contemporary Western culture, in section 1, I will first explore the aspects of Western life that are portrayed in the novels as contributing to the increased reflexivity of the contemporary individual's existence (and, thus, to the corresponding rise of the problem of *hyper*reflexivity). I will do so by identifying in these works five factors described by Anthony Giddens as making the contemporary self into a necessarily '*reflexive project*'.[8] Having established that contemporary Western life indeed seems to require constant self-reflection, we then have to understand why this can have problematic effects. To that end, in section 2, I will first offer an outline of Sartre's view of being, (self-)consciousness and the self, and connect this to the (existentialist) view underlying Wallace's work. This will establish why, for Sartre, the problem of self-reflection lies in the fact that it turns consciousness into an object, which conflicts with its 'non-thinglike' character, and results in alienation from the self; this also connects Sartre's analysis to the above-quoted definition of hyperreflexivity, which,

---

[4] Sass and Parnas, 'Schizophrenia, Consciousness, and the Self', 427, 437.
[5] E.g. Hutcheon, *A Poetics of Postmodernism*, 53.
[6] Sass, 'Self and World in Schizophrenia', 266–7.
[7] Ryerson, 'Introduction: A Head That Throbbed Heartlike', 1.
[8] Giddens, *Modernity and Self-Identity*, 32.

as said, is based on a phenomenological view as well.[9] Subsequently, in section 3 I will analyse, from this heuristic perspective supplied by Sartre's philosophy, the different instances of reflexive self-alienation portrayed in the fiction of Wallace, Eggers and Foer. I will discuss the following five (Sartrean) instances of increasing reflexive self-alienation (which follow and build on each other) that can be identified in these works: (1) the internalization of the look; (2) language as objectification; (3) the 'poisoning' of experience; (4) bad faith; and (5) solipsism.

1. Factors of heightened contemporary reflexivity

The problem of excessive self-consciousness is portrayed in the works of Wallace, Eggers and Foer against the background of the Western world at the end of the twentieth or beginning of the twenty-first century. Though this problem is in no way unique to the current, postmodern period in Western culture, and probably not even to the past century, it has become exacerbated and more widespread in current times. Through their depiction of this problem, the literary works in question offer insight into different aspects of contemporary Western life that contribute to the increased reflexivity of the contemporary individual's existence and, thereby, to the rise of the problem of *hyper*reflexivity. This section offers a brief exploration of these contributive aspects.

In *Modernity and Self-Identity* (1991) Anthony Giddens describes five factors that can also be discerned in the works of Wallace, Eggers and Foer. For Giddens, as in the novels, '[t]he backdrop here is the existential terrain of late modern life'. He writes that '[i]n the settings of what I call "high" or "late" modernity – our present-day world – the self' has become 'a *reflexive project*'. Giddens explains: 'Modernity's reflexivity refers to the susceptibility of most aspects of [social life] [. . .] to chronic revision in the light of new information or knowledge.' Contemporary Western life forces individuals to constantly perform reflexive operations: to reconsider, to doubt previous insights and decisions. According to Giddens this 'radical doubt is an issue which [. . .] is not only disturbing to philosophers but is *existentially troubling* for ordinary individuals'.[10] Giddens mentions the following five factors as contributing to the contemporary Western individual's heightened reflexivity: (1) 'living in a post-traditional order'; (2) the 'pluralisation of life-worlds'; (3) 'the contextual nature of warranted beliefs under conditions of modernity'; (4) 'the prevalence of mediated

---

[9] Cf. Sass's description of the dynamic of consciousness and self-consciousness: 'There is a potential for estrangement in every act of consciousness. To become aware of something, to know it as an object, is necessarily to become aware of its separateness, its nonidentity with the knowing self that one feels oneself to be at that very instant. [. . .] And since this is an *essential* fact about consciousness, it must surely apply to self-awareness as well: to know my own self is, inevitably, to multiply or fractionate myself; it is to create a division between my knowing consciousness and my existence as a perceivable individual who interacts with others or subsists as a body of flesh and blood' (Sass, *Madness and Modernism*, 75).

[10] Giddens, *Modernity and Self-Identity*, 80, 3, 32, 20, 21.

experience'; and (5) 'the transformation of intimacy'.[11] I will use these factors listed by Giddens to outline the general portrayal of the contemporary Western individual's life (and its heightened reflexivity) offered in the literary works of Wallace, Eggers and Foer.[12]

1.1. Living in a post-traditional order

First of all, contemporary Western culture can be characterized as 'a post-traditional social universe'. Giddens writes: 'by definition, tradition or established habit orders life within relatively set channels'. He adds that, however, 'the signposts established by tradition now are blank'.[13] The lives of most Western individuals are no longer guided by a clear tradition, something that orders and directs all of their choices. In his essay 'E Unibus Pluram', Wallace describes the effect of the fact that there are 'no sources of insight on comparative worth, no guides to *why* and *how* to choose among experiences, fantasies, beliefs, and predilections', as follows: 'When all experience can be deconstructed and reconfigured, there become simply too many choices. And in the absence of any credible, noncommercial guides for living, the freedom to choose is about as "liberating" as a bad acid trip.'[14]

In Eggers's *A Heartbreaking Work of Staggering Genius* the absence of tradition and authority has a very tangible, tragic cause: Dave's parents both die of cancer within a short period of time, after which he becomes in charge of his little brother's upbringing, 'an orphan raising an orphan', 'rootless, ripped from all foundations'. Dave says that at first he was confident about their independence, about their ability to build their own life, from the ground up, as they saw fit. But it turns out there is simply too much to do, too much that has to be thought about.[15] The resulting problem of choice (how and what to choose) continues into Eggers's second book *You Shall Know Our Velocity*, where it frustrates main character and first-person narrator Will in a more general sense: 'All I ever wanted was to know what to do.'[16]

In Foer's *Extremely Loud & Incredibly Close* one way in which the contemporary absence of tradition and decisive criteria is symbolized, is through the last game of 'Reconnaissance Expedition' that Oskar is sent on by his father, before the latter dies in the 9/11 attacks. Oskar gets a map of Central Park, but no clues whatsoever: 'I didn't know what I was looking for. [. . .] There was nothing, which would have been unfortunate, unless nothing was a clue. Was nothing a clue?' Oskar tries to connect the

---

[11] Ibid., 82–7.
[12] The listed developments form the general cultural decor of contemporary Western existence, and thus the starting point for all kinds of problems, analyses and possible solutions. But, as such, they also form the background of the worlds portrayed (and the specific aspects emphasized) in the novels under review. Also, to be clear: I will not try to describe the *causes* of these developments, of these (changed) aspects of Western life; this section is limited to the description of the influence of these aspects on contemporary reflexivity.
[13] Giddens, *Modernity and Self-Identity*, 80, 82.
[14] EUP, 75–6, 79.
[15] AHWOSG, 235–6, 61, 66.
[16] YSKOV, 323.

things he has found in the park into some meaningful pattern, but: 'I could connect them to make almost anything I wanted, which meant I wasn't getting closer to anything. And now I'll never know what I was supposed to find.'[17]

Wallace's *Infinite Jest* describes a world in which all guidelines to meaningful life seem to have been lost. Marathe, a Quebecois terrorist, states that all '*free* choices follow from this: what is our temple. What is the temple, thus, for U.S.A.'s?', to which he adds: 'You stand on nothing. [. . .] You fall; you blow here and there. How does one say: "tragically, unvoluntarily, lost."' In the absence of any meaningful criteria, addiction, as a self-absorbed, reflexive state of non-decision, is widespread in *Infinite Jest*. Most of the characters are involved with drugs: 'Like who isn't, at some lifestage, in the U.S.A. and Interdependent regions, in these troubled times.'[18]

1.2. Pluralisation of life-worlds

The second factor of heightened contemporary reflexivity is the 'pluralisation of life-worlds', Giddens writes: 'throughout most of human history, people lived in social settings that were fairly closely connected with each other. [. . .] The settings of modern social life are much more diverse and segmented.'[19] Contemporary Western individuals are exposed to numerous different life-worlds, different cultures or subcultures – countries, nationalities, languages, religions, life-views, et cetera. The different aspects of these life-worlds reflect back on the life of the individual confronted with them. All of the works of Wallace, Eggers and Foer offer Western perspectives, but they also show the enormous diversity within that cultural hemisphere, and the impression that the rest of the world is close at hand. Often this plurality ties in with the above-mentioned, post-traditional nature of the world described in their fictions.

In Foer's *Everything Is Illuminated* one of the main characters and narrators is an American young man, 'Jonathan Safran Foer', who goes to the Ukraine to document his Jewish ancestry, but, finding nothing, ends up turning the history of his family into a highly fantasized, escapist fable. Alexei Perchov, the other main character and narrator, is a young post-Soviet Ukrainian, who regularly expresses his adoration of American pop culture, and, though having been raised in an anti-Semitic domestic climate, discovers the Jewish roots of his own family.

In Eggers's *You Shall Know Our Velocity* Will and Hand travel (halfway) around the world in eight days: from Chicago to Greenland, on to Senegal, Morocco and (via London) to Estonia. The erratic 'plurality' of their travel schedule is mirrored by the different life-directions Will envisions for himself: a life in Senegal, a life sailing, and one organizing rafting tours in Alaska. 'So choose one', Hand says. 'That's the problem, dumbshit', replies Will.[20]

---

[17] ELIC, 8, 10.
[18] IJ, 107, 108, 53.
[19] Giddens, *Modernity and Self-Identity*, 83.
[20] YSKOV, 123, 112–13.

Although all the novels being examined portray characters from different (American) subcultures, *Infinite Jest* offers a veritable abundance of representatives from different US sociocultural strata. The novel features more than 200 characters, from Hal Incandenza, hyperintelligent tennis prodigy, to Don Gately, ex-burglar, -convict and -drug addict; from Joelle van Dyne, who is both the 'Prettiest Girl of All Time' and the mysterious, despair-filled radio personality 'Madame Psychosis', to Mario Incandenza, who 'doesn't seem to resemble much of anyone'[21] in the novel, because he suffers from severe physical handicaps, but also because he is compassionate and kind, contrary to the cynical, self-absorbed nature of most of the other characters; and from Rémy Marathe, Quebecois wheelchair terrorist, to Poor Tony Krause, homosexual prostitute and desperate heroin addict. The wide diversity of life experiences and existential circumstances of these characters is described in great detail, as life-worlds worthy of attention in their own right.

1.3. Contextual nature of warranted beliefs

A third factor in the heightening of reflexivity lies in what Giddens describes as 'the existential impact of the contextual nature of warranted beliefs under conditions of modernity'. He writes: 'The reflexivity of modernity operates, not in a situation of greater and greater certainty, but in one of methodological doubt.' Contemporary individuals cannot regard the things they 'know' as absolute certainties anymore; all of our insights have become temporary, Giddens writes: 'Even the most reliable authorities can be trusted only "until further notice".' The self-conscious provisionality of our convictions, like the aspects contributing to contemporary Western reflexivity, is not an academic issue, but something that is *'existentially troubling'* for everybody.[22] We can find this contributive factor and its disturbing existential impact illustrated in countless places in the works of Wallace, Eggers and Foer, often as a leitmotiv, as a quest for meaning.

As mentioned above, in Foer's *Extremely Loud & Incredibly Close*, Oskar is sent on a search for meaning by the map of Central Park that his father gives him. Because his father does not give him any clues about what to look for, Oskar wonders how he will ever find the right thing, what he is supposed to find, to which his father replies that it could also mean that there is no wrong thing to find. Elsewhere in the book, the father elaborates on the felt contextuality and provisionality of our insights: 'There's nothing that could convince someone who doesn't want to be convinced. But there is an abundance of clues that would give the wanting believer something to hold on to.' To which he adds: 'Maybe we're just missing things we've lost, or hoping for what we want to come.'[23] The rest of the novel shows Oskar learning to cope with this aspect of contemporary life, and finding his own 'clues' in his search for meaning.

---

[21] IJ, 239, 170, 101.
[22] Giddens, *Modernity and Self-Identity*, 83–4, 21.
[23] ELIC, 9, 221–2.

In Eggers's *You Shall Know Our Velocity* the troubling effect of this aspect of contemporary Western existence becomes very clear through the descriptions of the thoughts of first-person narrator Will. He finds that the constant discussion of insights in his own head does not lead anywhere: 'There was nothing left to debate, no heated discussion that seemed to progress toward any healing solution.' To which he adds: 'we insisted on distorting things to make it seem like we were all, with each other, in such profound disagreement about everything – that first and foremost there are two sides to everything'. Will is tired, worn down by these constant reflexive reconsiderations: 'I wanted them to end. I wanted the voices silenced and I wanted less of my head generally. I didn't want the arguments.' Instead, Will desires some form of meaning: 'I wanted agreement now, I wanted synthesis and the plain truth – without the formalities of debate.'[24]

In Wallace's works this 'methodological doubt' and its troubling effects are a recurrent theme as well. In *Infinite Jest* addiction is connected to excessive self-reflectivity, as both are states in which it becomes impossible for an individual to reach conclusions. Also, Wallace's works frequently describe double-binds that result from the constant reflexive reconsideration of viewpoints. 'Brief Interview #28', from the short story collection *Brief Interviews with Hideous Men*, offers the following example: 'Schizophrenic media discourse exemplified by like for example *Cosmo* – on one hand [women today are now expected to] be liberated, on the other make sure you get a husband.' The 'hideous men' discussing this are themselves highly reflexive, and seem to maliciously enjoy theorizing about these difficulties: '[T]oday's women are in an impossible situation in terms of what their perceived sexual responsibilities are.'[25] Wallace often describes characters using double-binds to justify apathy or disingenuity, as there seems to be no preferable alternative.

1.4. Prevalence of mediated experience

The fourth influence Giddens lists, is 'the prevalence of mediated experience'. Many of our experiences are mediated, which means that we have not experienced the objects or events in question firsthand, but indirectly, through a medium that brings them to us, allowing us to witness them, to experience them secondhand. Giddens mentions television, newspapers and magazines, but since the publication of his book the world has seen the rise of the internet, as an information exchange medium with an enormous impact on the way we experience the world. In today's world, Giddens's assertion that '[w]ith the increasing globalization of media, a multifarious number of milieux are, in principle, rendered visible to anyone who cares to glean the relevant information' is applicable more than ever.[26]

This development is also an integral part of the contemporary Western world portrayed in the works of Wallace, Eggers and Foer. In a sense it has even become old

---

[24] YSKOV, 27.
[25] Wallace, 'Brief Interviews with Hideous Men III', *Brief Interviews with Hideous Men*, 196.
[26] Giddens, *Modernity and Self-Identity*, 83.

news, a simple fact of life in these books. *Extremely Loud & Incredibly Close*'s Oskar, for example, is a child of the information age. He has learned much of what he knows on the internet, through Google – about 'sharks, who die if they don't swim, which I know about', about the meaning of the word 'decapitated', 'which I know about but really, really wish I didn't', and when he comes up with the plan to dig up his father's coffin, which was buried empty because there were no bodily remains recovered after the 9/11 attacks: 'I could fill the coffin with jewelry, like they used to do with famous Egyptians, which I know about.'[27]

But what exactly is the influence of these developments on heightened reflexivity, besides the fact that there is simply so much more information to take into account? The fictions of Wallace, Eggers and Foer show that the enormous amounts of mediated experiences that the contemporary Western individual is exposed to do not simply function descriptively, as a disclosure of things individuals might not have witnessed otherwise; they also, and maybe even more so, function prescriptively: the effect of these mediated experiences is not just that they offer information, but that they become the standard by which individuals judge their own experience.[28] In *Everything Is Illuminated* Alex idolizes (the image he has formed of) American life, and makes it the benchmark for how he wants his own life to be: 'I dig American movies', he says, and, clearly, these movies determine the other things Alex 'digs', namely: 'to disseminate very much currency at famous nightclubs in Odessa. Lamborghini Countaches are excellent, and so are cappuccinos.'[29] A large section in the middle of *A Heartbreaking Work of Staggering Genius* is structured as a (mock) interview between Dave and a casting producer from the MTV reality show *The Real World*. Throughout the interview Dave defines himself almost exclusively through how he is seen, or wants to be seen, by others, as if he were already a participant on a reality-TV show; he could be the 'normal', 'average' character, 'one whose tragic recent past touches everyone's heart, whose struggles become universal and inspiring'.[30] In *Infinite Jest* the narrator states: 'the lively arts of the millennial U.S.A. [. . .] are our guide to inclusion. A how-to'.[31] One of Wallace's short stories, with the telling title 'Think', describes a man's experience of the onset of an extramarital affair: 'We see these things a dozen times a day in entertainment [. . .]. A different man might have said what he'd seen was her hand moved to her bra and *freed* her breasts.' He sees the woman 'replaying a scene from some movie she loves': 'Her expression is from Page 18 of the Victoria's Secret catalogue [. . .] [,] a combination of seductive and aroused, with an overlay of slight amusement meant to convey sophistication, the loss of all illusions long ago.'[32] In his essay 'E Unibus Pluram', Wallace writes that individuals will become 'vastly

---

[27] ELIC, 87, 317, 321.
[28] Cf. Eggers's *The Circle*, in which the prevalence of mediated experience, and the effects thereof, is one of major themes – e.g. 'You comment on things, and that substitutes for doing them. You look at pictures of Nepal, push a smile button, and you think that's the same as going there' (Eggers, *The Circle*, 261).
[29] EII, 2.
[30] AHWOSG, 183, 205.
[31] IJ, 694.
[32] Wallace, 'Think', *Brief Interviews with Hideous Men*, 61–2.

more spectatorial, self-conscious', as a result of the increasing amounts of mediated experiences they undergo in addition to their limited, direct experience. These mediated experiences become an enormous frame of reference, on the basis of which individuals watch, compare and direct their own, personal experience (in Wallace's words: people start to 'experience "experiences"').[33]

1.5. Transformation of intimacy

The fifth and final factor in heightened contemporary reflexivity is 'the transformation of intimacy'. Giddens states: 'It is characteristic of modern systems of sexual intimacy and friendship that partners are voluntarily chosen from a diversity of possibilities.' Modern-day individuals want to engage in a romantic relationship or friendship mainly for the sake of the emotional satisfaction, the happiness that this relationship itself brings them. Therefore, these relationships with others entail frequent reflection; from time to time the question arises as to whether they are still satisfactory and a source of happiness. Giddens writes about these 'pure relationships' that: 'The more a relationship depends only upon itself, the more such a reflexive questioning comes to be its core.'[34] So, the reflexive nature of the contemporary relationship is at the same time a constant threat to that relationship.

In fact, the works of Wallace, Eggers and Foer describe a world in which this reflexive examination is carried through, eventually at the *expense* of individuals' meaningful relationships with other people: many characters are so caught up in their self-reflective processes – they are truly self-absorbed – that profound interpersonal connections have been lost. The self-reflecting individual always places himself over against the world and others, who are objects of the individual's evaluation at best. It is in this sense that we should understand Oskar's remark, in *Extremely Loud & Incredibly Close*, that: 'It probably gets pretty lonely to be anyone.'[35] In *You Shall Know Our Velocity* the distancing, self-reflective attitude of the individual is frequently symbolized by the simple image of 'eyes', referring to the individual as observing but not participating. Will says: 'There wasn't one thread connecting us to anyone [. . .] it was just us, ghosts, irrelevant and unbound, not people but only eyes.'[36] And in *Infinite Jest* Hal says: 'Welcome to the meaning of individual. We're each deeply alone here.'[37]

By identifying the above-mentioned factors contributing to heightened reflexivity, we have established that contemporary Western life indeed requires almost constant self-reflection. Having done so, we will now, in section 2, turn to Sartre's analysis of what consciousness and self-reflection are exactly, so that we can start to understand how heightened contemporary reflexivity (of which we have seen the contributive

---

[33] EUP, 34.
[34] Giddens, *Modernity and Self-Identity*, 87, 91.
[35] ELIC, 69.
[36] YSKOV, 324.
[37] IJ, 112.

factors above) can lead to the alienating effects portrayed in the fiction of Wallace, Eggers and Foer.

2. Sartre's view of consciousness and self-reflection

This section will offer an outline of the Sartrean view of consciousness and self-reflection underlying the descriptions of reflexive self-alienation which will be further analysed in section 3. Here, I will first describe Sartre's general view of being and consciousness, and subsequently, focus specifically on his view of the self and self-reflection. Finally, I will connect this view to the one underlying Wallace's works.

2.1. Being and consciousness

From the perspective of human consciousness we can distinguish between two 'types' of being, says Sartre: the being of the objects that *appear to* consciousness (that is: the things that a human being 'sees' in the world), which Sartre calls 'being-in-itself', and the being of that perceiving consciousness *itself* (that is, conscious, human being), which Sartre calls 'being-for-itself'.

Being-in-itself, according to Sartre, simply 'is what it is'. It is the thing-like being of objects. Think, for example, of when you see a stone. That stone lies in front of you, limited to what it is, a unity: 'The in-itself has nothing secret: it is *solid*. [. . .] It is full positivity', Sartre writes. Therefore, this type of being is called 'in-itself': it is fully enclosed within itself – it completely coincides with what it is: a stone is simply a stone. 'In-itself' also means that it is closed off from the rest of the world: it 'does not enter into any connection with what is not itself', argues Sartre; 'Being-in-itself has no *within* which is opposed to a *without*', it is 'isolated in its being', it 'knows no otherness'.[38] A stone does not relate itself to the rest of the world; it simply is, in itself.

We should understand this description of thing-like being, of objects that appear to consciousness, in contrast to Sartre's description of the being of consciousness itself. Sartre defines consciousness as follows: 'All consciousness is consciousness *of* something'.[39] The fact that it is always consciousness *of* something, means that being-for-itself, contrary to thing-like being (being-in-itself), does not coincide with itself, and does enter into connection with what is outside itself. It is, after all, consciousness of something, something other, something that is not itself. While being-in-itself is contained 'in itself', being-for-itself has something 'before' it: there is a world 'for' it, of which it is consciousness, to which it relates itself. In phenomenology this is called the 'intentionality' of consciousness: consciousness always has a certain intention, in the sense that it is always directed at something (intends something). Indeed, this is exactly and solely what consciousness is, according to Sartre: 'for consciousness there

---

[38] BN, 21, 22.
[39] Ibid., 16 [emphasis added, AdD; cf. ibid., 17].

is no being outside of that precise obligation to be a revealing intuition of something'.[40] Consciousness is *sheer* intentionality, claims Sartre: it is solely a directedness *at* something. Consciousness itself has no substance: it does not exist as a thing-like something. To be clear: Sartre regards a human being to be a body as well; but as conscious being, a human being is always more than this: because of consciousness, he does not fully coincide with what he 'is' at a certain moment – I will return to this further on in this section.

Sartre concludes that consciousness is in fact 'nothingness'.[41] This means, first of all, that, as outlined above, consciousness 'is' not something, it has no substance, no thing-like being. But Sartre's point stretches further: consciousness is 'nothingness' in the sense that it is the source of '*nothings*', of 'non-beings' in the world;[42] it is the 'origin of nothingness', he writes.[43] Catalano describes a familiar experience to illustrate what Sartre is getting at: '[the immediate] awareness of someone as missing. For example, while walking with someone in a crowd, I suddenly turn and *perceive* that the person is not there'. This 'perception of absence' is an immediate awareness of someone not being there, or, in other words, of consciousness negating, distancing itself from what 'is', and thereby bringing nothingness, non-being (someone who should be there but is not) into the world.[44] Similarly, '[i]n posing a question I stand facing being in a certain way', writes Sartre, 'the questioner must be able to effect in relation to the questioned a kind of nihilating withdrawal [. . .]; he detaches himself from being'. These situations reveal consciousness (being-for-itself) as nothingness, as sheer distance (to being) in which non-being can arise. As Sartre writes: 'Nothingness is the putting into question of being by being – that is, precisely consciousness or for-self'.[45]

For Sartre, the consequence of consciousness existing as nothingness is that human being has two aspects: transcendence and facticity. As nothingness, the human being is characterized by 'transcendence', the freedom to 'transcend' all the determinations of his existence: 'the condition on which human reality' – by which Sartre means being-for-itself – 'can deny all or part of the world is that human reality carry nothingness within itself as the *nothing* which separates its present from all its past'. To which Sartre adds: 'the for-itself is perpetually determining itself *not to be*'. At any moment, man is free to distance himself from, to transcend what he is (which means: what he has been until now), and choose new attachments. This transcendence does not just manifest itself at a particular moment; it is the continuous process that characterizes conscious being: 'consciousness continually experiences itself as the nihilation of its past being'.[46]

Yet, observes Sartre, the for-itself '*is*', in spite of this constant nihilation. He explains: 'It *is* in so far as there is in it something of which it is not the foundation – its *presence to the world*'.[47] A human being always finds himself in a factual situation, with a factual

[40] Ibid., 17.
[41] Cf. BN, 47: '*The being by which Nothingness comes to the world must be its own Nothingness*'.
[42] Catalano, *Commentary*, 57.
[43] BN, 45.
[44] Catalano, *Commentary*, 57.
[45] BN, 31, 47, 103.
[46] Ibid., 52, 110, 109, 52.
[47] Ibid., 103.

past: he is born in a certain country, raised in a certain family, environment and culture, with a certain education. Sartre calls this situatedness 'facticity'. It is on the basis of this facticity that we can say that being-for-itself 'is', exists. It does so, however, without ever coinciding with this facticity: as 'transcendence', the human being can always distance himself from the facticities that situate him; he 'transcends' them, does not fully coincide with them, is able to relate to and distance himself from them. For example, I am not a Dutchman in the same way that a stone is a stone. I am Dutch, but at the same time I do not completely coincide with my being-Dutch. I am more than my nationality, if only because I am conscious of that nationality, and therefore already at a certain distance to it; I am always free to be more than what I am at a certain moment.

So, for Sartre, human being is characterized by both facticity and transcendence. On the one hand, being-for-itself (consciousness) 'is', has a certain factual existence; on the other hand, it exists as a nothingness, as a relation – that is: a distance, a non-coincidence – to what it 'is'. Therefore, Sartre sometimes describes being-for-itself as a 'being which is what it is not and which is not what it is'.[48]

2.2. Self and self-reflection

What does this mean for Sartre's view of the self and self-reflection? As noted in the previous section, consciousness has no substance; it is sheer intentionality, solely the awareness of something other than itself. From this relational, non-substantial nature of consciousness Sartre concludes that there is no self – no 'I' or 'Ego' – that precedes and unifies consciousness.

'For most philosophers, the Ego is an "inhabitant" of consciousness', Sartre remarks; they regard this Ego as the 'principle of unification', the principle that keeps consciousness together and determines its relations with the world. However, according to Sartre, 'the unifying and individualizing role of the *I* [is] completely useless': it is based on a misconception of consciousness. When we look at the normal, everyday situations that constitute the majority of our conscious states, we can see that there is no 'I' present in these experiences; instead, our consciousness is completely immersed in the world, focusing on what it is consciousness of (and not on consciousness itself). Sartre writes: 'there is no *I* on the unreflected level. When I run after a tram, when I look at the time, when I become absorbed in the contemplation of a portrait, there is no *I*. There is a consciousness of the *tram-needing-to-be-caught*, etc.'[49]

Moreover, this intentionality is what unifies consciousness. In the example above, it might seem that, even though in everyday experience consciousness is indeed not explicitly accompanied by an 'I', an implicit, underlying self is still required to unify consciousness. But this is not the case. Sartre writes: 'consciousness is defined by intentionality. Through intentionality it transcends itself, it unifies itself by going outside itself'.[50] The first part of this passage is clear, I think: consciousness is intentionality, an

---

[48] Ibid., 81.
[49] TE, 1, 7, 13.
[50] Ibid., 6.

awareness of something that is not itself. But what does Sartre mean by the assertion that through this intentionality, by 'going outside itself', consciousness 'unifies itself'? He means that consciousness acquires unity from its being-over-against objects, or as Sartre sometimes formulates it, by 'being what it is not'. Consciousness does not need an 'I' to hold it together and to delimit what it is and what it is not; consciousness unifies and identifies itself by not being its objects.

But what is the 'I', then, if it is not an immanent structure of consciousness itself? Sartre acknowledges that we exist as individuals, and that we ascribe an 'I' to ourselves. He holds, however, that this is not the result of something that inhabits, and resides over, consciousness. On the contrary: he regards the 'I', the Ego, the self as a secondary phenomenon that we derive from our experience of 'the unity of our representations'. So, according to Sartre it is not 'the *I* that in fact unifies the representations among themselves'; the 'I' is not the cause but 'merely an expression' of the unity of intentional consciousness.[51] Catalano formulates it as follows: 'the self is a product and not an *a priori* principle of activity'.[52]

As such, argues Sartre, 'as a unifying pole of *Erlebnisse* the Ego is in-itself, not for-itself'. That the 'I' is something that consciousness derives from its own relations to the world – in other words: something that consciousness becomes conscious *of* –, by definition means that the 'I' lies *outside of* consciousness, as an object it encounters in the world: 'the Ego appears to consciousness as a transcendent in-itself, as an existent in the human world, not as *of the nature* of consciousness', writes Sartre. This perhaps somewhat counterintuitive suggestion receives further plausibility from the fact that if our Ego or self were immanent to consciousness, we would have to have a complete awareness of it; the self is, after all, 'in' consciousness. However, this is clearly not the case: getting to know ourselves is a gradual, ongoing process. Or as Sartre puts it: 'the consciousness which I have of the "I" never exhausts it'.[53] This further illustrates the claim that the self is transcendent to consciousness, an object that consciousness discovers in the world.

For the Ego to appear, consciousness has to turn itself into its own object; in other words: it has to perform a reflective operation. Sartre writes: 'The *I* only ever appears on the occasion of a reflective act'.[54] Sartre distinguishes between three 'orders', or 'degrees', of consciousness.[55] The first degree is the aforementioned consciousness that is 'with the world' and, therefore, not explicitly aware of itself; Sartre speaks of 'unreflective' or 'pre-reflective' consciousness. First-order consciousness is 'positional' consciousness of a transcendent object, an object 'outside' itself; here, the term 'positional' (or 'thetic') refers to what is explicitly 'posited' (or 'thematized') by consciousness. For example, in the case of the immediate consciousness of the '*tram-needing-to-be-caught*', the '*tram-that-needs-to-be-caught*' is what is posited by consciousness (what it is about).

[51] Ibid., 3, 4, 7.
[52] Catalano, *Good Faith*, 156.
[53] BN, 127.
[54] TE, 16.
[55] Fretz, 'Individuality in Sartre's Philosophy', 76–7; Priest, *The Subject in Question*, 18; Raynova, 'Jean-Paul Sartre, a Profound Revision of Husserlian Phenomenology', 325.

Aside from positional consciousness of its object, this first-order consciousness is also 'non-positional' consciousness of itself, claims Sartre (with the term 'non-positional' indicating that this is something not explicitly posited by consciousness). What Sartre means by this is that consciousness has to be 'conscious of itself *insofar as it is consciousness of a transcendent object*'; otherwise 'it would be a consciousness ignorant of itself, an unconscious [consciousness] – which is absurd', he writes.[56] Leo Fretz illustrates this first degree as follows: 'when Peter sees a tree, he is *positionally* conscious of the consciousness-transcendent object "tree". As such, he is at the same time *non*positionally conscious of himself, insofar as he is that positing activity'. However, this does not point to some underlying Ego or self. Fretz explains: 'the term "himself" does not in this instance denote a mysterious selfhood lying hidden *within* Peter's consciousness' – an immanent, 'true' self – 'but only his consciousness insofar as this is a tree-positing activity'.[57] In fact, this non-positional awareness is consciousness grasping its own unity through the transcendent object which it intends, which it is consciousness of: 'The object is transcendent to the consciousnesses' – the moments of consciousness – 'which grasp it, and it is within the object that their unity is found. [. . .] In this way, consciousness continually refers back to itself'.[58]

Subsequently, second-order consciousness performs a 'reflective operation' by directing itself at this non-positional consciousness of (the unity of) itself.[59] To take up Fretz's example again: Peter keeps looking at the three, which remains the object of his positional consciousness; but the non-positional consciousness now directs itself towards the non-positional consciousness of itself of the first order.[60] So, instead of referring to the seeing-the-tree itself, it now refers to the (non-positional) consciousness of that seeing. This might sound laboured, but in fact describes an important step in Sartre's understanding of (self-)consciousness, because here the 'I' enters the stage (although the 'I' itself remains unreflected), as the reflective designation of the pre-reflectively experienced unity of consciousness.[61] While first-order consciousness translates as 'seeing a tree', second-order consciousness equals 'I see a tree', but without this 'I' being made into an explicit object. Therefore, second-order consciousness is reflective but not self-reflective.

For this, 'a new, third-order act is needed', Sartre writes.[62] Self-reflection means a third-order consciousness that takes the unreflected 'I' of second-order consciousness as its *explicit* object. Third-order consciousness is thus 'positional' consciousness of itself, while also remaining positional consciousness of the object at which it was directed in first- and second-order consciousness. 'Both the *perception* and the *subject* of this perception are thematized', writes Fretz.[63] Here consciousness has arrived at a

---

56 TE, 8, 13, 7; BN, 8.
57 Fretz, 'Individuality in Sartre's Philosophy', 74.
58 TE, 6–7; cf. Fretz, 'Individuality in Sartre's Philosophy', 73; Priest, *The Subject in Question*, 34–9.
59 TE, 10.
60 Fretz, 'Individuality in Sartre's Philosophy', 75–7.
61 In bad faith one uses this reflective objectification to turn the unity of consciousness into an in-itself (see the next section).
62 TE, 11.
63 Fretz, 'Inleiding', 25.

state of self-reflection. In self-reflection, consciousness takes the 'I' that designates the unity of consciousness as its (transcendent) object.

So, according to Sartre, the self is a product of consciousness's relations to the world, and is thus to be found 'in' the world, and is therefore a public, non-private phenomenon. As previously discussed, in the existentialist view, the self is not some true, inner core the individual already has, and perhaps has to discover and develop; rather, the self arises through the individual's choices and actions in the world. Furthermore, we have seen that Sartre sees self-reflection as turning consciousness into an object (an in-itself); this forms the basis for an analysis, offered in the next section, of hyperreflexive alienation.[64]

2.3. Wallace's existentialist view

Despite the specificity of Sartre's view of consciousness, it fits the general existentialist view of the individual having to become a self, instead of having a self as some sort of inner core. For example, Kierkegaard – as we will see further on in this study – describes the self in similar terms.

In a talk that he gave on Franz Kafka, a writer who is also an important representative of the existentialist tradition, Wallace formulates an almost identical view of the self.[65] Wallace remarks that in our present age it is a common mistake to think 'that a self is something you just *have*'. According to Wallace, we should acknowledge the central insight of existentialism, 'that the horrific struggle to establish a human self results in a self whose humanity is inseparable from that horrific struggle. That our endless and impossible journey toward home is in fact our home' (Wallace also explicitly compares Kafka to Kierkegaard in this respect).[66] And in this context Wallace's statement, 'Although of course you end up becoming yourself' (which became the title of David Lipsky's 300-page 'road trip' interview with Wallace from which it is derived), has a strong existentialist ring to it, asserting the need to *become* yourself.[67] Also, the Sartrean view that the self arises outside consciousness, that consciousness has to be directed towards the world in order to discover the self, fits Wallace's (in this respect quite Sartrean) credo – mentioned in the Introduction – that consciousness needs to be facing outward and not be bent-inwards.

That individuals evade this task of becoming a self (of the self arising in the relations of consciousness to the world) is a classic existentialist motif, namely that of 'anxiety'. In this sense, Wallace again formulates a typically existentialist view when he says that 'the fear is the basic condition, and there are all kinds of reasons for why

---

[64]   Cf. 'The claim that our ego is transcendent is thus to claim two things: First, it is to insist that we interiorize only what we have first encountered in the world. Thus what we call our character, or our self, is the product of the way we interiorize what is given to us in the world. Second, it is to claim that there is no a priori privileged perspective on what I call my self or ego. [Much later in his career] Sartre will refine this view in relation to language, but what he says there can be extended to the self' (Catalano, *Good Faith*, 155).

[65]   Bennett, 'Franz Kafka', 236; Marino, 'Introduction', xv.

[66]   Wallace, 'Some Remarks on Kafka's Funniness', 64–5.

[67]   Lipsky, *Although of Course You End Up Becoming Yourself*, 52.

we're so afraid', but that 'the job that we're here to do is to learn how to live in a way that we're not terrified all the time. And not in a position of using all kinds of different things, and using *people* to keep that kind of terror at bay'.[68] The individual feels anxiety when confronted with existential responsibilities and therefore constantly tries to distract himself, to flee from existential questions that have to be faced if a meaningful life is to be attained.

This motif plays an important role in Wallace's work. In *Infinite Jest*, Avril Incandenza, the mother of main characters Hal and Mario, explains the unhappiness of all the addicted and depressed people that Mario observes around him as follows, explicitly connecting the underlying view of the self to existentialism:

> There are, apparently, persons who are deeply afraid of their own emotions, particularly the painful ones. [. . .] As if something truly and thoroughly felt would have no end or bottom. Would become infinite and engulf them. [. . .] such persons usually have a very fragile sense of themselves as persons. As existing at all. This interpretation is 'existential', Mario, which means vague and slightly flaky. But I think it may hold true in certain cases.[69]

In the works of Wallace, Eggers and Foer such self-alienation is inherently connected to excessive reflexivity. This will be analysed in the following section.

3. The alienation of self-reflection

Now that we have seen that contemporary Western life requires almost constant self-reflection, and have established a Sartrean, existentialist perspective on consciousness and self-reflection, we can proceed to analysing the alienating effect of this excessive contemporary self-consciousness. We have seen that for Sartre the self can never be something fixed, as consciousness is constantly entering into new relations with the world (it is being-for-itself). However, in performing a reflective operation, consciousness makes itself, and no longer its relations to the world, into object. Consciousness objectifying itself means that it will try to ascribe to itself the same being as it does to all objects that appear to consciousness, namely: being-in-itself; in other words, consciousness will try to attribute to itself a fixed being that precedes all its relations to the world. Sartre writes: 'This effort to be to itself its own foundation, to recover and to dominate within itself its own flight [. . .] inevitably results in failure; and it is precisely this failure which is reflection'.[70]

In reflective objectification consciousness is turned into a thing, but because consciousness is a nothingness that cannot be determined as a thing-like essence, the

---

[68]   Ibid., 292; although Wallace uses the term 'fear' instead of 'anxiety' (while according to Kierkegaard these two terms should be distinguished on the basis of the fact that fear is always directed at a more or less specific object, while anxiety lacks a clear object, and is brought forth by the nothingness of the freedom of existence), it is clear from Wallace's explanation that what he is referring to is, or is connected to, anxiety.

[69]   IJ, 765.

[70]   BN, 176–7.

objectification of consciousness will always remain strained: it causes an insoluble tension, because it tries to determine something that can never be fully determined. Therefore, Sartre calls self-reflective objectification 'a perpetually deceptive mirage': it goes against the freedom (transcendence) that consciousness 'is'.[71] It is in this context that Sartre states: 'myself-as-object' is an 'uneasiness'. Elsewhere, he uses the more well-known term 'alienation': objectification is an alienation from myself, an 'alienation of my own possibilities'.[72]

In this section, I will analyse, from the heuristic perspective supplied by Sartre's philosophy, phenomena of increasing uneasiness or alienation resulting from self-reflection, as portrayed in the novels of Wallace, Eggers and Foer. The first four phenomena of reflexive self-alienation, which follow and build on each other, are well-known Sartrean motifs, namely: (1) the internalization of the look; (2) language as objectification; (3) the 'poisoning' of experience; and (4) bad faith, in which self-reflective objectification (and thus alienation) becomes an attitude towards existence. Additionally, Wallace's novels show this attitude escalating into (5) psychological disorders which could be brought together under the philosophical label of ·'solipsism'.[73]

3.1. The internalization of the look

Consciousness experiences itself as an object, for the first time, through the look of the other, when consciousness is turned into an object by another consciousness. Sartre writes: 'If someone looks at me, I am conscious of *being* an object. But this consciousness can be produced only in and through the existence of the Other.' Sartre says that, in this sense, 'the Other is the indispensable mediator between myself and me'.[74] With this objectification by the other comes the experience of uneasiness, of alienation. This is a well-known aspect of Sartre's analysis of the look. In the encounter with the other, I experience how his look reduces me to an object (in *Being and Nothingness* Sartre holds that the confrontation with the other necessarily has this effect on me, but in *Notebooks for an Ethics* it is described as a *possible* effect).[75] For the other, I am part of the world, and I am, in a sense, an object, just like a stone or a tree. The other sees me as a thing, with certain properties and perhaps a certain use, and I have no control over how he defines me.[76]

---

[71] TE, 39; Sartre also says that consciousness can only become a 'quasi-object' for itself (BN, 323).

[72] BN, 299, 286.

[73] As a result of the constant self-reflection required by contemporary Western life (see section 1), the instances of self-alienation that will be analysed below are not merely frequent or recurrent in nature, but a constant and increasingly all-encompassing aspect of the existence-reality of many of the characters in the studied novels.

[74] BN, 295, 246.

[75] E.g. Sartre, *Notebooks*, 280–1; cf. 'The general tenor of *Notebooks* is to move away from the notion of conflict as essential to human relations, and to show how, through generosity, we may overcome conflict and opposition that is initiated by "the look"' (Linsenbard, *An Investigation of Jean-Paul Sartre's Posthumously Published Notebooks for an Ethics*, 125).

[76] Cf. BN, 286.

It is important to note that the main effect of the look of the other, in Sartre's analysis, is that it makes me highly self-conscious. Sartre offers the example of looking through a keyhole: 'I am alone and on the level of a non-thetic self-consciousness. This means first of all that there is no self to inhabit my consciousness.' But then, I hear footsteps: 'Someone is looking at me! [. . .] I now exist as *myself* for my unreflective consciousness [. . .]: I see *myself* because *somebody* sees me.' Sartre writes that the look is first of all an 'intermediary which refers from me to myself'.[77] I appear to myself as an object, which does not do justice to the free (transcending) consciousness that I am.

The opening chapter of Wallace's *Infinite Jest* offers a striking example of this experience when Hal Incandenza is reduced to a thing by the look of others. This example prefigures the *self-reflective* alienation that forms an important theme in the novel. The chapter is narrated in the first person from Hal's perspective. Hal – 17 years old, hyperintelligent, a gifted tennis player, and marihuana addict – is seated in an office of the University of Arizona, for an admission interview. However, he has recently lost the power of speech, and can only utter unintelligible, terrifying sounds. Therefore, he has been instructed by the headmaster and coach from his current school, the Enfield Tennis Academy, to keep quiet and let them do the talking. Because he cannot speak, Hal is not able to prevent being turned into an object by all the people involved. 'I am in here', Hal wants to say, indicating that he himself is present during the interview, but more importantly: that he is his own person, a (free, transcendent) consciousness. The admission committee does not believe that Hal's fabulous test scores and his academic-level essays are really *his*, are his own legitimate achievements; instead, the committee members regard Hal as an object shaped by external forces (his instructors), as a fraudulent product that his institution is now trying to sell to the university. In other words, the committee members deny that Hal has a legitimate self. That Hal is not acknowledged as a self, as being-for-itself, causes him increasing uneasiness and frustration: the 'familiar panic at feeling misperceived is rising'.[78] Eventually, Hal breaks his silence in an attempt to reclaim control, and he tries to explain himself, but his attempts are perceived by the committee members as primal noises and spasms.[79] Subsequently, Hal is pushed to the floor and an ambulance is called. With his face on the ground, re-submitted to external forces, or, as Sartre would say, objectified and denied a human self, Hal thinks:

'I am not what you see and hear.'
Distant sirens. A crude half nelson. Forms at the door. A young Hispanic woman holds her palm against her mouth, looking.
'I'm not,' I say.[80]

---

[77] BN, 283, 284, 282.
[78] IJ, 3, 7, 8.
[79] Perhaps the perceived 'primitivity' of Hal's self-expression symbolizes Hal's desire for a more 'sincere' – and therefore perceived by the committee members as a 'primitive', outmoded – conception of the self; see Chapter 6 of this study.
[80] IJ, 13.

Hal's last remark, 'I'm not', is especially significant when viewing the scene from the perspective of Sartre's theory of consciousness. Hal is a human consciousness, a nothingness. That he is nevertheless regarded as a thing determined by external forces (note the woman who is 'looking'), means that Hal experiences himself as objectified, as alienated from himself.

Sartre's analysis of the look is connected to the problem of hyperreflexivity because human beings subsequently *internalize* this objectifying gaze. Contemporary heightened reflexivity is such that we look upon ourselves as if we were under the constant scrutiny of others. This is one of the many aspects in which addiction is connected to self-reflection in *Infinite Jest*. The many addicted characters in the novel are constantly looking at themselves, trying to manipulate how they are perceived by others but even more so by themselves; so that they can keep telling themselves they are not ('really') addicted. One character, Kate Gompert, for example, is 'like so obsessed with Do They Know, Can They Tell'; while, Ken Erdedy 'considered himself creepy when it came to dope, and he was afraid that others would see that he was creepy about it as well'.[81]

Sartre strikingly illustrates the internalization of the look of the other through the example of shame.[82] In his analysis of this phenomenon he shows that the other need not be present for the objectifying gaze to be felt. Sartre offers the example of shame (think back to the example of peeking through a keyhole): '[I]t is in its primary structure shame *before somebody*. I have just made an awkward or vulgar gesture. [. . .] I neither judge it nor blame it. I simply live it.' But then I look up, realizing someone was there and has seen me: 'Suddenly I realize the vulgarity of my gesture, and I am ashamed.'[83]

As mentioned above, the look of the other is above all an 'intermediary' that refers me to myself. Sartre reiterates this by describing shame as the 'shameful apprehension *of* something and this something is *me*. I am ashamed of what I *am*'. In shame, I appear as an object to myself: I become '*in-itself*, writes Sartre.[84] For this, the physical presence of the other is no longer required. In *A Heartbreaking Work of Staggering Genius*, Dave describes himself in his living room late at night, singing along with a favourite song, moving his hands through his hair while singing, until he messes up the words to the song:

> I became quickly, deeply embarrassed about my singing gaffe, convinced that there was a very good chance that someone could see me – through the window, across the dark, across the street. I was sure, saw vividly that someone – or more likely a someone and his friends – over there was having a hearty laugh at my expense.[85]

[81]   Ibid., 77, 18.
[82]   Note, in this respect, a relatively minor plot element in *Infinite Jest*, the 'Union of the Hideously and Improbably Deformed' (U.H.I.D.), whose members wear a veil to visibly display (instead of being ashamed of) their desire to be hidden from sight (cf. IJ, 534); I will further explore this in Chapter 2.
[83]   BN, 245.
[84]   Ibid., 282, 245, 286.
[85]   AHWOSG, 214.

This example, and the alienation it describes, is clearly of a more light-hearted kind than Sartre's. But it is alienation, nonetheless. Feeling objectified, consciousness suddenly experiences itself as alienated from itself. The (pre-reflective) spontaneity that consciousness was just now, has suddenly been dispelled, seemingly from outside. But no one was there. Reflective consciousness is responsible by putting itself in between its former pre-reflective spontaneity and the world.

3.2. Language as objectification

In self-reflection, I look at myself, isolating aspects of my being from their context, from their connections to the world, and place myself at a distance from them. The danger of self-reflection is that, by objectifying aspects of myself in this way, I truly start to regard these aspects – thoughts and actions I have undertaken – as 'objects' that I somehow 'possess', residing 'inside' me, and that only I truly 'know'. For Sartre, as we have seen above, this is a misconception of the self; according to him, we find the self in the world, and not inside ourselves. But *Being and Nothingness* is in many ways an analysis of such misconceptions of the self, and their (alienating) implications. The next problem the self-objectifying individual runs into is language.

When the individual, trying to reclaim himself from the grasp of the other, wants to express himself, he has to use language. However, the self-reflective individual, as a result of his introspection, has come to regard himself as consisting of unique, private contents, while language consists of terms that are necessarily public, that acquire their meaning by being meaningful *for others*. When the individual expresses himself, his words are subject to the meaning that the listener, as a free consciousness, attributes to them. Sartre writes: '[Language] is the fact that a subjectivity experiences itself as an object for the Other.'[86] To which he adds:

> I cannot even conceive what effect my gestures and attitudes will have since they will always be taken up and founded by a freedom which will surpass them and since they can have a meaning only if this freedom confers one on them. Thus the 'meaning' of my expressions always escapes me. I never know exactly if I signify what I wish to signify nor even if I am signifying anything.[87]

So, the self-reflective individual experiences language as a threat to his self, as a means of objectifying him in improper terms: language has an alienating effect upon him. This experience is a recurrent aspect of the portrayal of the problem of hyperreflexivity offered in the works of Wallace, Eggers and Foer.

Although the connection between depression and self-reflection in *Infinite Jest* and Wallace's other works will be explored mainly in the last subsection of this chapter, it is interesting to note, here, that in the cycle of self-reflectivity that leads up to and is part of depression, the felt inability to express oneself and one's pain, adds to the spiralling

---

[86] BN, 394.
[87] Ibid., 395.

of self-reflectivity and further alienation from oneself.[88] The opening sentence of Wallace's short story 'The Depressed Person' reads: 'The depressed person was in terrible and unceasing emotional pain, and the impossibility of sharing or articulating this pain was itself a component of the pain and a contributing factor in its essential horror.'[89] The portrayal of this 'depressed person' – whose namelessness throughout the story can be regarded as an additional symbol of her self-alienation – ties in with the subject of the previous subsection: the self-reflective objectification of her pain makes the depressed person *ashamed* of relating her problems; she worries that her problems sound like boring clichés and that she comes across as self-pitying:

> [H]ow painful and frightening it was not to feel able to articulate the chronic depression's excruciating pain itself but to have to resort to recounting examples that probably sounded, she always took care to acknowledge, dreary and self-pitying or like one of those people who are narcissistically obsessed with their 'painful childhoods' and 'painful lives' and wallow in their burdens and insist on recounting them at tiresome length to friends who are trying to be supportive and nurturing, and bore them and repel them.[90]

The depressed person's shame and felt inability to express herself aggravate each other, and thereby further her self-alienation. We will return to this story later on in this section.[91]

In *A Heartbreaking Work of Staggering Genius* Dave curses his inability to describe the life that he and his brother Toph are leading. It turns out to be impossible to render a complete picture of their life. Everything he writes fails to match the lived reality he wants to describe: 'To adequately relate even five minutes of internal thought-making would take forever – It's maddening.'[92] However, it is exactly the hyperactivity of that 'internal thought-making', Dave's ceaseless self-reflection, that makes it impossible for him to describe anything, above all his constant thought-making itself.

The alienating effect of language is also a recurrent theme in Foer's works. Many of his characters experience language as not allowing them to adequately express themselves. In *Everything Is Illuminated* the character Safran repeatedly refuses to

---

[88]   The above-mentioned fact that, in the opening chapter of *Infinite Jest*, Hal Incandenza has lost the power of speech, symbolizing his inability to prevent others from objectifying him, might be seen to symbolize a felt, self-reflective inability to express himself adequately on the part of Hal (which, in turn, could be seen as a symptom of his addiction and/or depression). However, the problem here does not seem to be caused by an uneasiness on the part of Hal about relating himself through language; in fact, his 'internal' self-descriptions (to which the reader has access in this chapter through the first-person perspective) are clear and self-confident. The problem, here, seems to lie in how Hal's expressions are *understood* by the people around him (cf. IJ, 9, 10). So, perhaps the fact that these other people only hear 'primal noises' when Hal speaks, tells us more about these people than about Hal himself. I will return to this in Chapter 6.

[89]   Wallace, 'The Depressed Person', *Brief Interviews with Hideous Men*, 31.

[90]   Ibid., 32.

[91]   The further impact of hyperreflexivity on language, especially on fiction-writing, will be discussed in detail in Chapters 3 and 5; in the current section, the goal was to describe the role of language in this spiral of reflexivity.

[92]   AHWOSG, 114, 115.

employ certain commonly used words. He tells his lover, the 'Gypsy girl' that words have been hollowed out by their frequent use, and therefore can never do justice to what he thinks or feels.

Do you think I'm wonderful? She asked him one day as they leaned against the trunk of a petrified maple.
No, he said.
Why?
Because so many girls are wonderful. I imagine hundreds of men have called their loves wonderful today, and it's only noon. You couldn't be something that hundreds of others are.
Are you saying that I am not-wonderful?
Yes, I am. [. . .]
Do you think I am not-beautiful?
You are incredibly not-beautiful. You are the farthest possible thing from beautiful.
She unbuttoned his shirt.
Am I smart?
No. Of course not. I would never call you smart.
She kneeled to unbutton his pants.
Am I sexy?
No.
Funny?
You are not-funny.
Does that feel good?
No.
Do you like it?
No.
She unbuttoned her blouse. She leaned in against him.
Should I continue?[93]

In Foer's second novel, *Extremely Loud & Incredibly Close*, the grandfather loses the power of speech, word by word. In a process of increasing self-alienation, he loses the ability to express himself. The grandfather's self-alienation is caused by his self-reflection, his inwardness, which is symbolized by the fact that 'I' is the last word he is able to speak: 'the distance that wedged itself between me and my happiness wasn't the world, it wasn't the bombs and burning buildings, it was me, my thinking [. . .]. "I" was the last word I was able to speak aloud, which is a terrible thing, but there it is'.[94]

---

[93] EII, 229–30. Also see the conversation between the characters 'Jonathan Safran Foer' and Alex, in which they discuss the difficulty of expressing oneself – in writing and in life in general – and Jonathan remarks that he just wants to do something that he is not ashamed of (ibid., 70).
[94] ELIC, 17.

In closing, we should note that the alienation through language described in this subsection, follows from a self-reflective *misconception* of language: through the objectification of self-reflection, the individual comes to misunderstand his thoughts and feelings as unique objects that he has inside him and that language has to (but is unable to) express.[95]

3.3. The 'poisoning' of experience

Self-reflection, as the internalized look, does not only affect linguistic self-expression, but also experience and action. Sartre speaks of reflection 'poisoning' experience: distancing itself from the spontaneity of experience and turning it into an object, reflection will subsequently poison experience through judgements and the attribution of motives to certain actions. Sartre gives the following example:

> On the unreflected level I come to Peter's aid because Peter is 'needing-to-be-aided'. But if my state is suddenly transformed into a reflected state, then I am watching myself acting [. . .]. It is no longer Peter who attracts me, it is *my* helpful consciousness that appears to me as having to be perpetuated. [. . .] Before being 'poisoned', my desires were pure; it is the point of view I have adopted towards them that has poisoned them.[96]

This poisoning will also interfere with subsequent actions: spontaneity in itself becomes suspect, as self-reflection proves itself capable of always revealing poisonous considerations. Again, reflexivity results in self-alienation: reflection unmasks unselfishly offered help as possibly inspired by self-interest. The spontaneity of consciousness has disappeared and my motives have become unclear.

This poisoning is clearly visible in the portrayals of the experience of contemporary Western life in the works of Wallace, Eggers and Foer. The constant self-reflection of many of the characters interferes with the feeling of 'own-ness' of their experiences, of them being a true expression of themselves. In the case of the grandfather in *Extremely Loud & Incredibly Close*, this is explicitly connected to his loss of the power of speech. This linguistic alienation goes hand in hand with an alienation from experience and action, from a connection with the world. He says: 'the meaning of my thoughts started to float away from me, like leaves that fall from a tree into a river, I was the tree, the world was the river'. Self-reflection only seems to lead to the undoing, the negation of any joyful experience, he states: 'I think and think and think, I've thought myself out of happiness one million times, but never once into it.'[97]

In Wallace's story 'The Devil Is a Busy Man' someone describes having done 'a nice thing for someone' but having to remain nameless, unacknowledged by the beneficiary as having done this 'nice thing', because a 'lack of namelessness on my part would destroy the ultimate value of the nice act'. He describes being tempted to say something

---

[95] This misconception will be addressed in Chapters 5 and 6.
[96] TE, 20.
[97] ELIC, 16, 17.

about it, as he wants to be recognized as a 'good man', but at the same time realizes that, giving in to that desire would keep him from being that good man. These loops of self-consciousness make it impossible for the character to be exactly that; they poison his thoughts and actions, making it impossible for him to be good or sincere. Note the extreme 'black-and-white' contrast of the reproachful remarks that follow the self-reflective annihilation of the altruistic act: '[it] caused me to fail, again, in my attempts to sincerely be what someone would classify as truly a "nice" or "good" person, but, despairingly, cast me in a light to myself which could only be classified as "dark", "evil", or "beyond hope of ever sincerely becoming good"'.[98]

A Heartbreaking Work of Staggering Genius describes multiple situations (including the singing-at-night passage, quoted above) very much akin to Sartre's description of the poisoning of experience, for example: while Dave is scattering his mother's ashes, which starts with simple, pure intentions, his consciousness of this action is gradually poisoned by self-reflection. It makes his actions into an object and forces him to pass judgement on them: is this something beautiful or a terrible cliché? However, the problem is that, as soon as this question arises, the answer already does not matter anymore; through its questioning, self-reflection has robbed the action of its pure spontaneity, and further reflection on self-conscious action only exacerbates this lack of spontaneity – the thinking irrevocably destroys the action:

> I want to be doing something beautiful, but I'm afraid that this is too small, [. . .] this tossing of cremains from a gold tin box into a lake? Oh this is so plain, disgraceful, pathetic–
> Or beautiful and loving and glorious! Yes, beautiful and loving and glorious!
> But even if so, [. . .] I know what I am doing now, that I am doing something both beautiful but gruesome because I am destroying its beauty by knowing that it might be beautiful, know that if I know I am doing something beautiful, that it's no longer beautiful. [. . .] I am a monster. My poor mother. She would do this without the thinking, without the thinking about the thinking –[99]

This disruptive, alienating effect of self-reflection is visible in many places in the works of Wallace, Eggers and Foer, in connection with, among other things, mediated experience (an aspect of contemporary Western life described in the first section of this chapter). The self-reflective awareness of the influence of mediation (examples from the internet, movies or television) on our personal, firsthand experiences, can have the same poisoning effect as described above. For example, in *A Heartbreaking Work of Staggering Genius*, when Dave tries to comfort a friend who has tried to commit suicide, he feels he is basing himself on what he has seen and heard on TV and in movies, and this awareness, the 'obviousness' of his words, makes him nauseous.[100] Awareness of these possible influences can turn experiences into pastiches of mediated experiences, and consequently they no longer feel like one's own experiences, which

[98] Wallace, 'The Devil Is a Busy Man', *Brief Interviews with Hideous Men*, 162–4.
[99] AHWOSG, 399–400.
[100] Ibid., 279.

in turn results in increased self-reflective discretion towards one's own experiences.[101]
The individual is alienated even further from himself.

3.4. Bad faith

Sartre's notion of 'bad faith' is more wide-ranging than the phenomena discussed
above, and will therefore require a more elaborate account. Below, I will offer a brief
outline of Sartre's descriptions of the phenomenon of bad faith, and subsequently use
it to interpret the works of Wallace, Eggers and Foer.[102] However, in his writings Sartre
is inconsistent about one aspect of bad faith that is relevant here, namely whether it
implies a pre-reflective or reflective consciousness. In this respect, I will therefore
follow the analysis of Ronald Santoni, who has shown that, according to Sartre's own
view of consciousness, bad faith necessarily implies a reflective operation.[103]

3.4.1. Sartre on bad faith

We have already seen that, according to Sartre, the 'double property of the human
being' is that he is at once *facticity* and *transcendence*: a human being always finds
himself in a certain factual situation, but at the same time is always already beyond that
situation, in the sense that he is free to relate to it, in a new way.[104] Living this tension,
between being and non-being, is what characterizes human existence. However, in
bad faith, an individual tries to escape from this tension by trying to reduce himself
to one of the poles of his being; he tries to objectify himself as coinciding with either
his facticity or his transcendence (thereby trying to determine himself as thing-like
being). Below, I will briefly summarize both these forms of bad faith.

In the form of bad faith in which 'I *am* my transcendence in the mode of being of
a thing', I regard myself as always beyond any determination or responsibility, Sartre
writes: 'I flee from myself, I escape myself, I leave my tattered garment in the hands
of the fault-finder.'[105] I try to exploit the transcendence that human being, in part,
'is', by holding that this transcendence *determines* my whole being: transcendence
determines me as transcending any determination. Such an individual 'sees himself
as neither a part of, nor responsible for, the choices which he has chosen since he is
beyond his choosing, like the man who when grabbed by the collar always slips out of
the sleeves', as William Smoot aptly observes. Smoot continues: 'he sees himself not as a
situated freedom, but as a ghost-like freedom which glides untouched and untouching
through the world. It is a posture of extreme alienation.'[106] In this form of bad faith, the
individual objectifies himself as un-objectifiable.

---

[101]   Note that this 'awareness' follows from the same self-reflective misconception that was mentioned
        at the end of the previous subsection, and which will be addressed in Chapters 5 and 6.
[102]   I will elaborate on related notions like good faith, impure and pure reflection, sincerity and
        authenticity, and their relation to bad faith, in Chapter 6; here I will limit myself to discussing the
        aspects of bad faith relevant to the problem of hyperreflexivity.
[103]   Santoni, *Bad Faith, Good Faith, and Authenticity*, 45; Busch, *The Power of Consciousness*, 37–8.
[104]   BN, 79.
[105]   Ibid., 80.
[106]   Smoot, 'The Concept of Authenticity in Sartre', 138; cf. Kierkegaard's critique of 'total irony'
        (Chapter 2).

In the other form of bad faith the human being tries to identify himself as pure facticity. Here, the individual determines himself as a being that cannot determine itself, that simply 'is what it is', that is fully determined by what it is, by its nature. One flees from the tension of human-reality by stating the facticity of one's being, denying any self-determination and, with that, any responsibility – 'by affirming what he has chosen but denying its status as choice; in other words, by viewing himself as a *thing* and by giving his values, duties and obligations the status of beings or consequences of beings', Smoot again concisely summarizes. He adds: 'It is this worldview of "thingification" of human existence that the alcoholic in bad faith partakes of when he declares that he cannot help it that he gets drunk for he simply *is* an alcoholic as a tree *is* a tree.'[107] Here, bad faith implies an alienation from the self as a free, self-determining entity, by objectifying being as a facticity.

An individual is 'in bad faith' exactly because he is aware of the double nature of his being that he is trying to conceal from himself. Sartre writes: 'in bad faith it is from myself that I am hiding the truth'. Bad faith is a form of self-deceit. The individual knows that he is lying to himself, but at the same time believes the lie. According to Sartre, this is possible because bad faith is 'in bad faith' about the nature of faith, about the evidence that is required to believe something. In bad faith I formulate 'two-faced concepts' and decide ('in bad faith') that I am convinced by these concepts, while '[i]n truth, I have not persuaded myself'. According to Sartre, bad faith is characterized by the 'firm resolution *not to demand too much*, to count itself satisfied when it is barely persuaded, to force itself in decisions to adhere to uncertain truths'. With bad faith, writes Sartre, a 'peculiar type of evidence appears; non-persuasive evidence'.[108]

At this point in Sartre's description of the self-deceit of bad faith, an inconsistency arises, as we can see from the following statement: 'there is no question of a reflective, voluntary *decision*, but of a spontaneous determination of our being. One *puts oneself* in bad faith as one goes to sleep and one is in bad faith as one dreams'. However, Sartre's own view of consciousness and of the realization of bad faith makes it impossible for bad faith to be a fully spontaneous and pre-reflective attitude, for he claims that: '[s]ince the unreflective consciousness is a spontaneous self-projection toward its possibilities, it can never be deceived about itself'.[109] Pre-reflective consciousness is sheer intentionality, a relation to something it is not; and although consciousness is always consciousness of itself, in the pre-reflective order it remains non-positional: consciousness does not turn itself into an object, so it cannot decide anything about itself, it cannot deceive itself about itself. Santoni concludes: 'if, in fact bad faith is a pre-reflective consciousness, then it would appear to follow that, insofar as bad faith is self-deception, bad faith is not possible'.[110] Within Sartre's view of consciousness, bad faith as a form of self-deceit simply cannot be pre-reflective.

Moreover, looking at the descriptions of bad faith itself, it seems impossible to maintain that it is a phenomenon of spontaneous, pre-reflective consciousness. Bad faith is based on a 'firm resolution', forcing itself to believe things that, intuitively, it

[107] Smoot, 'The Concept of Authenticity in Sartre', 138.
[108] BN, 72, 91.
[109] Ibid., 91, 493.
[110] Santoni, *Bad Faith, Good Faith, and Authenticity*, 125.

does not believe. Bad faith does so by means of 'two-faced concepts' which, according to Sartre, 'we forge expressly to persuade ourselves', when we are not really persuaded.[111] These steps that consciousness undertakes to put itself in bad faith, require a reflective operation: consciousness has to turn its attention towards itself, at least in part, if it is to resolve anything about itself and 'forge expressly' the concepts for its own deception.[112]

Bad faith is a flight from the tension of human existence: the individual in bad faith tries to deceive himself about the true, double nature of his being, and tries to determine himself as a fixed, thing-like being.[113] Sartre summarizes the connection between reflection and bad faith as follows: 'reflection is in bad faith in so far as it constitutes itself as the revelation of *the object which I make-to-be-me*'.[114]

Although bad faith is based on '*non-persuasive* evidence', and therefore 'precarious', belonging to the 'kind of psychic structures' Sartre calls 'metastable', that does not mean that it is limited to being a temporary phenomenon, Sartre says that it is nonetheless an 'autonomous and durable form. It can even be the normal aspect of life for a very great number of people. A person can *live* in bad faith'.[115]

We can see this in many of the characters in the works of Wallace, Eggers and Foer. For the contemporary Western individual, existence has become an ever-present, unremitting question, ever-strengthening the temptation to flee the tension that lies at the heart of it, which is exactly what many of the characters do. Characteristically, their constant self-awareness makes these characters feel objectified as if by outside forces – that is, by the requirements of contemporary Western life –, which also means that they feel little control over the determination of their object-self. However, at the same time, their self-reflection offers them the solution of bad faith: to determine *themselves* as a certain fixed being. Bad faith comes to them as an apparent solution to their uneasiness, but will only add to it, will only aggravate their alienation.

3.4.2. David Foster Wallace

Infinite Jest describes addiction as functioning through bad faith mechanisms. The many addicts in the novel employ both above-described forms of bad faith, to escape acknowledgement and responsibility for their actions. Their desire to flee from the

---

[111] BN, 91.

[112] Santoni concludes: 'because the bad-faith consciousness exploits the autodestructiveness and evanescence of consciousness and forges for itself "two-faced" concepts by which to count itself satisfied or "persuaded" even when it is not persuaded, [. . .] [and] particularly because it makes "knowing preparations" for its own deception, then it would seem to follow that bad-faith consciousness is [. . .] at least in part, a reflective consciousness that is directed upon itself' (Santoni, *Bad Faith, Good Faith, and Authenticity*, 125–6).

[113] This is exactly the 'motivation' from which reflection arises, argues Sartre, as the attempt to ascribe being to oneself, as the 'effort to be to itself its own foundation, to recover and to dominate within itself its own flight' (BN, 176–7); and this effort, as we have now seen, is in bad faith: through reflective objectification the individual tries to escape from the task of human being; cf. 'In self-deceit they become objects through their own look or lock themselves up in their own subjectivity' (Fretz, 'Individuality in Sartre's Philosophy', 88).

[114] BN, 184.

[115] Ibid., 91, 73.

tension of existence can be regarded as the principal motivation of their addiction (connecting it to reflection, which, as we have seen, has the same motivation, according to Sartre). On the one hand, there is the bad faith attitude of regarding oneself as pure transcendence. The addicts deny that they are addicts: for example, they refuse to be determined as such by appealing to the inadequacy or inaccuracy of language, which (the addict claims) can never express the particularity of the addict's situation. Thus, Michael Pemulis, a friend of Hal Incandenza and fellow student at Enfield Tennis Academy, claims that 'addict' is just a 'word'; and Tiny Ewell, when confronted with his alcohol addiction, insists on hearing the exact definition of the word 'alcoholic'. The same attitude can be seen in new members of AA, who – although they are encouraged to 'Identify' with other addicts speaking at a meeting – are eager to 'Compare', to look for differences between themselves and the (other) addicts, as Gately explains: 'I'd just sit there and Compare, I'd go to myself, like, "I never rolled a car", "I never lost a wife", "I never bled from the rectum"', instead of hearing 'how fucking similar the way he felt and the way I felt were, Out There, at the Bottom, before we each Came In'.[116] In this way, the addict 'convinces' himself that no comparison can determine what he 'is'; he always escapes every determination and remains free.

On the other hand, there is the attitude, when the addiction has become an undeniable reality for the addict, of regarding the self's addicted nature as a thing-like facticity, as something that is impossible to change – which it subsequently becomes, more or less, because of the constant self-conscious thinking about this impossibility. For example, Joelle van Dyne compares her attempts to quit drugs to the motorcycle jumps of stuntman Evel Knievel, counting the days she stayed off and adding them up: 'And soon it would get . . . improbable. As if each day was a car Knievel had to clear. One car, two cars. By the time I'd get up to say like maybe about 14 cars, it would begin to seem like this staggering number.' After which Joelle thinks about the rest of the year, the rest of her life, the time that she will have to stay clean: 'looking ahead, hundreds and hundreds of cars, me in the air trying to clear them. [. . .] How did I ever think anyone could do it that way?' We can clearly see how the addict's obsessive self-reflection creates the illusion that addiction is somehow his or her nature, which then makes that addiction appear impossible to kick. As Kate Gompert describes: 'I'm getting more and more miserable and fed up with myself for smoking so much, [. . .] and I start getting high and thinking about nothing except how I have to quit smoking all this Bob."[117] We can recognize Smoot's above-quoted example of the alcoholic claiming to be an alcoholic 'like a tree is a tree': the addict confesses that he or she is an addict, but denies having a real choice in matter, and, therefore, also denies being truly responsible for it.

3.4.3. Dave Eggers

In *You Shall Know Our Velocity* Will is weighed down by the constant, uncontrollable, self-reflective 'debates' in his head. He says: 'I wanted less of my head generally.' Similar

---

[116] IJ, 1066, 205, 365.
[117] Ibid., 859, 77.

expressions appear repeatedly throughout the novel: 'I need sections of my head removed. I need less memory. No memory. I need –' (the end of this sentence seems to mark silence, the emptiness of thought, as a simple but apt reference to 'thoughtless', thing-like being).[118] Will admits that for quite some time he had desired limitations, boundaries, and that for this reason he had even fantasized about car crashes, injuring himself – to limit his choices: 'I wanted something to happen so my choices would be fewer, so my map would have a route straight through, in red.'[119]

These wishes are in bad faith: they express the desire to be relieved of the (constant self-reflective awareness of the) difficulty of being, by sustaining some sort of limitation, in one of the most horrible ways imaginable. (What makes his wish even worse is that Will confesses to it in an imagined conversation with his childhood friend Jack, who actually died in a car accident; at the same time, the fact that Will realizes how horrible this is, and that he speaks about it in the past tense, indicates that, at this point – towards the end of the novel –, he no longer deceives himself with this 'fantasy'.) At an earlier stage in his life, Will had tried to escape the tension of his existence through 'withdrawal', not expressing or participating in human emotions anymore, earning him the nickname 'Robotman'. Also, Will's eight-day trip around the world, which forms the time span of the novel, is prompted by the bad faith reasoning of 'unmitigated movement, of serving any or maybe every impulse'. Every minute has to be exploited. The ambition to seize *every* opportunity is intended to take away the need to reflect upon which opportunity to *choose*. Will refuses to sleep, because sleep means losing time and opportunity, even though part of him knows better.[120] Initially, for Will the only purpose of his trip is 'speed', for speed drowns out the question of being (speeds by it) – it allows him to experience himself as simply an object among objects.[121]

3.4.4. Jonathan Safran Foer

Foer's novels feature various characters who, for different reasons, try to place themselves completely beyond the grasp of others; to repeat Smoot's formulation, these characters 'glide untouched and untouching through the world'. For example, the grandfather in *Extremely Loud & Incredibly Close*, leaves his wife when she is pregnant with their son, and subsequently, for 40 years, writes a letter to his child every day, but he only mails the envelopes – which function as a sign that he exists, but he keeps evading determination by content.[122] Something similar applies to the

---

[118]   YSKOV, 27, 184, 157.

[119]   Ibid., 323.

[120]   Ibid., 152, 153, 9, 252.

[121]   Such bad faith behaviour, the desire to the escape the tension and uncertainty of human-being, is also clearly recognizable throughout Eggers's *The Circle*, e.g., when Mae thinks: '[It occurred to her] that what had always caused her anxiety [. . .] – it wasn't danger to herself or the constant calamity of other people and their problems. It was internal: it was subjective: it was *not knowing*. [. . .] If she could eliminate this kind of uncertainty [. . .] you would eliminate most of the stressors of the world, and maybe, too, the wave of despair that was gathering in Mae's chest' (Eggers, *The Circle*, 194–5).

[122]   ELIC, 233.

young girl Brod, in *Everything Is Illuminated*, who has a reflective aversion to reality: existing things are not good, not beautiful enough for her: '*They were good and fine, but not beautiful. No, not if I'm being honest with myself. They are only the best of what exists*.' She distances herself from the world: 'It was not the world that was the great and saving lie, but her willingness to make it beautiful and fair, to live a once-removed life, in a world once-removed from the one in which everyone else seemed to exist.'[123] She lives in a world 'once-removed', and remains 'untouchable', not committed to anything or anyone – not to Yankel, her adoptive father, and not to The Kolker, her husband.

3.5. Solipsism

In the foregoing, we have seen different instances of excessive self-reflection leading to (increasing degrees of) self-alienation. This hyperreflexivity (and the resulting self-alienation) can, in the final instance, take on such an excessive, problematic form, that it is regarded as a psychological disorder, which we can label solipsism. Often, psychological disorders are associated with a decrease in the rational, critical and self-reflective faculties of a person, but, as Sass writes, '[madness, in at least some of its forms] derive[s] from a heightening rather than a dimming of conscious awareness'. This form of madness is 'generated from within rationality itself rather than by the loss of rationality'. It is 'the endpoint of the trajectory consciousness follows when it separates from the body and the passions, and from the social and practical world, and turns in upon itself; it is what might be called the mind's perverse self-apotheosis.'[124]

Sartre, too, connects self-reflective alienation to psychological disorder. In *The Transcendence of the Ego*, for example, he speaks of the 'various types of psychasthenia' tied up with the self-reflective masking of the tension that underlies human existence.[125] Sass approvingly summarizes Sartre's suggestion that 'delusions' are an 'escape' from 'not so much the content as the form of the real – its ultimate frightening unknowability and its tendency both to demand and resist real-world action';[126] in other words, for Sartre too, they are the result, not of the loss of rational consciousness, but of its 'hyperactivity', resulting in anxious frustration and escape from its dependency upon the world – an exacerbation of the dynamic also underlying bad faith.[127] Subsequently, however, Sartre in some places notoriously concludes that mental illness is a choice, 'an invention so as to be able to live an unlivable situation.'[128] Here, Sass parts ways with Sartre: '[To stress the role of hyperreflexivity is not] to suggest that these developments

---

[123] EII, 79, 80.
[124] Sass, *Madness and Modernism*, 5; Sass, *The Paradoxes of Delusion*, 12; cf. Sass, 'Self and World in Schizophrenia', 252.
[125] TE, 47.
[126] Sass, *The Paradoxes of Delusion*, 49.
[127] Sass speaks of 'a noonday rather than a midnight world'; perhaps we could compare this description of hyperreflexive experience of the world, to Sartre's descriptions of 'nausea', in which the individual experiences the world in overwhelming detail (Sass, *Madness and Modernism*, 5).
[128] Sartre, 'Foreword', 7 ('invente pour pouvoir vivre une situation invivable'); translation quoted in: Busch, *The Power of Consciousness*, 13.

are essentially volitional in nature, as if the fragmentation and dislocation in question were purely the result of some perverse strategy engaged in wilfully.' What, in my opinion, Sartre is wrong to rule out, and Sass is absolutely right to suggest, is that, in these psychological disorders, the '[very processes of introspection] *dissolve* the sense of volition or active engagement', that hyperreflexivity 'can seem, in fact, to be imposed', as an 'irresistible seeing'. In fact, this irresistibility is probably the main reason why we regard this form of self-reflection as a psychological *disorder*. '[What patients like those] cannot seem to control is self-control itself; what they cannot get distance from is their own endless need for distancing', observes Sass. He argues that they suffer from 'an inability to let themselves be caught up in and carried along by the ongoing flow of practical activity in which normal existence is grounded'.[129] These descriptions fit the psychological disorders portrayed in the novels of Wallace, Eggers and Foer. Also, both Sass and Wallace connect the problem of hyperreflexivity to solipsism, as a state in which the above-described self-alienating effects of hyperreflexivity come together.

Let us take a short look at the symptoms ('prodromes') associated with hyperreflexivity, so that we can subsequently view the novels in light of these descriptions:

> Complaints may range from a seemingly trivial 'I don't feel myself' or 'I am not myself', to 'I am losing contact with myself' [. . .] Prodromal patients usually feel detached from the standard cornerstones of identity. They may complain of being 'occupied by, and scrutinizing, my own inner world', of 'excessive brooding [and] analyzing and defining myself and my thoughts', of feeling 'like a spectator to my own life', of 'painful distance to self'.[130]

Elsewhere, Sass quotes a patient describing her symptoms as follows: 'I am somehow strange to myself; I am not myself'; 'It is as if I watched from somewhere outside the whole bustle of the world'; 'It is impossible to stop myself from thinking.'[131]

We have already encountered some of these symptoms, implicitly or explicitly, in the above-quoted descriptions of self-alienation from the novels of Wallace, Eggers and Foer. Indeed, some of these portrayals already pointed towards psychological problems. This is clearly the case, for example, with the grandfather's loss of speech in *Extremely Loud & Incredibly Close*; his affliction is caused by his constant self-reflection, which subsequently isolates him from the world and from his own thought. In *Everything Is Illuminated* Brod suffers from a similar affliction: she seems to exist at a distance from everything, not just from the world and its objects, but also from her own thoughts and feelings – she 'experiences experience', to borrow an expression that both Sass and Wallace use.[132] When Brod falls in love with the Kolker, her future husband, it is because she is in love with the idea of being in love ('She loved what it felt like').[133] In *You Shall Know Our Velocity*, Will's hyperreflexivity causes him to fantasize about 'mental silence' through self-effacement; although he never appears

---

[129]   Sass, *Madness and Modernism*, 240, 241.
[130]   Sass and Parnas, 'Schizophrenia, Consciousness, and the Self', 437–8.
[131]   Sass, 'Self and World in Schizophrenia', 258–9.
[132]   E.g. Sass, *The Paradoxes of Delusion*, 36; EUP, 34.
[133]   EII, 122.

to be truly suicidal, many of his metaphors refer to 'getting rid of' or 'damaging' his head, and his exhausting trip around the world often seems to be an attempt to use himself up. Self-obsession and its damaging effects are also an important theme in *A Heartbreaking Work of Staggering Genius*. One of the most extreme examples of this is John, who tries to commit suicide. Although Dave initially states that there is a right and a wrong way to deal with self-obsession, and that John deals with it the wrong way ('channelling' everything inward), which Dave suggests lies at the root of his suicide attempt, the book is critical of all self-obsession, including Dave's own extroverted version of it.[134]

However, it is only in Wallace's work that psychological disorders connected to hyperreflexivity and self-alienation form a truly explicit and central theme.[135] In his story 'The Depressed Person', for example, the main element of the eponymous main character's depression is that she is caught in a hyperreflexive spiral that makes it impossible for her to focus on anything other than her 'self', as becomes clear when her therapist commits suicide: 'all her agonized pain and despair since the therapist's suicide had in fact been all and only for *herself*, i.e. for *her* loss, *her* abandonment, *her* grief, *her* trauma and pain and primal affective survival'; and, subsequently, this insight can only contribute to the continuation of her hyperreflexive spiral: 'these shatteringly frightening realizations had seemed, terrifyingly, merely to have brought up and created still more and further feelings in the depressed person about *herself*.[136] The story describes symptoms that are strikingly similar to the ones listed by Sass, culminating in the depressed person's fear of losing her 'self': 'she was frightened for herself, for as it were "{her}*self*" – i.e. for her own so-called "character" or "spirit" or as it were "soul"'.[137]

In *Infinite Jest* addiction and depression are inextricably connected, and both psychological disorders are characterized by hyperreflexivity. Almost every character in the novel is addicted, and all these addicts are addicted to thinking, *obsessing* about themselves, in a myriad of ways. About this 'addictive-type thinking' we read: 'it all gets too abstract and twined up to lead to anything'. It just leads to getting 'lost in a paralytic thought-helix', sometimes called 'Marijuana Thinking': they 'Marijuana-Think themselves into labyrinths of reflexive abstraction that seem to cast doubt on the very possibility of practical functioning'.[138] Slowly, this leads to an alienation from one's own thoughts and feelings, as becomes clear in the following description of the mental life of Ken Erdedy, one of the addicts living in Ennet House:

> [Erdedy] thought very broadly of desires and ideas being watched but not acted upon, he thought of impulses being starved of expression and drying out and floating dryly away, and felt on some level that this had something to do with him and his circumstances and [. . .] would surely have to be called his problem.[139]

---

[134] Cf. AHWOSG, 201.

[135] Marshall Boswell offers a detailed analysis of Wallace's short-story collection *Oblivion* as a bleak, merciless portrayal of the 'prison-house of interiority' (Boswell, '"The Constant Monologue Inside Your Head": *Oblivion* and the Nightmare of Consciousness', 168).

[136] Wallace, 'The Depressed Person', *Brief Interviews with Hideous Men*, 56, 57.

[137] Ibid., 57.

[138] IJ, 54, 335, 1048.

[139] Ibid., 26–7.

In the end, the addict's hyperreflexivity leads to a total alienation from the self, where the 'cliché "I don't know who I am"' unfortunately turns out to be more than a cliché'.[140]

This is how, in *Infinite Jest*, addiction inevitably leads to depression, which is therefore just as omnipresent as addiction. In the novel, depression is mostly referred to as 'anhedonia',[141] which is described as a 'kind of spiritual torpor in which one loses the ability to feel pleasure or attachment to things formerly important', 'a kind of radical abstracting of everything, a hollowing out of stuff that used to have affective content'. Terms – like '*happiness, joie de vivre, preference, love*' – are 'stripped to their skeletons and reduced to abstract ideas. They have, as it were, denotation but not connotation', that is, the 'anhedonic' can still use these terms, speak about them, but has become 'incapable of feeling anything in them, [. . .] or believing them to exist as anything more than concepts. Everything becomes an outline of the thing. Objects become schemata. The world becomes a map of the world. An anhedonic can navigate, but has no location'.[142]

The anhedonic cannot 'feel' himself anymore. He stands at a distance from himself, no longer truly in contact with the interaction between self and world, as the result of his continuous objectification of that self. For these characters in *Infinite Jest* the constant reflecting on the self clouds and, eventually, completely impedes assuming the self and its involvements in the world, which in turn leads to the experience of emptiness and loss of self. In the novel, anhedonia is also described as 'complete psychic numbing. I.e. death in life'.[143] Sass uses the same characterization – 'a sort of death-in-life' – in relation to the self-disorders he discusses, and he emphasizes the same reflective abstracting leading to loss of feeling and self-alienation: 'what dies in these cases is not the rational so much as the appetitive soul [. . .]; this results in detachment [. . .][,] and entrapment in a sort of morbid wakefulness or hyperawareness'.[144]

As mentioned above, both Sass and Wallace repeatedly refer to this final outcome of hyperreflexivity as a state of *solipsism*. Sass describes solipsism as a state of mind in which 'the whole of reality, including the external world and other persons, is [regarded as] but a representation appearing to a single individual self'.[145] The solipsist regards only himself – that is, his thoughts and perceptions – as real; the outside world and other people 'disappear' as independently real and meaningful entities. According to Sass, the solipsistic conviction is brought on by 'not a loss but an exacerbation of various forms of self-conscious awareness'.[146] As such, solipsism can be seen as

---

[140] Ibid., 204.
[141] Sass speaks of the same 'diminishment of the sense of vitality, or of existence itself', but feels that the 'term "anhedonia" does not capture the phenomenon, for not merely pleasure but *all* experiences are affected' (Sass, 'Self and World in Schizophrenia', 255). However, in *Infinite Jest* 'anhedonia' is portrayed in this broader sense (i.e. not limited to a diminishment of pleasure), as is clearly shown in the passage quoted.
[142] IJ, 692–3.
[143] Ibid., 698.
[144] Sass, *Madness and Modernism*, 7–8.
[145] Sass, *The Paradoxes of Delusion*, 8 ['regarded as' added, AdD].
[146] Ibid., 12.

the result of hyperreflexivity.[147] In Wallace's work, too, the alienation resulting from hyperreflexivity is repeatedly and explicitly equated with solipsism. *Infinite Jest*, for example, speaks of the 'fall into the womb of solipsism, anhedonia, death in life'.[148] In general, we could say that many of the characters described in this chapter are subject to this '[disease] of thought',[149] which is brought about by their exacerbated self-consciousness: these characters show little interest in others (since they assume that they do not have access to other people anyway) and are convinced of the singularity of their thoughts and feelings. In other words, they seem to have become completely encaged in their own head.[150]

Conclusion

This chapter has offered an analysis of the problem of hyperreflexivity as portrayed in the novels of Wallace, Eggers and Foer. Sartre's view of consciousness has allowed us to understand that, in self-reflection, consciousness is turned into a thing, and that this objectification conflicts with the non-thinglike nature of consciousness, which thereby alienates from itself. The fact that contemporary Western life forces the individual to almost constant reflexivity, aggravates this potential conflict. The final section of this chapter analysed successive instances of this excessive self-reflection leading to increasing self-alienation. The portrayed hyperreflexivity was shown to lead to an eventual loss of the self, or at least to a gradual inability to feel the self (and therefore, to feel that one is or has a self, at all), to what could be called a state of solipsism.

[147] Coming from a phenomenological standpoint which is akin to that of Sartre, Sass also connects this to the later Wittgenstein's philosophy, specifically the latter's view of self-reflection and solipsism: 'Wittgenstein speaks of solipsism as "a serious and deep-seated disease of language (one might also say 'of thought')"'. As we have seen in this chapter, Sartre regards real self-knowledge as looking at one's involvement in the world, not at oneself as if one were an object, or a consciousness filled with object-like states. Compare this to what Sass writes about Wittgenstein's view of the self and self-reflection: 'such thinglike mental states do not exist, except as artifacts of reflection, conceptual postulates for philosophers or psychologists who reflect on experience [. . .] but who have lost touch with the lived reality of prereflective existence' (Sass, *The Paradoxes of Delusion*, 34, 89). In Chapter 5, I will elaborate this Wittgensteinian view.

[148] IJ, 839; cf. Wallace stating, in an interview: 'Das Grausame an der Depression ist, dass sie eine Krankheit mit so viel Selbstbezogenheit ist – Dostojewski zeigt das sehr gut in seinen *Aufzeichnungen aus dem Kellerloch*. Die Depression ist schmerzvoll, man wird aufgezehrt von sich selbst' (Diez, 'Der Klang der Gedanken. Ein Gespräch mit David Foster Wallace', 6).

[149] Cf. Sass, *The Paradoxes of Delusion*, 34.

[150] E.g. Mario's older brother Orin, who regards some of his thoughts as exceptionally horrible, while they are in fact completely average (cf. IJ, 737). The perceived singularity of thoughts and fears that are in fact widely shared, is a recurrent motive in Wallace's work; e.g., in the short story 'Westward the Course of Empire Takes Its Way', Mark Nechtr's 'solipsistic delusion [. . .] that he's the only person in the world who feels like the only person in the world' (Wallace, 'Westward the Course of Empire Takes Its Way', *Girl with Curious Hair*, 304–5).

Endless Irony

Introduction

Problematic irony can be said to follow from the problem of hyperreflexivity: a person who cannot stop thinking about himself and his possible actions, cannot or can only just barely come to conclusions and actions, let alone conclusions and actions to which he is fully committed. The attitude that follows from this is the attitude of irony. Constant self-reflection leads to never being able to fully stand behind one's actions, for one is constantly reconsidering them, and this awareness is expressed through irony: by not taking those actions seriously, not fully claiming them as one's own. The outside-world relations of *Infinite Jest*'s hyperreflexive addicts are characterized as the 'coyly sincere, ironic, self-presenting fortifications they'd had to construct in order to carry on Out There'. The incessant ironic conduct of these addicts is described as functioning, at the same time, as the 'bottle in which clinical depressives sent out their most plangent screams for someone to care and help them'.[1] In this portrayal, the ironic attitude is shown, just like self-reflection, to take on an excessive, endless form: the ironization is infinite, and not aimed at any goal or end.

The works of Wallace and Eggers formulate a clear and sharp critique of irony through their explicit portrayal of the above-described ironic attitude.[2] Although Foer's work seems to imply a similar critique, it does not directly address this problematic form of irony; rather, Foer's work seems to focus on exploring the attitudes that might, or should, come in stead of the ironic attitude – which is, of course, an indispensable addendum to such a critique.[3] However, as this chapter is concerned with the analysis of the problem of endless irony, it will focus on its portrayal in the work of Wallace and Eggers.[4]

Unless otherwise indicated, translations are mine.

[1] IJ, 369, 71.

[2] For earlier versions of my interpretation of this critique, see: Den Dulk, 'Voorbij de doelloze ironie'; Den Dulk, 'Beyond Endless "Aesthetic" Irony.'

[3] For the further exploration of this alternative attitude, see Part 2 of this study.

[4] In the interview I conducted with Foer, he was critical of irony as a form of cynicism, without dismissing all forms of irony and their possible value (e.g. in relation to unquestioned truths) outright: 'I think that a kind of cynicism is dangerous, but so is its opposite, being unquestioning, undoubting. You want to be somewhere in the middle' (Interview with Jonathan Safran Foer by

Although Wallace's and Eggers's critique of irony is the most widely discussed topic in the critical and scholarly literature on their work, perhaps the most illuminating perspective on this critique has been largely ignored, namely the one offered by Kierkegaard's philosophy. Boswell has noted the relevance of Kierkegaard's philosophy in relation to Wallace's writing.[5] Wallace himself wrote, in my correspondence with him: 'I too believe that most of the problems of what might be called "the tyranny of irony" in today's West can be explained almost perfectly in terms of Kierkegaard's distinction between the aesthetic and the ethical life.'[6] I will use Kierkegaard's analysis of irony, and the related distinction between the aesthetic and the ethical life-view, as a heuristic perspective for the analysis of the irony critique formulated in the works of Wallace and Eggers. This perspective will help us to see that their critique is aimed at a specific form of irony and also to better understand the problematic nature of this form of irony and its disastrous consequences for the self.

In this chapter, I will analyse the resemblance between Kierkegaard's, Wallace's and Eggers's critique of irony on four crucial aspects: (1) their critique is concerned with irony as an attitude towards existence, not as just a verbal strategy; (2) they agree irony constitutes a negative independence; and (3) that things go wrong when irony becomes permanent – Kierkegaard calls this endless form of irony the 'aesthetic' attitude; and (4) that liberation from this empty, aimless form of irony cannot be achieved through the ironizing of irony, that is, through meta-irony, as this is simply a continuation of the spiral of negation. For Kierkegaard, Wallace and Eggers liberation from irony is only possible through (what Kierkegaard calls) a 'leap', by ethically choosing the responsibility to give shape and meaning to one's freedom. This last important parallel forms part of the engagement of the studied novels, and therefore the analysis of this alternative to irony will be performed in Part 2 of this study.

Under the influence of postmodernist thought, most interpretations of Wallace's and Eggers's critique of irony have approached irony as a linguistic phenomenon, and not as an existential attitude, which I think is the actual aim of the critique. Taking this latter approach also prevents the discussion from being narrowed down to the question whether alleged instances of ironic language use in the novels contradict the critique of irony formulated therein.[7] To be sure: I am not claiming that these works do not contain any irony; rather I argue that their critique of irony is aimed at a specific, ironic view of life, portrayed as being widespread in contemporary Western culture, and that the possible presence of other, verbal forms of irony in those works does not contradict or refute their critique of the specific form of irony as a life-view.[8]

Allard den Dulk, dd. 26 June 2006). This is very similar to the import of Wallace's and Eggers's critique, as will become clear in this chapter.

[5]   Boswell, *Understanding David Foster Wallace*, 137–40, 143–4.

[6]   Letter from David Foster Wallace to Allard den Dulk, dd. 20 March 2006.

[7]   Determining whether or not something 'is' irony, is, in the case of the criticized form of irony (as an existential attitude) less a matter of irony being in the eye of the beholder than in the case of a verbal expression of irony; for irony as an attitude towards existence has quite distinct markers, as we will see in this chapter.

[8]   Of course, an exception to this point seems to be the title of *A Heartbreaking Work of Staggering Genius*. This can be perceived as a joke, an exaggeration, a mocking of one's attempt to write a memoir about the tragedy of one's recent family history, but as such it can indeed be perceived

Here, it is also important to see that describing irony in order to critique it is not the same as being (verbally) ironic about irony. Such an equation would rely on a simplistic reading of irony as covering all instances of 'not saying what you mean' or 'saying what you do not mean', whereby '(not) *meaning* something' also takes on a signification – that is, words (not) 'referring' to a 'real' state of affairs – that, in my opinion, does not properly apply to the context of fictional texts; it would imply that these texts do not mean anything. Such a reading would, in fact, render all fiction (verbally) ironic. In Kierkegaard's *Concluding Unscientific Postscript*, the difference is formulated as follows: 'there is indeed irony in the book – but that does not mean that the book is irony'.[9] As in Kierkegaard's case, the ultimate test for the critique formulated in the works of Wallace and Eggers, because it concerns an all-negating ironic attitude, is whether these works succeed in realizing a positive content, an affirmation of value or meaning. This aspect of the novels in question (that is: their engagement) is the main subject of Part 2 of this study.

1. Irony as an attitude towards existence

Kierkegaard, Wallace and Eggers are not critical of irony in general. They do not regard irony as a single, monolithic phenomenon that is to be rejected in all of its forms, as, Michael Little, for example claims is the case for Wallace.[10] In the current section, I will argue that in their critique of irony, Kierkegaard, Wallace and Eggers are not concerned with irony as merely a verbal strategy, a figure of speech, an indirect or ambiguous form of language use, but with irony as an *attitude towards existence*.

1.1. Kierkegaard on irony as an attitude towards existence

In *Concluding Unscientific Postscript*, one of Kierkegaard's pseudonyms, Johannes Climacus, writes: 'Irony is an existence-qualification, and thus nothing is more ludicrous than regarding it as a style of speaking or an author's counting himself lucky

---

as what below will be further defined as verbal irony. Although an instance of verbal irony will be shown not per se to entail the total negativity that Wallace and Eggers criticize, it does carry the threat in it of ironizing the whole book, because it concerns the title of the work, and as such 'encompasses' it as a whole. I think it is clear, as I will show in this chapter, that the rest of the book does not signal such a reading (on the contrary, I will argue). Nevertheless, Eggers has repeatedly expressed his regrets about the title: 'the title is the fuck-up. The title is the problem. I've tried to change that title many times. And everybody yells at me and says I can't change the title, but to a lot of people that's all they need to see. Oh, well, fuck it, it's totally insincere. And they can't get passed it. But if I had called the book "Two Boys", then none of that would've happened, or a lot less misunderstanding would've happened. In some countries they changed the title, and I was happy. I was fine with it' (Interview with Dave Eggers by Allard den Dulk, dd. 23 May 2006).

9   CUP 2, 66; cf. Alastair Hannay on Kierkegaard's dissertation on irony: 'The dissertation is serious in what it says about irony' (Hannay, *Kierkegaard*, 152). Also, Kierkegaard's structural use of pseudonyms is not an instance of the ironic attitude that he criticizes; it functions as a way to portray different existence attitudes (compare the above explanation that we should not make the mistake of rendering all fiction ironic).

10 Little, *Novel Affirmations*, 66.

to express himself ironically once in a while. The person who has essential irony has it all day long and is not bound to any style'.[11]

Irony as 'a figure of speech' has, as Kierkegaard formulates it, 'the characteristic of saying the opposite of what is meant'.[12] An oft-cited example is the person who stands in the pouring rain and says 'Lovely weather today', meaning that the weather is terrible.[13] 'The ironic figure of speech cancels itself', writes Kierkegaard, 'inasmuch as the one who is speaking assumes that his hearers understand him; [. . .] it is like a riddle to which one at the same time has the solution'. Of course, verbal irony can take on forms that are much more complicated (that are not so overtly 'un-earnest' and, therefore, do not directly cancel themselves) and that are meant to be exclusionary (to remain uncomprehended by 'lay people' who are not part of a certain 'inner circle' – which, in the most extreme case, can consist of just the ironic speaker himself). But, in any case, irony as a figure of speech targets a more or less delimited part of reality, and implies some sort of positive content (what is truly meant as opposed to what is said) – however vague or hidden – lying behind the ironic expression.[14] Kierkegaard is not concerned with this form of irony.

Instead, he is interested in analysing, as Cross formulates it, 'what it is to be an ironist "all the way down"'.[15] Kierkegaard calls this, 'irony as a position', or 'pure irony'. The distinctive aspect, in comparison to verbal irony, is that this 'irony *sensu eminentiori* [in the eminent sense] is directed not against this or that particular existing entity but against the entire given actuality at a certain time and under certain conditions', writes Kierkegaard. He continues: 'It is not this or that phenomenon but the totality of existence that it contemplates *sub specie ironiae* [under the aspect of irony]'.[16] Here, irony becomes an attitude towards existence, a way of life, or, in a formulation that we have already seen above, 'an existence-qualification'. 'Existential' irony means taking up an ironic relation to the whole of reality. This also means that no positive content lies behind it, because existential irony places the totality of existence under negation, and, therefore, no possible meaning remains for it. Verbal irony can of course be expressive of such existential irony, or lead up to it.[17] But, in itself, an ironic expression is not necessarily indicative of existential irony; that depends on (that is, it requires further analysis of) the underlying attitude towards existence.

1.2. Irony as an attitude towards existence in Wallace and Eggers

With this Kierkegaardian analysis in mind, we can better understand the critique of irony offered in Wallace's and Eggers's works, by seeing that it is aimed at existential irony and that this does not imply all instances of ironic speech per se. The critique

---

[11] CUP, 1, 503–4.
[12] CI, 247.
[13] E.g. Cross, 'Neither Either nor Or: The Perils of Reflexive Irony', 127.
[14] CI, 248, 249.
[15] Cross, 'Neither Either nor Or: The Perils of Reflexive Irony', 126.
[16] CI, 253, 254.
[17] Lansink, *Vrijheid en ironie*, 6–8.

of irony in these works lies, not, as some scholars seem to think, in an intention to completely abstain from ironic language use.[18] Rather it lies in their critical portrayal of the ironic life-view: of individuals – or almost an entire society, even – living their lives through the perspective of irony. In Wallace's and Eggers's works, irony as a way of life is associated with contemporary Western culture.

More specifically, it is portrayed in *A Heartbreaking Work of Staggering Genius*, above all, through the descriptions of *Might Magazine* (which is characterized by 'immediate opinion-reversal and self-devouring. Whatever the prevailing thinking, especially our own, we contradict it'),[19] and in *You Shall Know Our Velocity* through Will's initial hyperreflexivity leading him to ironize his every move.

In Wallace's work the critical portrayal of the ironic life-view is an even more dominant theme. This is perhaps most apparent in *Infinite Jest*. Wallace's magnum opus clearly deals with 'irony as a position', through its portrayal of the life-view of the many addicted characters, for whom irony is inextricably tied in with addiction, as an escape from responsibility and from their problems.[20] *Infinite Jest* describes this addict-type attitude as a culture-wide phenomenon.[21] I will elaborate on these portrayals of the ironic life-view in subsequent sections; here, these references are merely meant to illustrate that the critique of irony in Wallace's and Eggers's works is aimed not so much at verbal irony, but at irony *as a way of life*.

However, many scholars and critics interpreting the critique have failed either to make this distinction, or to fully implement it in their interpretation. Although most of them acknowledge that Wallace and Eggers are concerned with irony as an all-encompassing 'attitude' that dominates contemporary Western culture,[22] many subsequently call into question the validity and consistency of this critique by pointing out possible instances of ironic language use in these works.[23] Some of these interpretations are the result of an overly broad use of the term 'irony', resulting, for instance, in the equivocation of irony and humour.[24] Other interpretations are based on a more informed reading and offer more thoroughly argued objections, but, nevertheless, stem from a similar misunderstanding. Below, I will address some of these interpretations.[25]

---

[18] Wallace has explicitly stated that he thinks that verbal irony, in itself, 'is fantastic. It's one of the primary rhetorical modes. It's been around forever. It's intensely powerful. There's nothing wrong with it' (Wiley, 'Interview').

[19] AHWOSG, 240.

[20] IJ, 369 (the 'coyly sincere, ironic, self-presenting fortifications they'd had to construct in order to carry on Out There'); cf. Aubry, *Literature As Self-Help*, 248.

[21] Cf. IJ, 385; the novel describes a culture that shows its members 'how to fashion masks of ennui and jaded irony at a young age where the face is fictile enough to assume the shape of whatever it wears. And then it's stuck there' (IJ, 694).

[22] E.g. Scott, 'The Panic of Influence', 40; Harris, 'Infinite Jest', 47.

[23] E.g. Holland, 'The Art's Heart's Purpose', 218, 220; Hultkrans, 'Books – *A Supposedly Fun Thing I'll Never Do Again* by David Foster Wallace', 15–22; McInerney, 'The Year of the Whopper'; Messud, 'Crushed by a Killing Joke'; Korthals Altes, *'Blessedly Post-ironic'?*, 11.

[24] Hutcheon describes the 'conflation of irony and humor' as one of the main misinterpretations of irony (Hutcheon, *Irony's Edge*, 5).

[25] This discussion also touches upon the problem of meta-irony, the supposed use of irony to 'overcome' irony, but I will address this in detail, separately, in section 4.

In a typical example of this misunderstanding, Andrew Hultkrans, after saying that he agrees with the general critique of the ironic attitude, speaks of Wallace's 'struggle with his own ironic impulses', referring, among other things, to the pop references in Wallace's work – the fact that his 'fictional characters appear on Late Night with David Letterman' –, and to his occasionally absurd humour – for example the acronym 'O.N.A.N.', short for 'Organization of North American Nations', in *Infinite Jest*.[26] But, first of all, references to popular culture are not necessarily ironic: not in the verbal sense, wherein such a reference would undercut the seriousness of a specific expression or part of a story; and not in the existential sense, wherein it would negate the whole reality that is portrayed. Secondly, a relatively isolated linguistic joke, such as the acronym O.N.A.N., perhaps amounts to verbal but not to existential irony. And, as we saw above, verbal irony always has a more or less delimited target and therefore does not automatically infect the novel's entire existence-qualification.

In a more complicated example, Mary K. Holland bases her claim that *Infinite Jest* 'fails to eschew empty irony' on what she regards as the 'ironic ambivalence' in the depiction of certain 'sincere' characters and experiences. For instance, Holland writes that by giving the sincere character Mario Incandenza a long list of physical ailments, the novel 'only punishes' him, instead of 'celebrat[ing]' him as one of 'those who resist the infantile fear of earnest emotion'. Here, Holland focuses on the far-fetched notion of a novel 'punishing' a character by describing him as disabled, instead of relating that Mario is unreservedly portrayed as the happiest and most exemplary character in the novel. Similarly, when the other sincere hero of the novel, Don Gately, after being shot, refuses all pain medication (because of his former drug addiction) and experiences pain-delusional dreams of his former drug use, Holland faults this description of the character, because '[r]ather than recalling the drug indignantly, [. . .] Gately remembers it as "delicious" and "obscenely pleasant", a welcome escape from the horror'. According to Holland, this completely undercuts the portrayal of Gately as embodying a successful critique of irony: 'these ironic wakings void any notion of heroic transformation'. First: again it seems very far-fetched (disproportionate, to say the least) to regard the heroic fact that Gately succeeds in handling the immense pain on willpower and dreams alone, as ironically negated by the fact that some of those dreams are about drug use. Secondly, Holland fails to stress the fact that in these drug dreams Gately is not simply 'indulging the infantile desire to escape the pain of the world', as Holland puts it, but is also confronted with horrifying memories of his life as an addict, and as such these drug dreams are actually part of AA's recovery process – 'you'll begin to start to "Get in Touch" with why it was that you used Substances in the first place' –, and, therefore, of the novel's critique of irony. Above all, even if these supposed contrasts – Mario's disabilities, Gately's drug dreams – were to be labelled ironic, these are verbal ironies, describing a contrast in a certain situation, that, as I have just described, cannot be rightly interpreted as undermining the novel's overall portrayal of sincerity and critique of irony – for that, the contrasts

---

[26] Hultkrans, 'Books – *A Supposedly Fun Thing I'll Never Do Again* by David Foster Wallace', 15–22.

that Holland discerns are much too strained. If anything, these contrasts, in the case of Gately, make him more real and human; and in the case of Mario we see that none of these potential ironies can prevent him from being the warmest, most empathetic and humane character in the novel.[27]

Turning to Eggers we can see a similar misreading of his critique of irony. Liesbeth Korthals Altes writes about Eggers, in relation to *A Heartbreaking Work of Staggering Genius*, that '[i]n his indictment of irony he is in fact gunning for that "postmodern" all-affecting relativism'.[28] This remark seems to indicate an awareness that Eggers's critique is aimed at an all-encompassing attitude. However, Korthals subsequently calls into question the success or even the sincerity of this critique by pointing to the presence of verbal irony in the book: 'Meanwhile, despite Eggers's rejection of the phenomenon, this book is filled with all forms of irony as a figure of speech.' Here, the equivocation of verbal and existential irony is obvious. To illustrate that *A Heartbreaking Work of Staggering Genius* is 'truly a work from "the Age of Irony"', Korthals mentions that the work is 'full of postmodern games with typography, expanding footnotes et cetera', and asks, rhetorically: 'How post-ironic can an author with such a media-conscious and self-conscious main character be?'[29] However, the elements that Korthals mentions (further on, she also adds 'polyphony' and 'ambiguity')[30] are not necessarily even expressions of *verbal* irony (compare the aforementioned pop references in Wallace); they might just as well be regarded – perhaps even more plausibly – as normal aspects of the portrayal of contemporary reality. Above all, the mere presence of these elements in the book, even as potential *verbal* ironies, does not automatically undercut its critique of *existential* irony. Also, how could one then ever critique contemporary reality, if just describing that reality would by definition imply ironizing one's critique of it?

The question of whether Wallace's and Eggers's works live up to their own critique of existential irony does not depend on the absence of ironic language use, but on the attitude towards existence embodied in those works – whether they succeed in replacing irony's total negation by positive meaning.

In this section, we have seen that Kierkegaard, Wallace and Eggers regard irony as an attitude towards existence. So, from now on, I will use the term 'irony' in the sense of 'existential irony', unless otherwise specified. Next, we shall examine what exactly irony as an existence-qualification means and what the effects of this attitude are.

2. Irony as negative independence

According to Kierkegaard, Wallace and Eggers, the attitude of irony has an enormous impact on an individual's existence. Although they all criticize the possible escalation

---

[27] Holland, 'The Art's Heart's Purpose', 218, 220, 230–1, 236; IJ, 446.
[28] Korthals Altes, *'Blessedly Post-Ironic?'*, 10.
[29] Korthals Altes, *'Blessedly Post-Ironic?'*, 11, 4, 12. Also: Korthals seems to wrongfully equate author and main character here.
[30] Ibid., 15.

of this attitude, it is also important to see that they recognize the first onset of irony as a valuable step, not in itself, but as making possible a transition in the development of the self. How should we understand this?

2.1. Kierkegaard on irony as negative independence

Kierkegaard writes: 'no genuinely human life is possible without irony'. To which he adds: 'just as philosophy begins with doubt, so also a life that may be called human begins with irony'.[31] What does he mean by this?

Kierkegaard (and existentialist thought in general) holds that an individual is not automatically a self, but has to become one: *becoming* a self is the *task* of human existence. To become aware of this task, the individual has to free himself from what Kierkegaard calls 'immediacy', which is to say that the individual has to realize that he does not coincide with what is 'given': his upbringing, his social background, his culture. In *Concluding Unscientific Postscript*, we read: '*the life-view of immediacy is good fortune.* If one were to ask from whence he has this life-view, this essential relation to good fortune, he might naively answer: I do not understand it myself'.[32] In the attitude of immediacy, the individual regards himself and his values as determined by the world around him (this is similar to what Sartre calls the 'spirit of seriousness', or the bad faith attitude of regarding oneself as possessing the fully determined nature of a thing).[33]

Through irony, the individual frees himself from this immediate attitude: irony breaches the individual's identification with the given reality. Kierkegaard writes that at 'any such turning point in history', when an individual frees himself from the given and wants to give shape to himself, 'two movements must be noted. On the one hand, the new must forge ahead; on the other, the old must be displaced'. However, for the old to be 'superseded', Kierkegaard writes, it 'must be perceived in all its imperfection'. Herein lies the function and value of irony: it 'destroys' actuality by revealing it in its imperfection, or in Kierkegaard's words: '[the ironist] destroys the given actuality by the given actuality itself [since the ironist does not have the new in his power]'.[34]

So, for the ironist, 'the given actuality has lost its validity entirely; it has become for him an imperfect form that is a hindrance everywhere. But on the other hand, he does not possess the new. He knows only that the present does not match the idea'.[35] Kierkegaard values this initial, disassociating potential of irony. In *Either/Or*, Kierkegaard's pseudonym Judge William writes: 'irony is and remains the

---

[31] CI, 326, 6.
[32] CUP 1, 433.
[33] Cf. 'The serious attitude involves starting from the world and attributing more reality to the world than to oneself'. In this context, Sartre mentions Kierkegaard's irony as a means of 'getting out' of this attitude (BN, 601).
[34] CI, 260–1, 262.
[35] Ibid., 261.

disciplinarian of the immediate life'.[36] Cross summarizes Kierkegaard's assessment of irony as follows:

> Kierkegaard argues that this form of radical dissociation from one's society and one's social self, though not fully admirable or desirable as a way of life, constitutes an important improvement on the way of life it rejects. For the movement of irony constitutes the self's break with 'immediacy'.[37]

It is important to note that irony is a purely negative movement: it destroys what is given, thereby liberating the individual, but it does not contribute anything to the formulation of the new, to the content of the individual's self-becoming. Therefore, the freedom that arises from this break with immediacy, is a negative freedom: a freedom-from. Kierkegaard writes that in irony, 'the subject is negatively free, since the actuality that is supposed to give the subject content is not there. He is free from the constraint in which the given actuality holds the subject, but he is negatively free and as such is suspended, because there is nothing that holds him'.[38]

Kierkegaard calls this form of irony, *Socratic*. According to Kierkegaard, existential irony came into the world with Socrates. Socrates used irony to topple the immediate actuality of his time, which to him had lost its validity. For Kierkegaard, the liberation that Socrates brings about, is the essential stepping stone towards a personal moral interpretation of one's existence. The negative freedom that it brings about is a necessary condition for the subsequent formulation of a positive freedom (a freedom-to), in which one gives actual content (positivity) to one's freedom and establishes one's self-chosen moral framework. However, because irony is pure negation, it cannot be the source of that positivity.[39] Consequently, Kierkegaard concludes that irony should only be employed temporarily, and that subsequently one should start to give positive meaning to one's freedom.

It is also important to note that, although this liberating, Socratic irony performs a total negation – it negates the whole of reality –, this total negation is aimed at the totality of a *specific* reality. As we already saw above, existential irony is initially directed against 'the entire given actuality *at a certain time and under certain conditions*'. Kierkegaard writes about Socrates: 'to him the established actuality was unactual, not in this or that particular aspect but in its totality as such [. . .]. But it was not actuality in general that he negated; it was the given actuality at a particular time'.[40] We will see that this is a crucial difference from the problem of endless irony, which is not directed against a specific reality anymore but against *any* reality.

2.2. Irony as negative independence in Wallace and Eggers

Wallace and Eggers, too, acknowledge this valuable effect that irony can initially have, but also see that it results in a negative independence that cannot be a goal in itself, but

---

[36] EO 1, 120.
[37] Cross, 'Neither Either nor Or: The Perils of Reflexive Irony', 136.
[38] CI, 262.
[39] Ibid., 257.
[40] CI, 254 [emphasis added, AdD], 270–1.

merely makes possible the transition to something else. Since essays by and interviews with both authors have played an important role in the discussion on their critique of irony, it seems relevant to briefly point out the comments made, especially by Wallace, about the value of both verbal and existential irony, before looking at the fictional works themselves.

On the value of irony as a critique of reality, Wallace states: 'The great thing about irony is that it splits things apart, gets us up above them so we can see the flaws and hypocrisies and duplicities. [. . .] Sarcasm, parody, absurdism and irony are great ways to strip off stuff's masks and show the unpleasant reality behind it.'[41] As mentioned above, for Wallace the contemporary problem of endless irony has its origins in postmodernist thinking being absorbed into mass culture. But Wallace acknowledges that postmodernist irony started off with an idealistic purpose: 'the ironic function like in postmodern fiction started out with a rehabilitative agenda. Largely it was supposed to explode hypocrisy – certain hypocritically smug ways the country saw itself that just weren't holding true anymore.'[42]

These comments tie in with Kierkegaard's view of irony as a valuable initial means of overthrowing a 'given actuality [that] has lost its validity', of freeing oneself from what has become the standard, immediate way of seeing things that does not hold true anymore. In this context, Wallace notes, like Kierkegaard, that irony should only be employed temporarily. In his essay 'E Unibus Pluram', Wallace quotes Lewis Hyde: 'Irony has only emergency use. Carried over time, it is the voice of the trapped who have come to enjoy their cage.'[43] (The significance of this image of being 'trapped in irony' will be explored in the next section, on the problem of endless irony.) To this, Wallace adds that irony 'serves an almost exclusively negative function. It's critical and destructive, a ground-clearing. Surely this is the way our postmodern fathers saw it. But irony's singularly unuseful when it comes to constructing anything to replace the hypocrisies it debunks.'[44]

Although Wallace's and Eggers's novels mostly portray instances of existential irony that have progressed into a problematic form (which will be analysed in the next section), we can recognize the initial liberating effect of irony in some elements of these portrayals. In *Infinite Jest*, the 'Union of the Hideously and Improbably Deformed' (U.H.I.D.) can be seen as an instance of irony as negative independence (the interpretation of this part of the story also reveals, indirectly, the connections between Kierkegaard and Sartre's view of the self – in this case, the latter's analysis of the look, specifically). Joelle van Dyne, recovering drug addict and member of the U.H.I.D., explains that most people want to hide the shame they feel before the gaze of others: 'you *hide* your deep need to hide', 'You stick your hideous face right in there into the wine-tasting crowd's visual meatgrinder, you smile so wide it hurts', concealing your desire to hide 'under a mask of acceptance'.[45]

[41] McCaffery, 'Interview', 147.
[42] Wiley, 'Interview'.
[43] Hyde, 'Alcohol and Poetry', 90; quoted in: EUP, 67.
[44] EUP, 67.
[45] IJ, 535.

According to Joelle, most people allow themselves to be objectified in this way (comforted, perhaps, by the fact that they do the same to others), or, in a more Kierkegaardian formulation: they accept themselves as an 'immediacy', as determined by the world, by others. Members of the U.H.I.D., by contrast, openly display their shame, their wish to remain unseen (and thus unobjectified, undetermined by others), by wearing a veil: 'unashamed about the fact that how we appear to others affects us deeply', 'we don the veil' and 'hide openly', says Joelle.[46]

What the members of U.H.I.D. do, in effect, is distance themselves from the rest of the world. Their veil is an ironic distancing mechanism that forms a separation between them and the world. In one sense, the veil functions as a barrier, a screen placed in-between. At the same time, by wearing the veil, the members of U.H.I.D. openly display their shame, which is indicated by their need to wear the veil, while simultaneously hiding that shame, placing it beyond reach, beyond determination by others, behind the veil. Thereby, in a sense, they become free. It is, in a twofold sense, a negative freedom: it is a freedom from the look of others, but no positive content has been given to their own identity; worse still, and this is the second sense of the negativity, it is an identity in hiding, and therefore at the same time not at all free. In the next section, we will see that freedom remaining isolated is part of the escalation of irony.

In *Infinite Jest*, the veils of the U.H.I.D. work as an interesting means of distancing their wearers from a culture that is itself 'deformed', but it does not offer a satisfactory alternative to that culture. In Joelle's case it can even be seen as part of the attachment to secrecy that is typical for the addicts in the novel. It is interesting to note, however, that the U.H.I.D. is described in *Infinite Jest* as a support-group for the 'aesthetically challenged'. As mentioned in the introduction to this chapter, Kierkegaard calls the problematic attitude of endless irony the *aesthetic* life-view. And all the characters in *Infinite Jest* who, at different points, seem to symbolize a digression or an alternative to the dominant culture portrayed in the novel, are subsequently described as physically repulsive, or, in other words, as aesthetically challenged. This is most clearly the case with Mario Incandenza's countless physical deformities, and – though less evidently – with Gately's big, ogre-like appearance. But it is also the case for Joelle, who is described as '[driving] anybody with a nervous system out of their fucking mind' – although we never find out for sure whether this is because she is unbearably beautiful or horribly disfigured (or both, at different stages in her life) –, and for Hal Incandenza, who, in the opening chapter, is described like 'some sort of animal with something in its mouth',[47] which I take as an indication that Hal is at that point actually 'becoming a self', in the Kierkegaardian sense, and not psychically damaged, as other (aesthetic) characters in the novel – and many interpreters of the novel – take him to be.

In *A Heartbreaking Work of Staggering Genius*, the descriptions of *Might Magazine* offer a critical portrayal of the very problem of endless irony. However, the origins

---

[46] IJ, 535.
[47] Ibid., 187, 538, 14.

of the magazine, its original ambitions, are portrayed more positively, and akin to Kierkegaard's comments about the initial effects of irony. Dave wants to clear away the 'slacker' label attached to his generation, and replace it with new and meaningful ideas about contemporary existence (although the actual formulation of these ideas will turn out to be the problem for *Might*).[48] In the book, *Might*'s 'underlying sensibility that at least something needed to be done' is not 'knocked down'; 'It is this underlying sensibility that holds up in the text', Nicoline Timmer notes, 'the "hope" with which *Might* was started is not completely ridiculed and debunked in the text'.[49]

Kierkegaard, Wallace and Eggers agree that through irony the individual obtains a negative freedom, a freedom-from, and that, as such, irony constitutes an indispensable step towards freely choosing a personal interpretation of one's moral life.[50] But they also emphasize that, to that end, irony's negative independence will have to be followed by a positive freedom, a freedom-to, that irony, as pure negation, by definition cannot provide. Therefore, irony should be employed only temporarily.

3. Endless 'aesthetic' irony

However, Kierkegaard, Wallace and Eggers all recognize the danger of the ironist getting wrapped up in his negative freedom, and turning irony into a permanent attitude. Irony implies distancing oneself from all determinations, not coinciding with anything. But endlessly continuing this process of negation will have disastrous existential consequences for the individual.

3.1. Kierkegaard on endless aesthetic irony

Kierkegaard writes: 'In irony, the subject is continually retreating, talking every phenomenon out of its reality in order to save itself – that is, in order to preserve itself in negative independence of everything.'[51] The individual can come to regard this process as needing to be continued endlessly, for its own sake. Thus, negative freedom can become, in a sense, the ironist's 'truth'.

Kierkegaard connects this to the problem of hyperreflexivity that was analysed in the previous chapter. Kierkegaard describes the perpetuation of the ironic attitude as following from a heightened, continuous form of self-reflection: 'Because reflection was continually reflecting about reflection, thinking went astray, and every step it advanced led further and further, of course, from any content.'[52] Constant self-reflection

---

[48] Cf. AHWOSG, 144, 147.

[49] Timmer, *'Do You Feel It Too?'*, 228, 231.

[50] Cf. 'Irony is the cultivation of the spirit and therefore follows next after immediacy; then comes the ethicist' (CUP 1, 504).

[51] CI, 257.

[52] CI, 272.

means constantly distancing oneself from one's thoughts and, as a result, from one's words and actions; in other words, it leads to a permanent ironic attitude.

Kierkegaard calls this attitude the aesthetic life-view, and the individual that holds it, the aesthete. The aesthetic life-view is characterized by an endless total irony through which the individual avoids all commitment, all responsibility, and retains his negative freedom at all cost. It is to this type of endless aesthetic irony that Kierkegaard is strongly opposed. He sometimes speaks of *Romantic irony*, as he associates this problematic form of irony mainly with the Romantic poets of the first half of the nineteenth century. The result of the aesthete's endless irony is that, by definition, all distinctions and values have become invalid, completely immaterial. As Kierkegaard writes: 'Irony now functioned as that for which nothing was established, as that which was finished with everything, and also as that which had the absolute power to do everything.' Kierkegaard summarizes this position as follows: 'subjectivity became the infinite, absolute negativity'.[53]

This position differs fundamentally from the total negation of Socratic irony, which is directed at a *specific* reality. The aesthete's irony, on the other hand, has no specific target: 'when the given actuality loses its validity for the ironist in this way, it is not because it is an antiquated actuality that must be replaced by a truer actuality, but because [no actuality is adequate]'.[54] For the aesthete, no actuality suffices, as his 'total negative irony'[55] dictates that a true actuality is by definition impossible, he is solely interested in his own 'ideality', in what his own head can make of things. Everything becomes secondary to the aesthete's fantasy and desire. In his striving to aestheticize his life, to merge it with the ideality in his head, the aesthete accepts no limitations: *everything* should be possible.

Initially, the aesthete revels in this infinite, absolute freedom. He can exploit the reflective powers of his mind to their full extent, occupying himself with rich, poetic imaginings on whatever subject strikes his fancy. The aesthete seems always in control, at least one step ahead of the people he manipulates. It is not an accident that the aesthete A portrayed in *Either/Or* is in many ways intellectually superior to the ethicist B, Judge William – something that the latter expressly admits to A: 'You are all too skilled in the art of talking in generalities about everything without letting yourself be personally involved for me to tempt you by setting your dialectical powers in motion.'[56] In *Either/Or*, the aesthetic individual is portrayed at the peak of his self-confidence and imaginative force through the figure of Johannes the Seducer (who is, in turn, one of A's literary creations):[57]

> If someone else could see my soul in this state, it would seem to him that it, like a skiff, plunged prow-first down into the ocean, as if in its dreadful momentum it

---

[53]   Ibid., 275, 273.
[54]   Ibid., 283.
[55]   Scholtens, 'Inleiding', 21.
[56]   EO 2, 5.
[57]   To be clear: from the standpoint of Kierkegaard's critique of irony, the figure Johannes the Seducer is *not* to be regarded as the final, most *advanced* form of the aesthetic life-view, since that would require an awareness of the futility of that life-view. In his 'Diapsalmata', in part one of *Either/Or*, the aesthete A *does* represent this awareness.

would have to steer down into the depths of the abyss. He does not see that high on the mast a sailor is on the lookout. Roar away, you wild forces, roar away, you powers of passion; even if your waves hurl foam toward the clouds, you still are not able to pile yourselves up over my head – I am sitting as calmly as the king of the mountain.[58]

Note that the aesthete's calm and his elevated position express his reflexive-ironic distancing from everything, from all the possible uproar around him. According to Kierkegaard's ethicist, Judge William, the aesthete A manages (through his ironic attitude) to escape everyone: 'Your occupation consists in preserving your hiding place, and you are successful, for your mask is the most enigmatical of all; that is, you are a nonentity.'[59]

However, this last remark also signals the problem that the aesthetic life-view eventually runs into: the aesthete remains a 'non-entity'. When Kierkegaard describes the connection between constant self-reflection and endless irony (quoted above), he also remarks that, in the end, the ensuing attitude will lead to a disintegration of the self: 'The more the *I* in criticism became absorbed in contemplation of the *I*, the leaner and leaner the *I* became, until it ended with becoming a ghost.' In *Either/Or* the aesthete A says about himself: 'I have, I believe, the courage to doubt everything; I have, I believe, the courage to fight against everything; but I do not have the courage to acknowledge anything, the courage to possess, to own, anything.'[60] All of A's abilities are negative: he can doubt and fight things. But he is not capable of placing anything in their stead, of realizing something positive in the ensuing void, of acknowledging or possessing something, a positivity: that is, something that is confirmed and made present by him. Cross aptly labels A 'the defeated aesthete': 'He fails, that is, to assume responsibility for himself; when his life-project founders, this is seen not as evidence that he has made an unwise choice of life-projects but as evidence that no life can be meaningful.'[61] Kierkegaard writes: 'Therefore, the ironist frequently becomes nothing.'[62] As a result of his endless irony, the aesthete lacks convictions, as all values have been emptied of meaning and therefore all actions seem immaterial. He lacks what Kierkegaard sometimes calls 'inwardness', a term that does not refer so much to a form of self-reflection, but rather to the individual's ability to act on the basis of a set of personal values. In other words, the aesthete lacks a self.[63]

3.2. Endless aesthetic irony in Wallace and Eggers

Kierkegaard's critique of endless, aesthetic irony corresponds with the irony critique offered in Wallace's and Eggers's works. This is the form of irony that, according to

---

[58] EO 1, 324–5.
[59] EO 2, 159.
[60] CI, 272; EO 1, 23.
[61] Cross, 'Neither Either nor Or: The Perils of Reflexive Irony', 145, 146–7.
[62] CI, 281.
[63] Cf. Lansink, *Vrijheid en ironie*, 25.

Wallace, has 'permeated the culture', has 'become our language', 'our environment', that has 'become an end in itself' and, as such, 'tyrannizes us'.[64] It has nothing to do anymore with the liberating, subversive effect that can rightly be attributed to certain (Socratic) ironic attitudes. Wallace writes: 'So what *does* irony as a cultural norm mean to say? That it's impossible to mean what you say? [. . .] Most likely, I think, today's irony ends up saying: "How totally *banal* of you to ask what I really mean."' To which he adds: 'herein lies the oppressiveness of institutionalized irony [. . .]: the ability to interdict the *question* without attending to its *subject* is, when exercised, tyranny', that uses irony 'to insulate itself'.[65] Note the similarity with the aesthete A's expression of his ironic imperviousness to any meaningful choice or distinction: 'These words Either/ Or are a double-edged dagger I carry with me and with which I can assassinate the whole of actuality. I just say: Either/Or. Either it is this or it is that; since nothing in life is either this or that, it does not, of course, exist.'[66] The contemporary ironic attitude has become 'poisonous', functioning as not more than a 'mechanism for avoiding some really thorny issues', says Wallace: it has resulted in 'the contemporary mood of jaded weltschmerz, self-mocking materialism, blank indifference' and, as such, is the cause of 'great despair and stasis in U.S. culture'.[67] Eggers expresses his agreement with Wallace, and explains that his own critique is aimed at the same, 'cynical' form of irony: '[It's] an attitude that just dismisses things left and right, and has an attitude about speaking out on anything. It's just worthless, totally vacant and empty and terrible. [. . .] I'm on the same page with [Wallace] in a lot of ways.'[68]

3.2.1. David Foster Wallace

In Wallace's works this ironic attitude is portrayed and critiqued, above all, in *Infinite Jest*, through the theme of addiction. Boswell points out the resemblance between Kierkegaard's aesthetes and the addicts portrayed in *Infinite Jest*:

> Wallace's desperate drug addicts are essentially 'aesthetes' in Kierkegaard's famous formulation. An aesthete is someone who [. . .] – as Kierkegaard explains in the great *Concluding Unscientific Postscript to 'Philosophical Fragments'* – 'holds existence at bay by the most subtle of all deceptions, by thinking. He has thought everything possible, and yet he has not existed at all.'[69]

We have already seen in the previous chapter that *Infinite Jest* connects addiction to self-reflection ('most Substance-addicted people are also addicted to thinking, meaning they have a compulsive and unhealthy relationship with their own thinking'). Just like we saw in Kierkegaard, this constant self-reflection brings with it an attitude of permanent irony. Through self-reflection, as the internalized look of other people, the

[64] McCaffery, 'Interview', 148; EUP, 67.
[65] EUP, 67–8.
[66] EO 1, 527.
[67] McCaffery, 'Interview', 146; Wiley, 'Interview'; EUP, 63, 49.
[68] Interview with Dave Eggers by Allard den Dulk, dd. 23 May 2006.
[69] Boswell, *Understanding David Foster Wallace*, 138; cf. CUP 1, 253; cf. 'Kierkegaard's aesthetes are *postmodernists* "avant la lettre"' (Scholtens, 'Inleiding', 21).

addicted characters are constantly manipulating how they (think they) are perceived by others. They are, in a sense, hiding; for instance, Kate Gompert, who is 'so obsessed with Do They Know, Can They Tell'.[70] In Kierkegaard's *Concluding Unscientific Postscript*, the aesthetic life-view is characterized as 'hiddenness'.[71] Irony serves to mask oneself. The addicted characters avoid taking responsibility for their actions, or committing themselves to anything. '[In performing such] functions, addiction finds its perfect companion in irony', writes Timothy Aubry: 'Irony is a "fortification"; it is like an outer layer, a mask on the self [. . .]. Drugs too are a fortification, a shield; they offer a basis for disclaiming responsibility for one's behavior.'[72] *Infinite Jest* describes it as the 'coyly sincere, ironic, self-presenting fortifications they'd had to construct in order to carry on Out There, under the ceaseless neon bottle'.[73]

Through irony, the addicted characters can deny the reality of their (addicted) existence, and instead continue to escape into the pleasure fantasy of their addiction. Like Kierkegaard's aesthetes, the addicts are trying to aestheticize their lives: they chase the pleasure-filled ideality in their head, and ignore the actuality of their lives. Addiction can be regarded as an attempt to soothe or evade existential anxiety, through alcohol, drugs, sex, entertainment, et cetera. An extreme example of this in *Infinite Jest*, is Gately's crime partner and fellow addict Gene Fackelmann, whose addiction drives him to scam his boss, a ruthless bookmaker, after which Fackelmann uses the money to buy and ingest an enormous amount of Dilaudid (a very strong, opioid painkiller) to forget about the probably fatal consequences (namely, his boss's revenge) of that same scam. Thereupon, Gately realizes that a drug addict is a 'thing that basically hides'.[74] This aesthetic escapism also explains why the U.H.I.D. (discussed in the previous section), with its motto of 'hiding openly', can eventually only add to the escalation of Joelle van Dyne's situation of addiction, and does not embody an exemplary attitude in itself.[75]

This aesthetic condition, however, does not only apply to the drug addicts in *Infinite Jest*. It holds true for almost everybody in the novel: the aesthetic attitude is the default life-view of the contemporary society portrayed in *Infinite Jest*. Another way to express it, is that almost everyone is addicted to something. In the novel, it is contemporary culture – recall Wallace's remarks about irony having become our 'environment' – that teaches everybody the ironic-aesthetic attitude early on:

> The U.S. arts are our guide to inclusion. A how-to. We are shown how to fashion masks of ennui and jaded irony at a young age where the face is fictile enough to assume the shape of whatever it wears. And then it's stuck there, the weary cynicism that saves us from gooey sentiment and unsophisticated naïveté.[76]

---

[70] IJ, 203, 77.
[71] CUP 1, 254; cf. Boswell, 140.
[72] Aubry, *Literature As Self-Help*, 248.
[73] IJ, 369.
[74] Ibid., 932.
[75] The preferable alternative in the novel is the model of AA; Gately tells Joelle that the empathy ('love') received from others in AA will lead to the ability of leaving one's 'cage' and stop 'hiding' (cf. IJ, 534).
[76] Ibid., 694.

Moreover, this widespread attitude is explicitly connected to an exclusive focus on *negative* freedom (resulting from the ironic life-view), through the words of the character Marathe, a Quebecois wheelchair terrorist. Marathe's conversation with Hugh Steeply, secret agent of a somewhat obscure American intelligence service (the U.S. Office of 'Unspecified Services', or: U.S.O.U.S.), functions as a general discussion of this cultural condition. That this conversation is not rendered as one, continuous scene, but rather in fragments interspersed throughout the novel, makes it into a thread that seems to 'underlie' the entire story. Steeply functions as the spokesperson for the American, aesthetic attitude, while Marathe says: 'Your freedom is the freedom-*from*: no one tells your precious individual U.S.A. selves what they must do. It is this meaning only, this freedom from constraint and forced duress. [. . .] But what of the freedom-*to*?' Marathe adds that, as a result, 'you all stumble about in the dark, this confusion of permissions. The without-end pursuit of happiness of which someone let you forget the old things which made happiness possible. How is it you say: "*Anything is going*"?'[77]

3.2.2. Dave Eggers

In *A Heartbreaking Work of Staggering Genius* the critique of the ironic attitude is most evident in the passages concerning *Might Magazine*. As mentioned in the previous section, the book offers a positive portrayal of the original (however vague) ambitions of the magazine. But soon these ambitions are lost to an attitude of total negative irony:

> We begin a pattern of almost immediate opinion-reversal and self-devouring. Whatever the prevailing thinking, especially our own, we contradict it. We change our minds about Wendy Kopp, the young go-getter we heralded in the first issue, and her much-celebrated Teach for America. [. . .] in a 6,000-word piece that dominates the second issue, we fault the nonprofit for attempting to solve inner-city problems, largely black problems, with white upper-middle-class college-educated solutions. 'Paternalistic condescension,' we say. 'Enlightened self-interest,' we sigh.[78]

This passage summarizes the ironic-aesthetic attitude of the editorial staff of *Might*: every position, every idea has a flip side that can and thus *has* to be exposed. Timmer writes: 'They are so accustomed to a negative dialectic or a deconstructive attitude that they are much better at articulating what they do *not* want than they are at formulating any constructive goals and visions.'[79] Initially, this 'deconstructive' activity might even seem like a viable and worthwhile activity in itself. But, as becomes clear from their choice of targeting vulnerable, idealistic initiatives, the editors' irony serves, above all, to liberate them from commitment to any of these positions, and insulates them from any criticism that might be brought against them. For *Might*'s editors, the ironic stance of 'immediate opinion-reversal' – that is, to be 'positionless' – seems to be the only viable, safe attitude.

---

[77]   Ibid., 320.
[78]   AHWOSG, 240–1.
[79]   Timmer, '*Do You Feel It Too?*', 232.

However, in the course of the book the editorial staff grow more and more frustrated with their own endless irony. The emptiness of the aesthetic attitude starts to dawn on them; their work becomes 'depressing, routine': 'We debunk the idea of college in general, and marriage, and makeup, and the Grateful Dead – it is our job to point out all this artifice, everywhere.'[80] In the end, *Might Magazine* loses out to general frustration. The editorial staff realize that their ironic efforts have led to nothing. They have exposed falsity and artificiality everywhere, but have offered no alternatives. As Timmer observes: '*Might*, in that sense, implodes. It implodes because their critical stance is deconstructive and eventually turns inwards.'[81] In the end, the editors stand empty-handed: 'all these hundreds of thousands of hours, were going to end without our having saved anyone [. . .] – what had it all been? It had been something to do, some small, small point to make, and the point was made, in a small way'.[82]

In the book, the above-quoted passages function as a critique of the attitude of endless irony, illustrating its futility and even its potentially harmful viciousness. However, some critics have mistaken this portrayal of the escalation of irony for an employment of irony, and subsequently faulted Eggers for being inconsistent with his own critique.[83] First of all, this accusation seems to be based on the equivocation of existential and verbal irony, discussed in section 1. Secondly, as already remarked above, describing irony in order to critique it is not the same as being (verbally) ironic about irony.

In the appendix to *A Heartbreaking Work of Staggering Genius*, we read that '*Might*, and its ironic contents, were included in the book simply so that they could be knocked down and picked apart'.[84] To me, this is an accurate description of what the passages in question do: they clearly aim to describe the futility and viciousness, and subsequent frustration and emptiness, resulting from the magazine's ironic attitude. 'What is dismissed', Timmer writes, 'is the *attitude*' of the editors[85] – their attitude of endless irony. The end of *Might* coincides, and stands in stark contrast to, the death of a friend: 'Skye's death humbles us all, makes us all feel like imbeciles for the time we've spent spitting acid stomach juices (ah!) onto everything we see.'[86] In the book, *Might* functions as the embodiment of the contemporary ironic attitude, and the magazine undergoes a development similar to that of Kierkegaard's aesthetes: their initial attitude, (socratically) striving towards a vague notion of liberation, quickly turns into an aesthetic irony that no longer serves to expose, but to hide. As Scholtens writes about the link between the contemporary ironic attitude and Kierkegaard's aesthetes: 'Their irony is a rampant growth and a fashion fad. They play with irony purely to play and avoid every existential implication.'[87]

---

[80] AHWOSG, 304.
[81] Timmer, '*Do You Feel It Too?*', 233.
[82] AHWOSG, 417.
[83] E.g. Star, 'Being and Knowingness', 39–40; Korthals Altes, '*Blessedly post-ironic*'?, 11–12.
[84] AHWOSG, 35 [appendix].
[85] Timmer, '*Do You Feel It Too?*', 228.
[86] AHWOSG, 35 [appendix].
[87] Scholtens, 'Inleiding', 26.

3.3. The disintegration of the self

In *Infinite Jest*, as in Kierkegaard's analysis, this aesthetic ironizing of values and actions, in the end, leads to the disintegration of the self. We arrive here at the same point as where we ended the previous chapter, only this time not via the route of excessive self-reflection but via that of excessive irony (as has been made clear, both phenomena are inextricably connected): at the point where the 'cliché "I don't know who I am"' unfortunately turns out to be more than a cliché'. The result of the addict's aesthetic attitude is the feeling of emptiness and despair that in *Infinite Jest* is labelled as 'anhedonia', more commonly known as depression (a term also used by Kierkegaard): a 'kind of emotional novocaine', a 'hollowing out of stuff that used to have affective content'.[88] The ironic-aesthetic attitude that for so long offered an escape from the limitations of reality, comes to imprison and destroy the individual, as is illustrated by the following passage: 'What looks like the cage's exit is actually the bars of the cage. [. . .] The entrance says *EXIT*. There isn't an exit [. . .] It is the cage that has entered her somehow. The ingenuity of the whole thing is beyond her. The Fun has long since dropped off the Too Much.'[89] Compare this to Lewis Hyde's above-quoted description of the ironist trapped in the cage of his own irony. Here we see the result of irony carried on for too long, the irony of the defeated aesthete. As Kierkegaard's ethicist Judge William writes to the aesthete A: 'you have seen through the vanity of everything, but you have not gone further. [. . .] You are like a dying person. You die daily, not in the profound, earnest sense [. . .], but life has lost its reality'.[90]

As the ironic-aesthetic attitude is the dominant life-view in the society portrayed in *Infinite Jest*, the resulting state of depression is, therefore, widespread as well. However, the sufferers of anhedonia try to carry their affliction as a badge of sophistication, just as Kierkegaard's aesthetes do – perhaps because the emptiness and meaninglessness of their existence is in a sense the grand conclusion of their reflexive-ironic tour de force. As we read in *Infinite Jest*: 'It's of some interest that the lively arts of the millennial U.S.A. treat anhedonia and internal emptiness as hip and cool. It's maybe the vestiges of the Romantic glorification of *Weltschmerz*, which means world-weariness or hip ennui.' Note that in this passage anhedonia and emptiness are connected, as in Kierkegaard's philosophy, to a Romantic – ironic – attitude. Marathe calls it: 'This irony and contempt for selves'.[91] According to Judge William, the aesthete laughs the 'laughter of despair' and Kierkegaard speaks of the 'superior indolence that cares for nothing at all, that does not care to work [. . .], that disperses and exhausts all the powers of the soul in soft enjoyment, and lets consciousness itself evaporate into a loathsome gloaming'.[92]

---

[88] IJ, 204, 692, 693; cf. CUP 1, 253; EO 2, 204.
[89] IJ, 222.
[90] EO 2, 194, 196.
[91] IJ, 694, 530.
[92] EO 2, 205; CI, 295.

3.4. Scepticism

Wallace has described the aesthetic world-weariness, in which all meaning and value have been ironized, as the 'congenital scepticism' of contemporary Western culture. Broadly speaking, scepticism is the refusal to grant that any knowledge or judgement is certain or justified. We can readily see the connection between such a refusal and the endless negation that characterizes aesthetic irony. With irony as our 'environment', as the new immediacy of Western society, we have been raised and conditioned to 'distrust strong belief, open conviction', writes Wallace.[93] As mentioned above, in *Infinite Jest* contemporary culture is blamed for teaching everybody the ironic-aesthetic attitude early on, including the young, (pre-)adolescent students at the Enfield Tennis Academy, who, as a result, already suffer from anhedonia. This is also labelled as the students' 'worldly scepticism'.[94] Just as hyperreflexivity and endless irony are connected – as we have seen –, so are the solipsism and scepticism that Wallace describes as the effects of endless self-reflection and irony. Distancing myself from all determinations that could be attached to the world or to my actions in it, requires constant self-reflection. My own thoughts become the sole place where meaning or value is formed but is also immediately relinquished again (through irony). And just as I become unable to ascribe any value or meaning to the reality outside me, I am equally incapable of ascribing, through self-reflection, any determination to my interior life, to my so-called self.

This sceptical world-weariness might be regarded as the new immediacy of contemporary Western culture. The ironic attitude that lies at the root of this scepticism, has become our environment, as Wallace would say. We are raised on irony. The feeling of ennui that accompanies the emptiness of ironic existence is described by Kierkegaard as boredom and his aesthete A calls this boredom an 'acquired immediacy'. Kierkegaard writes: 'Boredom is the only continuity the ironist has. Boredom, this eternity devoid of content, this salvation devoid of joy, this superficial profundity, this hungry glut.'[95] Boredom in the Kierkegaardian sense is the result of the negative freedom of the aesthete's irony: it follows from the conclusion that there is nothing left in the world with which the aesthete is connected, to which he is committed, that is of value to him. The aesthete A writes: 'Boredom rests upon the nothing that interlaces existence; its dizziness is infinite, like that which comes from looking down into a bottomless abyss.'[96] We use the term boredom to describe both an individual's basic, languid state of apathy, as well as the frenetic attempts that he might undertake, out of boredom, to distract himself from that boredom. It does not seem far-fetched to claim that many of the characters in *Infinite Jest* are in fact trying to dispel the boredom of their aesthetic existence, through innumerable forms of addiction, with disastrous

---

[93] Wallace, 'Joseph Frank's Dostoevsky', 272.
[94] IJ, 116; admittedly, this characterization is part of a remark made quite offhandedly by one of the older E.T.A. students, Michael Pemulis, while playing cards with a group of younger students. Still, in relation to the wider societal picture offered in the novel, it is a telling reference that ties in with remarks made by Wallace in other writings, such as the one quoted directly above.
[95] EO 1, 290; CI, 285.
[96] EO 1, 291.

existential consequences. Wallace's unfinished, posthumously published novel *The Pale King* further focuses on this notion of boredom.

Kierkegaard, Wallace and Eggers do not criticize irony *in general*, in all of its manifestations, they are critical, specifically, of irony as a permanent, default attitude. As an end in itself, irony becomes aimless and empty. The individual that Kierkegaard calls the aesthete, turns irony into a *permanent* attitude, and uses it to avoid all commitment, all responsibility, in order to retain his negative freedom. This total negative irony, described and criticized by Kierkegaard, is similar to the ironic attitude that both Wallace and Eggers critique.

In this form, irony is no longer a means to overthrow hypocritical, unquestioned truths, but rather an instrument of hypocrisy and cynicism, which makes it incredibly difficult for individuals to realize a meaningful life. For, in the end, the ironic-aesthetic life-view amounts to a gradual disintegration of the self: by neglecting reality through endless irony, not realizing a new, freely chosen relation to that reality, the self is also neglected – gradually, it is emptied out, ending up in a state of complete scepticism. And, as we read in Kierkegaard's *Repetition*, 'such a mistake is and remains a person's downfall'.[97]

4. Meta-irony

How to rid oneself of this tyrannizing form of irony? As mentioned in section 1, certain critics and scholars have faulted Wallace and Eggers for employing irony and thereby contradicting their own critique. Other critics, however, are of the opinion that in the works in question (especially Wallace's) the ironic attitude is successfully overcome by ironizing it, by being ironic about irony; that is, by employing meta-irony. Below, I will argue that this claim is incorrect, that the ironic attitude portrayed above cannot be regarded as being overcome by being ironic about it, and that such meta-irony, in fact, would amount to a continuation of the problem.

4.1. Wallace's meta-irony?

Critics and scholars have argued that the critique of irony in Wallace's works is executed through meta-irony; that in his fiction irony is criticized and overcome by ironizing it (the same has been suggested in relation to Eggers's work, but less substantially; therefore, I will limit myself, here, to the argument made in relation to Wallace).[98] A. O. Scott, for example, writes: 'If one way to escape from the blind alley of postmodern self-consciousness is simply to turn around and walk in another direction [. . .] – Wallace prefers to forge ahead in hopes of breaking through to the other side, whatever that may be.' Subsequently, Scott concludes that Wallace 'is less anti-ironic than (forgive

---

[97]   Kierkegaard, *Fear and Trembling/Repetition*, 137.
[98]   E.g. Korthals Altes, 'Sincerity, Reliability and Other Ironies', 123–4.

me) meta-ironic. That is, his gambit is to turn irony back on itself'.[99] Boswell holds a similar view. He writes that irony is a 'cage the doors of which [Wallace's] work wants to spring. He opens the cage of irony by *ironizing* it, the same way he uses self-reflexivity to disclose the subtle deceptions at work in literary self-reflexivity'.[100]

Both arguments, however, are flawed. The claim that the works of Wallace (and Eggers) are meta-ironic either implies an equivocation of different meanings or forms of irony, namely: being ironic – in the sense of a humorous, or even simply a fictional (and thus 'un-meant') portrayal – about irony – now in the sense of the total negative irony described above; or the claim implies an interpretation that overlooks passages from the texts themselves that seem to imply the contrary. Again, my point is not that irony, in all of its forms, is absent from Wallace's works or, more specifically, from his portrayal of the ironic attitude and its resulting problems. Rather my point is merely that Wallace's works cannot be rightly described as successfully overcoming or going beyond the problematic ironic attitude described in the previous section by ironizing it, that is, through meta-irony. Although the suggestion sounds reasonable, envisioning how it works proves to be more problematic: an analysis of the relevant aspects shows that the suggestion of a liberating ironization of total irony does not hold up.

First of all, the claim of meta-irony cannot imply that Wallace's work effects an ironization of irony simply by offering a (critical) fictional portrayal of irony and its resulting problems, for, as argued above, such a claim would render all fiction ironic (and the whole point moot). Secondly, we have to be careful not to equivocate irony, humour and self-consciousness, or, more importantly, verbal irony and existential irony. Certain passages in Wallace's fiction can perhaps be read as mocking, or joking, or employing irony as a figure of speech in relation to certain aspects of the ironic attitude. However, such instances of verbal irony, which are always limited to a specific target, can never amount to the total negation that is needed to ironize in turn the total negation that is existential irony. And even if such a total negation of existential irony could in fact be executed, the result would still be the same total negativity that one started out with, and not a specific positivity that functions as an alternative to irony, for irony is incapable of producing this. Boswell seems to overlook this problem when he writes that Wallace's fiction 'treats the culture's hip fear of sentiment with the same sort of ironic self-awareness with which sophisticates in the culture portray "gooey" sentimentality', and that 'the result is that hip irony is itself ironized in such a way that the *opposite* of hip irony – that is: gooey sentiment – can emerge as the work's indirectly intended mode'.[101] However, even Socratic total irony can, by definition, only expose the futility of, in this case, the 'hip fear of sentiment', but it cannot be seen to truly 'intend' any alternative (not even 'indirectly'); for even if such an ironic 'insight', in this case into the merits of 'gooey sentiment', were to present itself, it would immediately be subject to the same ironic self-awareness that gave rise to it, and, as a result, only continue irony's spiral of negation.

---

[99]   Scott, 'The Panic of Influence', 40.
[100] Boswell, *Understanding David Foster Wallace*, 207.
[101] Ibid., 17.

4.2. Meta-irony from a Kierkegaardian perspective

For Kierkegaard, meta-irony as the ironization of irony remains an integral, undisruptive part of the ironic-aesthetic attitude. Meta-irony forms part of what was described in the previous section as the perspective of the defeated aesthete: he who has recognized the futility of his life-view and submitted his own ironic attitude to the viewpoint of irony. However, this meta-ironic movement does not give rise to a change in life-view. Recall what Judge William says to the aesthete A: 'you have seen through the vanity of everything, but you have not gone further'.[102] Instead, the preference for one thing or the other becomes a matter of complete indifference to the defeated aesthete. The crucial reason why, for Kierkegaard, meta-irony cannot constitute a move beyond the aesthetic stage, is that it merely emphasizes the futility of irony itself, but does not, and cannot, replace it with something else, a positivity, a freedom-to, which forms the only possible liberation from the suppression of negative freedom. For the defeated aesthete nothing remains but mocking and tripping up all human actions. The aesthete A meta-ironically mocks his own ironic life-view, by describing himself as having become, as a result of that view, 'the unhappiest one'; at the end of the eponymous essay, however, he writes: 'But what am I saying – "the unhappiest"? I ought to say "the happiest" [. . .] See, language breaks down, and thought is confused.'[103] Meta-irony is simply another thought-movement in the spiral of 'reflection reflecting upon itself'; it does not break out of it, and as such does not constitute a liberation from the ironic-aesthetic attitude: 'As [Kierkegaard] put it in his journals', writes George Stack, 'one does not overcome a stultifying state of being by more knowledge or more thought.'[104] Meta-irony, or the ironization of irony, and the resulting insight that the ironic attitude is futile, does not function as an overcoming of the aesthetic attitude; instead, it forms a continuation of it.

4.3. Arguments against meta-irony in Wallace

We find a similar assessment of meta-irony in both Wallace's essays and fiction writing. We have already seen that Wallace regards irony as an instrument of negation, of destructive exposure, that should only be employed temporarily, precisely because of its negative character. In 'E Unibus Pluram', Wallace invites us to think of irony in terms of 'Third World rebels and coups'. He writes: '[they] are great at exposing and overthrowing corrupt hypocritical regimes, but they seem noticeably less great at the mundane, non-negative task of then establishing a superior governing alternative'. To which he adds a remark that ties in with the above claims about meta-irony: 'Victorious rebels, in fact, seem best at using their tough, cynical rebel-skills to avoid being rebelled against themselves – in other words, they just become better tyrants.'[105] These remarks seem to be at odds with Boswell's claim that in Wallace's

---

[102] EO 2, 194.
[103] EO 1, 230.
[104] Stack, *Kierkegaard's Existential Ethics*, 33.
[105] EUP, 67.

own work irony *does* succeed in being both 'diagnosis and cure'.[106] In fact, Boswell's claim brings to mind another remark by Wallace, concerning the 'assumptions *behind* early postmodern irony', namely that it 'assumed that etiology and diagnosis pointed toward cure, that a revelation of imprisonment led to freedom'. The import of Wallace's remark is precisely that this assumption – of irony functioning as both diagnosis and cure – has turned out to be mistaken, that irony has turned out to be 'not liberating but enfeebling'. Also, this passage is directly followed by the remark discussed in the previous sections about irony becoming a cage and continued irony the song of the trapped coming to enjoy that cage. Wallace is saying here that irony, in addition to 'diagnosis', cannot possibly present a proper 'cure', because, as he writes, irony serves an 'almost exclusively negative function' and is therefore 'singularly unuseful when it comes to constructing anything to replace the hypocrisies it debunks'.[107]

In 'E Unibus Pluram', Wallace offers a further argument against meta-irony with his view of the 'literary subgenre' he labels 'Image-Fiction'. Wallace applauds Image-Fiction's intention, of wanting to offer a contemporary 'response' to the irony and hyperreflexivity of contemporary culture. However, he criticizes its conviction that this can be done by being '*reverently ironic*' – by portraying the ironic culture through its own irony, that is, by being 'meta-ironic'. Wallace concludes that, as a result, Image-Fiction 'doesn't satisfy its own agenda'; its response 'via ironic genuflection is all too easily subsumed' into the ironic attitude: 'It is dead on the page.'[108] This is, in my opinion, a clear and direct argument against meta-irony as a solution to the ironic attitude that Wallace wants to overcome.

Scott connects his attribution of meta-irony to Wallace to the latter's appreciation of David Lynch. Scott writes: 'Wallace is temperamentally committed to multiplicity – to a quality he has called, with reference to the filmmaker David Lynch, "*both*ness." He wants to be at once earnest and ironical.'[109] However, what Wallace means by Lynch's 'bothness' has little to do with irony or meta-irony. An important part of his fascination with Lynch lies precisely in the fact that, as Wallace writes, 'nobody in Lynch's movies analyzes or metacriticizes or hermeneuticizes or anything, including Lynch himself. This set of restrictions makes Lynch's movies fundamentally unironic'. Wallace adds: 'Lynch's lack of irony is the real reason some cinéastes – in this age when ironic self-consciousness is the one and only universally recognized badge of sophistication – see him as a naïf or a buffoon.' Wallace's point about Lynch's 'bothness' actually has to do with existential complexity: 'Laura Palmer in *Fire Walk with Me* is *both* "good" and "bad", and yet also neither: she's complex, contradictory, real', Wallace writes: 'Laura's muddy *both*ness [. . .] [requires] of us an empathetic confrontation with the exact same muddy *both*ness in ourselves and our intimates that makes the real world of moral selves so tense and uncomfortable.' It may be useful to recall here the connection, briefly discussed in the Introduction, made in *Infinite Jest* between Lynch and Kierkegaard when a movie is described as being a 'Kierkegaard/Lynch (?) parody'.

---

[106]   Boswell, *Understanding David Foster Wallace*, 17.
[107]   EUP, 66–7.
[108]   Ibid., 50, 80, 76, 52, 81.
[109]   Scott, 'The Panic of Influence', 40.

Perhaps we should connect this to the need (which, according to Wallace, both men have perceived) to overcome irony, to be 'unironic'.[110]

Perhaps most importantly, *Infinite Jest* itself contains a clear, explicit reference to the futility of meta-irony. The novel describes the movie 'The Joke', which is advertised as: "*The JOKE*": *You Are Strongly Advised NOT To Shell Out Money To See This Film*'.[111] However, 'art film habitués of course thought [this] was a cleverly ironic anti-ad joke'. Against the advice of the ads, people go to the theatre, where the screen simply shows a live recording of the very same people entering the theatre and taking their seats. So, the film *is* a joke and the advice on the posters a meta-ironic trick aimed at an ironic audience, who will not take the warning at face value.[112] This meta-ironic trick is clearly portrayed in the novel as a failure, as a continuation of the problem it supposedly points out. In his reading of 'The Joke', Iannis Goerlandt writes: 'a meta-ironic stance still employs irony and is not an authentic solution to the problem'.[113] The example of 'The Joke' makes clear that meta-irony is not a satisfying solution to the ironic attitude; it is a trick that partakes in and therefore continues the exact structures it claims to subvert. And this self-preserving character of irony is an important part of what makes it so tyrannical.

So, meta-irony is not a solution to the problem of irony, but a continuation of it. In the end, it is only through the literary execution of what Kierkegaard calls the 'leap' towards the ethical, that the ironic-aesthetic attitude can be overcome. However, the correct place for the analysis of this aspect of the works of Wallace and Eggers – even though it follows from their critique of endless, aesthetic irony – is Part 2 of this study, as it concerns the engagement that characterizes these works.

Conclusion

This chapter has provided an analysis of the problem of endless irony portrayed in the novels of Wallace and Eggers. By viewing their work in light of Kierkegaard's critique of irony, we have been able to see that their common object is not irony as merely a verbal strategy, but irony as an attitude towards existence, which implies a total negation of all given meaning or value (and not just verbal irony's indirect expression of something, however vague or hidden). Also, the works in question all illustrate that the ironic attitude can initially have a liberating effect: through it, the individual can socratically free himself from his given, immediate situation, and as such irony forms an indispensable step towards becoming a self, realizing an

---

[110]   Wallace, 'David Lynch Keeps His Head', 199, 211; IJ, 992.

[111]   The film was made, just like the 'Kierkegaard/Lynch (?) parody', by James Incandenza, whose tragic fate – he commits suicide by sticking his head into a microwave – functions as another emblem of the destructiveness of the ironic attitude. In *Infinite Jest*, it is repeatedly pointed out that the several characters who commit suicide (or attempt to), opt to do so by 'destroying' their head, the 'headquarters' of their reflexive-ironic mind.

[112]   IJ, 397–8.

[113]   Goerlandt, 'Put The Book Down and Slowly Walk Away', 315–16.

existence informed by self-chosen values. For Kierkegaard, Wallace and Eggers the problem lies in irony becoming a permanent attitude, escaping all determinations and responsibilities. This aesthetic or Romantic irony has disastrous consequences for the self: because no content or value is attached to one's life, the self is gradually emptied out. This disintegration of the self as a result of the attitude of endless, aesthetic irony is what the works of Wallace and Eggers criticize, as we have seen in the examples of the addicts in *Infinite Jest* and the editors of *Might Magazine* in *A Heartbreaking Work of Staggering Genius*. Finally, it is important to note that meta-irony – even though some critics have erroneously described it as part of the critical strategy of Wallace's and Eggers's works – cannot lead to liberation from empty irony, because ironizing irony is simply a continuation of the endless spiral of aesthetic negation.

Problematic Fiction

The two previous chapters have provided an analysis of the problems of hyperreflexivity and endless irony as portrayed in the novels of Wallace, Eggers and Foer. But, as explained in the Introduction to this study, these literary works do not just critique these problems on the 'existential' level of their story-worlds, but also on a more 'theoretical' level; that is, hyperreflexivity and endless irony can be regarded as determinant characteristics of the view of fiction underlying the 'postmodernist metafiction' of John Barth and the 'postmodernist minimalism' of Bret Easton Ellis.

The next two chapters serve to bring out the reflexive-ironic strategy that lies at the heart of these two literary trends, and to show how, in both cases, this goes wrong. The hyperreflexivity and endless irony of the works of Barth and Ellis result in two forms of fiction that are both unable to give meaning to the world we live in. In Barth's highly theoretical writing, it leads to fiction that can only affirm or express its own artificiality, the fact that it is not real (that fiction is pretence). This will be explored in Chapter 3. In Ellis's work, the distinction between fiction and reality seems to implode: in his writing there simply remains no deeper ('real', 'true') meaning or value to express, only the description of surface, appearance. This will be explored in Chapter 4. Their hyperreflexivity and endless irony, and the resulting effects of solipsism and scepticism, makes these works into what we might call 'problematic fiction'.

3

Postmodernist Metafiction: John Barth

Introduction

In this chapter and the following one I will analyse two embodiments of hyperreflexive irony in American literary fiction, which are criticized as such, implicitly and explicitly, in the works of Wallace, Eggers and Foer, namely, the postmodernist metafiction of (mainly) the 1960s and 1970s, specifically the work of John Barth; and the postmodernist minimalism of (mainly) the 1980s and (first half of the) 1990s, specifically the work of Bret Easton Ellis.[1] These two literary trends can be seen to represent the two senses in which the term postmodernism is most often employed: on the one hand, a theoretical postmodernism, signifying a predominantly 'academic' problematization and subversion of beliefs considered to be central to modernist thought or Western thought in general; and on the other hand, a popular postmodernism, referring to a broader, societal situation, namely, the widely shared perception of reality as having become uncertain and devoid of value.[2] However, there is a clear connection between these two postmodernist forms, as I will show in this and in the following chapter.

'Oh God comma I abhor self-consciousness.'[3] This sentence from John Barth's *Lost in the Funhouse* is emblematic of the reflexive irony of Barth's fiction: it professes an aversion to self-reflectivity, while actually wallowing in it. In the two previous chapters we have seen that in the portrayal of contemporary existence in the works of Wallace, Eggers and Foer, hyperreflexivity and endless irony are the two main issues that impede the realization of a meaningful life. As such, their works carry out an implicit and, in the case of Wallace, explicit critique of the role of these phenomena in

Unless otherwise indicated, translations are mine.
[1] Annesley, 'Review Essay: David Foster Wallace', 132; Boswell, *Understanding David Foster Wallace*, 66, 70, 78, 103, 207; Max, 'The Unfinished', 52; McCaffery, 'Interview', 144; Wallace, 'Fictional Futures and the Conspicuously Young', Other terms used to label this wave of 'minimalist' postmodernist literature are: 'Brat Pack', 'Blank Generation', 'Punk Fiction', 'Blank Fiction' (Annesley, *Blank Fictions*; Young and Caveney, 'Introduction', iii).
[2] This distinction is similar to the one drawn by Yra van Dijk and Thomas Vaessens, between 'intellectualist' and 'popular' postmodernism (Vaessens and Van Dijk, 'Introduction', 10).
[3] LF, 113.

other fiction. An analysis of such 'problematic' works is needed to further clarify the shared philosophical dimension of the novels of Wallace, Eggers and Foer, especially since certain scholars have erroneously described the latter works as instances of either postmodernist metafiction or minimalism.[4] By analysing these problematic forms of fiction, and their underlying view of language and literature, I will be able to contrast them with the view that underlies the novels of Wallace, Eggers and Foer. On the basis of this view, which we will examine in Chapter 5, the latter works are able to speak meaningfully again about the notions of sincerity, reality-commitment and community. We will see that Barth's fiction, as a result of its hyperreflexive irony, is unable to do so; it portrays the alleged impossibility of giving meaningful substance to such notions. We will see that this follows from the metafictional problematization of the notion of reality, which (allegedly) cannot be adequately expressed through language, leaving the individual in a situation in which he cannot communicate anything truthful about himself, others or the world – in other words, in a situation of solipsism and scepticism.

The current chapter will be structured as follows: In section 1, I will outline what postmodernist metafiction is, and show that Barth's writing (specifically *Lost in the Funhouse* and his essay 'The Literature of Exhaustion') is a pre-eminent expression of this literary movement. In section 2, in order to further illustrate its reflexive-ironic dynamic, I will view Barth's fiction in light of Derrida's 'strategy' of deconstruction, which can be seen to consist of two parts, two double movements, 'construction and undermining', and 'overturning and displacement'. I will show that Barth's metafiction performs a very similar strategy, resulting in a similar cycle of endless self-reflection and irony. In the conclusion to this chapter I will briefly examine Wallace's similar critique of Barth and Derrida's shared postmodern strategies.

Also, I would like to emphasize that, in this chapter (and throughout this study), I will be referring to the notion of deconstruction as it was interpreted in the United States, based on Derrida's earlier, highly language-focused writings, and will not be taking into account, for example, the so-called ethical turn of Derrida's later works. Because of the innumerable discussions and interpretations associated with the name 'Derrida' and the concept of 'deconstruction', it is important to clearly mark the limits of what can be critically discussed within the scope of this study (especially since Derrida is not its main focus). The suggested distinction is a widely accepted one. Moreover, the relevance of Derrida and the notion of deconstruction for this study follows from the enormous impact that the interpretation of these earlier writings on deconstruction have had in American fiction, literary theory and criticism. Looking at the aspects of deconstruction that were picked up by or can be aligned with postmodernist literature and literary theory, will best illuminate the primary concerns of this study. With this specification in mind, we can say that in both postmodernist metafiction and deconstruction the impossibility of connecting language to reality leads to the conclusion that language must fail.

---

[4] E.g. Korthals Altes, 'Blessedly post-ironic'?, 11–12; Myers, 'A Bag of Tired Tricks', 115–16, 120; Scott, 'The Panic of Influence', 43; Theuwis, *The Quest for Infinite Jest*.

1. Metafiction

First of all, what does the term 'metafiction' mean? Patricia Waugh defines it as follows: '*Metafiction* is a term given to fictional writing which self-consciously and systematically draws attention to its status as an artefact in order to pose questions about the relationship between fiction and reality.'[5] Examples of metafictional techniques are: the so-called author – the authorial voice that, as a narrative structure of the text, is itself part of the fiction, in other words, the fictional author – intruding into the narrative and declaring, for instance, the incompleteness or simply the complete fictitiousness of the story; the use of excessively difficult language to describe simple events; or the use of a strange lay-out (different typography, sudden use of colour), thereby stressing the linguistic or material character of the story. In such instances, a literary text is described as self-consciously displaying its constructed, artificial character.

As a literary technique, such textual reflexivity is not a recent invention. Waugh writes: 'although the *term* "metafiction" might be new, the *practice* is as old (if not older) than the novel itself.' But she also notes that in certain texts, mainly from 1960s and 1970s America, 'metafictional practice has become particularly prominent.'[6] As a result, the term metafiction has also come to designate these texts as a specific literary trend or genre, namely *postmodernist* metafiction. From now on, my use of the term metafiction will refer to this specific literary movement, unless specified otherwise. At the same time it is important to keep in mind that these works do more than employ metafictional techniques. To label this literary trend 'metafiction' is a *pars pro toto*, symbolic of its larger postmodernist project of unveiling artificiality and problematizing reality.

This trend in American literature is closely connected with the sociocultural transformation of the time. Raymond Federman, for example, argues that the new 'self-reflexive fiction' that came into prominence during the 1960s, is attempting 'to render concrete and even visual in its language, in its syntax, in its typography and topology, the disorder, the chaos, the violence, the incongruity, but also the energy and vitality, of American reality.'[7] Waugh holds a similar view and also explains the difference between this new, strongly metafictional trend and previous literary trends:

> The historical period we are living through has been singularly uncertain, insecure, self-questioning and culturally pluralistic. Contemporary fiction clearly reflects this dissatisfaction with, and breakdown of, traditional values. Previously, as in the case of nineteenth-century realism, the forms of fiction derived from a firm belief in a commonly experienced, objectively existing world of history. Modernist fiction, written in the earlier part of this century, responded to the initial loss of belief in such a world. [...] Contemporary metafictional writing is both a response and a contribution to an even more thoroughgoing sense that reality or history

---

[5]   Waugh, *Metafiction*, 2.
[6]   Ibid., 5; cf. Federman, 'Self-Reflexive Fiction', 1142.
[7]   Federman, 'Self-Reflexive Fiction', 1146.

are provisional: no longer a world of eternal verities but a series of constructions, artifices, impermanent structures.[8]

This 'thoroughgoing' awareness of the 'provisional', 'constructed' character of reality and history is expressed, according to Brian McHale, by a shift from mainly '*epistemological*' questions as the 'dominant' (the position from which the world is interrogated) of the previous literary period, for example 'How can I interpret this world of which I am part?', to mainly '*ontological*' questions, for example 'what and how is this world?', as the 'dominant' of the new trend of metafictional literature.[9] This shift in the literary interrogation of the world is equated by Waugh, Federman and McHale to the shift from modernist to postmodernist literature.[10] Therefore, this literary trend is often labelled as '*postmodernist* metafiction' (which is also the term that Wallace uses).

What exactly does the above-mentioned ontological awareness amount to? We have already seen that, in light of radical sociocultural changes, the world has come to be regarded as chaotic, without order, and all attempts to unify (or cover up) that chaos as temporary, artificial constructs. In other words, in the metafictional works in question the notion of 'reality' as something apparent and unequivocal has become problematic. What these works aim to express, prompted by the circumstances of their time, is the 'mess of reality' or the 'unreality of reality', to quote Federman.[11] The notion of reality comes to be regarded as constructed, artificial, fake – that is, as an 'unreality'.

The *meta*fictional character of these works follows from this problematization. As Waugh writes: 'for metafictional writers the most fundamental assumption is that composing a novel is basically no different from composing or constructing one's "reality"'.[12] This assumption implies the following, initial 'opposition between fictional and real':[13] on the one hand, there is the notion of reality (critiqued in the metafictional works in question) as an unproblematic (or perhaps, immanent, spontaneous) unity; and on the other hand, there is the notion of fiction as an artificial construct that creates the illusion of such a reality (expressed by the common characterization of the reader's attitude as a 'suspension of disbelief'),[14] but that is, in fact, not real; it is made-up, in other words, it is an unreality constructed to be experienced as a coherent reality. Subsequently, these metafictional works conclude that, as the experience of unified reality has become problematic, illusory (what we regard as) reality can, in fact, be rightly and insightfully equated to fiction: reality is always an artificial construct,

---

[8] Waugh, *Metafiction*, 6–7.
[9] Higgins, *A Dialectic of Centuries*, 101; McHale, *Postmodernist Fiction*, 7–11.
[10] Waugh, *Metafiction*, 6–7; Federman, 'Self-Reflexive Fiction', 1147; McHale, *Postmodernist Fiction*, 11.
[11] Federman, 'Self-Reflexive Fiction', 1156.
[12] Waugh, *Metafiction*, 24.
[13] McHale, *Postmodernist Fiction*, 28. To be sure: this opposition 'between fictional and real' is quite debatable; however, here, I simply aim to summarize the metafictional critique of reality; Chapter 5 will offer a (in my opinion) preferable take on this matter that also implies a critique of the opposition phrased here.
[14] Waugh speaks of 'the concept of "pretence"' and 'ensur[ing]' the reader's absorption' (Waugh, *Metafiction*, 41, 40).

an unreality, in other words, a fiction. As a result of this line of reasoning, from the perspective of postmodernist metafictional writing, fiction, and its conventions of reality-projection, come to be regarded as, writes Waugh, 'a useful model for learning about the construction of "reality" itself'.[15]

Postmodernist metafictional writing, by reflecting on itself, that is, by showing how it is structured, how it has come into being, openly *displays* its artificial character (compare the examples of oft-used metafictional techniques, given at the beginning of this section). In doing so, these works expressly deny that they are trying to project a reality by offering a credible story. These metafictional texts *pierce* their own illusionary reality (and thereby, that of other pieces of fiction) by revealing the artificiality that underlies it. Such a text, writes Waugh, 'lays bare its rules in order to investigate the relation of "fiction" to "reality", the concept of "pretence"'.[16] '[I]t systematically disturbs the air of reality by foregrounding the ontological structure of texts and of fictional worlds', writes McHale: 'we are left facing the words on the page: this happens again and again in postmodernist writing, [. . .] our attention is distracted from the projected world and made to fix on its linguistic medium'. This 'disturbance' of the 'air of reality' is meant to contribute to an awareness of the fact that what we regard, outside literary texts, as our normal, unproblematic everyday reality, is likewise a fictional, artificial construct. McHale speaks of 'destabilizing the ontology of this projected world and simultaneously laying bare the process of world construction'.[17]

The reflexive-ironic nature of postmodernist metafiction is clear: its essential operation is a constant ironic self-distancing through the self-conscious unveiling of its own structures. This strategy has an idealistic purpose: it wants to unmask the illusions that we regard as reality.[18]

As we have seen in Chapter 2, Wallace acknowledges that, like Kierkegaard's Socratic irony, initially the irony of postmodernist metafiction is aimed at liberation. He writes: 'the best postmodern fiction wasn't just credible as art; it seemed downright socially useful in its capacity for what counterculture critics called "a *critical negation* that would make it self-evident to everyone that the world is not as it seems"'. According to Wallace, at that time, these were 'not just literary devices but sensible responses to a ridiculous world', meant 'to explode hypocrisy – certain hypocritically smug ways the country saw itself that just weren't holding true anymore'.[19]

As mentioned, the most important figure of this literary trend, is John Barth (1930–).[20] Marjorie Worthington writes that Barth is 'widely considered to be the preeminent American metafictionist'.[21] According to Stan Fogel and Gordon Slethaug, Barth, together with a few other postmodernist writers, is 'responsible for the redefinition of fiction in America' since the 1960s: 'he has helped to give fiction a theoretical turn, steering it away from the conventionally realistic use of plot and

---

[15]   Waugh, *Metafiction*, 3.
[16]   Ibid., 41.
[17]   McHale, *Postmodernist Fiction*, 221, 148, 101.
[18]   Cf. EUP, 65–6.
[19]   EUP, 65–8; Wiley, 'Interview'.
[20]   Cf. Worthington, 'Done with Mirrors', 114; Fogel and Slethaug, *Understanding John Barth*, 1.
[21]   Worthington, 'Done with Mirrors', 114.

character, [. . .] toward a concern with the writings of fiction itself'.[22] Two pieces of work in particular are of decisive importance in establishing Barth's pre-eminent position in postmodernist metafiction: the literary work *Lost in the Funhouse* (1968) and the essay 'The Literature of Exhaustion' (1967).

Lost in the Funhouse 'has often been touted [. . .] as the preeminent postmodern urtext', writes Worthington.[23] It has become the classic example of postmodernist metafiction. The work consists of a series of short stories that, according to the 'Foreword', are nonetheless meant 'to be received "all at once"'. This suggestion is strengthened by the strong thematic connection between the stories. This connection is forged, above all, by their shared metafictional intention, 'to acknowledge what I'm doing while I'm doing it is exactly the point', as it is summarized by the authorial voice in the story 'Title'.[24]

Barth expounds the ideas behind the extreme metafictional strategy of *Lost in the Funhouse* in the essay 'The Literature of Exhaustion', which was published the year before the literary work.[25] The essay 'has since become', writes Charles B. Harris, 'one of the more frequently reprinted, widely commented upon, and highly influential documents of the "postmodern" literary esthetic'.[26] Frank D. McConnell even posits: 'It may well be the most famous and influential essay of the decade; it has certainly been reprinted, quoted, and "explained" by any number of critics and teachers anxious to clarify and celebrate the fiction, not only of Barth, but of his contemporaries.'[27] In the essay, Barth declares that all literary means have been 'exhausted': everything has been done already, there is nothing new to be said, and no new way of saying it. Barth's main assertion seems to be that literary means are not (or: no longer) able to express the world nor what the writer wants to say about it. Subsequently, the only option that is left, according to Barth, is turning this exhaustion against itself, as it were, namely by representing this exhaustion of literary means, portraying it through new literary texts, and thereby, through the portrayal of the impossibility of creating or expressing anything new, creating new literary works nonetheless. Or, as summarized in the story 'Title': 'To turn ultimacy against itself to make something new and valid, the essence whereof would be the impossibility of making something new.'[28]

2. Deconstruction and metafiction

Several scholars – including Harris, McConnell, Boswell, and Fogel and Slethaug[29] – have remarked on the strong affinity between the metafictional strategy of Barth's

[22] Fogel and Slethaug, *Understanding John Barth*, 1.
[23] Worthington, 'Done with Mirrors', 118.
[24] LF, xi, 111.
[25] Worthington, 'Done with Mirrors', 134.
[26] Harris, *Passionate Virtuosity*, 1.
[27] McConnell, *Four Postwar American Novelists*, xxvi.
[28] LF, 109.
[29] Harris, *Passionate Virtuosity*, 165; Fogel and Slethaug, *Understanding John Barth*, 9, 14, 104; McConnell, *Four Postwar American Novelists*, 110; Boswell, *Understanding David Foster Wallace*, 26.

'literature of exhaustion' and Derrida's 'strategy of deconstruction'. Barth has written that 'the true postmodernist [. . .] keeps one foot always in the narrative past [. . .] and one foot in, one might say, the Parisian structuralist present'.[30] Fogel and Slethaug write that with the term 'structuralist' (used somewhat loosely, here) Barth is referring to, among others, Derrida. They describe the affinity between the methods of Barth and Derrida as follows: 'These traits have come to be called deconstructive – taking apart the structures, patterns and expectations of text, context, author, and reader. [Deconstruction] can be understood as a vital postmodern practice akin to the experimentation and focuses of Barth's literary practice.'[31]

This description, however, is quite general and unspecific. Therefore, in this section, I will compare Barth's literary practice and Derrida's strategy of deconstruction in greater detail. This is not a simple task: first of all, because one of the main features of deconstruction seems to be the impossibility of a message, text or philosophy having a clear, unequivocal meaning. This means that Derrida's philosophy of deconstruction, as Eddo Evink formulates it, 'cannot be discussed as "Derrida's philosophy" without opposing the leading idea of that philosophy – and this assertion, too, struggles with the same problem'.[32] Nevertheless, it seems possible to describe the general outlines of deconstruction.[33] Even in Derrida's own work, it is repeatedly described 'schematically', as 'a general strategy of deconstruction'.[34] Furthermore, I will be approaching Derrida's notion of deconstruction from a specific perspective, limiting myself to the comparison with Barth's literature of exhaustion (and, later on in this study, the opposition between the similar views of Derrida and Barth, on the one hand, and, on the other, the late-Wittgensteinian view of language and literature that underpins Wallace's fiction).

Like postmodernist metafiction, Derrida's philosophy of deconstruction has an idealistic, liberating motivation: it wants to expose illusory notions and thereby transform our way of thinking. Below, I will begin by explaining that Derrida's philosophy is aimed at exposing the illusion of presence that dominates Western thought. I will show that, according to Derrida, this notion is illusory and inevitable at the same time. Subsequently, I will turn to deconstruction, the strategy that, according to Derrida, allows us to expose, without ever being able to completely shake off, this illusion. I will focus on two aspects of deconstruction that invite a comparison with metafiction. These two aspects can best be regarded as the two double movements that characterize deconstruction. First of all, a general characteristic of deconstruction is that it implies both *construction* and *undermining* (deconstruction does not destroy the illusions at which it is aimed; it both 'constructs' and 'destructs' them).[35] The second aspect, or second double movement, is actually a specification

---

[30] Barth, 'The Literature of Replenishment', 204.
[31] Fogel and Slethaug, *Understanding John Barth*, 14.
[32] Evink, *Transcendentie en inscriptie*, 55.
[33] Cf. the several authoritative introductions to Derrida and deconstruction; e.g. Culler, *On Deconstruction*.
[34] Derrida, *Margins of Philosophy*, 329; Derrida, *Positions*, 41; cf. Evink, *Transcendentie en inscriptie*, 75.
[35] Cf. Brill, *Wittgenstein and Critical Theory*, 98; Culler, *On Deconstruction*, 86; Moyaert, 'Jacques Derrida en de filosofie van de differentie', 82.

of the process of undermining, namely that it is executed through the, as Derrida writes, 'double gesture' of '*overturning*' and '*displacement*'.[36]

2.1. Derrida: The indispensable illusion of presence

According to Derrida, the most fundamental notions of Western thought – that is, the notions of metaphysics, the branch of philosophy that tries to contemplate the deepest ground, the first causes of existence – are based on illusions. The illusion that dominates Western thought, and that therefore is deconstruction's target, is the ideal of *presence*. All Western philosophy, according to Derrida, strives to reach a fundamental level where truth and meaning are fully *present*.[37] All philosophical attempts at definition, at indicating the determining grounds for something, the principle on which something is based – all these attempts imply the ideal of presence. They all imply that, if one could only go (back) deep or far enough, one could clearly determine the essence, the 'pure' meaning of something. This ideal of metaphysical essences expressed in perfect, pure definitions is an illusion, an impossible dream, according to Derrida.

However, at the same time, it is an impossible dream from which we cannot free ourselves, without which our language would not be able to function, argues Derrida.[38] Seen by themselves, words seem nothing more than a series of marks or sounds, 'without life', one could say; a word seems to require something that accompanies it, that is 'present' to it and, as such, gives meaning to that word. Derrida says that we necessarily regard a word as a supplement for something else, as *referring* to something – to a thing in the world, or a thought in my head. Without that connection, a word would appear to be dead, meaningless.

By presupposing that a word functions as a supplement to something, as referring to something outside itself, a gap opens up between language and what it seeks to express in the world (for example, an object, or a thought in my head). If that gap is to be bridged, if language is to express the world, a clear and unequivocal connection between language and world is required, that infuses words with accurate meaning,

---

[36]   Derrida, *Margins of Philosophy*, 329.

[37]   In his later writings, Derrida has tried to play down this perhaps overly generalized characterization of all Western philosophy as a uniform product of a metaphysics of presence. However, this is the characterization offered in his early language-focused writings; e.g. 'Western metaphysics, as the limitation of sense of being within the field of presence, is produced as the domination of a linguistic form. To question the origin of that domination does not amount to hypostatizing a transcendental signified, but to a questioning of what constitutes our history and what produced transcendentality itself' (Derrida, *Of Grammatology*, 23); cf. Evink, *Transcendentie en inscriptie*, 57.

[38]   Cf. 'There is no sense in doing without the concepts of metaphysics in order to shake metaphysics. We have no language – no syntax and no lexicon – which is foreign to this history; we can pronounce not a single destructive proposition which has not already had to slip into the form, the logic, and the implicit postulations of precisely what it seeks to contest' (Derrida, *Writing and Difference*, 354); 'what indeed I try to deconstruct, seems to me, insofar as it is desire or need, to be indestructible, or, I would even venture to say, "immortal", and moreover, for the same reasons, mortal, or rather, deadly, in the sense of death-bearing. Is not the "pure realization of self-presence" itself also death?' (Derrida, *Limited Inc*, 116); also see footnote 40.

and thereby, their capacity to describe the world. However, such an accurate reflection of language and world requires a shared metaphysical 'origin', a system of essences, of transcendental signifieds that underlies both the being of the world and the possibility for its accurate expression in language.[39]

Derrida explicitly acknowledges the inevitability and legitimacy of this ideal of pure essences underlying our language use. According to him, the connection between word and world has to be pure and unequivocal, if a word is to have meaning at all – because any remaining ambiguity would be contrary to the whole idea of meaning: 'Every concept that lays claim to any rigor whatsoever implies the alternative of "all or nothing"', Derrida writes in *Limited Inc.*[40] So, a set of pure, transcendental essences – the 'all or nothing' or, elsewhere, the 'pure realization of self-presence' that Derrida speaks of – is the only possible foundation for meaningful language use (pure concepts connecting words and world). 'If the connection with that impossible presence disappears, the supplement will not be perceived as meaningful anymore', explains Paul Moyaert. He adds: 'Saying that the supplement produces meaning without surrendering to the call to make present the impossible presence, actually means that the inscription has already lost its meaning and does not really speak to us anymore.'[41] According to Derrida, a language that does not make an appeal to (impossible, illusory) metaphysical presence, cannot exist, because we cannot rid ourselves of this illusion, because without it language would appear to be without meaning. These illusory notions are deep-seated habits of thought that are virtually unalterable, for they concern 'the founding categories of our understanding of reality, our interpretation of the world and the functioning of thought in general', writes Ger Groot.[42]

But why, then, does Derrida regard the ideal of presence as an illusion? Because the striving for presence always implies absence, distance, opacity. According to Derrida, there is always a gap between language and world, and language and thought. My words can never mean exactly what I want them to mean, because of the fact that my words can be repeated by others – without being accompanied by my intentions –, which means that my intentions are not determinative, that my words will evoke unintended associations and their meaning will shift. Similarly, words can never offer a pure, complete signification of the world, if only because word and world do not coincide; there is always a certain distance between the words and the objects they refer to in the world. This essential indeterminacy of language is an important 'outcome' of deconstruction (further elaborated by Derrida through terms such as 'différance', 'dissemination', 'trace').

---

[39] Cf. Hacker, *Meaning and Mind*, 16; Hacker, *Mind and Will*, 36–7; also: 'Once words and things are seen as constituting separate, self-enclosed realms, one can only avoid skepticism by positing some metaphysical entity, or "origin," an absolute mind, a synthetic *a priori*, logical simples, or an idea of forms or essences – to explain how the two come together' (Altieri, 'Wittgenstein on Consciousness and Language', 1409).

[40] Also: 'when a concept is to be treated as a concept I believe that one has to accept the logic of all or nothing, I always try to do this and I believe it always has to be done, at any rate, in a theoretical-philosophical discussion of concepts or of things conceptualizable' (Derrida, *Limited Inc*, 116–17).

[41] Moyaert, 'Jacques Derrida en de filosofie van de differentie', 54, 61.

[42] Groot, 'Inleiding', 7.

We should note, however, that this analysis presupposes the traditional (referential) picture of language. Derrida explicitly states that we cannot simply correct or step out of this referential picture of language:

> to determine language as representation is not the effect of an accidental prejudice, a theoretical fault or a manner of thinking, a limit or closure among others, a form of representation, precisely which came about one day and of which we could rid ourselves by a decision when the time comes.[43]

Derrida's exposure of the inevitability of absence presupposes a system that is motivated by a striving towards presence. One can only speak, as Derrida does, of a gap between language and world, and between language and thought, if one assumes that language acquires (or tries to acquire) meaning by referring to the world or thought (by attempting to bridge that gap).[44] 'Derrida's concept of writing, with its associated metaphors of trace, hymen, supplement, restance, parergon, and dissemination, can be seen as a precise rendering of this problematic relation between representation and its other', writes Charles Altieri, '[because language] does not picture what it purports to refer to, meanings depend on structures of signs or other meanings, none of which is securely anchored in a reality outside language'.[45] It is this failure to connect words and world (that is, to realize presence) that, for Derrida, opens up the space from which meanings arise, always imperfectly, not uniquely signifying what is meant to be described, carrying with them other possible connotations.[46] But this failure presupposes the attempt to refer, to make present.

2.2. Construction and undermining

To further understand how deconstruction works, we have to see that 'to deconstruct a discourse is to show how it undermines the philosophy it asserts, or the hierarchical oppositions on which it relies', writes Jonathan Culler. The first double movement of deconstruction – construction and undermining – implies that a certain philosophical discourse first has to be constructed, confirmed, before it can subsequently be shown to be based on an illusion. Culler: 'The practitioner of deconstruction works within

---

[43] Derrida, 'Envoi [Sending: On Representation]', 102.

[44] In certain aspects, Derrida's description of what he regards as the inability of language to describe the world, resembles, perhaps surprisingly, the view of early Wittgenstein. After all, the latter concludes that forms of language that do not 'picture' the world do not have sense; they try to 'say' something that cannot be said. Ralph Shain remarks: 'metaphilosophically, Derrida's views are closer to the *Tractatus* than to the *Investigations*. The failures of philosophy are not simply failures but gaps which mark the limits of what can be said' (Shain, 'Derrida's References to Wittgenstein', 83). An important difference lies in the fact that Derrida carries through the purity ideal of meaningful language use so 'strictly', that for him everything becomes 'unsayable': language never succeeds in bridging the gap, in 'picturing' the world.

[45] Altieri, *Act & Quality*, 35.

[46] For Derrida, this justifies the contention that every utterance requires interpretation (e.g. Derrida, 'Force of Law', 23).

the terms of the system but in order to breach it.'[47] Deconstruction shows that a system undermines itself by revealing its contradictory, 'illusory' grounds. Although deconstruction breaches the system in question, it does not destroy it, and it does not replace it with something new. Moreover, deconstruction always remains *within* the system that it deconstructs, retaining it, simultaneously showing its impossibility *and* its necessity. '[B]y maintaining the dichotomies as such, actual subversion never occurs, as can be seen even in the name of the project that includes the "construction" one struggles against', writes Susan B. Brill, '[w]ithin "deconstruction", we thus see the hierarchies of the reigning status quo being constructed (asserted) and then violently "destructed" (not destroyed, but shown to be groundless)'.[48]

Here, the notion of presence can serve as an example. As we have seen, Western thought is motivated by the attempt to establish the complete presence of meaning and truth, but when we take a closer look at such attempts, we will find that its ambition does not hold up. Thought can never survey reality in its entirety: there is always something that escapes its 'gaze', if only that gaze itself, trying to see everything, but by definition unable to see itself; there is always a remainder of absence that disrupts the striving towards presence. Indeed, absence is vital to thought: for thinking itself always functions at a certain distance towards the things that it is considering; there is always a certain amount of opacity that has to be *thought through*. So, by constructing an attempt to establish presence, deconstruction exposes an ineluctable, ineffaceable element of absence that undermines the ideal of presence.

Because of this dynamic of construction and undermining, Derrida's deconstructions often start as a reading of texts of other, influential philosophers. In doing so, a certain way of thinking is first established, constructed. Subsequently, Derrida places his remarks in the 'margins' of those texts, as it were, thereby undermining them, from their own edges. Therefore, irony can be said to form a central tenet of the deconstructive strategy: it aims to undermine what it asserts.[49]

A similar dynamic of construction and undermining can be discerned in Barth's metafictional writings. The examples of metafictional techniques given at the start of section 1, illustrate that metafiction always depends on the construction of something (a fiction) that it subsequently breaches (reflects upon, distances itself from: a *meta*-fiction), for instance, a story is first constructed and then suddenly interrupted by the authorial voice stating the fictitiousness of the story. As Waugh writes, on the workings of metafiction: 'Frames are set up only to be continually broken. Contexts are ostentatiously constructed, only to be subsequently *deconstructed*.'[50]

A prime example is Barth's story 'Lost in the Funhouse' from the eponymous book. In the story, the dynamic of construction and undermining is constantly at work:

---

[47] Culler, *On Deconstruction*, 86.
[48] Brill, *Wittgenstein and Critical Theory*, 98.
[49] Cf. a 'style of writing' that fits deconstruction, 'to disrupt the logic of a text and lift it off his hinges, is *parody*, the caricatural double of a text', writes Paul Moyaert: 'In the parody the original remains directly recognizable', but subsequently 'a text is radically stripped of its singularity' (Moyaert, 'Jacques Derrida en de filosofie van de differentie', 33–4).
[50] Waugh, *Metafiction*, 101 [emphasis added, AdD].

the text repeatedly creates the impression of starting to narrate a seemingly normal, credible story – in this case about the young Ambrose Mensch spending a day in Ocean City with his family (where, among other things, he enters a funhouse) –, but each time the story is interrupted, disrupted, undermined by different metafictional techniques. The following passage offers a typical example:

> For whom is the funhouse fun? Perhaps for lovers. For Ambrose it is *a place of fear and confusion*. He has come to the seashore with his family for the holiday, *the occasion of their visit is Independence Day, the most secular holiday of the United States of America*. A single straight underline is the manuscript mark for italic type, *which in turn* is the printed equivalent to oral emphasis of words and phrases as well as the customary type for titles of complete works, not to mention.[51]

First, a story is set up about a boy going to the seashore with this family. Then, the subordinate clause on the status of Independence Day already has a slightly estranging effect, but can perhaps still be ignored, or, better said, be read as a (somewhat irrelevant) part of the story. However, the subsequent digression on the function of underlining and italicization can definitively not be ignored, as it points out the artificial, constructed character of the text by referring to its own layout, thereby breaching the fictional illusion.

So, whereas Derridean deconstruction is aimed at exposing the illusion of presence (haunting all of our notions), the *metafictional* deconstruction in Barth's *Lost in the Funhouse* is aimed at exposing the illusion of reality. The metafictionalist problematization of reality as an artificial construction (and therefore, an illusion) was already outlined in the previous section. Now we can see the strong affinities between the main targets of metafiction and deconstruction, respectively (the illusion of) reality and (the illusion of) presence. The notion of reality brings with it associations of 'truth', 'genuineness' and 'purity', just as Derrida's notion of presence entails pure, metaphysical essences. The reality of something equates to how something truly is; and saying of something that it is a reality, is saying that it is really there, that it is really *present*.

The notion of reality was not as problematic for preceding literary movements as for postmodernist metafiction. McHale writes that, although reality is not a completely unproblematic notion in modernist literature, the difficulties surrounding it are regarded as the result of the shortcomings of the knowing subject trying to attain knowledge of that reality (that is, the problem of reality is regarded as an epistemological problem), and does not greatly affect the possibility of reality itself being an unequivocal and pure entity.[52] However, for postmodernist metafiction such a (metaphysical) notion of reality has become untenable: just as deconstruction shows that the notion of presence always implies absence, postmodernist metafiction shows that reality cannot be unequivocal and pure, but always contains elements of ambiguity, chaos, incongruence and opacity.

As discussed in the previous section, the view of (traditional) fiction underlying postmodernist metafiction, is that fiction is based on preserving the illusion of

---

[51] LF, 72.
[52] McHale, *Postmodernist Fiction*, 9, 234.

reality: the successful functioning of a fiction is based on its believability – we have to (temporarily) believe what we read (the so-called suspension of disbelief). The text has to conjure up a world that feels 'real' to the reader, or rather: the descriptions offered in the text have to be experienced by the reader as, in a sense, 'credible' or 'realistic', meaning that the reader is able to project a world on the basis of his reading of the text. If this is not the case, a story is generally considered a failure, badly written. However, this believability is an illusion, and fiction itself is an illusion, according to the postmodernist metafictionists, and, in this sense, fiction is opposed to reality – it is unreal.[53]

Postmodernist metafiction, by exposing the underlying structures of the illusory reality of fiction, aims to provide insight into the fact that (what we regard as) reality is the result of structures that are comparable to those of a fictional text. The reality we live in is turned into an orderly, unequivocal whole by omitting inevitable elements of disorder and unclarity. In other words, the world we live in is fictionalized in order to become the unequivocal reality that we expect it to be. Thus, our reality is always, partly, a fiction.

This does not lead postmodernist metafiction to a complete erasure of reality: its final conclusion is not that *everything* is a complete unreality or illusion. Analogous to deconstruction, which does not aim to destroy its target, postmodernist metafiction functions through a continuous dynamic of construction and undermining. As Waugh writes:

> Metafiction functions through the problematization rather than the destruction of the concept of 'reality'. It depends on the regular construction and subversion of rules and systems. Such novels usually set up an internally consistent [. . .] world which ensures the reader's absorption, and then lays bare its rules in order to investigate the relation of 'fiction' to 'reality', the concept of 'pretence'.[54]

Both deconstruction and postmodernist metafiction are dependent on the frameworks they try to subvert. As Evink writes about Derrida: 'his thoughts and interpretations *presuppose* the project of the metaphysical intention and therein play their game of disruption and postponement'.[55]

An illuminating instance of the simultaneously constructive and undermining character of the deconstructive strategy is Derrida's so-called writing 'sous rature' ('under erasure').[56] The most famous example appears in *Of Grammatology* (1967): 'the sign ~~is~~ that ill-named ~~thing~~'.[57] It is not necessary to perform an in-depth examination of this technique, to be able to conclude that it offers a striking expression of the first double movement of deconstruction: words are written and subsequently stricken

---

[53]   In the previous section I have already remarked on the fact that this opposition of fiction and reality can be regarded as off, or even fallacious, as contrasting incommensurables – or at least: notions that are not fully diametrically opposed. In Chapter 5, I will describe a view of the relation between fiction and reality that is, in my opinion, preferable to the metafictionalist view outlined here.

[54]   Waugh, *Metafiction*, 40–1.

[55]   Evink, *Transcendentie en inscriptie*, 102 [emphasis added, AdD].

[56]   Cf. Van der Sijde, *De visie op literatuur van Jacques Derrida*, 58–9.

[57]   Derrida, *Of Grammatology*, 19.

through. McHale rightly remarks: 'Physically cancelled, yet still legible beneath the cancellation, these signs *sous rature* continue to function in the discourse.' McHale remarks on the obvious parallel between this technique, 'Derrida's practice of placing certain verbal signs *sous rature*, under erasure', and the essence of all metafictional techniques, namely projecting a credible, realistic world to subsequently undermine it, a practice that McHale describes as 'un-projection'. Postmodernist metafictions also write 'sous rature': '[they] place under erasure [. . .] presented objects in a projected world'. They construct a reality, to subsequently 'strike it through', 'un-project', undermine it.[58]

This dependence on that which is being undermined, is also expressed by Barth's term 'literature of exhaustion': the fiction writer is to take exhausted literary means, 'the felt ultimacies of our time', and bend them into 'material and means for his work'.[59] It is interesting to note that Derrida, in his description of the strategy of deconstruction, has occasionally employed a terminology similar to Barth's. In *Positions*, Derrida states that deconstruction is aimed at the 'exhaustion' of metaphysical 'philosophemes':

> by means of this double play, marked in certain decisive places by an erasure which allows what it obliterates to be read, [. . .] I try to respect as rigorously as possible the [. . .] philosophemes or epistemes by making them slide – without mistreating them – to the point of their nonpertinence, their *exhaustion*, their closure.[60]

This process of 'exhaustion' (undermining, disruption) can be further specified as a second double movement of 'overturning and displacement'. This will be described, in relation to both deconstruction and metafiction, in the following subsection.

2.3. Overturning and displacement

In the essay 'Signature Event Context', from *Margins of Philosophy*, Derrida provides, 'very schematically', a description of this second double movement of the strategy of deconstruction:

> Very schematically: an opposition of metaphysical concepts (for example, speech/writing, presence/absence, etc.) is never the face-to-face of two terms, but a hierarchy and an order of subordination. Deconstruction cannot limit itself or proceed immediately to a neutralization: it must, by means of a double gesture, a double science, a double writing, practice an *overturning* of the classical opposition *and* a general *displacement* of the system. It is only on this condition that deconstruction will provide itself the means with which to *intervene* in the field of oppositions that it criticizes [. . .]. Deconstruction does not consist in passing from one concept to another, but in overturning and displacing.[61]

---

[58] McHale, *Postmodernist Fiction*, 100.
[59] Barth, 'The Literature of Exhaustion', 71.
[60] Derrida, *Positions*, 6.
[61] Derrida, *Margins of Philosophy*, 329; cf. Derrida, *Positions*, 41.

The first three sentences of this passage summarize what we have seen in the previous subsection, namely that, as part of the strategy of deconstruction, a hierarchical order of metaphysical concepts (for example, presence/absence) is first constructed to be subsequently undermined. Here, Derrida adds that this undermining does not amount to a straightforward 'neutralization' of this order of metaphysical concepts: the disruption of such an order requires a more elaborate process, already implied by the term 'exhaustion', which we encountered at the end of the previous subsection. The disruption that deconstruction aims to effect requires a 'double gesture' of 'overturning' the classical opposition (for example not presence but absence, is essential, fundamental), *and* a 'displacement' of the whole order, or 'system'. What the latter, the 'general *displacement*' amounts to, is not fully explicated in this passage or in the essay. What we do know is that this displacement has to follow the overturning, for Derrida emphasizes that deconstruction cannot consist of (that is, limit itself to) 'passing from one concept to another', and 'overturning' (for example, privileging absence over presence) appears to be exactly such a 'passing' from one to the other. Therefore, this first step of overturning has to be followed by a displacement that ensures that deconstruction not simply replaces the old metaphysical hierarchy for the other, but truly disrupts and contorts the whole functioning of the idea of hierarchical, metaphysical order.[62]

Let us start with the first step. An illuminating example of the *overturning* of the traditional hierarchy within a metaphysical opposition, of temporarily privileging (as implied in the term 'overturning') the inverse (previously subordinate) pole of a metaphysical order, is provided by Derrida's discussion of the relation between speech and writing. According to Derrida, Western philosophy has always privileged speech over writing, and he calls this engrained preference 'phonocentrism'.[63] The spoken word is accompanied by the presence of the speaker. And for the speaker the meaning of the words he speaks is present in his consciousness. Therefore, with the spoken word, the presence of unequivocal meaning appears to be guaranteed. As Culler writes: 'Speech is seen as in direct contact with meaning: words issue from the speaker as the spontaneous and nearly transparent signs of his present thought, which the attendant listener hopes to grasp.'[64] The written word, on the other hand, usually functions in the absence of the writer, whose consciousness contains and thus guarantees the meaning of his words. Thus, the written word is coupled with uncertainty. Furthermore, writing consists of material signs, which are relatively permanent and more likely to assume a life of their own than speech, which 'evaporates' more quickly and is therefore much more controllable.[65] In the phonocentric view, writing is regarded as a 'derivative, auxiliary form of language', a 'supplement to the spoken word', confined

---

[62] Cf. Evink, *Transcendentie en inscriptie*, 75.

[63] Cf. 'We already have a foreboding that phonocentrism merges with the historical determination of the meaning of being in general as *presence*' (Derrida, *Of Grammatology*, 12); 'The system of this interpretation [. . .] has been *represented* in the entire history of philosophy' (Derrida, *Margins of Philosophy*, 311).

[64] Culler, *On Deconstruction*, 100.

[65] Cf. Evink, *Transcendentie en inscriptie*, 60.

to a 'secondary and instrumental function: translator of a full speech'.[66] Writing serves simply to 'record' speech, so that it can be repeated at a later moment, in the absence of the speaker (the repeatability, or 'iterability' as Derrida calls it, of writing); but this absence also points towards its essential shortcoming, namely, the absence of the original meaningful intention.[67]

However, Derrida asks, are these supposed shortcomings of writing 'not also to be found in all language'?[68] 'Iterability' is not just characteristic of writing, but also of speech. For, the sounds that I produce when speaking can only function as signs, as words, when they can be understood and potentially repeated by others. If speech sounds were non-repeatable, secret, reserved for the speaker alone, these sounds would not be able to enter into communication between people as potentially meaningful signs. Or, as Derrida formulates it:

> This implies that there is no code – an organon of iterability – that is structurally secret. The possibility of repeating, and therefore of identifying, marks is implied in every code, making of it a communicable, transmittable, decipherable grid that is iterable for a third party, and thus for any possible user in general.[69]

All linguistic codes are characterized by iterability, by the possibility of being repeated in the absence of the original meaning-giving intention. Derrida: 'If "writing" means inscription and especially the durable instituting of signs (and this is the only irreducible kernel of the concept of writing), then writing in general covers the entire domain of linguistic signs.'[70] In other words, all language is characterized by absence: *all language is writing*. This is a prime example of a deconstructivist overturning of a traditional, philosophical opposition of metaphysical concepts (to be followed, by displacement; this will be described further on in this subsection).

In Barth's postmodernist metafiction a similar overturning or reversal of the leading principle – in this case, of fiction – can be perceived. Whereas in Derridean deconstruction the disruption of the metaphysics of presence is initiated by stressing the primacy of *absence* (in the example above, the primacy of writing, which is characterized by the absence of the speaker and his meaning-intention), in Barth's metafictional 'deconstructions' the primary literary principle of aiming to project a credible reality in which truths concerning the world can be expressed, is initially replaced by the principle that in fiction nothing real can be projected and nothing

---

[66] Derrida, *Of Grammatology*, 7; cf. Derrida, *Margins of Philosophy*, 311–15.

[67] As with all aspects of the metaphysics of presence, phonocentrism is an illusion that, according to Derrida, is deep-seated and necessary: 'These disguises are not historical contingencies that one might admire or regret. Their movement was absolutely necessary, with a necessity which cannot be judged by any other tribunal. The privilege of the *phonè* does not depend upon a choice that could have been avoided. The system of "hearing (understanding)-oneself speak" through the phonic substance [. . .] has necessarily dominated the history of the world during an entire epoch, and has even produced the idea of the world, the idea of world-origin, that arises from the difference between the worldly and the non-worldly, the outside and the inside, ideality and nonideality, universal and nonuniversal, transcendental and empirical, etc' (Derrida, *Of Grammatology*, 6–7).

[68] Derrida, *Margins of Philosophy*, 318.

[69] Ibid., 315.

[70] Derrida, *Of Grammatology*, 102.

truthful can be expressed. The traditional principle is overturned: the supposed credibility and truthfulness of fiction are an illusion, thus, in fact, the opposite of credible and truthful.

Barth's *Lost in the Funhouse* performs this radical reversal through what Harris calls a series of 'weary fictions'. The sole subject of most of the stories in the first half of the book is their inability or refusal to realize a story. For example, in the story 'Title', 'The final question is, Can nothing be made meaningful? Isn't that the final question. If not, the end is at hand. Literally, as it were. Can't stand any more of this.' Followed by: 'What now. Everything's been said already, over and over; I'm as sick of this as you are; there's nothing to say. Say nothing. What's new? Nothing.'[71] Harris writes: 'many of the early stories in *Funhouse* do embody this weariness'.[72] All of these stories have first-person narrators, acting as the so-called self-conscious 'voice' of the story, who solely narrate their own inability or refusal to be a story and stress the fact that they are an unreality, an artificial construct incapable of portraying anything real, or expressing anything truthful. The story 'Autobiography' supposedly addresses its author who is writing and thereby continuing the story: '*Wretched old fabricator, where's your shame? Put an end to this, for pity's sake! Now! Now!*'[73] Similarly, 'Life-Story', at a certain point, addresses its reader and faults him for still reading, continuing the story:

> The reader! You dogged, uninsultable, print-oriented bastard, it's you I'm addressing, who else, from inside this monstrous fiction. You've read me this far, then? Even this far? For what discreditable motive? How is it you don't go to a movie, watch TV, stare at a wall, play tennis with a friend, make amorous advances to the person who comes to your mind when I speak of amorous advances? Can nothing surfeit, saturate you, turn you off? Where's your shame?[74]

In 'Night-Sea Journey', a spermatozoid describes the 'swimming journey' to the ovum that it is expected to partake in. The story functions as an allegory of fiction writing and the doubts that have arisen in postmodernist metafiction concerning the purpose and possibilities of the 'project' of fiction. The spermatozoid doubts its own reality (that is, the reality of the story): 'Do the night, the sea, exist at all, I ask myself, apart from my experience of them? [. . .] My trouble is, I lack conviction.' In (this example of) postmodernist metafiction, it is solely these doubts (regarding fiction) that keep the story 'afloat', keep the spermatozoid 'swimming', but at the same time this continuation is only the increasing realization that it is unreal and without meaning: '[these] reflective intervals that keep me afloat have led me into wonder, doubt, despair – strange emotions for a swimmer! – have led me, even, to suspect . . . that our night-sea journey is without meaning'. The increasing 'weariness' of the story and the spermatozoid is expressed as follows: 'I find it no meaningfuller to drown myself than to go on swimming.' Further on, the story even suggests that perhaps it would be better to completely abandon the project of fiction, abandon its 'calling' (for credible

[71] LF, 105.
[72] Harris, *Passionate Virtuosity*, 5.
[73] LF, 38.
[74] Ibid., 127.

and meaningful stories): 'the hero of heroes would be the swimmer who, in the very presence of the Other, refused Her proffered "immortality" and thus put an end to at least one cycle of catastrophes'.[75]

So far we have discussed the strategy of overturning in both deconstruction and metafiction. The old order has been reversed: presence has been replaced by absence, and the literary ideal of meaningful and truth-expressing fiction has been replaced by the conviction that fiction cannot express anything. But these reversals are not the final aim of deconstruction and metafiction; they are followed by displacement.

We shall look at deconstruction first. According to Derrida, our language use is motivated by the (illusory) ideal of presence, by the idea that our words are accompanied by meaning (that, with our words, meaning is present, for example, through the intention we have while speaking, or through the object in the world that our words refer to). On the most fundamental level, our words would derive their meaning from the presence of the pure essences of meaning and truth (which form the foundation of the metaphysics of presence): Derrida calls this pure and direct meaning derived from the order of things the 'transcendental signified'.[76] However, this ideal is undermined by the absence that characterizes all language use; returning to the above-discussed example of speech and writing, it is through their iterability that words are able to function as signs that communicate meaning. Writing, which was traditionally seen as an imperfect, auxiliary form of language use (a 'supplement'), turns out to embody the 'original', in the sense of 'fundamental', qualities of language. Therefore, Derrida sometimes refers to writing with the paradoxical terms the 'originary supplement' and the 'supplement of origin'.[77]

However, these deliberately paradoxical terms – 'originary supplement' and 'supplement of origin' – used to describe the role of absence in the functioning of language, already indicate that we cannot simply substitute absence as the new origin, the new essence of meaningful language. In fact, what deconstruction has shown, is that thinking in terms of such transcendental essences goes awry, because it always entails, and tries to suppress, that which cannot be brought in line with the preferred origin or essence. When Derrida speaks of realizing a displacement, he seems to refer to this realization, that hierarchical oppositions can never be completely comprehensive and accurate. Evink describes the displacement of these oppositions resulting from deconstruction as follows: 'both poles are no longer exactly distinguishable, their relation is undecidable, a displacement takes place in the field of structures and

---

[75] Ibid., 3, 4, 11.
[76] Derrida, *Of Grammatology*, 20; 'There has to be a transcendental signified for the difference between signifier and signified to be somewhere absolute and irreducible. [. . .] This illusion is the history of truth and it cannot be dissipated so quickly' (ibid., 20); '[reading] cannot legitimately transgress the text toward something other than it, toward a referent (a reality that is metaphysical, historical, psychobiographical, etc.) or toward a signified outside the text whose content could take place, could have taken place outside language, that is to say, in the sense that we give here to that word, outside of writing in general [. . .]; as regards the absence of the referent or the transcendental signified. *There is nothing outside the text* [there is no outside-text; *il n'y a pas de hors-texte*]' (ibid., 158).
[77] Ibid., 313.

denotations that can no longer be organized [. . .] the oppositions have been thrown out of plumb, the organization is disrupted'.[78]

A similar paradox characterizes Barth's work. *Lost in the Funhouse*, after it has overturned the traditional literary ideal, expresses through fiction that there is nothing left to express in fiction. This is the aim of the literature of exhaustion that Barth describes in his eponymous essay. As discussed above, the stories in the first half of *Lost in the Funhouse* express 'weariness', and seem to represent the 'impulse to get it all said, to exhaust the possible permutations of words and yield at last to the all-encompassing silence', as Harris writes. He adds, however, 'this eschatological tendency is counteracted by a stronger if paradoxically weary desire to continue filling in the blank'.[79] After all, even Barth's weary fictions continue their weary telling. And in the second half of *Lost in the Funhouse*, the stories – although they are still regularly interrupted and undermined through the use of metafictional techniques – no longer focus on explicitly expressing that there is nothing to express. The final conclusion is not that all fiction is a meaningless fabrication that has absolutely no potential for expressing aspects of the world we live in. The initial overturning of the traditional literary ideal is aimed at effecting the realization that every so-called reality (whether it is the reality of our everyday lives, or the fictional projection of a reality) is an artificial construction, and not as comprehensive, unequivocal and pure as its believability suggests. As Waugh writes: 'Contemporary metafiction draws attention to the fact that life, as well as novels, is constructed through frames, and that it is impossible to know where one frame ends and another begins. [. . .] there is no simple dichotomy "reality/fiction".'[80] In Barth's postmodernist metafiction, too, after an initial overturning (temporarily asserting that fiction is meaningless unreality), a displacement takes place that disrupts the old oppositions, making it impossible to organize and distinguish between fiction and reality in an accurate and hierarchical way.

2.4. The endless postponement of meaning

What is the result of the deconstructions that Derrida and Barth have performed? They regard the ideals of presence and reality as impossible and unattainable, but at the same time as indispensable for philosophy and fiction, respectively. This is what Derrida and Barth want to show in their work.

'Deconstruction is aimed at the unresolvability of each boundary and each distinction and at the postponement of judgment', writes Evink. Thought inevitably means excluding options, not being able to take everything into account. Therefore thought should postpone each judgement, to retain an openness towards the 'alterity' that otherwise will be excluded. As such, deconstruction has no end: it constrains thought to a constant self-reflection that exposes 'each articulation of a question and each attempt at an answer' as incomplete, to thereby 'retain the

---

[78] Evink, *Transcendentie en inscriptie*, 75.
[79] Harris, *Passionate Virtuosity*, 121.
[80] Waugh, *Metafiction*, 29.

question and the appeal of the other as such', explains Evink.[81] In *Positions* Derrida says deconstruction aims 'to avoid both simply *neutralizing* the binary oppositions of metaphysics and simply *residing* within the closed field of these oppositions, and thereby confirming it'.[82] However, as the postponement of judgement and disruption of the field are to be continued without end, deconstruction runs the risk of not only exhausting its targets, but also itself, and by not offering anything new, can appear to reside in the criticized but irreplaceable order.

Barth's postmodernist metafiction is based on a view of language strikingly similar to that of Derrida, and has a very similar aim. As Boswell summarizes, 'Barth foregrounds the artificial means by which literature creates an illusion of reality; as such, he acknowledges the unbreachable gap between text and world – or, to use Derrida's terminology, between signifier and signified concept.'[83] Harris writes: '[If language] is by nature *irreal* since it does not refer except in the most arbitrary sense to an antecedent reality, then how can the writer become a writer-in-the-world?'[84] As words cannot be connected to the world, how can fiction express anything meaningful about the world? From Barth's view, the only thing that fiction is able to express, is exactly that impossibility; in Beverly Gross's formulation, for Barth, fiction is merely capable of 'denying the possibility of meaning, identity, and answers in a world in which these things are always shifting, masked and unattainable'. For this reason, Gross describes Barth's works as 'anti-novels', as 'an anti-novelistic assault on itself': '[At the end] one sees their madly complicated structures have led nowhere: one suspects that the whole point of each book was to express the fraudulence of narrative art and one wonders how Barth was able to write them at all.'[85]

Similar to Derrida's deconstruction, Barth's postmodernist metafiction consists of constantly exposing the fictional framework it has just constructed, revoking the reality it has just posited. With that, metafiction, like deconstruction, is aimed at unresolvability. The constant undermining of every description as fictional, write Fogel and Slethaug, 'permits art without affirmation [. . .] the postmodern writer wishes to write something without wanting to emphasize or value some *thing*'. They add that, in this respect, *Lost in the Funhouse* 'engages the means of fiction almost at the expense of content'.[86] Waugh writes about the radical metafictionality of Barth's text that, 'almost every sentence is undermined and exposed as fictional'.[87] Joseph Waldmeir assesses that Barth 'seems often actively to reject the taking of a position' and that 'his work has gradually turned in upon itself, has become increasingly self-conscious, reflexive, like a Moebius strip seen in a set of mirrors'.[88]

---

[81] Evink, *Transcendentie en inscriptie*, 76, 99.
[82] Derrida, *Positions*, 41.
[83] Boswell, *Understanding David Foster Wallace*, 27.
[84] Harris, *Passionate Virtuosity*, ix.
[85] Gross, 'The Anti-Novels of John Barth', 31, 36.
[86] Fogel and Slethaug, *Understanding John Barth*, 12, 4.
[87] Waugh, *Metafiction*, 95.
[88] Waldmeir, 'Introduction', x. Barth himself has written, in an essay: 'Muse spare me (at the desk, I mean) from Social-Historical Responsibility, and in the last analysis from every other kind, except Artistic' (Barth, 'Muse, Spare Me', 55); Fogel and Slethaug quote this passage and, in relation to it,

Conclusion

In this chapter, Barth's postmodernist metafiction was analysed by viewing it in light of Derrida's strategy of deconstruction. We have seen that, according to Derrida and Barth, philosophy and literature are motivated by similar ideals, namely 'presence' and 'reality', that disrupt themselves, because presence is never complete and reality is never unequivocal. At the same time, both these illusions are regarded as indispensable and irrepressible aspects of thought and fiction. Both deconstruction and metafiction work from within the exact frameworks they try to subvert and, therefore, also embody a confirmation and continuation of these frameworks. Derrida and Barth's goals are not to destroy what they regard as both illusory and indispensable notions, but to maintain their unresolvability, endlessly revoking, postponing the determination of meaning.

Here, in this endless cycle of affirmation and undermining, we can readily see that deconstruction and metafiction turn into forms of hyperreflexive irony. Barth's postmodernist metafiction is solely occupied with the ironic exposure of its own fictional structures. It cannot breach its obsession with itself, for it perceives its task as endless, and it cannot put anything – no positivity, no 'positive freedom' to use a Kierkegaardian term – in the place of that which it exposes. This results in what Wallace describes as scepticism and solipsism. Postmodernist metafiction constantly 'crosses out' its own descriptions of reality, because they inevitably contain fictional elements; Barth's fiction cannot express anything truthful about reality; it can only express its own *un*reality, its own fictionality. Wallace writes: 'It gets empty and solipsistic real fast. It spirals in on itself.'[89] As a result, postmodernist metafiction can be seen as withering away into non-committal introversion.[90]

---

remark that Barth, indeed, in most of his writing, has 'no interest in contemporary social issues' (Fogel and Slethaug, *Understanding John Barth*, 167).

[89] McCaffery, 'Interview', 142.

[90] Cf. in Wallace's novella 'Westward the Course of Empire Takes Its Way': '[metafiction] can only reveal. Itself is its only object. It's the act of a lonely solipsist's self-love, a night-light on the black fifth wall of being a subject, a face in a crowd. It's lovers not being lovers. Kissing their own spine. Fucking themselves' (Wallace, 'Westward', *Girl with Curious Hair*, 332).

4

Postmodernist Minimalism: Bret Easton Ellis

Introduction

In relation to Barth's work, the postmodernist minimalism of Bret Easton Ellis takes the problem of hyperreflexive irony, and the resulting effects of scepticism and solipsism, to an even further extreme. As we have seen, postmodernist metafiction problematizes the relation between reality and fiction, asserting that fiction is always constructed and therefore unreal, and that we inherently construct what we regard as reality in a similar way, as a result of which reality should always be considered as (partly) a fiction. However, in Ellis's work, this problematization has evolved into an implosion of the notions of reality and fiction (and the relation between them), into the outright negation that there is anything real, anything meaningful or valuable, left to express.

Whereas in the postmodernist metafiction of the 1960s and 1970s reflexive irony constitutes an ongoing theoretical problematization of notions like meaning and reality through the disruption of fictional forms, two decades later, the reflexive-ironic problematization of such notions has been turned into fact (that is, that there 'is' no real meaning or value) and, as such, has become a widely held intuitive perception of the world. Robert McLaughlin describes the corresponding cultural development as follows: 'postmodernism's main qualities, irony and self-referentiality, percolated into the culture at large'.[1]

This new perception of things can clearly be seen in the accompanying literary trend of postmodernist minimalism. Elizabeth Young explains that, compared to the writers of metafiction, the authors of these minimalist works 'have a very different engagement with postmodernism'. Young: 'Their fiction arises directly out of their own observations and experiences of postmodern culture, from out of the streets with no name; they are reporting from within a lived reality, not dissecting its constituents from the academic perimeters'.[2] But, *as* in postmodernist metafiction, there is a sense of turning a felt 'ultimacy' against itself, only this time an ultimacy experienced in

---

Unless otherwise indicated, translations are mine.
[1] McLaughlin, 'Post-Postmodern Discontent', 64.
[2] Young, 'Children of the Revolution', 14.

daily life.[3] The internalizing of the (presumed) 'lessons' of postmodernist irony leads to the conviction that nothing is intrinsically valuable, that no choice is superior to other options. Accordingly, for this new group of writers in the 1980s the only thing left to express is exactly this: an American reality saturated by the conviction that nothing has value. And the best way to do this: through extremely 'flat', *minimalist* writing (hence the term postmodernist minimalism): terse prose consisting of present tense descriptions, often from a first-person perspective, of events and conversations of which the content and value are equally flat – so, for example, a rape or a murder is described in the same style and tone as a new car. James Annesley summarizes:

> Their novels are predominantly urban in focus and concerned with the relationship between the individual and consumer culture. Instead of [. . .] dense plots, elaborate styles and political subjects [. . .], [these fictions] prefer blank, atonal perspectives and fragile, glassy visions. [. . .] [They are] preoccupied with 'sex, death and subversion'.[4]

Bret Easton Ellis (1970–) is generally considered to be the most important and influential representative of the literary trend of postmodernist minimalism, and Ellis's 1991 novel *American Psycho* as the most extreme and consistent embodiment of this fixed style and subject matter.[5] The novel's first-person narrator, Patrick Bateman, is a rich, attractive and intelligent investment banker, but also a bloodthirsty psychopath, whose acts of torture, rape and murder are described in the novel in great detail.

American Psycho narrates Bateman's perception of the world, almost without interruption, in the present tense; no other voices or perspectives become even remotely visible. So, understanding the novel means understanding Patrick Bateman: who (or what) is he? What is his significance? In my opinion, *American Psycho* can be seen as expressing the escalation of the ironic-aesthetic life-view as criticized by Søren Kierkegaard. Kierkegaard's critique of this attitude has already been outlined in Chapter 2. Here, I will develop this reading of *American Psycho* by comparing the novel to Kierkegaard's 'The Seducer's Diary', from *Either/Or*.

In what follows, I will first offer a general comparison of the ironic attitudes expressed by 'The Seducer's Diary' and *American Psycho*. Subsequently, I will develop this comparison by describing four aspects that, according to Kierkegaard scholar Bradley Dewey, characterize the escalation of the ill-fated aesthetic life-view (other Kierkegaard scholars describe these aspects as well, though not as systematically as Dewey).[6] These aspects are largely phenomena that we have already – both implicitly

---

[3] Bran Nicol calls it 'fiction of the "postmodern condition" [. . .] [that] deals head on with the "death of affect" in contemporary society' (Nicol, *The Cambridge Introduction to Postmodern Fiction*, 183,197).

[4] Annesley, *Blank Fictions*, 2.

[5] Jay McInerney and Tama Janowitz are regarded as other prominent representatives of this literary trend; cf. Young, 'Vacant Possession', 93.

[6] Dewey, 'The Erotic-Demonic in Kierkegaard's "Diary of the Seducer"', 2; cf. Rehm, *Kierkegaard und der Verführer* [e.g. 'die Kritik an der romantischen Daseinshaltung, an [1] ihren ironisch-ästhetischen Wesen, [2] ihrer unverbindlichen substanzlosen Art, [3] ihrer Abwendung von jener entschiedenen Wirklichkeit zugunsten des abenteuerlichen Reizes, [4] der unendlichen Fülle blosser lockender Möglichkeiten, die der Phantasiewelt entströmen'; 'die Gefahr der "inneren Lüge", der

and explicitly – encountered in previous chapters, namely: 'alienation from others', 'self-alienation', 'solipsism', and 'sceptic frenzy'. Together, these four phenomena lead up to the aesthetic disintegration of the self, as can also be seen to happen to Patrick Bateman in *American Psycho*.

The reason for analysing *American Psycho* lies in the fact that the novel embodies a type of fiction that is bred by excessive reflexivity and irony, and thereby to further illustrate the fundamentally different approach that the works of Wallace, Eggers and Foer offer to these two problems of contemporary Western existence. I share Wallace's opinion[7] that *American Psycho* cannot be regarded – as some critics have suggested[8] – as a successful critique of the ironic-aesthetic attitude but instead functions as a reflexive-ironic confirmation and continuation of the problematic life-view that it portrays. I will explores this further in section 3.

1. General comparison

'The Seducer's Diary' forms part of Kierkegaard's *Either/Or*. The 'Diary' is presented as a work of fiction by the aesthete A with the character 'Johannes the Seducer' as its fictive author and first-person narrator.[9] For Kierkegaard, Johannes is the most extreme embodiment of the ironic-aesthetic life-view; in the 'Diary' the aesthete is shown at the peak of his abilities and self-confidence (because the 'Diary' forms part of a larger unity, my interpretation will also refer to other parts of *Either/Or*).[10] Patrick Bateman bears a strong resemblance to Johannes. Just like the aesthete, Bateman is an embodiment of the attitude of total negative irony. He does not accept responsibility for his actions, nor any limitations to them: *everything* should be possible – the violent acts he commits are the most obvious example of this attitude.

"interessanten Genialität", der Verzauberung in ein Märchenhaft-Unwirkliches, um die Gefahr der Selbstspaltung und des Selbstverlustes, der Ichersetzung, der Vernichtung des Gefühls der eigenen Person im Zwei- und Vieldeutigen. Auch das Abenteuer des Doppelgängertums, das Auswandern der Phantasie in ferne, fremde, unbekannte Reiche und Gestalten ist ihm vertraut, nicht minder dier seltsam bedrohliche Vorgang der Lebens- und Selbstentfremdung, das verwirrende Empfinden, sich selbst zum unerklärlichen Rätsel zu werden' (12, 14)]; Pulmer, *Die dementierte Alternative*, 50, 127, 133–4; Greve, 'Künstler versus Bürger', 50–1.

[7] Cf. McCaffery, 'Interview', 131–2.

[8] E.g. Weldon, 'An Honest American Psycho' ('American Psycho is a novel written out of the American tradition – the novelist's function to keep a running tag on the progress of the culture: and he's done it brilliantly'); Freccero, 'Historical Violence, Censorship and the Serial Killer' ('Ellis refuses us a consoling fantasy, a fetish for our disavowals; instead he returns us to that history, to the violence of historicity and to the historicity of violence' [56]).

[9] In his foreword to the 'Diary' A states that he is not the author but merely the 'transcriber' of the text, which he claims to have found on the desk of an acquaintance. However, Victor Eremita, the fictive editor of both parts of *Either/Or* (so, including all of A's writings) calls this an 'old literary device' and says that the Diary has to be regarded as a work of fiction written by A (EO 1, 9); cf. Hannay, *Kierkegaard*, 264; Pulmer, *Die dementierte Alternative*, 48, 53.

[10] In this respect, Johannes the Seducer precedes the stage of the defeated aesthete (described in Chapter 2) who has realized the futility of his life-view.

1.1. The aesthete, contemporary culture and the end of meaning

In Chapter 2, we examined the similarities between Kierkegaard's aesthete and the contemporary Western individual.[11] An aesthete is solely interested in *absolute* freedom: he ironically distances himself from any commitment to the world, which serves merely as an incitement for his fantasies. The contemporary individual, confronted with endless possible ways of shaping his life and therefore with the responsibility for shaping it into exactly what he wants it to be, can easily come to resemble such an aesthete. As discussed in Chapter 1, contemporary Western culture is characterized by the absence of clear, objective criteria by which to choose from the endless possibilities that have become available. In many cases, subjective preference is the only recognized decider that remains. This can easily lead to a situation in which individuals are *solely* concerned with the continuous satisfaction of their needs, as they strive to aestheticize their lives.[12]

Patrick Bateman and Johannes the Seducer represent the extreme consequence or extrapolation of this ironic-aesthetic attitude. Johannes is the 'extreme possibility of the aesthetic', and 'The Seducer's Diary' is the 'secret centre of the first part [of *Either/ Or*], around which all the other writings are arranged', writes Karin Pulmer.[13] With regard to Bateman, it might be tempting to regard him as 'simply' insane, a psychopath, a chance aberration. However, a clear line can be drawn from Bateman back to (the frustrations of) contemporary Western culture, of which the ironic-aesthetic attitude has become the default life-view. His sole interest is the continuous satisfaction of pleasure. Because Bateman is so thoroughly superficial, and commits horrible crimes, some critics have classified him as 'illiterate', as a character who is too 'stupid' to be ironic, arguing that 'Bateman cannot fathom irony because he has no layers, no sense of depth'.[14] But it is exactly because of irony that Bateman has no layers (he himself suspects that this levelling took place during his time at Harvard).[15] Like an aesthete, Bateman has ironically distanced himself from every content, and is merely interested in appearance, in running lightly across the surface of everything.[16]

In the following passage, Bateman utters an absurd monologue of a conflicting list of important political issues, revealing his total irony (even more so in light of his further, sharply contrasting statements and actions with regard to women and minorities):

> Well, we have to end apartheid for one. And slow down the nuclear arms race, stop terrorism and world hunger. Ensure a strong national defense, prevent the spread of communism in Central America, work for a Middle East peace settlement,

---

[11] Cf. Dewey, who writes that Kierkegaard's critique of the ironic-aesthetic attitude in general and 'The Seducer's Diary' in particular constitute a 'lens' offering an insightful view on 'the cluster of kindred challenges loosely labelled "the crisis of modernity" and reflected in "movements" such as "postmodernity". [T]he "Diary" addresses the current crisis of the spirit which our age now faces' (Dewey, 'Seven Seducers', 191–2).
[12] Cf. Greve, 'Künstler versus Bürger', 45–6.
[13] Pulmer, *Die dementierte Alternative*, 97, 102.
[14] Suglia, 'Bret Easton Ellis: Escape from Utopia'; Blazer, 'Chasms of Reality, Aberrations of Identity'.
[15] AP, 362.
[16] Cf. EO 1, 306.

prevent U.S. military involvement overseas. [. . .] But we can't ignore our social needs either. We have to stop people from abusing the welfare system. We have to provide food and shelter for the homeless and oppose racial discrimination and promote civil rights while also promoting equal rights for women but change the abortion laws to protect the right to life yet still somehow maintain women's freedom of choice. We also have to control the influx of illegal immigrants. We have to encourage a return to traditional moral values and curb graphic sex and violence on TV, in movies, in popular music, everywhere. Most importantly, we have to promote general social concern and less materialism in young people.[17]

In fact, all these things do not interest Bateman at all; he is not truly interested in anything. It is the permanent irony of contemporary existence that has made him indifferent and shallow. 'Surface, surface, surface was all that anyone found meaning in . . . this was civilization as I saw it, colossal and jagged . . .', as he formulates it himself.[18] Compare this to the descriptions of A's ironic indifference offered in Chapter 2 (among other things, his use of each 'Either/Or' as a means of eradicating any meaningful choice, as a 'dagger' with which to 'assassinate' the 'whole of actuality').[19] Wilfried Greve writes:

> [The aesthete] is completely indifferent towards existence. He does not see any meaning in it. He registers the misery, the social injustice, the narrow-mindedness of his contemporaries and cannot counterbalance this 'folly of the world' anywhere. For he does not recognize a comprehensive belief, a world view that could explain or help carry the wretchedness of existence[20]

Like the aesthete, Bateman is not stupid, even though a lot of what he says is stupid or even gruesome. René Boomkens aptly describes Bateman as an 'intelligent featherbrain'.[21]

1.2. 'Anything goes'

The aesthete's permanent irony means that his actions cannot be limited by anything; everything should be possible. As Walter Rehm formulates it: 'all objective life values evaporate or destroy themselves in play and careless pleasure'.[22] Both Johannes and Bateman do not accept responsibility for, or any limitation to, their actions. Their violent acts are the most obvious example of this, and also form the most striking similarity between both characters, even though the *type* of violence they commit is different. In *American Psycho*, Bateman commits torture, rape and murder. Whereas Bateman abuses his victims *physically*, Johannes does so *mentally*: he manipulates every new girl that he chooses to seduce, constantly stirring up her love to greater heights,

---

[17] AP, 14–15.
[18] Ibid., 360.
[19] EO 1, 527.
[20] Greve, 'Künstler versus Bürger', 40.
[21] Boomkens, *De angstmachine*, 138.
[22] Rehm, *Kierkegaard und der Verführer*, 13.

until, at the peak of her love, Johannes suddenly terminates their relationship, leaving the young girl behind, completely broken. Thus, Johannes systematically subjects his victims to a form of mental torment.

When every distinction has become immaterial, nothing can prevent such violent acts from happening. Indeed, Rehm points out that the extremes of human action, formerly hidden or forbidden, and regarded as 'evil', even contain a certain attraction or urgency for the aesthete.[23] Kierkegaard describes the motive behind this 'malignant curiosity for evil' as the aesthete's desire to know 'the world including its most extreme, horrific consequence'.[24] This description directly calls to mind Clay, the main character of Ellis's debut novel *Less than Zero*, who – after having watched, among other things, how a couple of his friends repeatedly rape a 12-year-old girl they have tied to a bed, and how one of his friends prostitutes himself to a rich, older man – says of himself: 'I want to see the worst' – a conclusion that could be the motto of Ellis's entire oeuvre.[25]

In this respect, it is also important to note the similarity of the form or genre of *American Psycho* and 'The Seducer's Diary'. Bateman characterizes his story as a 'confession', which is also how Rehm characterizes 'The Seducer's Diary'.[26] In the 'Diary' Johannes describes the seduction of his latest victim, Cordelia, in minute detail. We could also view *American Psycho* as a sort of diary: in it, Bateman describes, in great (often excessive) detail and from a first-person perspective, different events in his life, varying from quotidian, even banal things (such as his skin care and fitness regime, his favourite music, and innumerable meaningless social gatherings and dinners with friends and colleagues), to the horrible molestations and murders he commits. Furthermore, both Bateman and Johannes seem to be aware of the fact that the actions they 'confess' to, are, at least in the eyes of some people, morally reprehensible, but neither of them seems to let this insight influence his actions.[27]

Therefore, we should expect 'the worst', the limitless, the amoral from these 'confessional diaries'. 'ABANDON ALL HOPE YE WHO ENTER HERE', reads the opening line of *American Psycho*.[28] These words echo the inscription that, in Dante's *Divina Commedia*,[29] adorns the gate of hell; but they also indicate the starting point of the 'artistic', ironic-aesthetic life: 'Not until hope has been thrown overboard does one begin to live artistically', writes the aesthete A.[30] Hope implies a commitment, a lack of control (hope is directed at something that lies outside someone's power); this does

[23] Rehm writes that the aesthete, 'in der Neugier nach dem Bösen sich in allen Möglichkeiten, auch des Bösen, des Schrecklichen versuchen muss' (Rehm, *Kierkegaard und der Verführer*, 207).
[24] Quoted in: ibid., 85, 81.
[25] Ellis, *Less than Zero*, 160.
[26] Rehm, *Kierkegaard und der Verführer*, 87 (Rehm calls it a 'Beichte', a confession).
[27] E.g. Johannes: 'Am I stealing her heart? By no means – [. . .] I am shaping for myself a heart like unto hers. [. . .] She does not know that I possess this image and therein really lies my falsification. I obtained it secretively, and in that sense I have stolen her heart' (EO 1, 388–9); Bateman: 'I sign off by concluding, "Uh, I'm a pretty sick guy"'; '"Listen, it's Bateman again, and if you get back tomorrow, I may show up at Da Umberto's tonight, so, you know, keep your eyes open"' (AP, 338–9).
[28] AP, 3.
[29] Originally: 'Lasciate ogne speranza, voi ch'intrate'; Dante Alighieri, *De goddelijke komedie* [*Divina Commedia*] II, 26.
[30] EO 1, 292.

not fit into the aesthete's life-view. His life is, as Pulmer formulates it, a 'zero point existence', an existence that is not tied to anything, in which every event or decision can be revoked, and the aesthete just starts anew, without accounting for the old.[31]

1.3. The tragic fate of the aesthete

However, as we have already seen in Chapter 2, the ironic-aesthetic life-view is ill-fated. Although, initially, the permanent ironic attitude grants the aesthete freedom and possibility, in the end it leads to a situation in which, as Rehm formulates it, 'irony is no longer mastered, but has itself become the Master'. Irony robs everything of its binding force, as a result of which, the aesthete's existence is, ultimately, completely emptied out. In 'The Seducer's Diary' Johannes is still unaware of this inevitable downfall: 'the Seducer has not yet seen this total nothingness. He still finds himself in the flowering season of his sins', writes Rehm.[32] But the Seducer's eventual fate will be terrible, writes A in his introduction to the 'Diary', 'more terrible it will be for him – this I can conclude from the fact that I myself can scarcely control the anxiety that grips me every time I think about the affair'. Some of A's writings indicate that he himself has already been seized by this inevitable fate of the ironic-aesthetic life-view; for example, when he writes: 'Life for me has become a bitter drink, and yet it must be taken in drops, slowly, counting.'[33]

We can recognize this inevitable fate in *American Psycho* as well. Gradually, Bateman is completely numbed by his aesthetic existence, and it is precisely this numbness that leads him to increasingly extreme actions: 'Patrick Bateman suffers from a typically *decadent* disease: his nerves have been dulled. He needs very extreme stimuli to feel anything', writes Rob van Erkelens.[34] His mind has been deadened, like that of the aesthete A (who describes himself as a member of the 'Fellowship of the Dead' or 'Society of Buried Lives').[35] Bateman embodies the frustrations of contemporary consumer culture: nothing can satisfy his needs, because nothing has true value or meaning for him anymore. Only emptiness remains, and Bateman's violent excesses are an attempt to fill that void. In this respect he resembles Johannes, who likewise tries to ward off despair through an endless continuation of malicious seductions.

2. Four aspects of the escalation of ironic-aesthetic existence

In this section, this self-destructive escalation of aesthetic existence will be analysed in further detail, by distinguishing four phenomena that we have already encountered,

---

[31] Pulmer, *Die dementierte Alternative*, 133.
[32] Rehm, *Kierkegaard und der Verführer*, 220, 144; cf. ibid., 274. In some publications (cf. Doedens, *Het eenvoudige leven volgens Søren Kierkegaard*, 152) the 'reflected seducer' (i.e. Johannes) is described (in my opinion, mistakenly so) as a stage *following* the 'unhappy', 'defeated' existence of A. However, although the seducer embodies the aesthetic existence at the peak of its power and self-confidence, the 'despairing' aesthete is described in Kierkegaard's works as the final aesthetic stage.
[33] EO 1, 310, 26.
[34] Van Erkelens, 'Patrick B.', 16.
[35] EO 1, 165, 623.

im- and explicitly, in Chapters 1 and 2, as effects resulting from hyperreflexivity and endless irony. As we have seen, endless self-reflection and ironization result in a radical and calamitous distancing from others ('alienation from others'), from oneself ('self-alienation'), and from reality ('solipsism'), and all in a manic, endless spiral of scepticism, that can only deepen and thus become worse, in which everything is necessarily and increasingly regarded as meaningless and without value ('sceptic frenzy'). These four phenomena can be distinguished in both Kierkegaard's writing and in *American Psycho*, and can be regarded as leading up to the aesthetic disintegration of the self.

2.1. Alienation from others

First of all, the ironic-aesthetic life-style is characterized by an extreme alienation from other people. Johannes and Bateman maintain a great distance from other people, who do not really play a significant role in their narratives. Their permanent ironic-aesthetic distancing also causes a detachment from others. The previous section cited part of Bateman's ironic monologue on different political issues. His friends' reactions indicate the distancing effect of Bateman's ironic speech; they simply do not know how to respond: 'The table sits facing me in total silence. [. . .] Timothy just shakes his head in bemused disbelief. Evelyn is completely mystified by the turn the conversation has taken and she stands, unsteadily, and asks if anyone would like dessert.'[36] Nobody knows Bateman: he has no substantial ties to others, his relationships and friendships are utterly shallow and meaningless – nobody knows what he really thinks and does. The same goes for Johannes, who, according to Dewey, is 'forever cut off from the rest of the human community by the very aesthetic distance that he can no longer do without.'[37] And Rehm writes that Johannes 'avoids every bond to an outside, to a you, and evades every responsibility and therefore every answer, every deeper, inner community or the awareness, the possibility thereof, for instance in marriage, as well.'[38] The aesthete A describes himself and the other members of the 'Society of Buried Lives' as '*segregati*' (that is, 'separated', 'set apart', 'cut off', 'expelled') 'without association with men, having no share in their griefs and their joys.'[39]

For Bateman and Johannes, the outside world in general and other people in particular merely serve as an incitement, as base material that can be manipulated and utilized to satisfy their desires. Bateman sees other people as objects that he ascribes an identity to on the basis of the clothes they wear and the restaurants they go to, and that form possible 'ingredients' for the execution of his violent fantasies. In other words, Bateman reduces people to 'mere objects of desire, to be manipulated and played with

---

[36] AP, 15. That Timothy Price perhaps understands *something* of what Bateman is saying, shaking his head in (knowing, ironic) amusement, is in line with Price's position in the novel, as he is described by Bateman as the only interesting person he knows (ibid., 21).
[37] Dewey, 'The Erotic-Demonic in Kierkegaard's "Diary of the Seducer"', 7.
[38] Rehm, *Kierkegaard und der Verführer*, 221.
[39] EO 1, 220, 633.

until they satiate his need', as Blazer writes.[40] That, similarly, Johannes regards Cordelia as merely an occasion, as base material, becomes clear from his descriptions of his 'love' for her: 'Almost too much does Cordelia preoccupy me [. . .] – not face-to-face with her when she is present, but when I am alone with her in the strictest sense. I may yearn for her, not in order to speak with her but merely to have her image float past me.'[41] Johannes's interest in her is described as follows by Rehm: 'his business with Cordelia was for him basically "incitement".'[42]

The aesthetic attitude prescribes: 'in enjoyment you are to enjoy yourself'. That is what both Bateman and Johannes do. A telling statement by Johannes reads: 'How beautiful it is to be in love; how interesting it is to know that one is in love.'[43] Johannes enjoys 'himself', his own fantasy, and his ability to execute that fantasy by manipulating and controlling the world outside him. His enjoyment has virtually nothing to do with the supposed object of his desire, in this case Cordelia. She is just malleable base material that he can shape into whatever he wants, while enjoying his ability to do so. As Pulmer formulates it: 'While shaping Cordelia in accordance with his image, making her interesting, he in the end enjoys, as he enjoys Cordelia, only himself.'[44] Bateman's life, too, is solely about what he wants and by no means about others. Sex is purely a cold, mathematical execution of his desire, and the women involved are just 'implements' in service of that execution.

Such an alienated, instrumental view of other people leads to aggressive, predatory acts. In the case of *American Psycho* this requires little elaboration. Bateman describes countless acts of violence in horrific detail: as a predator, urged on by the 'smell of blood', he picks out his victims, after which he molests and usually kills them.[45] Although the violence of Johannes's acts is clearly of a different, more subtle kind, it is motivated by a similar aggression. Dewey, for example, notes the 'regular use of "military parlance"' in 'The Seducer's Diary', such as when Johannes decides on Cordelia becoming his next victim 'she is marked out, she shall be run down'.[46] In addition, Johannes speaks of his 'war with Cordelia, [. . .] a war of conquest; it is a life-and-death struggle'. And he remarks, sadistically: '[Like an archer] I am pulling the bow of love tighter in order to wound all the deeper.'[47]

In the context of Johannes's alienation from others, Dewey writes, 'he may at times feel stirring within him the human desire for open, candid relationships with other people. But no matter how tempted he might be to reveal himself to another human being, he cannot afford to succumb.'[48] This description likewise applies to Bateman's relation to Jean, his secretary, who is in love with him. Jean's defenceless character

[40] Blazer, 'Chasms of Reality, Aberrations of Identity'.
[41] EO 1, 361.
[42] Rehm, *Kierkegaard und der Verführer*, 282.
[43] EO 2, 190; EO 1, 334.
[44] Pulmer, *Die dementierte Alternative*, 110.
[45] AP, 356.
[46] Quoted in: Dewey, 'The Erotic-Demonic in Kierkegaard's "Diary of the Seducer"', 2. Another translation reads: 'she is selected, she will be overtaken' (EO 1, 317).
[47] EO 1, 384–5, 349.
[48] Dewey, 'The Erotic-Demonic in Kierkegaard's "Diary of the Seducer"', 6.

fills Bateman with disgust: the 'crush she has on me rendering her powerless – [. . .] I find this lack of defense oddly unerotic'. Bateman even comes to the verge of turning Jean into his next victim, but forgoes the opportunity. A part of Bateman desires what he loathes, the helplessness, the vulnerability towards the other: 'I imagine running around Central Park on a cool spring afternoon with Jean, laughing, holding hands. We buy balloons, we let them go.'[49] However, Bateman's alienation runs so deep that while these thoughts perhaps point towards his last bit of humanity, they remain unpursued. The aesthete's fatal alienation from the other turns out to be irreversible.

2.2. Self-alienation

The second aspect of the escalation of the ironic-aesthetic attitude is *self*-alienation,[50] which should be understood here, above all, as a splitting of the self into two parts: on the one hand, there is, to use Dewey's formulation, an 'agent self' that performs actions in the world, and on the other hand a 'hovering self' that reflects on the act that is performed and distances itself from it. This split is the result of the reflexive irony of the aesthetic attitude.[51]

Johannes the Seducer states that such a division is required to be able to experience something in an 'aesthetic' manner: 'to enjoy it properly, one ought to be on a somewhat higher level – not just as someone being baptized but also as the priest'. Johannes is proud of the way he manages to always stand at a distance from what is happening to and around him, to always control what he does and feels, as the 'director' of these experiences. From this standpoint, he aestheticizes life, bringing reality into accord with personal desire and fantasy. However, this 'self-direction' amounts to a form of self-deceit, as we can gather from Johannes's own words: 'I certainly am in love, but not in the ordinary sense [. . .] the god of love is blind, and if one is clever, he can surely be fooled'. In effect, this means: fooling *oneself*, by being – again, quoting Johannes – 'as receptive as possible to impressions'. He adds: 'In that way, one can be in love with many girls at the same time, because one is in love in a different way with each one.'[52] Initially, Johannes seems to fully control this self-deceit and to enjoy 'himself' in it, but gradually – and as we have seen in Chapters 1 and 2 – this reflexive split will lead to 'the feeling of one's self being shattered into two or multiple selves', writes Rehm.[53] A writes that, in the end, the Seducer 'goes astray within himself'. To which he adds: 'I can think of nothing more tormenting than a scheming mind that loses the thread and then

---

49   AP, 253, 255.
50   Dewey speaks of 'schizophrenia' ('While true that special demands of the aesthetic life-style create an unbridgeable gulf between the aesthete and the rest of the human community, they also produce a split deep within the aesthete himself'; Dewey, 'The Erotic-Demonic in Kierkegaard's "Diary of the Seducer"', 7). However, I think the term 'self-alienation' better fits the described phenomenon, because 'schizophrenia', in my opinion, refers too specifically to a mental disorder; plus, 'self-alienation' is the term used to describe the problem at hand in earlier chapters of this study.
51   Cf. Chapters 1 and 2.
52   EO 1, 342, 361.
53   Rehm, *Kierkegaard und der Verführer*, 14.

directs all its keenness against itself.'[54] Johannes's aesthetic self-splitting will lead to complete self-alienation, to 'the bewildering feeling of having become an inexplicable riddle to oneself', 'the frightening feeling', says Rehm, 'of believing to be something, that we really are not, and instead being something that we are afraid of being.'[55]

This is also what happens to Bateman, in the course of *American Pyscho*. His fantasy-driven mind places him at a constant distance from his real, agent self and the surrounding, real world. Frequently, Bateman describes events happening 'like in a movie'.[56] He remarks, for example:

> I am so used to imagining everything happening the way it occurs in movies, visualizing things falling somehow into the shape of events on the screen, that I almost hear the swelling of an orchestra, can almost hallucinate the camera panning low around us, fireworks bursting in slow motion overhead, the seventy-millimeter image of her lips parting and the subsequent murmur of 'I *want* you' in Dolby sound.[57]

In Bateman's case, this self-division also escalates to self-loss, to a situation where he has become a riddle to himself. At a certain point, he remarks: 'Something horrible was happening and yet I couldn't figure out why – I couldn't put my finger on it.' It is true that Bateman has his self-imposed persona – 'I . . . want . . . to . . . fit . . . in', he says to a former girlfriend – as a typical yuppie (so typical that he is constantly mistaken for other people). His lawyer describes him as 'such a bloody ass-kisser, such a brown-nosing goody-goody', while Bateman's girlfriend says: 'He's the boy next door, aren't you honey?' But Bateman whispers to himself: '"No I'm not, [. . .] I'm a fucking evil psychopath".' For he is gradually losing his grip on himself, on his controlled persona: 'My mask of sanity was a victim of impending slippage.'[58] He no longer feels in control, and becomes afraid of what appears from under the reflective mask of his imagined self. Under that slipping mask something terrible appears over which he has no control and which fills him with a deep anxiety. Bateman has gone astray within himself and is unable to avert his terrible fate.

2.3. Solipsism

The third aspect of the escalation of the ironic-aesthetic attitude is described by Dewey as follows:

> As the reader surveys the landscape of the 'Diary' through Johannes' eyes, the disquieting feeling creeps over him that the whole scene is dissolving before his very eyes. What appeared as solid people in conventional situations begins to shift subtly toward some strange half-life and they become transfigured into a

[54] EO 1, 308.
[55] Rehm, *Kierkegaard und der Verführer*, 14.
[56] See, e.g., the opening page of the novel *American Psycho* (AP, 3).
[57] Ibid., 254–5.
[58] Ibid., 271, 228, 372, 19, 268.

constellation of floating, shimmering, abstract impressions. Johannes seems beset by a kind of aesthetic solipsism.[59]

We have already encountered solipsism as a state of mind in which the individual regards only himself – that is, his thoughts and perceptions – as real, and the outside world and other people disappear as independently real and meaningful entities. Both 'The Seducer's Diary' and *American Psycho* gradually create the impression that (at least part of) the events reported, take place solely in the heads of their narrators. Both Bateman and Johannes are so alienated from the outside world and others, and from their own self that is part of that outside world, that, on and off, they *disappear* completely into the *un*reality of their own aesthetic fantasy. The aesthete wants to aestheticize his existence by bringing it into accord with his fantasy. In the case of Bateman and Johannes, their fantasy often replaces reality (comes to constitute its own pseudo-reality). Pulmer describes this as the 'demonic negation of all objective reality in absolute subjectivity'.[60] The only thing that has reality for Bateman and Johannes at these moments, is what their own minds produce; they can be said to subside in a purely solipsistic state.

Here, solipsism does not mean a permanent denial or disappearance of reality; it means that where reality does not suffice, does not offer enough stimuli, it is immediately and smoothly replaced by a fantasy that *does* offer that stimulus. Pulmer writes: 'Johannes's connections to reality are characterized by the fact that he is not able or willing to separate poetry and reality'.[61] In this respect, A offers a telling description of Johannes, connecting his solipsism to the aesthete's hyperreflexive, ironic distancing from reality:

He did not belong to the world of actuality, and yet he had very much to do with it. He continually ran lightly over it, but even when he most abandoned himself to it, he was beyond it. [. . .] He has suffered from an *exaberbatio cerebri* [exacerbation of the brain], for which actuality did not have enough stimulation, at most only momentarily.[62]

Bateman can be said to suffer from a similar 'exacerbation of the brain', in his case the hyperreflexive irony of contemporary existence. In the course of *American Psycho*, Bateman's descriptions raise more and more doubts as to their reliability. Certain scenes come across as abundantly unreal. The chapter 'Chase, Manhattan', for example, is cited by several critics as a clear indication that in Bateman's head reality is sometimes replaced by fantasy.[63]

In the chapter in question Bateman causes a bloodbath in Manhattan. First, he kills a busker, and, next, a cab driver. Then the narrative perspective changes from first to third person (an additional indication of the self-alienated splitting of Bateman's self),

[59] Dewey, 'The Erotic-Demonic in Kierkegaard's "Diary of the Seducer"', 11.
[60] Pulmer, *Die dementierte Alternative*, 50.
[61] Ibid., 127.
[62] EO 1, 306.
[63] Cf. Young, 'The Beast in the Jungle, the Figure in the Carpet', 114–15; Boomkens, *De Angstmachine*, 139; Murphet, *American Psycho. A Reader's Guide*, 47.

and Bateman gets into a gunfight with the police, at which point the narrative attains a grotesque character. The following fragment is illustrative:

> [the cops] start shooting and he returns their gunfire from his belly, getting a glimpse of both cops behind the open doors of the squad car, guns flashing like in a movie and this makes Patrick realize that he's in an actual gunfight of sorts, that he's trying to dodge bullets, that the dream threatens to break, is gone, that he's not aiming carefully, just obliviously returning gunfire, lying there, when a stray bullet, sixth in a new round, hits the gas tank of the police car, the headlights dim before it bursts apart, sending a fireball billowing up into the darkness, the bulb of a streetlamp above it exploding unexpectedly in a burst of yellow-green sparks, flames washing over the bodies of the policemen both living and dead, shattering all the windows of Lotus Blossom, Patrick's ears ringing . . .[64]

Confronted, so obviously, with the unreality of the description of this event, the thought begins to thrust itself upon us that all the violence we have experienced up until that point in the novel has perhaps just been a figment of Bateman's imagination. Julian Murphet rightly remarks: 'The "movie" reference [. . .] is a key to the status of Bateman's violent activities.'[65] This passage calls to mind all of Bateman's other descriptions that were accompanied by the qualifications 'like' or 'as in a movie', and leaves the impression that all of the horrific events described may only have been a fantasy of Bateman's overheated mind.

But it is not just reality disappearing for Bateman and Johannes. The reverse also is true: they disappear in reality, in the outside world as well. Dewey writes: 'the entire story might have taken place *only* in Johannes' mind. If so, [. . .] he, re the actual world, becomes "nothing" in order to accomplish it.'[66] The flip side of Johannes's rise above the actual world, is that he himself becomes a 'nothingness', or as A describes Johannes's 'sickness', a 'fading away in this manner, indeed, almost vanishing from actuality'. A describes Johannes's physical appearance as a 'parastatic body' (a 'feigned' body), and Cordelia says that he sometimes resembles a 'cloud'.[67] Johannes is well aware of this; it is an integral part of his aesthetic life-view:

> I myself am almost invisibly present when I am sitting visible at her side. My relationship to her is like a dance that is supposed to be danced by two people but is danced by only one. That is, I am the other dancer, but invisible. [. . .] I am flexible, supple, impersonal, almost like a mood.[68]

Also, think of Judge William's descriptions of the aesthete A: 'your mask is the most enigmatical of all; that is, you are a nonentity'.[69]

---

[64] AP, 336–7.
[65] Murphet, *American Psycho. A Reader's Guide*, 47.
[66] Dewey, 'The Erotic-Demonic in Kierkegaard's "Diary of the Seducer"', 14.
[67] EO 1, 306, 307–8, 309.
[68] Ibid., 380.
[69] EO 2, 159.

Invisible, a nonentity: that is how Bateman can be characterized as well. 'His character is a mask covering a void [. . .] he is a hollow shell', Blazer writes.[70] Bateman himself says: 'I was simply imitating reality, a rough resemblance of a human being.' Throughout *American Psycho*, there is constant confusion of identity. Bateman is mistaken for, among others, his colleagues Halberstam, Davis and Hamilton. It becomes clear that Bateman has no defining characteristics (another indication of the loss, the disintegration of self). Most revealing, in this respect, are probably Bateman's own words: 'though I can hide my cold gaze and you can shake my hand and feel flesh gripping yours and maybe you can even sense our lifestyles are probably comparable: *I simply am not there*'.[71]

The generic 'nothingness' of Bateman and Johannes also has to do with the fact that they are expressions of an idea, embody a certain life-view, and, as a result, are an 'ideal type'.[72] Rehm remarks on the fact that Johannes's Diary is called '*The* Seducer's Diary' and not '*A* Seducer's Diary': it is about 'the portrayal of the type'.[73] Towards the end of the 'Diary', Johannes himself formulates it as follows: 'Everything is a metaphor; I myself am a myth about myself. [. . .] Who I am is irrelevant; everything finite and temporal is forgotten, only the eternal remains'.[74] Similarly, Bateman, towards the end of the novel, says about himself: '. . . there is an idea of a Patrick Bateman, some kind of abstraction, but there is no real me, only an entity, something illusory'.[75]

2.4. Sceptic frenzy

The fourth and final aspect of the escalation of the ironic-aesthetic attitude is that, as Dewey writes, its 'demonic drive progressively accelerates its demands and eventually pushes the aesthete to a self-destructive frenzy'.[76] The aesthetic life-style requires a constant acceleration of the speed at which pleasures are to succeed each other; evermore quickly, the *sceptical* mind of the aesthete has to regard each sensation as meaningless. For the aesthete, pleasure is always short-lived: he constantly craves new sources of enjoyment, and in this respect his mind becomes increasingly demanding and tires ever more quickly of what is offered. As A remarks about Johannes: 'it is a circle from which he cannot find an exit'.[77] Similarly, Bateman is driven by an insatiable desire, for status, the right clothes, the right restaurants et cetera, as a result of which he describes himself as 'lethal, on the verge of frenzy'.[78] The 'Chase, Manhattan' chapter,

---

[70] Blazer, 'Chasms of Reality, Aberrations of Identity'.
[71] AP, 271, 362.
[72] Cf. Boomkens, *De Angstmachine*, 138.
[73] Rehm, *Kierkegaard und der Verführer*, 103.
[74] EO 1, 444.
[75] AP, 362.
[76] Dewey, 'Søren Kierkegaard's *Diary of the Seducer*', 152. I have labelled this phenomenon as '*sceptic frenzy*' as it is clearly in line with the spiralling loss of all meaning and value, as a result of aesthetic irony, that in Chapter 2 was described as scepticism.
[77] EO 1, 308.
[78] AP, 268.

discussed in the previous subsection, is a clear example of how Bateman's incessant desire has gradually accelerated into an absurd, frenzied mania.

Still, this excess does not constitute a solution or an end point: Bateman escapes, and everything continues as before, his bloodthirst unquenched and more demanding. As Dewey writes: 'After some momentary aesthetic diversions [. . .] the malaise of "modernity" returns and aesthetes are left, once again, facing the void. And the void appears more ominous now, because yet another option has failed.'[79] This marks an utter scepticism towards all thoughts or sensations, a saturation without satisfaction, or as A describes it: 'my eyes are surfeited and bored with everything, and yet I hunger.'[80] Although each new venture has a certain 'sweetness' for Johannes, '[w]hat awaits him after that is something of an anti-climax', according to Dewey.[81] This disappointment becomes ever more predominant: 'the pleasure becomes stale and boring', writes Greve.[82] Compare this to Bateman, who indulges himself in increasingly violent excesses, but remarks, while torturing a victim: 'it fails to interest me'. He says: 'Everything failed to subdue me. Soon everything seemed dull.'[83] Nothing can satisfy the needs of the aesthete anymore. A formulates this realization as follows: 'My soul is dull and slack; in vain do I jab the spur of desire into its side; it is exhausted, it can no longer raise itself up in its royal jump. I have lost all my illusions.'[84]

This disillusion leads to frustration: 'Once light and ethereal, he comes more and more under the sway of the actual world's pulls. [. . .] It pains him. He will rage against it', writes Dewey.[85] A says of himself: 'My soul is like the Dead Sea, over which no bird is able to fly; when it has come midway, it sinks down, exhausted, to death and destruction.'[86] Frustrated that nothing can invigorate him anymore, the aesthete becomes a sort of 'black hole' that destroys everything within its reach. Judge William tells A:

> I know no condition of the soul that can better be described as damnation – halt this wild flight, this passion for annihilation that rages within you, for that is what you want: you want to annihilate everything; you want to satisfy the hunger of your doubt by consuming existence.[87]

Bateman's frustration adds to the spiral of his increasingly extreme acts of violence. He is subjected to incessant stimulation without satisfaction. Bateman's violence starts to serve less as a means of satisfaction and more as an expression of frustration, taken out on others: 'My pain is constant and sharp and I do not hope for a better world for anyone. In fact I want my pain to be inflicted on others. I want no one to escape.'[88] Blazer aptly formulates this transition in Bateman's violent acts: '[other

---

[79] Dewey, 'Seven Seducers', 197–8.
[80] EO 1, 25.
[81] Dewey, 'The Erotic-Demonic in Kierkegaard's "Diary of the Seducer"', 18.
[82] Greve, 'Künstler versus Bürger', 50.
[83] AP, 315, 271.
[84] EO 1, 41.
[85] Dewey, 'The Erotic-Demonic in Kierkegaard's "Diary of the Seducer"', 19.
[86] EO 1, 37.
[87] EO 2, 160.
[88] AP, 362.

human beings] are reduced, in his image-conscious mind, to mere objects of desire, to be manipulated and played with until they satiate his need. But because they never can, he [. . .] aggresses; he destroys what displeases him; he rips life apart.'[89]

Initially, these 'discharges' can perhaps be seen to have some alleviating effect. Young notes that '[a]fter each of the major killings – those of the black bum Al, Bethany, and the several in the chapter "Chase, Manhattan" – there follows, either immediately or very shortly afterwards, an extremely strange, bland analysis of pop music.'[90] In these music chapters, Bateman respectively praises Genesis, Whitney Houston and Huey Lewis & the News. Murphet rightly states that 'Bateman's "mask of sanity" is seemingly nowhere more securely in place than when he commits entire chapters to enthusing over his favorite popular music. [. . .] It is in the chapters devoted to them that Bateman's confidence is at its highest pitch.'[91] It seems as if these murders have a somewhat calming effect on Bateman's frustrated mind, enabling him to muse lyrically and quasi-profoundly on superficial pop music.[92]

But this also quickly grows thin: the effect decreases and Bateman remains locked in the frenzied spiral of his life-view. What is there left for him to do, when even the most gruesome acts of torture, rape and murder – Kierkegaard's 'most horrific consequence' and Clay's 'the worst' – cannot appease him? At the end of the novel, Bateman states:

> There are no more barriers to cross. All I have in common with the uncontrollable and the insane, the vicious and the evil, all the mayhem I have caused and my utter indifference toward it, I have now surpassed. [. . .] But even after admitting this – and I have, countless times, in just about every act I've committed – and coming face-to-face with these truths, there is no catharsis. I gain no deeper knowledge about myself, no new understanding can be extracted from my telling. There has been no reason for me to tell you any of this. This confession has meant *nothing . . .*[93]

The aesthete's frustration and resulting destructive urge ultimately lead to *self*-destruction, to the aesthete's doom, in the sense that he is fated, in Dewey's words, 'to run his life as a demanding, frenzied uphill race. [. . .] the aesthetic life style permits no rest and cuts off the various avenues of escape. [. . .] It now turns out to be an inescapable, frenzied, compulsively driven nightmare.'[94] This is the aesthete's inevitable, tragic fate: 'thus will Johannes the Seducer, too, "carry out" his character and perish in

---

[89] Blazer, 'Chasms of Reality, Aberrations of Identity'.
[90] Young, 'The Beast in the Jungle, the Figure in the Carpet', 112.
[91] Murphet, *American Psycho. A Reader's Guide*, 33.
[92] Murphet himself does not connect this to the violent eruptions in the preceding chapters. Young mainly points out the change in style, the feeling that the same person cannot be the source of both narratives, which Young regards as proof for the 'unreality' of Bateman as a character. According to Sonia Baelo-Allué the relative calm of the music chapters serves to 'stress the horror narrated in the previous pages' (Baelo-Allué, 'Serial Murder, Serial Consumerism: Bret Easton Ellis's *American Psycho*', 79–80).
[93] AP, 362.
[94] Dewey, 'The Erotic-Demonic in Kierkegaard's "Diary of the Seducer"', 20.

the Tartarus of his burned out, arbitrary life', writes Rehm, adding that Kierkegaard describes the end the aesthete meets as 'forlornness in the cold, in the inferno, in nothingness'.[95]

Thus, the aesthete becomes the victim of a terror of his own making. His existence deteriorates into a nightmare that is filled with the terrible images brought forth by his own fantasy.[96] Johannes's aesthetic 'hell' will consist of, as A describes, 'the pale, bloodless, tenacious-of-life nocturnal forms with which I battle and to which I myself give life and existence'. Johannes wanders 'into that kingdom of mist, into that dreamland where one is frightened by one's own shadow at every moment'.[97] Bateman, too, concludes: 'Something horrible was happening'. He has confessed his crimes, on the phone to his lawyer, and through his narrative in general, but, as we read above, there follows neither catharsis nor punishment. There is no escape from the spiralling horror of Bateman's existence, as expressed by the novel's final words: 'THIS IS NOT AN EXIT.'[98]

3. A continuation of reflexive irony

So, we can conclude that *American Psycho* is a literary portrayal of the problematic ironic-aesthetic attitude. However, the novel cannot be regarded as a successful critique of that attitude.[99] The only way in which the novel can be said to critique its main character, and thereby the life-view that he embodies, is by forcing the reader to perform a constant ironic distancing from what he or she reads. *American Psycho* (like all of Ellis's novels) is written completely in the 'idiom', the voice of its first-person narrator, Patrick Bateman, who at the same time is meant to be the critical target of the novel. Because the expressive possibilities of the text are limited to the voice of the narrator, irony, in this case the ironic interpretation of the novel's 'excesses of stupidity and hollowness', is the only available critical instrument.[100]

In *American Psycho* there is no 'possibility of offering even the outline of another vision', writes Murphet.[101] There is no alternative, change is impossible, nothing escapes ironization. The novel offers no outer perspective that can function as an alternative to the life-view that is ironized. Bateman's secretary, Jean, seems to be about the only person in the novel who is not as horrible as Bateman himself, but she functions as

---

[95] Rehm, *Kierkegaard und der Verführer*, 226, 276.
[96] Cf. 'die Angst des Ästhetikers ist eine Angst vor dem eigenen Schatten' (Pulmer, *Die dementierte Alternative*, 133).
[97] EO 1, 23, 310.
[98] AP, 271, 384.
[99] I would like to stress that I am not interested in labelling *American Psycho* an immoral book and Bret Easton Ellis as some sort of evil, diabolic novelist. But I would like to question the designation of the novel as a successful indictment of the life-view that is at the base of what it portrays; e.g. Weldon, 'An Honest American Psycho'; Freccero, 'Historical Violence, Censorship and the Serial Killer'.
[100] Murphet, *American Psycho. A Reader's Guide*, 20.
[101] Ibid.

an emblem of unacceptable naïveté that will be crushed sooner or later, and not as a symbol of a possible way out. There indeed seems to be no exit, as Bateman's last words in the novel indicate.

Note that, in the end, Bateman's behaviour is apparently deemed to be completely normal in the world that the novel portrays. This is why nothing happens. This is not to say that Bateman should have been caught and punished, so as to soothe our desire for a clear distinction between right and wrong. But it is important to note that, while Bateman seems to have crossed all barriers and borders of acceptable behaviour, these transgressions are of no consequence; in fact, they do not truly qualify as transgressions, for the moral restrictions implied in that term simply do not exist anymore, and, as a result, there are no more actions that qualify as abnormal. It might well be that many of the other characters are psychopaths as well.

Completely in line with the aesthetic life-view, Ellis's work – described by himself as 'patch-braided satires of the culture I live in, pin-pointing the things that disgust me and make me angry and cause me a lot of anxiety and ridiculing them' – consists solely of the ridiculing of their own subject.[102] His novels ironically distance themselves from a world that is completely empty, shallow, affectless, materialistic and sadistic, but thereby, at the same time, conceive the world to be like that, without any room to truly attribute value or meaning to anything – 'rigidly nihilistic', as Ellis himself characterizes his worldview.[103] Young writes about Ellis: 'It is as if, having articulated the affectlessness and shallowness that so obsesses him he lacks the imagination with which to create anything other. He can only go deeper into surfaces and this he does.'[104]

Wallace has explicitly criticized Ellis's work, for exactly this reason.[105] Wallace writes that there is no actual discerning commentary on contemporary Western culture to be found in 'all this "literary" fiction that simply monotones that we're all becoming less and less human, that presents characters without souls or love, characters who really are exhaustively describable in terms of what brands of stuff they wear'. The conviction that this type of fiction does embody such a critique, attests, according to Wallace, to a 'black cynicism about today's world' that Ellis uses to mislead his readers: 'If readers simply believe the world is stupid and shallow and mean, then Ellis can write a mean shallow stupid novel that becomes a mordant deadpan commentary on the badness of everything.' To which he adds:

> Look, if the contemporary condition is hopelessly shitty, insipid, materialistic, emotionally retarded, sadomasochistic and stupid, then I (or any writer) can get away with slapping together stories with characters who are stupid, vapid, emotionally retarded, which is easy, because these sorts of characters require no development. With descriptions that are simply lists of brand-name consumer

[102] Quoted in: Grimshaw, 'Cultural Pessimism and Rock Criticism: Bret Easton Ellis' Writing (as) Hell'.
[103] Love, 'Psycho Analysis'.
[104] Young, 'Vacant Possession', 41.
[105] Cf. Wallace's short story 'Girl with Curious Hair' (from the eponymous collection), which, as Marshall Boswell formulates it, 'eerily forecasts Ellis's 1991 slasher novel *American Psycho*' (Boswell, *Understanding David Foster Wallace*, 79).

products. Where stupid people say insipid stuff to each other. If what's always distinguished bad writing – flat characters, a narrative world that's clichéd and not recognizably human, etc. – is also a description of today's world, then bad writing becomes an ingenious mimesis of a bad world.[106]

Wallace reproaches Ellis for failing to offer any alternative, or any insight in addition to what he mocks and ridicules as the 'darkness of the time'. This critique is directly in line with Kierkegaard's view of irony, and the need for realizing a positivity in its wake.

Thus *American Psycho* falls prey to the same attitude of which it shows us the extreme escalation, namely the total negative irony of the aesthetic life-view. This is not to say that the novel or Ellis somehow 'condone' – if it even makes sense to say such a thing – the violence that it portrays, but it *is* to say that the novel cannot truly criticize the attitude that lies at the *root* of these escalations, since its only way to do so, is to desire from its readers the same thing it portrays in its main character: endless irony.

The fact that Ellis's novels only ridicule and ironize, and are unable to formulate any meaning or value, shows us the underlying aggravation of the postmodernist view of language and fiction (and the formulation of meaning therein). Ellis regards the meaningful description of the world, whether it is seen as 'reality' or as 'fiction', as a simple impossibility. His works do not display a search for a way around this problem; they merely ridicule all attempts to find a way out, as well as the excesses that inevitably follow from the lack of a way out. There is, indeed, no exit.

Conclusion

In this chapter, Ellis's postmodernist minimalism, embodied by the novel *American Psycho*, was analysed by viewing it in light of Kierkegaard's conception of the ironic-aesthetic life-view, specifically by comparing the novel to 'The Seducer's Diary', which is part of Kierkegaard's *Either/Or*. We have seen that Patrick Bateman's perspective – which is the novel's *only* perspective – can be characterized as an extreme embodiment of the aesthetic attitude, which has ironized all meaning and value. We have also seen that this attitude escalates, through the phenomena of alienation from others, self-alienation, solipsism and sceptic frenzy, into a disintegration of the self.

However, as we concluded in the final section of this chapter, *American Psycho* cannot be considered as just a portrayal (or, even less so, a truly *critical* portrayal) of the aesthetic attitude, as the novel is also an expression of that same attitude. For although *American Psycho* can perhaps be said to reveal the viciousness of the ironic-aesthetic attitude, the novel also portrays it as the only *possible* attitude, as the world is seen to lack meaning and value, and all attempts to formulate them as useless and naïve. Moreover, the futile and potentially horrific nature of the aesthetic attitude can only be revealed through a constant ironic distancing from the portrayal of that

[106] McCaffery, 'Interview', 131.

attitude. However, this 'compulsory' ironic movement essentially continues the same endless spiral of detachment that characterizes Bateman's existence. The inability of *American Psycho* to formulate any meaning or value is an effect of the aggravation of the postmodernist view of language and fiction, of the preceding (deconstructive-metafictional) problematization of the connection between reality and language being turned into 'fact': the supposed fact that the world has no meaning and all attempts to formulate meaning are equally arbitrary and unreal, and therefore useless.

As a result of this reflexive-ironic conviction, *American Psycho* cannot offer any alternative. Wallace has reproached Ellis's work for exactly this reason. We have already seen that this viewpoint is, again, in line with Kierkegaard's critique of irony. Wallace and Kierkegaard express the need for realizing a positivity in the wake of reflexive-ironic negation. Wallace writes: 'Really good fiction could have as dark a worldview as it wished, but it'd find a way both to depict this dark world *and* to illuminate the possibilities for being alive and human in it.'[107] These possibilities are the subject of Part 2 of this study.

---

[107] McCaffery, 'Interview', 131.

Part Two

Engaged Fiction

In his fiction, Wallace wants to overcome the problematic view that underlies the works of Barth and Ellis and makes it impossible for fiction to forge a meaningful connection with the world. Wallace wants his fiction, as we saw at the end of Chapter 4, 'to illuminate the possibilities for being alive and human in it'.[1] To that end, Wallace has found, in the view underlying *Infinite Jest*, an ally in the philosophy of the later Wittgenstein.

In the next chapter, I will give an outline of late-Wittgenstein's view of language and literature that can be seen to underlie Wallace's work, and that offers an alternative to the postmodernist view, which in the fiction of Barth and Ellis ultimately leads to non-committal introversion. Wittgenstein's thought enables Wallace to think of fiction in new and different ways while avoiding a return to traditional realism, acknowledging and portraying the contemporary existential problems of hyperreflexivity and endless irony, without ending up at the same solipsistic and scepticistic dead-end as Barth and Ellis. Rather, such a view helps supply contemporary Western culture with new sources of meaning. The late-Wittgensteinian view enables a mode of fiction as always engaged with the world, makes it possible for Wallace's work (and Eggers's and Foer's works following in his wake) to speak meaningfully again about notions that Wallace regards as crucial to human existence. These notions are sincerity, reality-commitment and community: they form the engagement that we find in the work of Wallace, Eggers and Foer, and will be elaborated separately in Chapters 6, 7 and 8.

---

[1] McCaffery, 'Interview', 131.

5

Wittgenstein and Wallace: The Meaning of Fiction

Introduction

Wallace has repeatedly asserted his adherence to later Wittgenstein's view of language: 'Wittgenstein's conclusions seem completely sound to me, always have.'[1] Moreover, for Wallace, these conclusions seem to function against what he regards as the vacuity of the strategies of Barth and Derrida: 'I personally have grown weary of most texts that are narrated self-consciously as *written*, as "textes" [. . .] [,] the Barthian/post-Derridean self-referential hosts.'[2] Boswell suggests that 'Wallace uses Wittgenstein's elegant model to escape from what he regards as the dead end of postmodern self-reflexivity, particularly as practised by John Barth.'[3] In this chapter, I hope to further explore Boswell's suggestion. In Chapter 3, we have seen that the strategy underlying Barth's metafiction (as suggested by the preceding quote from Wallace) is similar to that of Derrida's philosophy of deconstruction. Therefore, the account of the Wittgensteinian 'model' underlying Wallace's fiction in this chapter will partly take the form of comparing and contrasting certain aspects of the philosophy of later Wittgenstein to that of Derrida.

Patricia De Martelaere writes that 'bringing together Wittgenstein and Derrida seems no small matter'. They are considered to belong to two completely different philosophical traditions – Anglo-American analytic philosophy and continental philosophy, respectively – described by De Martelaere as two 'rivalling philosophical "clubs" with their own members, their own slogans and (of course) their own secret language'. However, over the past decades, several critics have pointed to a number of significant connections between Wittgenstein and Derrida. As De Martelaere explains: 'both are concerned with and obsessed by language, both an enemy of metaphysical essentialism'.[4]

Unless otherwise indicated, translations are mine.

[1] McCaffery, 'Interview', 144.

[2] Wallace, 'The Empty Plenum', 221.

[3] Boswell, *Understanding David Foster Wallace*, 26.

[4] De Martelaere, 'Wittgenstein en Derrida', 96–7. On this similarity, see, e.g. Allison, 'Derrida and Wittgenstein: Playing the Game', 93–109; Garver and Lee, *Derrida and Wittgenstein*; Staten,

But as to the cause of, and solution to, the traditional essentialism of Western thought, they differ greatly.[5] According to Derrida and Barth there is an inevitable gap between language and reality, and between language and thought. But one can only speak of such a gap, if one assumes that language acquires (or tries to acquire) meaning by referring to the world or thought (by attempting to bridge that gap). Derrida regards this referential view as an illusion that, at the same time, is indestructible and indispensable for language to function. However, as we will see below, in sections 1 and 2, Wittgenstein shows that this 'illusion' of a connection between language and world or thought is a fallacy resulting from the reflective misperception of how words are actually used, and therefore *irrelevant* for the meaningful functioning of language. The focus of my analysis will be on Wittgenstein's account of ostensive definition and private language.

Subsequently, in section 3, I will demonstrate the specific benefits of the Wittgensteinian view of language in relation to the problems of hyperreflexivity and endless irony (and the resulting solipsism and scepticism) so evident in Derrida and Barth. I will also examine the various references in Wallace's work to these benefits.

Finally, in section 4, I will formulate a view of literature based on the late-Wittgensteinian view of language. This view amounts to understanding literature as a form of 'grammatical' investigation, that is, an investigation of our cultural semantic structures – an investigation that forms an important foundation for our use of complex, moral concepts (that is, concepts that are tied to what we regard as human virtue). Finally, I will argue that this Wittgensteinian view of language and literature forms the basis of the ability of Wallace's work (and that of Eggers and Foer) to speak meaningfully again of the notions of sincerity, reality-commitment and community which we will discuss in Chapters 6, 7 and 8.[6] There, the literary works in question will be shown to provide paradigmatic cases of these notions.

1. Wittgenstein: The temptation of essences

Wittgenstein does not regard the assumption of metaphysical essences as an inevitable (illusory) component of the functioning of language, but as a fallacy stemming from the metaphysical (mis)use of words, which takes place mainly in philosophy, distorting the meaning those words have when they are used in ordinary language.

Wittgenstein and Derrida; Wheeler, 'Wittgenstein as Conservative Deconstructor', 239–59. It does not seem as if Wittgenstein has influenced Derrida, who does not go into the former's philosophy in any of his writings: 'If it can be said that Derrida has never "deconstructed" Wittgenstein, perhaps it can also be said that the various references to Wittgenstein in his writings do not rise to the level of a response' (Shain, 'Derrida's References to Wittgenstein', 71; cf. Orbán, 'Die Herausforderung von Wittgenstein durch Derrida', 97).

[5] Cf. 'Derrida and Wittgenstein share a fundamental opposition to traditional essentialist forms of philosophy [. . .] but the more closely we examine this common point of origin the more the two men's differences emerge' (Altieri, 'Wittgenstein on Consciousness and Language', 1398); '[T]hey differ both in their diagnosis of the pathology and in their prescription for treatment' (Grene, 'Life, Death and Language', 265–6).

[6] Cf., for an earlier version of this analysis: Den Dulk, 'Wallace and Wittgenstein'.

This distinction, between philosophical and ordinary language, enables Wittgenstein to limit the problem of metaphysical essentialism to a specific area of language use and provide an alternative.

By contrast, Derrida thinks that the distinction between ordinary and philosophical language cannot be made. For Derrida, words always have a 'metaphysical appurtenance' ('attachment', 'appendage'), to employ Mireille Truong Rootham's formulation. Truong Rootham contrasts this with the view of Wittgenstein, who regards the illusion of essences as a matter of 'metaphysical *use*': words are used – or perhaps it is better to say: *mis*used – in a metaphysical way, but do not inevitably contain a built-in metaphysical element.[7] According to Derrida, such a distinction between metaphysical and normal language use is problematic, for such a limitation would itself imply a pure (that is, metaphysical) distinction that cannot be made: 'everyday language', says Derrida, always 'is the language of Western metaphysics, and it carries with it not only a considerable number of presuppositions of all types, but also presuppositions inseparable from metaphysics, which, although little attended to, are knotted into a system'.[8] So, the indeterminacy of language does not just pose a problem to metaphysical, philosophical or scientific language use, but 'infects' ordinary, everyday language use just as much. For Derrida, all language implies the metaphysics of presence, and its ideal of purity.

However, Derrida's rejection of the distinction between ordinary and philosophical language use presupposes his own affirmation of language as motivated by the ideal of metaphysical purity, that he subsequently deconstructs, resulting in the supposed impossibility of any clear conceptual distinction between metaphysical and normal language use.[9] Therefore, Derrida's critique does not affect Wittgenstein's argument: after all, this critique is based on the affirmation and subsequent deconstruction of an ideal that Wittgenstein regards as an avoidable, philosophical mistake.

'While Wittgenstein does reject much of the metaphysical endeavors of philosophy, he does not reject the possibility of grounds upon which a different sort of system can be built', writes Susan Brill, who adds that: 'It is this Wittgensteinian methodology of investigation that displays the greatest divergences from the deconstructive strategy.'[10] Henry McDonald concludes: 'What all of this does is to make Derrida's method at once *more sceptical* and *less radical* than Wittgenstein's. [. . .] Wittgenstein's project is more radical [. . .] in that he wishes us to give up the pursuit altogether.'[11] This difference between Wittgenstein and Derrida is of crucial importance: that we can actually free ourselves of what Derrida calls the 'illusion of

---

[7] Truong Rootham, 'Wittgenstein's Metaphysical Use and Derrida's Metaphysical Appurtenance', 35 [emphasis added, AdD].

[8] Derrida, *Positions*, 19; cf. 'For me *there is only ordinary language* – philosophy too is "ordinary language". But since there is no opposed term here, since there is only "ordinary language", this concept is empty' (Derrida, 'Response to Mulhall', 416).

[9] Cf. 'These pairs, for example natural language/formal language, language/speech, etc. having been produced by philosophical discourse, belong to the field which they are to dominate; which without stripping them of all authority, makes them incapable of mastering the relation of philosophical "discourse" to its constraints' (Derrida, *Margins of Philosophy*, 177).

[10] Brill, *Wittgenstein and Critical Theory*, 101.

[11] McDonald, 'Crossroads of Skepticism', 272.

presence', points towards an alternative from endless deconstruction, which is also what Wallace *cum suis* crave. Below, I will outline what Wittgenstein describes as the reasons why we are tempted to assume something like the illusory ideal of pure essences. In the next section, I will describe why this ideal is not just illusory but also *irrelevant* for the meaningful functioning of language.

Wittgenstein claims that Western philosophy is guided by the metaphysical urge to get 'behind' things and thereby discover their supposed essences. This philosophical 'craving for generality' – or '*theorizing* or *theoretical attitude*', as Marie McGinn calls it – results in a quest for the general qualities of certain concepts, asking: what are the essential characteristics of something – that is, what are the qualities that are not dependent on certain circumstances or contexts, but are always 'present' and therefore determinative of what a concept means?[12] Philosophers are convinced that, through these questions, they will discover the 'true core' of something. However, what actually happens, according to Wittgenstein, is that the examined concept is detached from the context within which it has a certain meaning.[13]

Philosophical problems arise because philosophers tend to remove linguistic utterances from their everyday use in order to scrutinize them without their connections to a certain practice, in what we could perhaps call a state of 'semantic zero-gravity'. Wittgenstein describes such analyses as situations in which 'language *goes on holiday*'. He writes: 'The confusions which occupy us arise when language is like an engine idling, not when it is doing work.'[14]

To illustrate this generalizing way in which philosophers analyse a concept, Wittgenstein offers the example of the question what exactly is 'thought' or 'thinking'? As a result of this line of questioning, phenomena that are normally unproblematic for us, become completely obscure. He writes:

> 'This queer thing, thought' – but it does not strike us as queer when we are thinking. Thought does not strike us as mysterious while we are thinking, but only when we say, as it were retrospectively: 'How was that possible?' How was it possible for thought to deal with the very object *itself*? We feel as if by means of it we had caught reality in our net.[15]

Philosophy makes us assume a reflexive stance: we start looking at the processes taking place in our heads from a distance, as 'objects' that we somehow 'possess': 'In order to get clear about the meaning of the word "think" we watch ourselves while we think; what we observe will be what the word means! But this concept is not used like that', writes Wittgenstein.[16] We assume that by looking, in this reflexive manner, at the

---

[12] Wittgenstein, *The Blue and Brown Books*, 18; McGinn, *Wittgenstein and the Philosophical Investigations*, 16.

[13] Cf. 'When philosophers use a word – "knowledge", "being", "object", "I", "proposition", "name" – and try to grasp the *essence* of the thing, one must always ask oneself: is the word ever actually used in this way in the language-game which is its original home? – What *we* do is to bring words back from their metaphysical to their everyday use' (PI, 42ᵉ [§116]).

[14] Ibid., 16ᵉ, 44ᵉ [§§38, 132].

[15] Ibid., 108ᵉ [§428].

[16] Ibid., 88ᵉ [§316].

phenomena that we call 'thinking', we can isolate that which is always present when we 'think', that is, what is essential to it. But that is not how the concept functions: '"Thinking", a widely ramified concept. A concept that comprises many manifestations of life. The *phenomena* of thinking are widely scattered', Wittgenstein writes.[17] P. M. S. Hacker adds:

> The verb 'to think' is multi-faceted, being connected with opining ('I think we ought to . . .'), believing ('I think she is in the garden'), conceiving, imagining, fancying, and envisaging ('That is just how I thought it would be'). It is also bound up with doing things attentively, carefully, with due consideration. And, what is prominent in philosophical investigation, it is related to reflecting, musing, meditating (whether aloud or *in foro interno*), as well as to deliberating, speculating, reasoning, and inferring.[18]

According to Hacker, the concept of thinking is 'like a traffic-network connecting many out-of-the-way places'. But if, instead of actually applying the concept in one of its actual uses, we start to reflect on the general meaning of the concept, then we are prone to passing over that diversity. Hacker: 'We suppose the concept of thinking to have a simple unified use with smooth contours. But that is an illusion. The use of this expression is far more erratic than we expect [. . .]; hence the danger of using "think" in a global, highly generalized way is great.'[19]

It is language that entices us to do this, says Wittgenstein, 'what confuses us is the uniform appearance of words when we hear them spoken or meet them in script and print'.[20] McGinn explains: 'The confusions arising from the theoretical attitude are not, therefore, mere mistakes. They are misunderstandings which, when we become reflective about it, language itself has the power to draw us into.'[21] According to Wittgenstein, these reflective misunderstandings are prompted by a 'bewitchment of our intelligence by means of language'.[22]

It is important to emphasize that saying that language entices us into assuming the existence of metaphysical essences is not the same as claiming, as Derrida does, that the illusion of metaphysical essences is inevitable and indispensable to the functioning of language. The only thing that Wittgenstein describes here, is how philosophers are tempted to think that behind language lies hidden a set of essences that bestow meaning onto it (he will go on to show that these essences, or the illusion of them, are completely *irrelevant* to the meaningful functioning of language – see the next section).

In Wittgenstein's own philosophical view, philosophy becomes a form of therapy that can cure us from metaphysical mistakes and the reflective tendencies from which these mistakes result: 'What we are destroying is nothing but houses of cards and we are clearing up the ground of language on which they stand.'[23] McGinn explains that

---

[17]   Wittgenstein, *Zettel*, 21^e [§110].
[18]   Hacker, *Meaning and Mind*, 301.
[19]   Ibid.
[20]   PI, 6^e [§11].
[21]   McGinn, *Wittgenstein and the Philosophical Investigations*, 21.
[22]   PI, 40^e [§109].
[23]   Ibid., 41^e [§118].

Wittgenstein's therapeutic philosophy aims 'to make us aware of the clash between our philosophically reflective idea of how a concept works and the way it actually functions'.[24] Wittgenstein is of the opinion that our language use 'must be freed from the self-consciousness that philosophical reflection chronically produces', writes Marjorie Grene, '[w]e should learn to be able to abandon reflection when we like and get on with the job'.[25]

According to Wittgenstein, we should look carefully at how language is actually used: 'It disperses the fog to study the phenomena of language [. . .] in which one can command a clear view of the aim and functioning of the words.' If we do this, we will be able to adjust our understanding of language in a way that does not fall victim to the illusion of essentialism, and thus be able to 'shew the fly the way out of the fly-bottle'.[26]

2. Wittgenstein: The irrelevance of essences

The previous section described how, according to Wittgenstein, philosophers are tempted to mistakenly assume the presence of metaphysical essences behind language. The current section will address the claim, which for Wittgenstein is equally mistaken, that such essences (or the illusion of them) are necessary for the meaningful functioning of language. Wittgenstein describes the idea that words have to be accompanied by something that gives them meaning, as quite common and understandable. He writes: 'Every sign *by itself* seems dead. *What* gives it life?'[27] A sign, a word points towards something – a thing in the world, a thought in my head. It might seem as if that referential connection 'causes' my words to have meaning, to be meaningful.

As we have already seen, the assumption that a word acquires meaning by referring to something outside itself, opens up a gap between language and what it seeks to express. Wittgenstein writes that this view suggests that 'lines of projection' are drawn between words and what they refer to: 'The lines of projection might be called the "connexion between the picture and what it depicts."'[28] Such a view of language and the world, as two separated, self-enclosed realms reflecting each other, requires the assumption that a set of metaphysical essences are their common source and explains their connection.[29] Concerning this common, metaphysical view, Hacker writes: 'This picture has seemed to many philosophers and psychologists to be persuasive, even unavoidable.'[30]

Derrida exposes this metaphysical essentialism as an impossible dream, resulting in the impossibility of bridging the gap between language and the world, resulting in scepticism (regarding others, communication, the world; after all, I cannot bridge the

---

24 McGinn, *Wittgenstein and the Philosophical Investigations*, 14.
25 Grene, 'Life, Death and Language', 275–6.
26 PI, 3ᵉ, 87ᵉ [§§5, 309].
27 Ibid., 108ᵉ [§432].
28 Wittgenstein, *Zettel*, 54ᵉ [§291].
29 Cf. Altieri, 'Wittgenstein on Consciousness and Language', 1409; Hacker, *Meaning and Mind*, 16; Hacker, *Mind and Will*, 36–7.
30 Hacker, *Meaning and Mind*, 25.

gap towards the world and do not know if what I say corresponds to that world) and solipsism (I can only assume that I have this feeling or this thought, but I cannot grasp the experiences of others and vice versa, because I do not know whether, for example, what I call pain is comparable to what they call pain).[31]

However, Wittgenstein avoids these problems, for in his view language does not strive to acquire meaning by referring (or *trying* to refer) to something outside itself, to something that 'accompanies' it. Therefore the supposed *failure* of such attempted connections, so crucial to deconstruction, can, from a Wittgensteinian perspective, be regarded as *irrelevant* for the meaningful functioning of language. Below, I will outline how the irrelevance of these two main aspects of this referential view, namely meaning through reference to an external object and meaning through reference to an accompanying mental intention, is demonstrated by Wittgenstein's discussion of ostensive definition and private language, respectively.[32]

2.1. Ostensive definition

Wittgenstein writes that there seem to be two ways of explaining the meaning of a word: through 'verbal' and through 'ostensive' definitions. A verbal definition explains a statement with the help of another statement. An ostensive definition is, in the words of McGinn, 'an act of giving the meaning of a word by pointing to an exemplar'.[33] Wittgenstein adds: 'The verbal definition, as it takes us from one verbal expression to another, in a sense gets us no further. In the ostensive definition however we seem to make a much more real step towards learning the meaning.'[34] Obviously, verbal definitions only make connections within language, and do not bring us from language to reality. Therefore, ostensive definitions appear to be the only way of connecting words with something outside language. Baker and Hacker offer the following summary of the enormous importance of ostensive definitions, at least for the view of language criticized by Wittgenstein:

> ostensive definitions provide the only possible means for correlating words with things. Only an utterance of the form 'That is . . .', together with the gesture of pointing at something, can be used to correlate a word with a thing. There must be ostensive definitions in *every* language. They are necessary for language to represent reality. [. . .] Every ostensive definition forges a link between language and the world.[35]

---

[31] Ibid., 25–6.
[32] Altieri points out that these two exponents, 'meaning by reference' and 'meaning as anchored in [. . .] an agent's intentions', are also the two main targets of Derrida's deconstructions of the referential picture of language (Altieri, *Act & Quality*, 32); cf. 'Derrida's two basic philosophical claims – that philosophy requires a notion of *propre sens* and cannot secure the concept, and that discourse is always plagued by overdetermined possibilities which cannot be adequately constrained. [In order to say what I mean (*vouloir dire*), I must use terms that can mean without my presence.] I want to argue, instead, that Wittgenstein can handle these claims' (ibid., 39, 36).
[33] McGinn, *Wittgenstein and the Philosophical Investigations*, 42.
[34] Wittgenstein, *The Blue and Brown Books*, 1.
[35] Baker and Hacker, *Understanding and Meaning*, 36.

Through ostensive definition 'we seem to pass beyond the limits of language and to establish a connection with reality itself', writes Wittgenstein.[36] But, to that end, the connection established by the ostensive definition must be unequivocal, infallible and definitive.[37] 'Otherwise, ostensive definition could not provide the foundations of language. If every ostensive definition were ambiguous or left open questions about the application of the defined word, it would require supplementation', conclude Baker and Hacker, '[a]ny attempt to supplement an ostensive definition [. . .] must be either redundant or inconsistent with the meaning already assigned to it'.[38]

However, ostensive definitions are not capable of fulfilling this lofty task assigned to them, argues Wittgenstein. They do not meet the heavy requirements mentioned. He writes:

> Now one can ostensively define a proper name, the name of a colour, the name of a material, a numeral, the name of a point of the compass and so on. The definition of the number two, 'That is called "two"' – pointing to two nuts – is perfectly exact. – But how can two be defined like that? The person one gives the definition to doesn't know what one wants to call 'two'; he will suppose that 'two' is the name given to *this* group of nuts! – He *may* suppose this; but perhaps he does not. He might make the opposite mistake; when I want to assign a name to this group of nuts, he might understand it as a numeral. And he might equally well take the name of a person, of which I give an ostensive definition, as that of a colour, of a race, or even of a point of the compass. That is to say: an ostensive definition can be variously interpreted in *every* case.[39]

Wittgenstein asks: what have we actually accomplished when we explain a word by pointing at an object in the world? We should picture this process as the afore-mentioned 'lines of projection' running from word to reality. That a certain connection has been made between word and object, does not say anything yet about how that connection should be understood. Peter Winch offers the following example: say that I have a desk with different labels attached to it – 'brown', 'rectangular', 'desk', 'furniture', 'late-Victorian', et cetera. Each of these labels can be regarded as an ostensive definition. But, in themselves, these designations do not say anything, after all, I do not know what – which aspect of the object – is explained by which label. 'I have got to understand how the label is being used, its grammar; otherwise I just don't know what has been labelled. In other words, the *lines* of projection don't do what is required of them; they only function in the context of a *method* of projection', writes Winch.[40]

However, that ostensive definitions are ambiguous and can be misunderstood, does not imply, as Derrida maintains, that language fails to (unequivocally) 'mean', as the gap between language and reality has proven to be unbridgeable. Rather it tells us that, in our philosophical questioning of how language acquires meaning,

[36] Quoted in ibid.
[37] Hacker, *Meaning and Mind*, 99.
[38] Baker and Hacker, *Understanding and Meaning*, 36.
[39] PI, 11ᵉ–12ᵉ [§28].
[40] Winch, 'Introduction: The Unity of Wittgenstein's Philosophy', 13.

we have attributed a role to ostensive definitions that they cannot and do not fulfil. Ostensive definitions appear to connect the structures of our language use with the reality outside those linguistic structures, as sort of 'pointers' that connect our words to a certain part of reality, which consequently fills those words with their meaning.[41] This is not the case: 'The thought that one can justify our grammatical rules by reference to reality confusedly trades on the misconception that an ostensive definition exits from language, links language to reality', writes Hacker.[42] Instead, an ostensive definition remains *within* language: it takes place completely 'intra-grammatically'. When I point at the afore-mentioned desk and say 'This is brown', then the words 'this', 'brown', my pointing finger and the brown object that I am pointing at are all part of the grammatical structures of language. They all function as symbols in a linguistic utterance, and, there, they have to behave according to the rules of grammar.[43] Although my pointing hand and the desk are not words, they have been absorbed into a linguistic utterance, and function as a part of language – as is shown by the fact that I can replace them by descriptions, for example, by saying, instead of 'this is brown': 'this desk that stands in front me is brown'.

So, it is not reference to something in the world, but the grammar, the structures of language, that make an utterance meaningful: the word 'brown' acquires meaning in the context of colour words, for example, as an answer to the question which colour something is, but not, for example, which shape it has. We tend to think that the meaning of something being 'brown', and that brown is darker than yellow, and that brown is not a primary colour, is determined by the 'nature' of colours in the reality outside language.[44] But Wittgenstein counters this idea. Grammar is autonomous, 'arbitrary' in relation to reality. He writes:

> One is tempted to justify rules of grammar by sentences like 'But there really are four primary colours.' And the saying that the rules of grammar are arbitrary is directed against the possibility of this justification, which is constructed on the model of justifying a sentence by pointing to what verifies it.[45]

Baker and Hacker emphasize that by calling grammatical rules autonomous and arbitrary, Wittgenstein does not mean that they are 'unimportant', 'a matter of caprice', of 'individual choice', that another system would work just as well, that it is easily replaceable, or that there are no reasons why grammar has a certain form.[46] Rather he means that the workings of grammar cannot be justified by referring to reality because that justification itself would have to be expressed using the grammar that one is trying to justify. Pointing out a colour is not a definition securing the meaning of the word 'brown', but a description of something according to the rules of grammar.[47] An ostensive definition supplies a linguistic rule, not a justification of that rule. Baker

[41] Hacker, *Meaning and Mind*, 99.
[42] Hacker, *Mind and Will*, 219.
[43] Baker and Hacker, *Understanding and Meaning*, 184.
[44] Cf. Baker and Hacker, *Rules, Grammar and Necessity*, 330–1.
[45] Wittgenstein, *Zettel*, 61ᵉ [§331].
[46] Baker and Hacker, *Rules, Grammar and Necessity*, 329–30, 336.
[47] Hacker, *Mind and Will*, 220–1.

and Hacker: 'There is no such thing as justifying grammar by reference to reality. For grammar determines the bounds of sense, what it makes sense to say. Hence it determines what is to be called "a description of reality".'[48] It is grammar that makes our words meaningful.

2.2. Private language

However, there is still the other aspect of the referential picture of language: meaning through reference to an accompanying mental intention. Even if I cannot unequivocally point out something in the world to someone else, do I not, for myself, have a clear idea in my head of what I am saying, of what I am pointing at? And could we not say, then, that the meaning of my words is anchored in the thoughts, the intentions that I have while speaking? As Hacker writes: 'So the fundamental form of correlation of words with things is mental ostension. Indeed, this must be the only form of correlation when the expressions thus correlated are names of sensations, feelings, or sense-data.'[49] It seems as if the meaning of processes that take place 'inside' me – for example, thinking, feeling, experiencing – can only be defined through this 'pointing-in-myself' (mental ostension). This view seems to be strengthened by the fact that my knowledge of what takes place inside me (for example, whether I am in pain right now) appears to be direct and indubitable. So, although my words do not acquire meaning by accurately mirroring objects in reality, it seems as if the mental processes that take place inside me, at least provide the source of meaning of my own language use.

However, Wittgenstein shows that this whole picture of the connection between words and mental intentions as the source of meaning is mistaken. He does so by means of his so-called private language arguments. These descriptions are directed against the misconception outlined in the previous paragraph, that we could call 'semi-solipsism', to use Hacker's term.[50] At its heart lies the conviction that a word spoken by me derives its meaning from a mental image that I have derived from my own experience. For example, I know what pain is from my own experience – I have experienced pain, have a certain mental image (memory) of it and that image gives meaning to my use of the word 'pain'. This view is *semi*-solipsistic because it assumes that this works the same for everybody else: everybody looks inside and names their mental images, which subsequently supply the meaning to their words, and thus everyone knows the meaning of pain from their own experience of pain.[51] According to Wittgenstein, however, language cannot possibly function in this way. He illustrates this impossibility by means of his thought experiment of the 'beetle in a box':

> If I say of myself that it is only from my own case that I know what the word 'pain' means – must I not say the same of other people too? And how can I generalize the *one* case so irresponsibly?

---

[48] Baker and Hacker, *Rules, Grammar and Necessity*, 332; also: 'whether that description is true or false is another matter, which is settled by reality' (ibid.).
[49] Hacker, *Meaning and Mind*, 99.
[50] Ibid., 206.
[51] PI, 88ᵉ [§315].

Now someone tells me that *he* knows what pain is only from his own case! –
Suppose everyone had a box with something in it: we call it a 'beetle'. No one
can look into anyone else's box, and everyone says he knows what a beetle is only
by looking at *his* beetle. – Here it would be quite possible for everyone to have
something different in his box. One might even imagine such a thing constantly
changing. – But suppose the word 'beetle' had a use in these people's language? –
If so it would not be used as the name of a thing. The thing in the box has no
place in the language-game at all; not even as a *something*: for the box might even
be empty. – No, one can 'divide through' by the thing in the box; it cancels out,
whatever it is.[52]

This thought experiment illustrates that, if we regard the meaning of a word as being
determined by essentially private images, everyone could have very different images in
their head (for how am I to know whether others have the same thing, the same image
in their heads as I do?), while the word in question continues to have a specific use
(meaning) in language. In other words: these private images simply cancel each other
out in the way language actually functions.

However, Wittgenstein's point extends further. It would not only be impossible
for us to understand *each other* if private images determined the meaning of our
words; if so, it might seem as if individuals would be able to use words according
to their common function while at the same time still associating those words with
very different, essentially private images that cannot be communicated.[53] But it
would also be impossible, according to Wittgenstein, for me to give meaning to *my
own words*: an individual cannot give meaning to such a private language.[54]

The whole idea that a word acquires meaning through a connection with a mental
image starts with the thought that Wittgenstein formulates as follows: 'now I simply
associate names with sensations and use these names in descriptions'. So, I have a
sensation and I apply a certain label to it. Wittgenstein adds: 'Let us imagine the
following case. I want to keep a diary about the recurrence of a certain sensation. To
this end I associate it with the sign "S" and write this sign in a calendar for every day
on which I have the sensation.'[55] This might seem in order, but we should wonder what
has actually been achieved by such a naming. 'Making a noise while concentrating
one's attention on a sensation does not make the noise a name of anything, for it
does not normatively determine what to do with this noise on subsequent occasions.
It does not lay down a norm of correct use', writes Hacker.[56] Being able to say that
'S' occurs, requires a justification of what 'S' means, a definition of what 'S' is; and

---

[52] Ibid., 85ᵉ [§293].
[53] This option (that Wittgenstein goes on to refute) calls to mind what Derrida says about being
essentially unable to communicate what I want to say; I cannot constrain the associations attributed
by the auditor to my words because of their iterability.
[54] Cf. 'The thrust of this argument is no that *others* cannot understand a radically private language,
hence such a language is of no great use or interest, but rather that *I* could not understand such a
putative language' (Hacker, *Meaning and Mind*, 97).
[55] PI, 78ᵉ [§258].
[56] Hacker, *Meaning and Mind*, 101.

simply saying 'S' to yourself, while having a certain sensation, does not provide such a definition. For how do I know whether I correctly remember that which I have impressed upon myself? When, the next time, I say 'Yes, this, too, seems "S" to me', I am doing so without any criteria to judge the correctness of my description. I say what I think is right, but it is impossible to judge whether it is right, whether it is the same sensation. So, I cannot have a consistent understanding of my own private images, and therefore of the meaning of words supposedly based on those images, for they stand in need of a criterion of correctness, which is something I cannot possibly formulate and uphold privately. Against what would I test my definition? Judging whether 'this', the feeling I have right now, is 'pain', within the limits of private language, is always left to the whims of memory. Wittgenstein writes: 'whatever is going to seem right to me is right. And that only means that here we can't talk about "right"'.[57]

This process of language use being accompanied by a looking-inside, by mental images that connect to our words, is irrelevant to language acquiring meaning. An individual can never maintain a private definition of, for instance, 'pain'. The individual's ability to name something and use that word in a meaningful way presupposes – is made possible by – the grammatical structures that are already in place in language, and that enable the use of that word. As Wittgenstein writes:

> When one says 'He gave a name to his sensation' one forgets that a great deal of stage-setting in the language is presupposed if the mere act of naming is to make sense. And when we speak of someone's having given a name to pain, what is presupposed is the existence of the grammar of the word 'pain'; it shews the post where the new word is stationed.[58]

McGinn explains: 'Wittgenstein is not suggesting, quite absurdly, that what a speaker feels is irrelevant to our concept of pain [. . .]. It is rather that there is nothing independent of [. . .] grammar that serves to fix what we mean by the word "pain"'.[59]

Here, as with his description of ostensive definitions, Wittgenstein shows that the meaning of a word (for example, 'pain') is not caused by the thing I am referring to – in this case, the feeling I am pointing to in myself – but by the grammatical structures that 'surround' my use of the word, and that determine what counts as a meaningful use of it. And again, this does not mean, as Derrida maintains, that language 'fails' in a certain way, by being unable to connect words to intentions, to mental images that are thought to provide those words with meaning. For, such a failure would depend on the undermining of an alleged aspect of language that is actually irrelevant, that plays no part in the process of meaning-acquisition by words. The criteria for meaningful language use lie in the grammar of our public language.

---

[57]   PI, 78ᵉ [§258]; cf. Hacker, *Meaning and Mind*, 97, 101.
[58]   PI, 78ᵉ [§257].
[59]   McGinn, *Wittgenstein and the Philosophical Investigations*, 140.

2.3. Language as life-form: Wittgenstein's 'Games' versus Derrida's 'Play'

Wittgenstein writes: 'to imagine a language means to imagine a life-form.'[60] This idea of the life-form applies 'to historical groups of individuals who are bound together into a community by a shared set of complex, language-involving practices', writes McGinn.[61] The rules of language are not determined by reality but result from the communal structures of groups of individuals. A language-game presupposes a group of people who relate to each other and to the world in a certain way. And although the grammar of a language-game is autonomous (in the sense that it cannot be justified by referring to an object or to mental images), that does not mean that language on the one hand, and the world on the other, are completely unrelated. On the contrary: the structures of life-forms and language-games *determine* the meaning we confer upon reality, and how we relate to it. The grammar of the word 'pain' determines what I can and cannot meaningfully describe as pain.

The difference between this Wittgensteinian account and the Derridean one is aptly summarized by the opposition between the Wittgensteinian notion of 'games' (*Spiele*) and the Derridean notion of 'play' (*jeu*). For Derrida, play is an activity of language itself, the uncontrollability of meaning: 'One could call *play* the absence of the transcendental signified as limitlessness of play, that is to say as the destruction of onto-theology and the metaphysics of presence.'[62] The play of language means that language always escapes man's grasp. As Grene writes: '[play] is the game *of* the world (*le jeu du monde*), it plays with us. As flies are to wanton boys, we could almost say, are we to our words.'[63] This uncontrollability, this ambiguity forms the 'seed-bed' of deconstruction, which is not a process resulting from (or controllable by) choices and decisions, but something that is 'at work' in language itself. As Truong Rootham writes: 'deconstruction is what language does of itself'.[64] For Wittgenstein, on the other hand, the notion of language-*games* stresses that language always functions within structures shared by a certain group of language users.[65] Boswell summarizes the difference as follows:

> A language-game in Wittgenstein must be played by more than one participant, whereas 'play' in Derrida is a dynamic property of language itself. [. . .] Derrida argues that there is no way to shut down the play of meanings. [. . .] the text in Derrida's vision remains always shut off and alienated, helplessly incapable of saying what it intends or of intending what it says. [. . .] [F]or Wittgenstein, language does not displace us from the world but rather takes place 'in' that world, specifically

---

[60] PI, 7^e [§19].
[61] McGinn, *Wittgenstein and the Philosophical Investigations*, 51.
[62] Derrida, *Of Grammatology*, 50.
[63] Grene, 'Life, Death and Language', 269.
[64] Truong Rootham, 'Wittgenstein's Metaphysical Use', 42.
[65] Cf. 'the term "language-*game*" is meant to bring into prominence the fact that the *speaking* of language is part of an activity, or of a life-form' (PI, 10^e [§23]).

among people in language-game situations. Far from alienating us from others, language can only exist as a product of communal agreement between others.[66]

Whereas for Derrida the play of language results in the impossibility to express ourselves or the world, Wittgenstein's descriptions of language-games show that community and reality are always implied when language is being used. A language-game always presupposes a limit to possible doubt, a limit that is set by the life-form shared by a group of people.

3. The virtues of the late-Wittgensteinian language view

When Derrida speaks of the autonomy of language, he means that language is not able to forge a connection with reality and, thereby, secure (accurate) meaning. As a result, according to Derrida, language functions as the free, uncontrollable play between signifiers. In Wittgenstein's opinion, in turn, assuming such a (failed) connection between language to reality is simply mistaken and irrelevant for the actual functioning of language: language does not seek or need a referential connection; meaning is secured through the structures of language-game and life-form, and not subject to endless play.

These differences have a decisive impact on the rest of Derrida's and Wittgenstein's philosophies, and on the fiction they can be seen to inform. According to Derrida, we are trapped in the impossible dream of language expressing essences (through reference and intention), while this striving must always inevitably fail. In Chapter 3, we have seen the problematic effects of this view of language in the postmodernist metafiction of John Barth; it ends in solipsism and scepticism, in non-committal introversion. However, given that, as I have shown, the processes allegedly disrupting language are irrelevant to its meaningful functioning, we can now use these insights to address the solipsism and scepticism tied to or resulting from deconstruction and metafiction. Below, we will see that, conversely, Wittgenstein emphasizes the importance of community, trust and commitment. In Wallace's work, too, these notions can be seen to be used against the threat of solipsism and scepticism.[67]

3.1. Hyperreflexive solipsism versus community and reality

In Chapter 1, we have already seen that the works of Wallace, Eggers and Foer portray hyperreflexivity as a considerable problem of contemporary existence. Such excessive,

---

[66] Boswell, *Understanding David Foster Wallace*, 28–30.
[67] Cf. D. T. Max's insightful comment that 'late Wittgenstein was Wallace well; early Wittgenstein, the author depressed' (Max, *Every Love Story Is a Ghost Story*, 45), together with Shain's remark, 'metaphilosophically, Derrida's views are closer to the *Tractatus* than to the *Investigations*' (Shain, 'Derrida's References to Wittgenstein', 83). The scepticism and solipsism that plague the depressed, addicted characters in *Infinite Jest*, and that can also be seen to follow from certain philosophical views, were existential realities for Wallace, who struggled with depression throughout his life.

continuous self-reflection underlies Derrida's deconstructionist philosophy and Barth's fiction (as well as that of Ellis, which embodies the acceptance of that theoretical problematization as fact) and can in their work be seen to lead, ultimately, to solipsism. In Barth, characters and text are caught, as fictional entities, in a necessarily ill-fated struggle to put into words (give reality to) their thinking, their selves (in Ellis, this struggle has been replaced by the acceptance of the lack of self).[68]

Wallace's debut novel *The Broom of the System* illustrates the hindering effect of such self-reflective objectification through a story that can best be read as a variation on Wittgenstein's thought experiment of the 'beetle in a box'. The story – which is actually more of a parable or allegory – is about a woman '[who] has a pale-green tree toad living in a pit at the base of her neck'. The woman completely identifies herself with this anomaly, can solely see herself as 'the woman with a toad in her neck', and as such cuts herself off from the rest of the world: 'The tree toad is the mechanism of nonconnection and alienation, the symbol and cause of the [...] woman's isolation; [...] she's got a reptile living in a pit in her neck, after all, and is to that extent alienated and different and comparatively disgusting, with respect to the world'. The story conjures up a solipsistic universe, in which the members of a group of people who, like the toad woman, turn out to each possess a different creature, and who define themselves on the basis of this difference. This creates a situation of non-connection in which everybody possesses something else (in their 'beetle-box', we could say), and therefore cannot know what the other is experiencing: 'the mother has a narrow-tailed salamander, one brother has a driver ant, one sister has a wolf spider, another has an axolotl, one of the little children has a sod webworm. Et cetera et cetera'.[69]

Wallace's story illustrates the solipsistic problems caused by the (hyper)reflexive attitude. For this attitude causes us to regard our so-called internal processes – thoughts, feelings, et cetera – as objects, 'as things that we have', and ourselves as the exclusive 'owners' of those objects. Although this might seem like an innocent line of thought, the effects are irrevocably far-reaching. Hacker writes: 'If we think of "pain" as the name of a sensation we have on the model of names of objects (in a generalized sense of 'object'), then solipsism is unavoidable. A public language cannot be construed as the confluence of private languages that happen to coincide'.[70] If I

---

[68] Because of its incorporation of self-reflection, Wallace's approach to fiction is sometimes interpreted as simply another instance of postmodernist writing, like that of Barth. However, such interpretations ignore that a 'key shift is that whereas in Barth self-referentiality is almost always calling attention to the text, so you are never allowed to forget that you are holding words in your hand and not a world', as Charles Harris explains. He states: 'In David's work, the self-referentiality reflects the work of the consciousness trying to rid itself of itself, and constantly second-guessing itself, so there is a psychological edge to it' (Harris quoted in 'Endnotes: David Foster Wallace', at 00:32:55–00:33:25). For Wallace, as we have seen, increased reflexivity is simply part of the reality of contemporary existence, and is portrayed as such; his inclusion of self-reflection in his works is not aimed at the exposure of the artificiality of its own fictional structures, but at the portrayal of what it is to live in current times. Therefore, it is a mistake to label these elements in the works of Wallace (and Eggers and Foer) as 'postmodernist' techniques, for they have a completely different aim. I will elaborate this, further on in this study (see Chapter 7).

[69] Wallace, *The Broom of the System*, 187, 189.

[70] Hacker, *Meaning and Mind*, 50, 207.

think that for me the meaning of the word 'pain' lies anchored in an essentially private experience, then I will never be able to speak meaningfully about my pain with others. It is impossible to connect myself to the outside world if I, from a reflexive attitude, regard the meaning of myself and the world to be derived from processes that take place inside me.

However, Wittgenstein has shown, through his private language arguments, that my understanding of myself and the world cannot and does not depend on such looking-inside. A word has a certain meaning because it has a certain use in language. That use is not invented by me at the moment that I pronounce a word while I point inside. Rather, it is the other way around, Wittgenstein writes: 'Grammar tells what kind of object anything is.'[71] It is grammar – the use a certain word has in language – that determines what I mean when I say 'I am in pain.' Or, as Wallace summarizes Wittgenstein's position: 'a word like *pain* means what it does for me because of the way the community I'm part of has tacitly agreed to use *pain*.'[72]

As we have seen: 'to imagine a language is to imagine a life-form.'[73] The grammar of language-games, the way language is used and, therefore, how words acquire meaning, is embedded in the activities and life structures of groups of people. I have learned how certain things are said, and that is also how I learned to use the utterance 'I am in pain.' A child is initiated, step by step, in these linguistic structures: first it expresses how it feels by crying, but gradually the child learns – as it learns to use language – to say 'I am in pain', instead of crying.[74] Wittgenstein's description of language use and acquisition, explains McGinn, shows that 'the adult human subject emerges slowly, as its life becomes structured through the acquisition of new and more complex language-games'. She continues: 'The human subject does not exist absolutely, either as consciousness or as body, but develops or evolves as it acquires a more and more intricate form of life, and as the phenomena that constitute its world become, thereby, ever richer and more complex.'[75]

According to Wittgenstein, the idea of 'introspection' – supposedly gaining 'knowledge' of myself by a reflexive looking-inside – rests on a misconception, leading to several absurdities, which he illustrates by means of the statement: 'only I can know whether I am really in pain'. Wittgenstein comments: 'In one way this is wrong, and in another nonsense.' First of all: 'If we are using the word "to know" as it is normally used (and how else are we to use it), then other people very often know when I am in pain.'

---

[71] PI, 99ᵉ [§373].

[72] Wallace, 'Tense Present', 47n23.

[73] PI, 7ᵉ [§19].

[74] Cf. 'A child has hurt himself and he cries; and then adults talk to him and teach him exclamations and, later, sentences. They teach the child new pain-behaviour' (PI, 75ᵉ [§244]). McGinn explains: '"I'm in pain" [. . .]. The way that these words connect with what the child feels is through his learning to use them as a technique for giving expression to how he feels. No act of inner ostensive definition is required for the words 'I'm in pain' to connect with what is felt; the connection is secured by the grammar of the concept, by virtue of the fact that it is used as a new means to express what is felt. The connection between 'pain' and what a subject feels is achieved, not by where the child looks when he learns the word, but by the grammar of the concept that he is being taught' (McGinn, *Wittgenstein and the Philosophical Investigations*, 121–2).

[75] Ibid., 52.

And, secondly, Wittgenstein says: '[It can't be said of me at all] that I *know* I am in pain. What is it supposed to mean – except perhaps that I *am* in pain?'[76] 'Knowing' that I am pain only makes sense when in a normal situation we can imagine the opposite being the case, that is, '*not* knowing' that I am in pain – and that is not possible.[77] 'There is no such thing as being ignorant of whether one is in pain; someone who said "Maybe I am in agony but I do not know whether I am" would not be understood', writes Hacker, who adds: 'Of course, I may be uncertain as to whether the sensation I have qualifies as a pain or is just a rather unpleasant feeling, but *that* doubt does not stem from ignorance' – this doubt is not a matter of knowing or not knowing. The utterance 'I am in pain' (or even, 'I know I am in pain') is not a knowledge statement, but an expression of how I feel, of my pain.[78]

Gaining self-knowledge is not a matter of introspection, of reflexively looking-inside, claims Wittgenstein. The whole idea of introspection is an illusion built on the above-discussed mistake of regarding thoughts and feelings as objects that we somehow have in possession, and, subsequently, of regarding gaining self-knowledge as observing (and thus knowing) these objects 'in' ourselves.[79] This does not mean, though, that according to Wittgenstein no real self-knowledge or self-observation is possible; only that an introspective account of them is a mistaken representation of what they signify. Hacker summarizes Wittgenstein's view as follows: 'There is indeed such a thing as self-knowledge and self-consciousness; but it does not consist in an array of reports and descriptions of one's sensations, perceptions, thoughts, and feelings' – it does not consist of looking-inside and expressing the acquired self-knowledge in 'statements or reports of what I know'. Rather I gain self-knowledge by observing how I express myself in the world, through 'expressions of what I think, manifestations of my will and purpose, and avowals of what I feel or perceive'. So, an individual can only gain meaningful self-knowledge, not by turning inside, but by turning to his connection to the world, a community of meaning that he shares with others, and there, in his relations to that community, by looking at 'the character of his reactions, the pattern of his desires, and the subtle nuances of his motives'.[80]

---

[76] PI, 76ᵉ [§246].

[77] Cf. 'But I can't be in error here; it means nothing to doubt whether I am in pain!' (ibid., 84ᵉ [§288]).

[78] Hacker, *Meaning and Mind*, 57–8; cf. 'It makes sense to say of a person that he knows such-and-such is the case only if it also makes *sense* to deny that he does. For "A knows that *p*" is meant to be an empirical epistemic proposition, and hence to exclude an alternative. But if there is no such thing as A's being ignorant of *p*, i.e. if it is unintelligible that *p* should be the case, yet A does *not* know it, then "A knows that *p*" says nothing about A's knowledge. So if the form of words "A was in pain but he did not know it" is ruled out, i.e. if it does not describe a specifiable possibility, the "A was in pain and he knew it" is likewise excluded' (ibid., 57).

[79] Cf. 'We confuse the ability to say how things are with us, what we are feeling of perceiving, what we think or want, with the ability to *see* – with the mind's eye, of course – and *therefore*, we think, we can say what is "within" us. [. . .] an avowal of pain is not the report of an observation. [. . .] To say another "I'm furious with you" is typically to express my anger, not to describe something accessible to me alone by introspection, just as to say "I love you" is to avow one's affections, not to describe oneself or one's emotion' (ibid., 58–9).

[80] Ibid., 60.

This view of self-consciousness and self-knowledge has a number of significant parallels with the view of Jean-Paul Sartre, which we examined in Chapter 1.[81] For Sartre, too, the tendency to regard thoughts, feelings and 'character' as objects that we somehow possess inside ourselves is a crucial mistake in how we view ourselves. Sartre's own view of how we gain knowledge of the self is very similar to that of Wittgenstein: self-knowledge, for Sartre, is not a result of consciousness looking at itself, as if it is an object (this is impossible, after all, consciousness is mere intentionality, a nothingness), but of consciousness looking at its own relations to the world. According to Wider: 'Sartre finds that his analysis of self-consciousness reveals that the Other's existence is necessary for a person to come to full self-consciousness', a finding which, argues Wider, resembles Wittgenstein's argument 'that the necessary condition for a person's ability to ascribe states of consciousness to himself is that others could do so as well'.[82] Both Sartre and Wittgenstein regard self-consciousness as inextricably tied in with the world outside consciousness, a view which undermines the threat of solipsism.[83] As Sartre writes:

> This conception of the Ego is, in my view, the sole possible refutation of solipsism. [. . .] So long as the *I* remains a structure of consciousness, it will always remain possible to contrast the consciousness with its *I* on the one hand and all other existents on the other. [. . .]
> But if the *I* becomes a transcendent, it participates in all the world's vicissitudes. [. . .] My I, indeed, *is no more certain for consciousness than the I of other men*. It is simply more intimate.[84]

Hacker's summary of Wittgenstein's view aptly illustrates the similarity with Sartre:

> To say to another 'I'm furious with you' is typically to express my anger, not to describe something accessible to me alone by introspection, just as to say 'I love you' is to avow one's affections, not to describe oneself or one's emotion. Hence too it is not necessarily the case that I am in a better position than others to say what I see, feel, or think. [. . .] What *is* true, [. . .] is that *my word* has privileged *status*. This is not because I have access to a private peep-show and so can describe what I see in it, whereas others cannot. Rather, it is because what I say is an expression

---

[81] Cf. 'what Sartre and Wittgenstein are trying to capture is a similar phenomenon. Sartre is trying to capture the difference between a self-consciousness that is irreflexive, not directed at *oneself*; and a self-consciousness that is expressly directed at oneself as an individuated entity among other entities in the world. Wittgenstein is trying to capture the difference between a use of the world "I" which does not, and one which does, refer to a particular entity in the world, individuated as an object of thought' (Longuenesse, 'Self-Consciousness and Self-Reference', 5).

[82] Wider, 'Hell and the Private Language Argument', 120; also: 'One of the strongest parallels to Sartre in Wittgenstein's rejection of the possibility of a private language for inner states or sensations is his rejection of the analogical argument', i.e. the argument that we base our understanding of concepts on 'knowledge' of our own case, while Wittgenstein shows that in fact there is no use of speaking, e.g. of 'knowing' that I am in pain (ibid., 125–6).

[83] Cf. Dwyer, 'Freedom and Rule-Following in Wittgenstein and Sartre'; Longuenesse, 'Self-Consciousness and Self-Reference: Sartre and Wittgenstein'.

[84] TE, 50.

or manifestation of my experience, whereas what others say of me is not. [. . .] The privileged status of my utterances is *grammatical*, not epistemic.[85]

However, within the context of the current study, one of the important differences between Wittgenstein and Sartre might be that the latter tends to qualify everything outside consciousness – including my own expressions and actions in the world – as 'objects' – except for the consciousness of the other, which is recognized as another 'being-for-itself', while Wittgenstein warns against the misleading effect of such a general use of the term 'object'.

3.2. Ironic scepticism versus reality and trust

The other problem outlined in Part 1 of this study is that of endless irony. In its constant postponement of all judgement and affirmation, irony leads to a condition of utter non-committal. In the philosophy of Derrida and the fiction of Barth and Ellis, this endless irony follows from the 'failure' of language: if there always remains a gap between language and world, how can I then speak of what is real? What can I trust, what can I commit to?

Wallace's work provides a critique of this postmodernist scepticism, this endless doubting of truth and reality. A striking example, especially when viewed in light of Wittgenstein's refutation of such linguistic scepticism, is the so-called Eschaton chapter from *Infinite Jest*. In the novel, 'Eschaton' is a nuclear war simulation game played by the students of the Enfield Tennis Academy.[86] During the Eschaton game that *Infinite Jest* describes in detail, it starts to snow in Enfield, and a quarrel breaks out among the participants (followed by a massive brawl) as to whether the snow falling on the tennis courts affects the nuclear war being simulated there.

This quarrel revolves around one of the issues central to the current chapter, namely the relation between reality and representation (in language, for instance).[87] The Eschaton story needs to be read in light of a fable by Jorge Luis Borges, about a map that completely coincides with reality (the territory described by the map), causing the territory (reality) to gradually disappear, leaving just the map (that is, the artificial representation). Borges's fable has come to symbolize the postmodernist idea that the 'artificiality' of representation infects or even completely usurps reality.[88] However, in the Eschaton episode in *Infinite Jest* the distinction between reality and representation is described as crystal-clear. For as one of the students, Michael Pemulis – the 'eminence gris' of

---

[85] Hacker, *Meaning and Mind*, 59–60.
[86] Eschaton is played with 8 to 12 people, divided into teams each representing a nuclear block (i.e. NATO, Warsaw Pact, China), on 4 adjacent tennis courts, representing the earth. The game is played with 400 intensively used, 'dead' tennis balls; each tennis ball represents a nuclear warhead, which a player can launch ('lob') with his or her racket (cf. IJ, 322–4, 333).
[87] Cf. Bell and Dowling, *A Reader's Companion to Infinite Jest*, 88.
[88] Borges is one of Barth's main literary forebears. The idea of reality having been replaced by artificial representation is akin to the notions of 'absence' and 'unreality' described by Derrida and Barth. Borges's fable is also used by postmodernist philosopher Jean Baudrillard in his book *Simulacres et simulation*, as an apt illustration of the contemporary, postmodern condition.

Eschaton – yells: 'It's snowing on the goddamn *map*, not the *territory*.' He adds: 'Real-world snow isn't a factor if it's falling on the fucking *map*!' However, the issue is exploited by some players to disrupt and frustrate the game play. The resulting debate is related to the hyperreflexive (postmodernist) inclination to abstraction and generalization, and thereby to losing sight of the practice of the specific situation concerned: Hal gets 'lost in a paralytic thought-helix', as he realizes that he finds the 'real-snow/unreal-snow snag in the Eschaton extremely abstract but somehow way more interesting than the Eschaton itself'. Pemulis characterizes the dispute as the result of 'equivocationary horseshit', which he subsequently counters with the following, Wittgensteinian arguments.

First of all, that a language or a game (language/game) presupposes the existence of reality. As Pemulis says: 'that is what makes Eschaton and its axioms fucking possible in the *first* place. [. . .] it's like *pre*axiomatic'. A language/game exists by the grace of a group of people dealing with each other and the world in a certain way. That reality outside the language/game cannot be doubted; it is presupposed. Subsequently, the fact that the grammar (that is, the rules or 'axioms', in Pemulis's case) of a language/game is autonomous (as explained in section 2 of this chapter) means that it cannot be justified by referring to reality (judging whether that reality is correctly expressed by that grammar), but that does not mean that the language/game is completely detached from reality. For the grammar of the language, or the rules of the game, are in fact a determination of the relation to reality: these rules determine how reality is to be handled. The grammar of the word 'pain' determines what can be signified as pain. The same holds for the Enfield students wanting to play Eschaton: to be able do so, they have to commit to the rules of the game that imply a certain relation to reality. It is not possible, says Pemulis, when 'asswipes like Jeffrey Joseph Penn run roughshod over the delimiting boundaries that are Eschaton's very life blood'.[89]

In his writings, Wittgenstein often compares the arbitrariness of the rules of a language to that of the rules of a game, for example, chess. The rules of chess are not an *expression* of the 'nature' of the game – of the nature of the different pieces: king, queen, knight, bishop, et cetera – rather they *determine* the nature of the game (which moves the different pieces are allowed to perform). 'The rules of grammar are arbitrary means: their *purpose* is not (e.g.) to correspond to the essence of negation or colour', writes Wittgenstein, '– but is the purpose of negation and of the concept of colour. As the purpose of the rules of chess is not to correspond to the essence of chess but to the purpose of the game of chess'.[90] We can of course decide, while playing chess, to ignore the existing rules and make up new ones, but then we are not playing chess anymore, and there is a good chance that our opponent does not understand what we are doing (as in the Eschaton game, which ends in a massive fight).[91] The space or freedom of movement within language is limited by the structures within which the language is used and that enable a certain utterance (movement) to have meaning.

For Derrida, conversely, the arbitrary character of language means that language is always equivocal, ambiguous, polysemic. As a result, Derrida maintains, for example,

---

[89] IJ, 333, 334, 335, 337, 338, 335.
[90] Quoted in Baker and Hacker, *Rules, Grammar and Necessity*, 331.
[91] Cf. Hacker, *Mind and Will*, 234

that there is no such thing as normal meaning directly understood: misapprehension is an essential, inevitable possibility with every utterance. Understanding an utterance always requires interpretation. That we regard certain utterances as normal and claim to understand them directly, does not mean that no interpretation takes place; it merely means that a certain interpretation has become dominant. In 'Force of Law' Derrida writes: 'Each case is other, each decision is different and requires an absolutely unique interpretation which no existing, coded rule can or ought to guarantee absolutely.'[92]

Wittgenstein strongly opposes such an interpretivist view.[93] He wants to show, above all, that with such a view the notion of interpretation loses meaning (we are not saying anything meaningful about it anymore). Wittgenstein establishes that the interpretation of an utterance must itself be an utterance too: 'an *interpretation* is something given in signs. It is this interpretation as opposed to a different one (running differently). – So when we wanted to say "Any sentence still stands in need of an interpretation", that meant: no sentence can be understood without a rider.'[94] But then: how can an interpretation offer us understanding, given that the interpretation itself is also an utterance, which, in turn, requires its own interpretation, if it is to be understood?[95] Wittgenstein adds: 'It would almost be like settling how much a toss [in a dice game, AdD] is to be worth by another toss.'[96] In other words: if every utterance would require an interpretation, we would enter into an infinite regress of interpretations, and all understanding would become impossible, including normal meanings that we seem to grasp directly. Altieri explains:

> [Wittgenstein] does not deny that some modes of activity require interpretation, but he shows that interpretation, like other forms of behavior, has characteristic marks [. . .]. It makes sense to talk about problematic situations; it makes no sense to generalize these situations as the basic reality for those cursed by consciousness and language.[97]

For Derrida, certainty (understanding) requires complete presence, which, as we have seen, is impossible: there is always absence, and therefore always doubt. Conversely, according to Wittgenstein it is simply impossible to make sense of the view that each utterance entails uncertainty and requires interpretation: 'If you tried to doubt everything you would not get as far as doubting anything. The game of doubting itself presupposes certainty.'[98]

---

[92] Derrida, 'Force of Law', 23.
[93] In one of Barth's works, the sentence 'There is one way to raise a cow', functions as an illustration of the supposedly inevitable ambiguity of language (thereby 'affirming Derrida's maxim', Fogel and Slethaug write). However, Wittgenstein would point out that to be able to begin communicating a sentence like that, all kinds of things would already have to be in place in language, and both speaker and receiver would already have to know how such utterances function, as a result of which any essential ambiguity is avoided (Fogel and Slethaug, *Understanding John Barth*, 103–4; cf. Altieri, *Act & Quality*, 43).
[94] Wittgenstein, *Zettel*, 41ᵉ [§229].
[95] Cf. 'if we now understand [the signs], by what token do we understand?' (PI, 109ᵉ [§433]).
[96] Wittgenstein, *Zettel*, 41ᵉ [§230].
[97] Altieri, 'Wittgenstein on Consciousness and Language', 1406.
[98] Wittgenstein, *On Certainty*, 18ᵉ [§115].

For Derrida, the inevitable ambiguity and uncertainty of language is connected to his contention, discussed above, that all concept-definition implies the metaphysical ideal of pure essences, which is simultaneously inevitable and impossible. To acquire (unequivocal) meaning, notions *have to* but *can never* be pure and precise. According to Derrida, this fundamental lack of clarity undermines the whole idea of meaningful speech.

However, Wittgenstein writes: 'Many words in this sense then don't have a strict meaning. But this is not a defect. To think it is would be like saying that the light of my reading lamp is no real light at all because it has no sharp boundary.'[99] Notions, utterances in general, do not have to be pure and exact in order to function. The ideal of purity is not derived from how language actually works, but imposed on language by philosophy, which then concludes that this criterion is not met: 'When we believe that we must find order, must find the ideal, in our actual language, we become dissatisfied with what are ordinarily "propositions", "words", "signs". The proposition and the word [. . .] are supposed to be something pure and clear-cut.' However: 'The more narrowly we examine actual language, the sharper becomes the conflict between it and our requirement. (For the crystalline purity of logic was, of course, not a *result of investigation*: it was a requirement.)' Wittgenstein concludes that we should free ourselves from this illegitimate requirement: 'We have got on to slippery ice where there is no friction and so in a certain sense the conditions are ideal, but also, just because of that, we are unable to walk. We want to walk: so we need *friction*. Back to the rough ground!' The requirement of exact definition, of ideal circumstances, by definition cannot be satisfied – we 'imagine that we have to describe extreme subtleties, which in turn we are after all quite unable to describe with the means at our disposal. We feel as if we had to repair a torn spider's web with our fingers', Wittgenstein writes. So, the ideal of purity sends us on a quest without end, and impedes – just like the endless postmodernist postponement of judgement, of affirmation – our ability to 'walk', that is, our ability to understand language in the right way. Such understanding can only be attained under non-ideal conditions (where there is 'friction'), in other words: in the actual use of language. Notions cannot and do not have to be pure. They have to 'do' what is 'asked' of them, namely, be meaningful within the context of their use. Wittgenstein writes: 'The sign-post is in order – if, under normal circumstances, it fulfils its purpose.'[100] Wittgenstein summarizes his analysis of the actual functioning of language in the following conclusion: 'ordinary language is all right.'[101]

In Wittgenstein's descriptions of how language functions, 'trust' plays an important role. He writes: 'I really want to say that a language-game is only possible if one trusts something (I did not say "can trust something").' The parenthesis is telling: Wittgenstein says that the language-game is not based on the reliability (infallibility) *of* language, but on my willingness to rely *on* (my trust *in*) language, the words and the meaning they have within a certain language-game. Again, Wittgenstein refers to the impossibility of doubting certain things (here, the fact that

[99] Wittgenstein, *The Blue and Brown Books*, 27.
[100] PI, 39ᵉ, 35ᵉ, 40ᵉ, 39ᵉ [§§105, 107, 106, 87].
[101] Wittgenstein, *The Blue and Brown Books*, 28.

he has two hands functions as an example): 'the fact that I use the word "hand" and all the other words in my sentence without a second thought, indeed that I should stand before the abyss if I wanted so much as to try doubting their meanings – shews that absence of doubt belongs to the essence of the language-game'.[102] Henry McDonald writes: 'without such trust, such affirmation of the reality that language describes and expresses, we could neither "believe" nor "deny", neither recognize truth nor perceive illusion'.[103] The trust that the language-game requires, that makes it possible, is not based on 'knowing' – on having certain propositional knowledge – but on a 'certainty' that results from the practice of action, of using language. Wittgenstein writes: 'You must bear in mind that the language-game is so to say something unpredictable. I mean: it is not based on grounds. It is not reasonable (or unreasonable). It is there – like our life'. Elsewhere, he writes: 'I would like to regard this certainty, not as something akin to hastiness or superficiality, but as a form of life.'[104]

4. A late-Wittgensteinian view of fiction

We now have to look at the collection of language-games that we call literary fiction.[105] In general, 'fiction' might be said to be 'whatever contrasts with what is a matter of fact'.[106] We might therefore ask: from what do these fictional texts, containing stories about non-existent persons and made-up events, derive their meaning? And how can these stories about non-existent things offer us insights – as we often assume they do – into our humanity and the world we live in? The so-called non-referentiality of literary fiction forms a problem for both the traditional (referential) and the postmodernist view of language. This problem, and the resulting confusions, are avoided, however, by the view of literature that results from the later Wittgenstein's descriptions of language. They imply a clear, preferable view of what literary fictions are and what they offer us, a view of literature as directly connected to our 'life-form', as an investigation of our cultural semantic structures – an investigation that forms an important foundation for our use of complex, moral concepts (that is, concepts that are tied in with what we regard as human virtue). The late-Wittgensteinian view offers a general description of literary fictions, and can therefore be applied to all such texts. However, in my opinion, the workings of this view are expressly illustrated by Wallace's fiction.

---

[102] Wittgenstein, *On Certainty*, 66ᵉ, 48ᵉ [§§509, 370].
[103] McDonald, 'Crossroads of Skepticism', 275.
[104] Wittgenstein, *On Certainty*, 73ᵉ, 46ᵉ [§§559, 358].
[105] As explained in the Introduction, throughout this study, I use the terms 'fiction' and 'literature' as interchangeable terms, referring to the works of Wallace, Eggers and Foer. For a further elaboration on the use of these terms, see footnote 11 in the Introduction.
[106] Gaut, 'Fiction', 309.

4.1. The problem with the traditional and postmodernist view

The non-referentiality of literary fictions poses a problem for both the traditional (referential) and the postmodernist view of language.[107] According to both views, language can only acquire meaning by referring to reality. The traditional view implies that fiction is inevitably cut off from reality; after all, fiction does not refer to anything existent. As we have seen, the postmodernist–deconstructivist view implies a similar gap between fiction and reality, in this case based on the assumption that not just fiction, but *all* language use fails in its attempts to refer to reality, and, as a result, fails to achieve unequivocal meaning.

So, both views lead to the conclusion that literary fictions have no meaning in the strict sense of the word, let alone make potentially truthful claims about the world. Literature must be regarded as a form of linguistic pretence, an atypical form of language use that is intrinsically cut off from expressing anything about the world. This is the outcome, despite the many differences between them, of both the postmodernist and the traditional referential view, of both 'the generally accepted position within literary studies which accepts Saussure's theory of the sign as an axiomatic demonstration that language and fiction are irrevocably cut off from the world', and 'the philosophical realism which assumes that the ideal model of language *tout court* is that of offering knowledge of the disposition of objects in the world and for which fiction therefore must a fortiori be secondary or derivative', writes David Schalkwyk.[108] This, perhaps surprising, consensus is the result of the fact that both views take the referential character of language as their starting point; consequently, 'to abandon the claim that a use of language, for instance literary language, is "referential", is to abandon the claim that that use of language is directly revelatory of the nature of anything extra-linguistic', explains Bernard Harrison.[109]

However, both views still try to ascribe to literary fiction a certain, indirect relevance for the acquisition of insight into the world we live in. In the postmodernist view, because language never succeeds in referring to reality, as a result of which meaning is always partly fictional, the value of literature lies in the fact that it explicates this fictionality and in doing so, indirectly teaches us that what we regard as reality is also always constructed, partly fictional. A popular suggestion, based on the traditional

---

[107] Wallace refers to these two positions as being involved in a 'battle' against each other, and also to the fact he himself prefers a third position (which he summarizes – too briefly – as a 'combination' of both): 'the real battle in fiction has been between writers and theorists who see fiction as essentially a recursive mechanism – William Gass and John Barth and the 60s guys [. . .]. The other side of it says that fiction is not recursive, it's referential – the old realistic "language is a system of pictures, of words, and I'm gonna write a story that makes you imagine that this stuff is really going on". [. . .] what I'm trying to do involves trying to write fiction that works both ways' (Wiley, 'Interview').

[108] Schalkwyk, 'Fiction as "Grammatical" Investigation', 287–8.

[109] Harrison, 'Imagined Worlds and the Real One', 101 [the printed text actually reads 'is *not* "referential"' (emphasis added, AdD], but the context makes abundantly clear that 'is referential' is the correct, intended formulation; AdD]; cf. 'if one accepts the basic insights of the referential picture of language, one faces difficulties [. . .], for it opens a gap [. . .] between literature and the world' (Huemer, 'Introduction: Wittgenstein, Language and Philosophy of Literature', 12–13).

view, is that fiction does not portray our reality, but that it does portray other, possible worlds, that function as alternatives to our own world. So, according to both views, fiction does not portray the reality of the world we live in, but can, indirectly, offer us other perspectives from which to view that reality.[110]

It is my opinion that these suggestions do not accurately describe what happens when we read fictional texts or do justice to the significance of literature to our use of language. The postmodernist suggestion that the value of literature lies in its demonstration of the constructed, fictional nature of our reality, seems far too narrow – for one thing, it would not do justice to the involvement we usually feel with what we are reading. Martin Stone writes that it does not take into account 'the kind of interest we take in literature, what literature means to us, and why we value it'.[111] John Gibson states that such views 'leave no room for speaking sensibly about one of the reasons we so value the literary work of art', and that important reason is, according to Gibson, 'that [literature] can be read, not only for fictions, but also for life'.[112] What is lost in the postmodernist view, 'is the possibility that the specialness of literature might consist in nothing more – but also nothing less – than the special sort of interest we take in texts we might call literary. Or perhaps we might say: in the use we make of them', writes Stone.[113]

The suggestion, from the traditional view, that fiction, through its creation of other worlds, can only provide indirect perspectives to our reality – alternatives that we can choose to contemplate in relation to our own reality – offers an artificial, roundabout way, the exact route of which I find very hard to trace. Moreover, can the suggested distinction, between indirect, 'literary' language use and direct, 'normal' language use, be made at all, in this manner? For example, do we always refer to reality in our supposed normal language use? And also, how can the apparently atypical, literary form of language use, that only acquires meaning indirectly, occupy such a central position in our language? We learn and refine our use of language partly by reading literary fictions. Furthermore, these texts often function, to quote Wolfgang Huemer, as 'paradigmatic cases of informed uses of language'. Huemer points out that the traditional view cannot explain, 'for example, why the *Oxford English Dictionary* often quotes from literary texts to illustrate the use of a word'.[114]

4.2. Wittgenstein: Fiction as grammatical investigation

The late-Wittgensteinian view of language and fiction avoids these problems and laboured solutions. We have already seen that, according to Wittgenstein, meaning is not determined by reference to the world or to the thoughts of the speaker, but results from the communal structures of language users. In light of this view,

---

[110] Gibson, 'Reading for Life', 111, 114–15.
[111] Stone, 'On the Old Saw, "Every Reading of a Text Is an Interpretation". Some Remarks', 191.
[112] Gibson, 'Reading for Life', 110.
[113] Stone, 'On the Old Saw', 191.
[114] Huemer, 'Introduction', 4.

the non-referentiality of literary texts does not pose a problem: fiction is not an atypical form of language use or a form of linguistic pretence intrinsically cut off from expressing anything about the world. As a result, the late-Wittgensteinian view enables us to see literature as most of us experience it: as directly concerned with our form of life, with the world we live in. Huemer writes: 'the meaning of a word is not radically altered when it is used in a literary text, [. . .] and the expressions used do not refer to other kinds of objects or other possible worlds; rather they are well grounded in our actual world'.[115]

For the world has already been brought 'into' language. When I want to define the colour brown and say 'This is brown', while pointing at a brown object, what happens is not the world – in this case the brown object – transferring meaning onto my utterance, but the world being transferred *into* the grammatical structures of language. This 'appropriation' of the world by language is logically prior to truthful or untruthful descriptions of the world by means of these appropriated terms.

So, before literary texts can present us with fictional descriptions (which perhaps do not *refer* to anything that *exists* in the world), the world has already been absorbed into language, and, therefore, there is no gap between fiction and the world. Wittgenstein writes that a word is first 'a *means* of representation' (and for that, the world has been entered into the structures of language through definitions), before it can be used to actually describe something, and we can rightfully speak of 'something that is represented' by that word.[116] In other words, as Schalkwyk writes: 'in terms of its *sense* [. . .] a work of fiction is no less beholden to the world than a factual report may be: each depends in the same way on prior appropriations of the world'.[117]

An oft-heard (formalistic) definition holds that literary fiction is not about *what* is said, but *how* it is said.[118] Literary language is language concerned with itself, language 'for its own sake'. But even if one were to define literary fiction in such a formalistic way, as 'language occupied solely with itself', it might, as Harrison writes, 'just in virtue of doing that, be occupied with exploring reality'.[119] Schalkwyk speaks, in this respect, of the 'logical dissolution of the traditional gap between word and world, form and content'.[120] In a fictional text, what is 'there', 'on hand', is the only thing we have. This is exactly what Wittgenstein wants us to realize about language in general, namely that 'everything lies open to view', in the words and social structures within which they

---

[115]   Ibid., 5.

[116]   PI, 21–22ᵉ [§50].

[117]   Schalkwyk, 'Fiction as "Grammatical" Investigation', 289.

[118]   Huemer, 'Introduction', 5.

[119]   Harrison, 'Imagined Worlds and the Real One', 102.

[120]   Schalkwyk, 'Fiction as "Grammatical" Investigation', 292. In this context, Schalkwyk also writes that this Wittgensteinian description of language 'accommodates both the "mimetic" notion that literature is concerned with what is "typical" of human beings and their engagement with each other and the world, and the formalist insistence that literature is concerned with its own representative status. To suggest that literary fiction is concerned with criterial or grammatical relations is, following Wittgenstein's specific conception of the relationship between grammar and objects, criteria and symptoms, necessarily to confirm both roles, and to do so, not in the spirit of a mix-and-match or golden-mean compromise, but as a direct result of the logical dissolution of the traditional gap between word and world, form and content' (ibid.).

are used – there, we can find everything we need: 'We want to *understand* something that is already in plain view.'[121] In fiction, we are limited to what is right before us. We cannot, for instance, ask characters for additional information about what they are thinking while they are saying something. A piece of fiction forces us to look solely at what is 'in plain view': the language, the words, but therefore automatically also the communal structures within which those words have meaning. 'A language occupied with bringing into consciousness the structure and rationale of the practices underlying its possibilities [. . .] will be a language occupied with language', writes Harrison, '[b]ut at the same time it will be concerned with reality, because it will be concerned with the specific modes of engagement of language with reality via the practices which ground its possibilities as language.'[122]

Perhaps, then, we could regard literary fiction as a form of grammatical investigation – in the Wittgensteinian sense – as showing and exploring the structures of our language use, of how certain concepts are used within our language communities, and, accordingly, which uses of those concepts we find meaningful or not: 'By telling stories [novels] provide the context necessary for exploring not only the grammar of our language, but also the limits of our form of life', writes Huemer.[123]

4.3. Wittgenstein: Fiction as source of paradigmatic cases

Moreover, as Gibson rightly suggests, this investigation into the grammatical structures of our communal reality should not only be regarded as purely 'reportive' but also, or perhaps *rather*, as 'foundational'.[124] In *Culture and Value*, Wittgenstein writes: 'Nothing is more important though than the construction of fictional concepts, which will teach us at last to understand our own.'[125] Fiction not only tells us how concepts are being used, but also plays an important role in establishing what certain complex concepts *mean*. Our meaningful language use – that we describe the world in similar terms, that we understand the descriptions offered by others and by ourselves – presupposes public standards. Wittgenstein gives the example of the 'standard meter' in the Paris archive, that, in its 'archived' capacity, determines what a meter 'is', what we mean by the word 'meter'. This example, according to Gibson, 'functions to draw our attention to the *institutional* setting of language [. . .]. We are expected to look for the *actual* places in which we store our instruments of representation.'[126] We should ask ourselves: where do we archive our more complex, cultural concepts? Gibson writes:

> Consider those words that are crucial to our more cultural – our more 'humanistic' – renderings of our world. [. . .] Think, for example, of 'love' or 'suffering', of 'exploitation' or 'devotion'. Consider our ability to cast ourselves as in possession

---

[121] PI, 43^c, 36^c [§§126, 89].
[122] Harrison, 'Imagined Worlds and the Real One', 102.
[123] Huemer, 'Introduction', 6.
[124] Gibson, 'Reading for Life', 122.
[125] Wittgenstein, *Culture and Value*, 85^c.
[126] Gibson, *Fiction and the Weave of Life*, 63–4.

of this or that sort of self, of our ability to depict others in very precise shades of moral, political and cultural identity. How is it that we can represent reality in *these* hues, that we can describe features of our world as expressive of or otherwise falling under *these* concepts?[127]

Contrary to the meaning of, for instance, brown, 'these words – these features of human circumstance (for they are much more than just words, of course) – would seem to have no corresponding "object" that could be archived. They designate extremely complex representational practices', writes Gibson.[128] On what public standards is our use of such notions based; how has their use been 'archived' in our social structures? Gibson writes that these complex concepts – contrary to words like 'brown' or 'meter' –

> are grounded on not 'things' or 'objects' at all but very elaborate visions of human life. And how could something like *that* be archived? How could we make something like that public such that a shared way of representing – of *seeing* – our world could be built upon it? [. . .] The claim I want to urge is that it is *the fact* of literature that most perspicuously represents this possibility.[129]

Gibson's suggestion is that our use of these concepts cannot take place without their being 'founded' by what we could call 'paradigmatic cases':[130] examples that are common knowledge within a certain life-form, that function as a sort of standard, and thereby form part of the foundation of our meaningful use of certain concepts. Literary fiction and other cultural products could be seen as important suppliers of these paradigmatic examples.

I have little difficulty explaining to somebody what I mean by the word 'brown' or 'meter'. But how do I explain other, more complex concepts, like 'love', to use Gibson's example? I could contend that my relationship with my wife is a perfect example of 'love', but most people do not know me or my wife, and will therefore not find my example very illuminating. If, on the other hand, I suggest the story of *Romeo & Juliet* as an example of 'love', then almost everybody will know what I mean. The concept of 'love' cannot be explained (or defined) in one sentence; it requires stories to acquire meaning.

The most influential of these stories we can regard as 'paradigmatic cases' that form the foundation of the meaning that we ascribe to certain concepts, that 'traverse' our talk of them. We can imagine that such complex concepts are not based on just one but many of these paradigmatic cases, and that they do not signify rigid standards, but change, together with the stories that, as time passes, we come to find either more or less meaningful. People make different selections from the

---

[127] Gibson, 'Reading for Life', 120–1.
[128] Ibid., 121.
[129] Ibid.
[130] I derive this term from an above-quoted statement by Huemer, who holds that from the late-Wittgensteinian position literature can be regarded as a 'practice central to our language without which we might not even be able to master a language as complex as ours in the first place' (Huemer, 'Introduction', 7).

available paradigmatic cases and emphasize different aspects. Concepts change as the paradigmatic cases, on which we base our understanding of them, change. Such transformations are changes of our life-form, of our socio-cultural identity. The novels of Wallace, Eggers and Foer are part of such transformation processes.[131]

Conclusion

Whereas the deconstructive strategy of showing that concepts can never meet their own standards and that words can never adequately express thoughts (there is always an element of absence in every striving towards presence) implies a referential picture of language (one can only speak of a gap between language and world, and between language and thought, if one assumes that language tries to acquire meaning by referring to the world or thought, by attempting to bridge that gap), Wittgenstein, on the other hand, holds that language does not acquire meaning by referring to something (a thing in the world, or a thought in my head). Instead, he views language as part of a form of life, as embedded in the communal structures of groups of individuals. This Wittgensteinian approach to the functioning of language entails a view of literature that does not regard fictional texts as expressing something unreal, but as a fundamental activity within a community of language users: literary fictions offer detailed depictions of concepts that are essential to our collective understanding of reality.

The fiction of Wallace, Eggers and Foer actively reassumes this function of literature; a function that was discredited by deconstruction and metafiction, which saw language and fiction as cut off from the world – a view that we have shown leads to solipsism and scepticism. Conversely, the novels analysed in this study emphasize a deep concern with the notions of sincerity, reality-commitment and community (in a close, but of course largely implicit accord with the Wittgensteinian 'virtues' of 'trust', 'reality' and 'community').

---

[131] When he set out to write *Infinite Jest*, Wallace wrote to editor Michael Pietsch: 'I want to author things that both restructure worlds and make living people feel stuff' (Max, *Every Love Story Is a Ghost Story*, 173).

Engagement

In an article on Dostoevsky (another cornerstone of existentialism),[1] Wallace states: 'Dostoevsky wrote fiction about the stuff that's really important. [. . .] His concern was always what it is to be a human being – that is, how to be an actual *person*, someone whose life is informed by values and principles.'[2]

We can recognize this view of the self underlying *Infinite Jest*'s portrayal of its characters. First, in a negative way, that is, through what happens when the self is not developed in such a manner – the characters suffering from addiction are described as having no self, as being 'empty' inside. Conversely, Don Gately is described as 'returned to himself', after his life, as a result of his participation in AA, has become informed by values and principles.[3]

In an interview, Wallace connects the afore-mentioned emptiness or sadness to a lack of exactly those values and principles that, according to Dostoevsky (and Wallace) are needed to be an actual person: 'some of the sadness' that seems to '[infuse] the culture right now has to do with this loss of a sense of purpose or organizing principles', and the 'addictive impulse which is very much in the cultural era right now, is interesting and powerful only because it's an obvious distortion of a religious impulse or an impulse to be part of something bigger'. To be clear: Wallace is not calling for a return to old truths and values. In other interviews, he says: 'we're going to have to *make up* a lot of our own morality, and a lot of our own values'. And: 'there's probably no absolute right in all situations handed down from God on the stone tablets. [. . .] it is our job as responsible decent spiritual human beings to arrive at sets of principles to guide our conduct in order to keep us from hurting ourselves and other people.'[4]

The following chapters will offer an analysis of the search for such values and principles, in the novels of Wallace, Eggers and Foer, through their portrayal of the notions of sincerity, reality-commitment and community.

---

[1] Marino, 'Introduction', xv.
[2] Wallace, 'Joseph Frank's Dostoevsky', 265.
[3] IJ, 694–5, 860.
[4] Silverblatt, 'Interview'; Lipsky, *Although of Course You End Up Becoming Yourself*, 159; Karmodi, 'Interview'.

6

Sincerity

Introduction

In response to the problems of hyperreflexivity and endless irony, analysed in Part 1 of this study, the novels of Wallace, Eggers and Foer portray the desire and search for an existential attitude that places (renewed) emphasis on qualities such as, honesty, openness, trust and vulnerability. I will call this attitude, which will be analysed in the course of this chapter, sincerity. Several scholars have viewed the desire for sincerity as an important theme in the novels of Wallace, Eggers and Foer, however, mostly without defining what that sincerity means exactly, and without adequately mapping out where we can find it in their work.[1] Also, the literary trend epitomized by these works has been labelled by certain critics as 'new sincerity'; after my initial restraint in using the term, I will adopt it throughout this chapter, and provide it with a philosophical foundation.

I regard the 'sincere' attitude sketched out in these novels as a basis from which the contemporary Western individual is again able to realize meaningful connections to the world and to others. These two aspects – the meaning of one's choices and actions in the world, and that of one's relation to others – will be addressed in Chapters 7 and 8, as relations that are made possible by the attitude of sincerity, and that, at the same time, give further substance to that attitude, and as such, are part of its realization. This inevitably means that certain topics will already be referred to in this chapter, to subsequently be elaborated in the following ones. I shall regard the sincere attitude as the striving towards a basic virtue that makes possible the realization of other virtues. As was explained in the Introduction to this study, the term 'virtue' refers to what is needed to 'be' (to be human, a self), to live. Or as André Comte-Sponville writes: 'In the general sense, virtue is capacity; in the particular sense, it is human capacity, the power to be human.'[2]

Unless otherwise indicated, translations are mine.

[1] E.g. Kirsch, 'The Importance of Being Earnest'; Scott, 'The Panic of Influence'. An exception is, e.g. Kelly, 'David Foster Wallace and the New Sincerity in American Fiction'. However, Kelly's broad approach is different from the more specific one employed in this chapter, which offers a philosophical analysis of the portrayal of sincerity in the studied works.

[2] Comte-Sponville, *A Short Treatise on the Great Virtues*, 3.

As with the novels' critique of hyperreflexivity and irony, their search for an attitude that overcomes these problems, can be seen in light of the existentialist tradition. The novels involve themselves in the discussion about the basic attitude that this tradition pursues, and, in my opinion, contribute a much-needed corrective to it. In section 1, I will outline the context of this discussion, by examining the two main 'ideals' of self-becoming, namely 'sincerity' and 'authenticity'. I will summarize how the self and its relations to the world and to others are regarded in both ideals. Thereupon, I will argue my choice for sincerity, as the virtue that is portrayed in the novels of Wallace, Eggers and Foer, and that provides a possible answer to contemporary problems. Subsequently, in section 2, I will use the heuristic perspective of Sartre's view of consciousness to rehabilitate sincerity as the contemporary individual's basic existentialist virtue (thereby showing Sartre's own critique of sincerity to be inconsistent with his own descriptions, and thus correcting and reconstructing the Sartrean view). This (redefined) virtue of sincerity implies a consciousness that has to 'exist' the tension of the becoming being that it is, and therefore has to constantly cast itself towards the world. On the basis of these connections to the world, consciousness can be seen to establish a sincere, stable self. It is important to note that the conceptual demarcations of this reconstruction of the Sartrean concept of sincerity are prompted by what the works of Wallace, Eggers and Foer describe. In section 3, the analysis of several case studies taken from these novels will show how therein we can recognize the formulated concept of sincerity. In turn, these case studies serve to underpin this new understanding of sincerity.

1. Sincerity versus authenticity

In this section, I will provide a critical overview of the notions of sincerity and authenticity. I will first outline both notions in a separate subsection, then sketch out what I perceive to be the consequences of both ideals (which priorities do they instil in an individual's existence?), and finally, I will argue that the virtue of sincerity best corresponds to the perspectives employed in this study.

1.1. Sincerity: Not for the self, but for the other?

'[A]t a certain point in its history the moral life of Europe added to itself a new element, the state or quality of the self which we call sincerity', writes Lionel Trilling. He defines sincerity as 'a congruence between avowal and actual feeling'.[3] The rise of the ideal of sincerity is connected to the birth of modern thought.[4] 'In distinctively premodern societies, [. . .] human beings experience themselves as placeholders in a

---

[3] Trilling, *Sincerity and Authenticity*, 2. Trilling's book counts as an influential study from which many of the other mentioned authors take their starting point as well (e.g. Taylor, Guignon and Sass – see further on in this section).

[4] Which, in turn, is of course the product of a whole series of developments, among other things: the religious individualism of the new, protestant forms of Christianity; the scientification of the view of the world; and the view of society as a human rather than a divine or cosmic product.

wider totality', writes Charles Guignon. But modernity gives rise to a split between the (inner) self on the one hand, and the (outer) totality of the world on the other: 'It is because of this split between inner and outer that the issue of sincerity becomes pressing in the seventeenth and early eighteenth centuries', Guignon observes.[5] As inner and outer are no longer seen to coincide, the self has to be (re)connected with the world by being 'sincere'.

Trilling opines that to us, in contemporary Western culture (although Trilling wrote this in the 1970s), sincerity comes across as an anachronism, about which we can only speak in a somewhat awkward or ironic way. Why is that? Because, claims Trilling, we realize that sincerity is an ideal that is pursued not for oneself but for the sake of others: sincerity is actually a social obligation, namely not to deceive others. The following words by Polonius, from Shakespeare's *Hamlet*, are often cited as a clear and distinctive expression of the nature and purpose of sincerity as a public duty: 'This above all – to thine own self be true, / And it must follow, as the night the day, / Thou canst not then be false to any man'.[6] Guignon writes: 'When we look at Polonius's words, [. . .] we see that he is thinking of being true to yourself not as an end in itself, but as a means to some other end.' With his words, Polonius is seen to be urging his son Laertes to be honest about himself, *in order* to be honest towards others. Guignon: 'there is no suggestion that being true to oneself is valuable in its own right. [. . .] It is a social virtue that is at issue here, not a personal virtue.'[7] The purpose of sincerity is always 'a public end', concludes Trilling, 'the correct fulfilment of a public role'.[8]

This is the main reason why Sartre, as well as other existentialist thinkers like Kierkegaard and Camus, seem so strongly opposed to the ideal of sincerity. After all, in light of the above, sincerity seems to be characterized by what Sartre describes as a striving to be in-itself (and what Kierkegaard calls 'immediacy'), that is, people who live according to this ideal, do so because they were taught to do so, without ever having thought about it themselves; they simply are what they are expected to be. Jacob Golomb summarizes this 'existentialist' view of sincerity as follows: 'sincerity is an externally imposed constraint. One is born to it and formed by the conditioning mechanisms of its educational institutions.'[9]

However, it remains to be seen whether this critique of sincerity is necessarily correct. Indeed, as a striving for a connection between the self and its actions in the world, sincerity has an undeniably public character, but in the above-quoted sources this has mistakenly led to a purely negative judgement. That sincerity reveals itself through action, and, consequently, is always public and (partly) aimed at the other, does not entail that it always involves fulfilling a public role and that it can therefore

---

[5] Guignon, *On Being Authentic*, 18, 35.
[6] Shakespeare, *The Complete Works of William Shakespeare*, 402.
[7] Guignon, *On Being Authentic*, 26–7.
[8] Trilling, *Sincerity and Authenticity*, 9.
[9] Golomb, *In Search of Authenticity*, 23. Eggers's *The Circle* ridicules such 'imposed' sincerity, in its portrayal of internet company 'The Circle', which advocates 'community' and 'sharing' as employee obligations. About main character Mae not sharing her kayaking hobby on her online profile, a colleague comments: 'How do you think other Circlers feel, knowing that you're so close to them physically, that you're ostensibly part of a community here, but you don't want them to know your hobbies and interests. How do you think they feel?' (Eggers, *The Circle*, 188).

not be undertaken for the self.[10] I will argue that this – the opening-up of the self, the connection of inner and outer that sincerity demands – is exactly what (according to the existentialist view, as well) the contemporary individual stands in need of, while the demands of the ideal of authenticity (a constant self-reflection and distancing from corrupting outside forces) largely contribute to the problems that were analysed in Part 1 of this study. I will return to this further on in this section.

1.2. Authenticity: The true I is autonomous

Just as sincerity is characterized by an outer-directedness, so authenticity, on the other hand, is characterized by a strong emphasis on the inner (at the expense of the outer). This is the 'improvement' that authenticity embodies, compared to sincerity. As a historical development, the replacement of the latter by the former is connected by Charles Lindholm to the rise of the 'notion of fundamental human equality', for it

> implies and even requires belief in a sacred and universal moral self, existing beneath the social framework. This premise not only supports the political right of each person to life, liberty, and the pursuit of happiness, it can also motivate a search for a transcendental spiritual essence that is assumed to lie beneath the surface of roles and convention. When individuals try to commune with and express this hypothetical inner source, sincerity has evolved into authenticity.[11]

Every individual has his own spiritual core, an uncorrupted self independent of the outside world. This view of the self as autonomous can be found in the work of Jean-Jacques Rousseau, who is probably the first important theorist of authenticity. According to Rousseau, man is good by nature, but societal structures and social bonds suppress the authentic, natural self and, thereby, cause sin to enter into the world. Therefore, Rousseau's ideal man, his famous 'noble savage', lives 'in himself', in complete autonomy.[12]

In Romanticism the self becomes 'the highest and most all-encompassing of all that is found in reality. [. . .] In the end, mind itself is the ultimate source and nature turns out to be its product', writes Guignon.[13] From these developments flows the ideal of

---

[10] Cf. Mariëtte Willemsen's suggestion that one can impossibly be sincere towards others and at the same time insincere, untruthful to oneself; and that sincerity, truthfulness towards oneself seems to be a condition of sincerity towards others (Willemsen, 'Friedrich Nietzsches getuigenis', 148).

[11] Lindholm, *Culture and Authenticity*, 6; cf. Sass, who points out the growing concentration on the self, on the individual's 'inside', that takes places in, among other things, the 'Copernican revolution' of Immanuel Kant's philosophy. Sass writes: 'Kant initiated the transcendental turn whereby the structures of reality came to be seen as subordinate to those of the knowing subject' (Sass, *Madness and Modernism*, 302, 327).

[12] Rousseau, *The Confessions*; e.g. '[My mind] needs to go forward in its own time, it cannot submit itself to anyone else's', 'For I knew that my experience did not apply to others' (118, 67). Quoted in Gutman, 'Rousseau's Confessions: A Technology of the Self', 100.

[13] Guignon, *On Being Authentic*, 51, 62 (cf. 64). This Romantic process of the subject becoming 'absolute' is what Kierkegaard reacts to in his philosophy in general and in his critique of irony specifically. The aesthete is led, by what Kierkegaard sometimes calls 'romantic' irony, to the denial of everything except his own consciousness, except the dream world he creates in his fantasy; cf. Chapters 2 and 4.

the autonomous subject, who is completely self-legislating, living purely according to his own self-acquired laws and insights, free from outside (social) constraints. Such a self embodies what we call authenticity, and it constitutes an ideal that still seems to be in place in our time. Sass writes: 'the point is not so much to be true to other human beings as to be true to oneself, to fulfil one's own inherent being and potential'.[14]

Now, most theorists of authenticity prefer to speak of authenticity as the product of continuous self-creation and development and not of an inherent, fixed self-*essence*. But if there is nothing 'inherent' about the authentic self, then the question arises as to whether we can even speak meaningfully about something – a self – that is at risk of being corrupted from the outside, in the first place. If authenticity requires the self to be fully autonomous – that is, not subject to any external influences, being completely self-determining – then that self-determination – if it is even possible – has to consist, by definition, of influences that are inherently present 'in' that self. In other words, the whole idea of an authentic self (over against the outer-directed ideal of sincerity) seems to depend on the implicit assumption of a profound, internal purity of the self that differs fundamentally from the impurity that lies outside it.

It is often suggested that our current age is still deeply influenced by Romanticism.[15] Sass, for example claims that, '[f]or some time now we have lived in a postromantic climate that [stresses] *authenticity*'.[16] Even the postmodernist deconstruction of the ideal of authenticity can be seen as motivated by a (Romantic) desire for authenticity. Deconstruction turns the ideal of being an autonomous, immanent self, free from external influences, against itself: it reveals authenticity to be impossible, as the subject is shown to be always the product of external forces, of societal structures that shape the individual. The result is a fragmented subject that can never be fully self-defining and that is, therefore, doomed to always be *in*authentic (this last conclusion follows from the fact that deconstruction always remains within the framework that it deconstructs). However, by presupposing the same ideal, that a subject can only be authentic if it is completely autonomous, and subsequently, through a self-reflective undermining of this ideal, exposing its impurity and thus inauthenticity, the deconstructivist drive to expose such self-undermining elements is itself a continuation of the same implicit longing for authenticity, for purity. Its drive to 'unmask' purports to offer, at a certain level, a truthful (authentic) disclosure of inauthenticity, aimed at liberating existence from such illusions. In this respect, postmodernism can be regarded as a continuation of Romantic thought.[17]

1.3. The consequences of both ideals

The ideal of *authenticity* requires constant self-reflection from the individual, analysing and securing his own autonomy, and distancing himself from the outside world, which

---

[14] Sass, *Madness and Modernism*, 99.
[15] E.g. Doorman, *De romantische orde*.
[16] Sass, *Madness and Modernism*, 99.
[17] Cf. Maarten Doorman, who writes: 'the fervour to unmask the authentic subject as fiction implies a utopian desire for an individual living freely, not burdened by the close-knit structures of the discourse that disciplines [the individual]' (Doorman, *De romantische orde*, 43).

is after all the source of inauthentic, corrupting influences. Therefore, authenticity, by its nature, cannot contribute to overcoming the existential problems discussed in Part 1. Indeed, it can be seen to greatly foster and aggravate these problems. As Guignon writes, in relation to such a striving for authenticity: 'One might begin to suspect that the true self [. . .] runs the risk of being maddeningly self-absorbed and selfish, constantly obsessed with herself, unable to let go and simply be part of the flow of things'.[18]

This becomes even more apparent when we look at the conception of art that has arisen in connection to the ideal of authenticity (and that, likewise, is still a very influential conception in our current age). According to this view, art, if it is to be authentic (that is, if it is to be regarded as art at all), has to be the expression of the creativity of the artist alone. Trilling explains: 'The work of art is itself authentic by reason of its entire self-definition: it is understood to exist wholly by the laws of its own being.'[19] This ideal has drastic consequences for what art 'does' and what it tries to accomplish, Guignon writes:

> [T]he new expressive conception of art drops both the interest in copying reality and the concern with pleasing an audience. All that really matters in art is that the creative genius authentically expresses him- or herself. It is expected that the audience will try to have the right experience in the presence of the work, and with luck a privileged few in the audience may have some inkling of what the genius imparts. But the artist is under no compulsion to communicate anything to anyone – indeed, the concern with communicating now begins to look like a sign that the work is not authentic.[20]

In fact, this ideal holds both for works of art and for the individual; these two 'categories' can be seen to melt into each other with the onset of the ideal of authenticity. With the above-described (exclusive) focus on the self and the disintegration of meaningful communication with the other (which is regarded as either unnecessary or impossible), solipsism and scepticism (the two philosophical 'diseases' following from the existential problems of hyperreflexivity and irony) are only a few steps away.

On the other hand, the objections against *sincerity*, outlined above, seem to me to be unfounded. The main objection is that sincerity implies a neglect of the self: it forces the individual to play a role, not for his own benefit, but for that of others, to conform to social patterns. However, there is no reason to think that sincerity, as the connection between self and action, necessarily leads to a neglect of the self, resulting from an exclusive focus on the other, or rather on the artificial role that the individual is expected to play.

There seems to be another objection against sincerity. If we think back to Trilling's definition of sincerity as 'a congruence between avowal and actual feeling', this seems to imply an individual, to quote Golomb, 'whose inner convictions

---

[18] Guignon, *On Being Authentic*, 92.
[19] Trilling, *Sincerity and Authenticity*, 99.
[20] Guignon, *On Being Authentic*, 75–6.

and commitments are congruent with that individual's behaviour', and '[such] correspondence presumes a static subject'.[21] In short, sincerity seems to imply a fixed, static self, with certain essential qualities that are sincerely communicated through an utterance or action. According to the existentialist view, the self does not possess such a fixed core; the self is not given but rather becomes, emerges, develops. For the existentialist thinkers included in this study, this second objection (assuming a static self) is linked to the first (performing social roles): the ideal of sincerity could be seen as making people think that they fully coincide with a certain being, namely, that which they should be according to the social order.

However, sincerity does not necessarily imply a static, essential self (as I have been arguing in the foregoing, it is rather the ideal of authenticity that necessarily implies some sort of true, inherent self). The connection between self and action means, above all, that the self *is* its actions (that the self comes into being in the world), and does not equal a naïve theory of the correspondence of inner and outer. When we speak of a sincere promise, the sincerity of that promise is judged by what I undertake to fulfil that promise, not by some internal state of being. Choosing, taking responsibility for my actions, is exactly what existentialist thinkers like Kierkegaard and Sartre desire from the individual.

1.4. 'New sincerity'

The terms authenticity and sincerity both have their inadequacies, due to their connotations. However, introducing a new term for the attitude that I want to describe would be overly pretentious and, more importantly, not very illuminating for the discussion at hand. Moreover, when we look closely at what seems to be the core of both notions, we can quite clearly make a distinction between them.

Authenticity implies a 'real' self – one's 'own' self – that is displayed in defiance of corrupting, external influences (authenticity requires autonomy). Sincerity, on the other hand, emphasizes the connection between self and action, and the importance of others in attributing meaning to these actions and to the self. Viewed in this way, both authenticity and sincerity could be seen to imply the erroneous conception of the self as something essential, fixed. But only the notion of sincerity, with its emphasis on the importance of the other and of the connection between the self and its actions, can also be regarded as expressive of a concept of the self as *external*, as shaped through choice and action (the subject of Chapter 7) and through community and dialogue with others (the subject of Chapter 8). Such a conception of the self arises from the works of Wallace, Eggers and Foer, in response to the problems of the self (hyperreflexivity, endless irony) analysed in Part 1.

The ideal of authenticity, as remarked above, can only foster and aggravate these problems. It requires constant self-reflection and autonomy (distance) in relation to the world and the other. It is what Charles Taylor calls a 'monological ideal': 'We are

---

[21] Golomb, *In Search of Authenticity*, 9.

expected to develop our own opinions, outlook, stances to things, to a considerable degree through solitary reflection. But this is not how things work with important issues, such as the definition of our identity.' Taylor and other philosophers who are critical of authenticity, such as Guignon, therefore propose a 'work of retrieval', that is similar to what I am suggesting in this chapter.[22] However, these authors retain the term authenticity for the adjusted ideal, ostensibly because they regard it as simply the term we use, the only viable term, when speaking of contemporary processes of self-becoming. As mentioned above, the self-ideal described by the existentialist philosophers employed in this study is also generally labelled as authenticity, although, to my knowledge, Sartre is the only one who explicitly employs the term as a label for what his existentialist philosophy can be seen to advocate.[23] Nevertheless, authenticity has become the standard term for the existentialist ideal of the self. In this study I critique this standard.

The biggest problem for the adjustment I would like to propose, is that all the existentialist philosophers we have discussed, at some point emphasize the importance of the autonomy of the individual. This aspect of existentialism generally receives a lot of attention, and accounts for its alleged social pessimism: existentialism is often seen as espousing the view that the individual, in his attempts to be a self, is in constant struggle with the outside world and with other people.

However, another important aspect of existentialism, which has remained relatively underexposed, casts a completely different light on its call to become a self and choose one's freedom, namely, the emphasis, by all the philosophers under consideration, on the importance of choice and action as well as the importance of others in self-becoming – this last aspect is, as will be shown in this and the following chapters, at its clearest in Camus and Wittgenstein. Furthermore, as we have seen, existentialism is opposed to the notion of an inner self, implied in the ideal of authenticity, and the related phenomenon of (isolated) self-reflection, which is seen to stifle choice, passion, action (reflection 'kills' action), the fundamental aspects of self-becoming. These important aspects are all better expressed by the term sincerity than by authenticity. Therefore, I will rename the attitude that accompanies existentialist self-becoming sincerity, and employ this term throughout the rest of this study. I will show that this 'forgotten' virtue, in a contemporary interpretation, is surprisingly attuned to our time and its problems.

---

[22] Taylor, *The Ethics of Authenticity*, 36, 35, 23.

[23] Kierkegaard does not use the term (although he is sometimes translated as doing so) – rather he speaks of 'passion', 'purity of will', et cetera, although his emphasis on the singular individual can be read as akin to the notion of authenticity described in section 1.2; however, the importance of choice and action fit the ideal of sincerity outlined in the rest of the chapter (also see Chapter 7, connecting this to Kierkegaard; in Chapter 8, I will also criticize Kierkegaard's underemphasis of the importance of others). Camus uses the term sporadically, but in a general sense, connected to something being real or true, not as embodying a clear notion of the self; e.g. 'Its movement, in order to remain authentic, must never abandon any of the terms of the contradiction that sustains it' (R, 285). For the rest, Camus can actually be seen as championing the importance of other-directedness for the meaningful existence of the self (especially in *The Rebel*), in a way that fits the notion outlined in the current chapter (also see Chapter 8, where this idea is elaborated in relation to Camus).

I regard sincerity as the attitude or virtue of wanting to form a stable self in the world; the individual who adopts this attitude, or aspires to this virtue, does not know whether or how he will succeed in striving towards it – just as the virtue of courage does not imply that the battle in which one acts courageously, is automatically won. Comte-Sponville writes: 'There is no such thing as absolute sincerity, [. . .] but this does not prevent us from aspiring to such absolutes, and making the effort to approximate them. [This effort] is itself already a virtue.' Defined as such, sincerity is the desire to show yourself in the public domain 'as yourself'; and it is only in such actions that the (sincere) self comes into being, just as a courageous self originates in courageous actions. Sincerity is a virtue that does not suffice by itself, but it does form the base that makes all virtuousness possible (for an insincere virtue is not a virtue).[24] In the next section, I will formulate a view of sincerity along these lines, in dialogue with Sartre's philosophy.

2. Sincerity: A Sartrean, existentialist ideal

The basic attitude of sincerity outlined in this chapter, serves as an alternative to the problems of hyperreflexivity and endless irony. These problems can be regarded as manifestations of bad faith. The reasoning that consciousness follows to endow itself with bad faith, strongly resembles the irony that Kierkegaard's aesthetes use to declare all distinctions to be invalid and immaterial (for example, the aesthete A, from *Either/Or*, who states: 'Marry, and you will regret it. Do not marry, and you will also regret it. Marry or do not marry, you will regret it either way').[25] Similarly, the individual in bad faith decides, on the basis of the insight that he can never believe enough, that he can therefore believe anything; that is, it does not matter what he believes, he can believe anything he wants. The connection is further strengthened by Sartre's description of irony at the beginning of the section on bad faith: 'In irony a man annihilates what he posits within one and the same act; he leads us to believe in order not to be believed; he affirms to deny and denies to affirm; he creates a positive object but it has no being other than its nothingness.'[26]

In this section, I will give further philosophical substance to the notion of sincerity, as the alternative to the bad faith of hyperreflexivity and endless irony. For that purpose, I will resume and extend the Sartrean perspective employed in Chapter 1. Sartre's early, existentialist writings contain multiple notions that, at first sight, might appear as an alternative to bad faith. He mentions, for instance, good faith, sincerity and authenticity. However, he employs these terms inconsistently, with varying meanings; as a result, it is unclear what the alternative to bad faith looks like, and what it is called. Therefore, with the portrayals offered by the novels in the back of

---

[24] Comte-Sponville, *A Short Treatise on the Great Virtues*, 196, 197.
[25] EO 1, 38.
[26] BN, 70; cf. 'In *Being and Nothingness*, irony is associated with bad faith' (LaCapra, *A Preface to Sartre*, 142).

our minds, and with the help of critical reconstructions of Sartre's philosophy (most importantly, those of Ronald Santoni and Joseph Catalano), I will try to formulate a consistent terminology, one that is in line with Sartre's general view of consciousness but, above all, serves as a fruitful heuristic perspective for understanding the case studies offered in the next section. Seeing that this interpretation is my final goal, and not a reading of Sartre per se, I am not concerned with being faithful to everything that Sartre has written. Moreover, I would like to emphasize that in this discussion with Sartre, which will result in a reconstruction of the concept of sincerity, I am already bringing along what I have found in Wallace, Eggers and Foer. I will further analyse how we can recognize the formulated concept of sincerity in their novels, in section 3.

2.1. Sartre: Good faith and bad faith

Sartre formulates the distinction between good and bad faith as follows: 'Bad faith does not hold the norms and criteria of truth as they are accepted by the critical thought of good faith. What it decides first, in fact, is the nature of truth.'[27] In Chapter 1, we have already seen that bad faith is a form of self-deceit.[28] The individual in bad faith tries to mask for himself the tension of his freedom, of his conscious being – that he is both transcendence (freedom, not coinciding with his current being) and facticity (the factuality of his free existence). To that end, the individual formulates 'two-faced concepts' and decides to be convinced by these concepts, while '[i]n truth, [he has] not persuaded [him]self'.[29] This is what Sartre means when he writes that bad faith does not 'hold' the norms and criteria of critical thought.

Sartre's description also implies that, conversely, good faith *does* hold the norms and criteria of critical thought. It demands persuasive evidence, while with bad faith 'a peculiar type of evidence appears; non-persuasive evidence'.[30] Santoni writes: '[whereas bad faith] is a closed, uncritical attitude toward available evidence, the fundamental attitude or original determination of being in good faith is an open, critical attitude toward evidence'.[31] Catalano explains:

> When I am in good faith, I first 'decide' what is reasonable evidence to believe. Although this may be different for each person, nevertheless, the criteria are faced consciously and some attempt is made to be critical. In good faith, we are willing to allow ourselves to be convinced on the basis of what we consider to be a reasonable amount of evidence.[32]

---

[27] BN, 91.
[28] Cf. 'in bad faith it is from myself that I am hiding the truth' (ibid., 72).
[29] Ibid., 91.
[30] Ibid.
[31] Santoni, *Bad Faith, Good Faith, and Authenticity*, 71.
[32] Catalano, *Commentary*, 87; also: 'We are in bad faith, however, when we first decide to believe and then decide not to require too much evidence for our belief [. . .]; it can choose to believe with almost no evidence' (ibid.).

Unfortunately, Sartre elaborates very little on the spontaneous-critical character of good faith. Further on in the text it even seems as if he qualifies good faith as a form of bad faith. However, we have to distinguish between normal good faith, and good faith that turns itself into an ideal, that is, that wants to coincide with its own belief. That there is nothing wrong with the former, is shown by Sartre's own example, that 'I believe [*in good faith*] that my friend Pierre feels friendship for me.' I believe it, even though 'I do not have for it any self-evident intuition, for the nature of the object does not lend itself to intuition.'[33] Friendship is not something that can be known with complete certainty, as, for example, a mathematical sum can: 'past and present actions seem to indicate this friendship, but this evidence can never present itself to me as apodictic, as proving his friendship in the sense that two and two is four', writes Catalano.[34] The friendship is something that I have to 'trust', says Sartre, 'I decide to believe in it, and to maintain myself in this decision', in good faith.[35] There is nothing wrong with believing in good faith, based on certain signals and indicators, in a certain friendship; all the more since, according to Sartre, friendship is something than can *never* be known to be there with complete certainty, you can only believe it.

Good faith only becomes problematic for Sartre when it turns its own belief into an ideal; that is, when faith in one's friendship with Pierre is not prompted by signs of that friendship, but by the wish to 'believe what one believes', to fully coincide with one's belief.[36] According to Sartre, the characteristic of believing is that 'every belief involves not quite believing'. 'Is Pierre my friend? I do not know; I believe so.' Believing is not knowing something for sure; when you would know for sure, it would cease to be belief, writes Sartre. '[T]o believe what one believes'[37] – that is, 'coinciding' with one's belief, no longer thinking about what and on what basis you believe – implies a denial of this uncertainty, of the norms and criteria of critical thought, and, therefore, a form of bad faith, according to Sartre.

But this does not apply to normal good faith. Catalano explains: 'good faith would seem to be a project of being spontaneously willing to be critical and open.'[38] As an 'immediate attitude', good faith implies a pre-reflective acceptance of the tension in human existence. Contrary to bad faith, good faith implies a truthful recognition of freedom, of our constant not-coinciding with ourselves: 'Sartre repeatedly states that bad faith is an attempt to flee from our freedom, whereas good faith is an attempt to face our freedom', writes Catalano.[39]

---

[33] BN, 92.
[34] Catalano, *Commentary*, 87.
[35] BN, 92.
[36] Cf. Catalano, *Good Faith*, 80–1; Santoni, *Bad Faith, Good Faith, and Authenticity*, 73–4.
[37] BN, 93, 92.
[38] Catalano, *Commentary*, 81.
[39] Ibid., 89. The difference lies, as Santoni formulates it, in 'how freedom "responds" to itself, how the free being of consciousness deals with its "troubled" freedom. Good faith is precisely the human being's (freedom's) project of accepting its abandonment to freedom and the anxiety of its ontological distance' (Santoni, *Bad Faith, Good Faith, and Authenticity*, 86); cf. 'good faith, as an *epistemological* attitude, accepts itself as faith and not certainty, retains a critical perspective on evidence, and refuses to construct two-faced concept by which to exploit the "self-distancing" of

So, bad faith is not the 'fundamental ontological condition of freedom', not the sole, original relation of man to his freedom (even though this is – partly due to Sartre's own inconsistencies and obscurities – quite a common reading of *Being and Nothingness*).[40] All consciousness is driven by the desire to 'be': after all, being-for-itself is characterized by a 'lack of being' (it is being-what-it-is-not and not-being-what-it-is), and, as a result of that lack, is driven by an unfulfillable '*desire to be*'[41] (consciousness casts itself towards the world, but can never coincide with it, can never 'be' as the world 'is'). That 'desire to be' cannot be suppressed, because that is what consciousness is – 'there would be nothing else', writes Sartre in *Notebooks for an Ethics*.[42] But at the same time, this lack of being and this desire to be, constitute a consciousness of not being able to 'be', of not being able to coincide with anything; in other words, it is consciousness of the freedom of consciousness and, thus, of the unfulfillability of its desire to be. Bad faith consciousness would imply trying to hide this impossibility for itself. Good faith, even though it shares the 'desire to be' that characterizes all consciousness, is an open, critical attitude that does not try to conceal the truth, but recognizes its own freedom, including its 'unhappy' character (being driven by a desire that never lets itself be fulfilled).[43]

Are good and bad faith two equally fundamental, spontaneous options that man has in relation to his freedom? In spite of his concise and sometimes inconsistent treatment of good faith, this seems to be Sartre's conclusion. He speaks of 'the two immediate attitudes which we can take in the face of our being'. However, even though Sartre himself writes that '[o]ne *puts oneself* in bad faith as one goes to sleep and one is in bad faith as one dreams',[44] we have already seen in Chapter 1 that bad faith necessarily implies reflection. Therefore, bad faith cannot be characterized as a pre-reflective, basic attitude of being (even though Sartre – erroneously – describes it as such).

This means that good faith is the only fundamental, spontaneous attitude. Sartre writes that pre-reflective consciousness 'can never be deceived about itself'.[45] He repeatedly emphasizes that consciousness is at all times (non-positional) consciousness of itself, that it 'knows' pre-reflectively that it 'is' freedom, that it can never fully coincide with anything, and that it cannot deceive itself about this (as a result of its own pre-reflective awareness thereof). For instance, Sartre gives the following description of the awareness of the 'impossibility' of the 'desire to be', as resulting from the pre-reflective consciousness of 'being' freedom: 'this impossibility is not hidden

---

consciousness and to "persuade" itself of its deceptive beliefs. [. . .] good faith is also – and perhaps more dominantly – what I have called an *ontological* attitude. That is, good faith is an "original" attitude toward human reality, toward our freedom, toward our "existing" as freedom' (ibid., 85–6).

[40] Catalano, *Good Faith*, 77.
[41] BN, 586.
[42] Sartre, *Notebooks*, 37; cf. Santoni, *Bad Faith, Good Faith, and Authenticity*, 83–4.
[43] BN, 114; cf. 'In good faith, we begin with a realization that we are our failure to *be* one with our body, our environment, and our entire situation, but we still recognize the necessity of struggling toward the being that we would be' (Catalano, *Commentary*, 90).
[44] BN, 93, 91.
[45] Ibid., 493 (cf. Chapter 1).

from consciousness; on the contrary, it is the very stuff of consciousness'.[46] And: 'at the very moment when I struggle to attain it, I have a vague prejudicative comprehension that I shall not attain it'.[47] Although Sartre is not consistent in some of his descriptions of this aspect of consciousness, bad faith is undeniably to be regarded as the flight of consciousness from its own freedom. In that case, 'there remains the question of how consciousness is aware that it is totally free, which is the necessary condition for flight behavior. One possible explanation is to push the issue on to the pre-reflective consciousness', suggests Thomas Busch, 'Against all attempts to reduce consciousness to a thing there persists "the contestation of non-thetic self-consciousness". In these cases pre-reflective self-consciousness is treated as an inescapable lucidity of freedom to itself.'[48]

This pre-reflective consciousness, which embodies a truthful awareness and acceptance of human-reality, clearly matches the heart of the attitude of good faith. Indeed, I contend that good faith *is* this pre-reflective awareness that cannot be deceived about itself. In other words, good faith is the imperative, pre-reflective (immediate) basic attitude of man, and bad faith the non-imperative but widespread reflective attitude of flight from, and thus ensuing, the pre-reflective insights of good faith.

2.2. Sartre: The role of reflection

As mentioned, consciousness is driven by a 'desire to be', which it, at the same time, pre-reflectively knows is unfulfillable. According to Sartre, reflection initially appears in service of, as accessory to, this 'desire to be', to found itself.[49] In reflection, consciousness is made into an object: the for-itself (freedom) tries to determine itself as an in-itself (thing), which is in bad faith. Sartre writes: 'reflection is in bad faith in so far as it constitutes itself as the revelation of *the object which I make-to-be-me*'. Sartre calls this 'impure reflection', which is an 'abortive effort on the part of the for-itself *to be another* while *remaining itself.* [. . .] Thus reflection is impure when it gives itself as an 'intuition of the for-itself in in-itself"'.[50]

Reflection is an impediment to the spontaneity of consciousness: it cuts consciousness off from that with which it was involved (what it was consciousness *of*, the action in which it was absorbed), which subsequently leads to self-alienation. Part of this is that reflection constructs the Ego (which is absent at the unreflected level): 'It is thus exactly as if consciousness constituted the Ego as a false representation of itself, as if consciousness hypnotized itself before this Ego which it has constituted, became absorbed in it, as if it made the Ego its safeguard and its law', writes Sartre, to which he adds: 'Perhaps its essential role is to mask from consciousness its own

---

[46] Ibid., 85–6.
[47] Ibid., 89. These passages are related to the 'desire to be' in what Sartre calls 'sincerity'; further on in this chapter I will show that Sartre, erroneously, describes sincerity as wanting to be what one is and therefore as a form of bad faith.
[48] Busch, *The Power of Consciousness*, 37–8.
[49] Cf. Sartre, *Notebooks*, 11; BN, 176–7.
[50] BN, 184.

spontaneity.' Reflective consciousness is 'a consciousness that imprisons itself in order to flee from itself'.[51] What happens, here, is that 'impure reflection confuses objectified consciousness with actual, existential consciousness', explains Busch.[52] The object-consciousness is not a consciousness that 'exists', that is with the world, while that is the only place where the self can take shape. As Sartre writes in the *Notebooks*: 'The one and only base of the moral life must be spontaneity that is, the immediate, the unreflective.'[53] Gail Evelyn Linsenbard explains Sartre's words as follows:

> We must be careful to note that when Sartre says that 'the base of the moral life' must be 'spontaneity', 'immediate', and 'unreflective', he is not talking about 'an ethics of sheer impulse or drive'. What he wants to suggest, rather, is that it is only through action, or through the way in which we *exist in the world*, that the world might be changed.[54]

To summarize: good faith is the pre-reflective basic attitude of the self, and reflection comes up as part of the self-deceit of bad faith. Sartre calls this bad faith reflection, impure reflection.

However, the emergence of impure reflection also carries with it the possibility of a conversion, of the emergence of a pure (or: purifying) reflection, that realizes the deceit of bad faith and impure reflection. Pure reflection represents a reflective resumption of the pre-reflective awareness and acceptation of human-reality in good faith. As Sartre states in *Notebooks*: 'Impure reflection is motivation for pure reflection.'[55] Elsewhere he writes: 'What is given first in daily life is impure or constituent reflection.' As such, it can form the occasion for a 'modification which it effects on itself and which is in the form of a katharsis'.[56] That 'katharsis' is pure reflection: in this form, reflection is no longer the attempt to determine consciousness as an in-itself (to found itself), but the acknowledgement of consciousness as for-itself.[57] Busch explains: 'Pure reflection can effect upon itself a "katharsis" and as a result, in its thematization of the pre-reflective, take cognizance of the "break in being", of the non-positional presence to self. [. . .] in pure reflection the self is grasped as "break in being" [. . .] and as "having to be".'[58]

Therefore, Sartre concludes, in *Notebooks*: 'Pure reflection is good faith.'[59] Pure reflection does not involve a new awareness – because it was there all along, masked by bad faith – but an internal modification that again reveals the pre-reflective insight of good faith. The realization that one has lived in bad faith 'implies a kind of ontological precomprehension of good faith', writes Santoni, who adds: '[the

---

[51] TE, 48, 34.
[52] Busch, *The Power of Consciousness*, 9.
[53] Sartre, *Notebooks*, 5.
[54] Linsenbard, *An Investigation of Jean-Paul Sartre's Posthumously Published Notebooks for an Ethics*, 135.
[55] Sartre, *Notebooks*, 12.
[56] BN, 182.
[57] Cf. ibid., 186.
[58] Busch, *The Power of Consciousness*, 32.
[59] Sartre, *Notebooks*, 12.

reflective conversion] adopts, or perhaps returns to, good faith's non-thetic, "joyful" affirmation of freedom'.[60] Pure reflection means that we are 'both inside and outside at the same time', and 'place spontaneity between parentheses', 'without depriving it of its affirmative force', Sartre writes in *Notebooks*.[61] Catalano describes pure reflection as 'a momentary grasp of ourselves while not ceasing in the activity and not turning the activity into an object of study'.[62]

Still, pure reflection and good faith are not identical, even though both attitudes entail the same awareness. However, their relation to that awareness differs. Good faith is pre-reflective, immediate, not effected by volition; for, as Sartre writes, the voluntary act 'requires the appearance of a reflective consciousness'.[63] Good faith is like an intuition, an immediate belief in what is important and what is not, occurring without what could be properly called a *choice*. One can only speak of choice, in the existentialist sense of the word, when there is the possibility of doing something differently. That possibility arises only with reflection, which emerges as the bad faith attempt to mask the insight of good faith, and subsequently with the possibility of reflectively acknowledging that self-deceit and (again: reflectively) *choosing* the insights of good faith. This reflective resumption of good faith is an act of volition, a choice to live in the awareness and acceptance of that insight, and give shape to the self.

2.3. Sartre: Sincerity – A reconstruction

It is this reflective attitude, resuming the awareness of good faith, that I would like to call 'sincerity', even though Sartre himself calls this attitude 'authenticity'[64] and describes 'sincerity' as a form of bad faith. However: first of all, with authenticity Sartre chooses a misleading term that implies the complete opposite of what he wants to recommend; secondly, his conception of sincerity is very limited (almost caricatural), and therefore does not do justice to the possibilities of that attitude.

Catalano aptly summarizes the problem with the term authenticity: 'If the task of living a moral life is ambiguous, the use of the term "authenticity", to describe that task, in a Sartrean context, seems not only ambiguous but wrong.' After all, the use of the term authenticity implies, as I have also argued in the first section of this chapter, 'the misguided task of developing an individualistic ethic', writes Catalano. This task is misguided (and therefore the term authenticity mistaken) because for Sartre the self

---

[60] Santoni, *Bad Faith, Good Faith, and Authenticity*, 124; cf. Hazel Barnes, who writes that, in this 'purifying' form, 'the purpose of reflection would not be to discover that self as object but to liberate it from the incrustations of the ego', i.e. free from the constructs of impure reflection (Barnes, 'Sartre's Concept of the Self', 75).

[61] Sartre, *Notebooks*, 4, 5; cf. Busch, *The Power of Consciousness*, 34.

[62] Catalano, *Good Faith*, 156.

[63] BN, 473.

[64] In a famous, concise footnote, Sartre writes: 'this supposes a self-recovery of being which was previously corrupted. This self-recovery we shall call authenticity, the description of which has no place here' (ibid., 94).

emerges in the world, in the interaction with others and with the social structures in which we encounter ourselves. This is sufficient reason to, as Catalano formulates it, 'be shy of using the term "authenticity"'.[65] To which he adds:

> It is clear that Sartre would be opposed to a use of the term 'authenticity' that referred either to being true to oneself or to a privileged reflection [. . .]. In all these senses, the term 'authenticity' implies that we have had an original bond either with our own true self or with Nature or Being, and that we have been led astray by the demands of the world.[66]

Most Sartre scholars choose to maintain the term authenticity and construe the concept in an idiosyncratic, Sartrean way. I will, however, replace Sartre's term of authenticity with sincerity. To do so, I will first discuss Sartre's own critique of (what he holds to be) sincerity, after which I will offer a reconstruction (that is much indebted to Santoni's analysis) of the attitude of sincerity, which not only does justice to what is normally meant by the term (in our normal use of it) but also is consistent with Sartre's general view of being and consciousness, corresponding with the reflective resumption of the awareness of good faith.

At the start of his discussion of the 'conducts of bad faith', Sartre promisingly calls sincerity the 'antithesis' of bad faith.[67] However, this quickly turns out to be a misleading formulation: based on the ensuing explanation, 'we can readily see that he does not view the two concepts as antithetical', concludes Santoni.[68] Sartre writes: 'what is the ideal to be attained in this case? It is necessary that a man be *for himself* only what he *is*. But is this not precisely the definition of the in-itself – or if you prefer – the principle of identity?' He concludes that the 'essential structure of sincerity does not differ from that of bad faith'.[69] In short, Sartre is of the opinion (like some of the authors mentioned in section 1) that sincerity implies the striving for a fixed, static subject, for 'being what you are', and, also, that it is undertaken for the other, a desire to merge into roles that society expects from the individual. Catalano writes that, for Sartre, sincerity is 'the obligation to make ourselves be what we are called. Thus a waiter, Sartre states, attempts to play the role of a waiter. He attempts to live up to the model that the world presents to him.'[70]

---

[65] Catalano, *Good Faith*, 151–3.

[66] Ibid., 153–4.

[67] BN, 81.

[68] Santoni, *Bad Faith, Good Faith, and Authenticity*, 7.

[69] BN, 81, 88.

[70] Catalano, *Commentary*, 84; cf. Sartre's example of the waiter: 'Let us consider this waiter in the café. His movement is quick and forward, a little too precise, a little too rapid. He comes toward the customers with a step a little too quick. He bends forward a little too eagerly [. . .]. All his behavior seems to us a game. [. . .] But what *is* he playing? We need not watch long before we can explain it: he is playing *at being* a waiter in a café. [. . .] In a parallel situation, from within, the waiter in the café can not be immediately a café waiter in the sense that this inkwell is an inkwell, or the glass is a glass. [. . .] What I attempt to realize is a being-in-itself of the café waiter, as if it were not in my power to confer value and urgency upon my duties and the rights of my position, as if it were not my free choice to get up each morning at five o'clock or to remain in bed, even though it meant getting fired' (BN, 82–3).

Following his characterization of sincerity as a demand coming from outside, Sartre goes on to describe sincerity as a 'confession' that we employ so as to no longer be responsible for what we have confessed to: after all, when we have admitted something, we no longer coincide with it, do we? Sartre writes:

> [T]he sincere man constitutes himself as what he is *in order not to be it*. [. . .] Total, constant sincerity as a constant effort to adhere to oneself is by nature a constant effort to dissociate oneself from oneself. A person frees himself from himself by the very act by which he makes himself an object for himself. To draw up a perpetual inventory of what one is means constantly to redeny oneself and to take refuge in a sphere where one is no longer anything but a pure, free regard.[71]

In Sartre's description, sincerity comes to correspond to what could actually be labelled, on the contrary, the insincere attitude that was described in Part 1, namely that of hyperreflexivity and endless irony: hyperreflexivity is a disassociating (alienating), perpetual 'drawing up inventory' of oneself, to ironically distance oneself from all responsibility and self-content. We could say that according to Sartre sincerity is insincere: it is in bad faith.

However, this description (which, according to Sartre, applies to all instances of supposed sincerity) does not do justice to what we generally take to be sincerity.[72] Within Sartre's philosophical system, sincerity attains a very specific meaning (being-sincere is being-merely-what-you-are, that is, being-in-itself), that, because of that limiting specificity, is simply inaccurate, not expressive of what we normally regard as sincerity.[73] In a sense, Sartre, like one of his bad faith characters, who does not want to acknowledge his facticity, 'plays on the word *being*': the man in question, 'slides surreptitiously towards a different connotation of the word "being". He understands "not being" in the sense of "not-being-in-itself"', writes Sartre.[74] In a similar way, Sartre himself slides, in his definition of sincerity, 'sneakily' from 'being' (I am a waiter) to 'being-in-itself' (I am a waiter, as in-itself).

Therefore, Santoni suggests the following 'reconstruction' of Sartre's conception of sincerity:

> I submit that to aim to be what I am or to express myself honestly as the person I am does not necessarily entail, even on Sartre's terms, constituting myself in the mode of *en-soi* or of a kind of fixed 'thing'. On the contrary, I suggest that a careful listening to the way 'sincerity' and 'being what [or who] one is' is used in ordinary language indicates a meaning that 'intends' *being* the person who I am – *not* hiding from,

---

[71] BN, 88–9.

[72] Of course, Sartre, as the acute 'psychologist' of bad faith, is right in holding that the individual could use expressions of seeming sincerity in such a way, thinking: 'I was honest about it, so now you cannot hold it against me anymore.' But, in my opinion, a confession for which an individual does not feel accountable to others, would rather seem to be an expression of the 'self-ideal' of authenticity.

[73] Cf. 'Sincerity is "made" to admit of "family relations" which, in common usage, it would not be said to have' (Santoni, *Bad Faith, Good Faith, and Authenticity*, 10–11; cf. xxi).

[74] BN, 87.

fleeing from, or thingifying that person. [. . .] If Sartre had paid greater respect to ordinary language, he might have recognized that 'being what one is' as employed in common usage may well mean 'being what it is not and not being what it is' when translated into the idiosyncratic discourse of his phenomenological ontology. [. . .] I submit that 'being what one is' ('being sincere') may involve being or living or existing in a mode in which one recognizes and accepts that 'one is not what one is and is what one is not'. That is to say sincerity is often intended to mean that one is 'what one is' in the mode of being of selfconsciousness, not in the mode of the objectification or thingification of consciousness, or of fleeing one's freedom.[75]

Generally, we regard someone as sincere when he is honest about himself, towards himself and towards the world; by that we mean exactly the acknowledgement of the multiplicities, the inconsistencies and the possibilities that every individual consists of at any moment. He is (in a more Sartrean formulation) someone who acknowledges and accepts that he is freedom, who 'exists' the tension between transcendence and facticity that he is. Such a conception of sincerity fits smoothly into Sartre's general philosophy and terminology. More than that: further on in his book, Santoni finds that the above-cited reconstruction corresponds to what Sartre intended to express through the (ill-chosen) term authenticity.[76]

Therefore, and considering the objections to the term authenticity discussed earlier, it seems to me that sincerity, as it was defined above, embodies the existential attitude of the individual who is conscious of his free being, and who, in the reflective resumption of good faith, realizes that he is responsible for the shaping and meaning of his own existence. In section 1, I have indicated that I will regard sincerity as the aspiration to form a self, in the acknowledgement that one's self is formed through one's actions, by being responsible for them, and that this process is never complete.

3. Case studies of sincerity: The fiction of Wallace, Eggers and Foer

As we have discussed, the understanding of sincerity outlined in the previous section has been prompted by considerations derived from the novels of Wallace, Eggers and Foer. Now that we have clearly outlined the concept of sincerity, we will examine its role in the works of Wallace, Eggers and Foer. This will be done through several case studies, offering detailed analyses of the most important characters from these works, in light of the philosophical perspective that has been outlined. These cases will both illuminate the alternative attitude that the works portray in response

---

[75] Santoni, *Bad Faith, Good Faith, and Authenticity*, 16–17.

[76] Ibid., xxi, 18. Santoni states that he nevertheless wants to differentiate between sincerity and authenticity, but does not make clear what that difference would consist of. Perhaps Santoni wants to equate sincerity and good faith (in a positive sense), in which case sincerity would be pre-reflective and authenticity reflective; but this is complicated by the fact that sincerity, in Santoni's own reconstruction is clearly reflective.

to the problems discussed in Part 1, and further underpin this new existentialist understanding of sincerity, by supplying paradigmatic cases and, as such, giving substance to the concept.

3.1. Good faith: Mario Incandenza

When we read in *Infinite Jest* that Mario Incandenza 'doesn't seem to resemble much of anyone', this might at first seem to refer solely to his physical appearance. At birth, he had to be 'more or less scraped out, Mario, like the meat of an oyster'. Prenatal anomalies and a difficult birth left Mario 'some lifelong character-building physical challenges'. But Mario's 'not resembling' anyone quickly turns out to refer to something 'deeper' than his physique. Whereas everybody else 'finds stuff that's really real uncomfortable and they get embarrassed. It's like there's some rule that real stuff can only get mentioned if everybody rolls their eyes or laughs in a way that isn't happy', Mario is different and likes to visit Ennet House, the nearby halfway facility because '[it's very real;] once he heard somebody say *God* with a straight face and nobody looked at them or looked down or smiled in any sort of way where you could tell they were worried inside'.[77] It is not Mario's physical appearance but his utter lack of cynicism, his focus on 'outside' – expressed through many passages like the above – that distinguishes him from everybody else in the novel.

Mario provides an alternative to the hyperreflexive irony of *Infinite Jest*'s many cynical, depressed characters. The novel remarks upon the fact that some readers will not take such a 'naïve' character seriously, finding him 'irritating', 'outright bats', 'dead inside in some essential way'. However, in *Infinite Jest* it is exactly this abhorrence of 'unsophisticated naïveté', this 'transcendence of sentiment' through hyperreflexivity and irony, that leads to emptiness, to 'anhedonia, death in life'. The desire to avoid naïveté at all costs is itself a form of naïveté – the 'queerly persistent U.S. myth that cynicism and naïveté are mutually exclusive' – that has catastrophic consequences for the self.[78]

Mentally, Mario is slow, but not, 'verifiably *not*, retarded'; he is more 'ever so slightly epistemically bent, a pole poked into mental water and just a little off and just taking a little bit longer'. Words like 'bent' and 'off' stress a deviation from the norm. Mario *is* a deviation, an abnormality: he stands for a different way of thinking about the self and its relation to the world, symbolizing the much-needed change that the rest of the novel illustrates. His younger brother Hal regards Mario as a 'miracle' and his mother Avril sees him as the family's 'real prodigy'.[79] Mario's role is in many ways akin to that of an 'angel' or a 'holy fool'. Mario can perhaps be compared to Alyosha from Dostoevsky's *The Brothers Karamazov*. Timothy Jacobs writes:

> [Mario is] the only character who is neither cynical nor ironic, who 'doesn't lie', is sincerely joyful, and displays a genuine charity toward all other characters,

---

[77] IJ, 101, 313, 592, 591.
[78] Ibid., 156, 694, 839.
[79] IJ, 314, 316, 317.

much like the patient, loving, and ever-listening Alyosha. Alyosha is ambiguously described at times as 'slow [and] underdeveloped', a 'sickly, ecstatic, poorly developed person . . . a meager, emaciated, little fellow', 'very strange', a 'holy fool', a 'novice', who always tells the truth, wears a 'foolish grin', and is a 'lover of mankind'. Both, after a fashion, are Dostoevskyean 'idiots'.

Furthermore, Jacobs identifies a passage from *Infinite Jest* on Mario and another character, Barry Loach, (which will be discussed in Chapter 8), as 'intertextually borrowed' from a chapter in *The Brothers Karamazov*. In that chapter Ivan tells Alyosha (as 'a lover of mankind') 'that he cannot understand "how it's possible to love one's neighbors" and then relates an anecdote about a saint who embraces and cares for "a hungry and frozen passerby" who had asked to be made warm, presumably by human contact', writes Jacobs.[80]

That Mario – like angels and fools – is perhaps 'neurologically' incapable of irony and cynicism, does not mean that his character cannot teach us anything valuable for overcoming the problems under consideration. The importance of the Mario character lies not in the (congenital) causes of his other way of thinking (causes that, after all, cannot be 'copied' by other characters) but in its results, its consequences: he shows us the structures of an alternative attitude, which regards the self as always already public and involved with others, and shows us that it works, as a life-view. Mario functions as an exemplary character, demonstrating the immediate, intuitive adaptation of a life-view that other characters – most importantly, Don Gately and Hal Incandenza – will only arrive at through a great deal of effort, through a route that requires reflection (see section 3.4).

Certain aspects of the character Mario Incandenza deserve additional attention, as they connect his attitude to the philosophical perspectives employed in this study. The first aspect that should arouse our interest is the fact that, despite being the most empathetic character in the novel who is always perceptive of other people's pain and suffering, Mario himself does not feel pain. He suffers from 'familial dysautonomia', a neurological disorder resulting in an insensitivity to physical pain.[81] Of course, we could regard this as simply another addition to the long list of Mario's physical ailments. However, this neurological deficit seems an unmistakable reference to Wittgenstein's question, which we encountered in Chapter 5: what determines the meaning of the utterance 'I am in pain'?

Mario cannot base his conception of what pain is on (the misguided conviction that he possesses) a private sample of pain because he cannot gaze inside and say 'this is pain'. Yet, where pain and suffering are concerned, he is the most understanding, empathetic character in the novel. Because of his neurological deficiency, Mario is immune to the self-reflective mistake of regarding inner processes as objects that an individual possesses and that only that individual can access as part of an immanent, inner process. Most other characters in *Infinite Jest* are subject to this illusion: they show little interest in others (since they – solipsistically – assume that they do not have

---

[80] Jacobs, 'The Brothers Incandenza', 272.
[81] Cf. IJ, 590.

access to the other anyway) and are convinced of the singularity of their individual thoughts and feelings. As we have seen in Chapter 1, this constant gazing inside can lead to a state of anhedonia, in which everything has become meaningless.[82]

Mario's existence seems to be based on the intuitive awareness that the self, the meaning of what he feels and thinks, is something that comes into being outside him, not in some immanent, private sphere but in what transcends his consciousness: in the world, in his actions. This seems to form an important aspect of his life-view. Mario is repeatedly described as 'leaning forward'. Again, at first this simply seems to be a reference to Mario's physical limitations. He moves 'body tilted way forward as if into a wind, right on the edge of pitching face-first onto the ground'. This posture is emphasized several times, in formulations such as: 'inclined ever forward' and 'Mario in his forward list'.[83] As a result of this repeated emphasis, his 'forward-inclination' becomes more and more a characterization not just of his posture but of his life-view (not just his body-position, but his life-position). As Greg Carlisle formulates it: 'Mario is "inclined ever forward", able to choose, to contribute, not caught in a cycle of stasis and passivity.'[84] Other characters *are* caught in such a cycle, are not 'inclined ever forward', such as, the many drug addicts, but above all, the people who have watched the film 'Infinite Jest', who just stare aimlessly, unresponsive and motionless; like those who suffer from anhedonia, they are empty shells, without real selves. Conversely, Mario is committed to the world outside, capable of acting and, therefore, of becoming a self.

As discussed, Mario displays this behaviour intuitively: he does not have to make any (reflective) effort to stay immune to the problems that affect other characters. Mario simply 'exists' his attitude, without having to think explicitly about what he has to do and why. That is, his virtue is completely pre-reflective. In Mario, therefore, we encounter an embodiment of *good faith* that contrasts sharply with the reflection-induced bad faith of most of the other characters. The fact that Mario does not feel pain symbolizes his innate immunity to the temptation of seeking all meaning inside himself, which would lead to bad faith; he does not find what he is inside himself, but in his relations to the world and others. As a result, Mario is focused on what is 'really real', that is, he intuitively and honestly acknowledges what is really important. Instead of fleeing from reality in (aesthetic/bad faith) fantasy, Mario takes on the reality of his existence, as expressed by his forward-inclination. He succeeds in becoming a stable self because he is aware that the self is connected to the world outside consciousness and takes shape through actions. As such, Mario is the paragon of what it means to be human. He shows the reality and desirability of the virtue that he embodies, thereby functioning as an example to other characters who will strive for a similar attitude, who will reflectively grasp the insight of good faith. As such, Mario 'is' good faith: he 'is' the life-view that is resumed by others through reflection.[85]

---

[82]   Cf. IJ, 692–3.
[83]   Ibid., 313, 315.
[84]   Carlisle, *Elegant Complexity*, 199.
[85]   Cf. about Mario: 'he becomes a strange and marvelous character, and a surprisingly potent source of hope amid so much unrelenting pain. Utterly lovable and emotionally insightful, Mario is truly

3.2. Good faith: Oskar Schell

One of the most important themes of Foer's second novel, *Extremely Loud & Incredibly Close*, is loneliness. Almost all the characters in the novel, living in post-9/11 New York, have turned inside and feel deeply alone. We see this in the main character, 9-year-old Oskar Schell, whose father died in the 9/11 attacks on the World Trade Center, but also in Oskar's grandparents, who survived the Holocaust.[86] In response to the incomprehensible madness and unreliability of the outside world, they flee inside, but there they are utterly alone with their horrible thoughts and memories. The results of such 'solitary self-confinement' we can see, above all, in the grandfather, who just cannot stop thinking, increasingly shuts out the world, and gradually loses the power of speech, word by word:

> I used to talk and talk and talk and talk, I couldn't keep my mouth shut, the silence overtook me like a cancer; [. . .] After a time, I had only a handful of words left [. . .] 'I' was the last word I was able to speak aloud, which is a terrible thing, but there it is. [. . .] I wanted to pull the thread, unravel the scarf of my silence and start from the beginning, but instead I said, 'I'. I know I'm not alone in this disease.[87]

That 'I' is the last word he loses is symbolic of his solipsism, of being completely taken up by his own thinking, and of the loss of meaning that this results in (which, as he says, is a 'disease' widespread in our times).

However, in the case of Oskar, we see a development in the other direction. On the one hand he does experience a similar existential loneliness – he feels a 'hole in the middle of [himself] that every happy thing fell into', and says: 'It probably gets pretty lonely to be anyone'.[88] But on the other hand he feels the closeness of everything, and gradually becomes more and more convinced that, if he is to find meaning in his existence, he will have to breach his confinement in his own thought and feelings:

> [I felt] incredibly close to everything in the universe, but also extremely alone. I wondered, for the first time in my life, if life was worth all the work it took to live. [. . .] Maybe it was because of everything that had happened [. . .]. Or maybe it was because I felt so close and alone that night. I just couldn't be dead any longer.[89]

Oskar's recent loneliness (following the death of his father) is offset by his natural, childlike naïveté. Oskar has a strong desire for openness, for honesty towards the other. This desire is expressed, above all, in the many inventions he thinks up: little microphones that everybody swallows ('you could hear everyone's heartbeat, and they

---

the heart of this long narrative.' And: 'Mario is ultimately the clearest instance of Wallace's effort to move past our deplorable inability to understand that cynicism is only another form of naïveté. [. . .] [He] is close to the center of *Infinite Jest*'s vast "retroironic" and deeply compelling story' (Bell and Dowling, *A Reader's Companion to Infinite Jest*, 132–3, 137–8).

[86] Cf. Uytterschout, 'An Extremely Loud Tin Drum. A Comparative Study of Jonathan Safran Foer's *Extremely Loud and Incredibly Close* and Gunter Grass's *The Tin Drum*', 185–6.
[87] ELIC, 16–17.
[88] Ibid., 71, 69; cf. Oskar's grandmother, who also speaks of such a 'hole' (83).
[89] Ibid., 145.

could hear yours, sort of like sonar') and wedding rings ('where each one takes the pulse of the person wearing it and sends a signal to the other ring to flash red with each heartbeat'),[90] or shower water that includes a chemical making your skin colour change according to your mood: 'Everyone could know what everyone else felt, and we could be more careful with each other.'[91] Oskar's inventions express his desire for meaning and sincerity: they are intended to make clear what someone's feeling or behaviour means, and this clarity and honesty would mean people would be more considerate of each other and of themselves.

As a character, Oskar is not just an embodiment of the commonplace of childish naïveté versus adult cynicism.[92] According to some critics the novel posits childishness as an ideal.[93] But because of Oskar's combination of occasional adult eloquence and childlike naïveté, he cannot be regarded as simply a 9-year-old child. Other critics have therefore described him as an unrealistic character.[94] However, such descriptions pass over the symbolic value of Oskar. Without unqualifiedly recommending him as an imitable ideal, the novel does portray in Oskar a symbol for what is needed and what has to change, to help deal with some of the problems of contemporary life.

In this respect, the role of Oskar is very comparable to that of Mario Incandenza in *Infinite Jest*. Like for Mario, for Oskar his own actions are natural, self-evident; he is surprised when people ask him questions about it, or when they act differently from how he would. So, likewise, Oskar's attitude is not the result of reflection; his virtue is pre-reflective, and should be characterized as good faith. Oskar's attitude is perhaps not as 'superior' as Mario's (Oskar sometimes displays annoying and even reprehensible behaviour).[95] Nevertheless, Oskar's good faith functions as an example, even though it cannot be directly imitated (because of its unrealistic, symbolic combination of adult eloquence and childlike naïveté) by other characters or the reader. The inventions that Oskar thinks up are symbolic recipes against the misleading thought that meaning is found inside oneself, that others cannot understand you anyway, and therefore one may just as well stay introverted; meaning and understanding are acquired by looking at the other, as well as at your own relations to the world and to that other. Like Mario, Oskar is a paragon of a consciousness without cynicism, and by simply being himself, being in good faith, he influences the world around him by displaying an insight that others can adopt through a process of reflection.[96]

---

[90] Ibid., 1, 106.

[91] Ibid., 163.

[92] Cf. Uytterschout and Versluys, 'Melancholy and Mourning in Jonathan Safran Foer's *Extremely Loud and Incredibly Close*', 228.

[93] E.g. Beck, 'Kinderkampf', 94; cf. LeClair, 'Two Cheers', 19; Douthat, 'After Tragedy', 49.

[94] E.g. Myers, 'A Bag of Tired Tricks', 118.

[95] E.g. when he sneaks away from his grandmother and subsequently observes her as she is increasingly seized by panic (cf. ELIC, 101).

[96] Cf. Mullins, 'Boroughs and Neighbors', 310–11. Mullins aptly describes that the significance of Oskar 'is precisely that other people experience a certain sense of community as a result of his actions' (311).

3.3. Sincerity: Will Chmielewski

As discussed, the virtue of sincerity functions as a counterweight to the problematic attitude of hyperreflexive irony. Sections 3.1 and 3.2 discussed 'exemplary' characters, who are immune to these problems, but whose good faith functions as a 'road sign' for other characters (and perhaps for the reader), pointing in the direction of sincerity. Unlike Mario and Oskar, Will Chmielewski, the main character and first-person narrator of Eggers' *You Shall Know Our Velocity*, does struggle with the problem of hyperreflexive irony. In the following passage, Will's desire for an end to these problems and for a more sincere life-view become clear:

> I wanted agreement now, I wanted synthesis and the plain truth – without the formalities of debate. There was nothing left to debate, no heated discussion that seemed to progress toward any healing solution. I wanted only truth, as simple as you could serve it, straight down the middle, not the product of dialectic but *sui generis*: Truth! We all knew the truth but we insisted on distorting things to make it seem like we were all, with each other, in such profound disagreement about everything – that first and foremost there are two sides to everything, when of course there were not; there was one side only, one side always: Just as this earth is round, the truth is round, not two-sided but *round*.[97]

The continuous, overpowering ('constant', 'loud', 'decisive', 'unavoidable') discussions in Will's head, amount to a hyperreflexivity that he cannot control (they have become a 'hobby' of his mind, that Will himself, 'after many years of enjoying the debates', does not take pleasure in anymore). These constant self-reflective debates result in an ironization that has neither purpose nor end ('no heated discussion that seemed to progress toward any healing solution') and that mainly causes problems (opposition, difference) where it is not needful at all ('we insisted on distorting things to make it seem like we were all, with each other, in such profound disagreement about everything'). Will wants to be able to stop this process in some way ('I wanted them to end'), and, instead of opposition, create space for the 'truth', which is always 'round'. This image of 'round truth' can best be understood as a recognition of plurality together with the negation that this necessitates a constant (self-)questioning (deconstruction): Will is aware of the multiplicity of possible perspectives but tries to get rid of the idea that this means that all of these individual perspectives (choices, actions) are therefore, by definition, unsatisfactory.

The desire for a head that is less 'full', not constantly brimming with debate and discussion, is symbolized, for instance, by the pleasure that Will takes in certain demolition work, tearing down ceilings, digging up floors: 'I loved the effect when both happened in the same space: the raising of a ceiling, the lowering of a floor, exposing the wood again above and below, the space growing, the usable space and air attendant swelling within immovable walls.'[98] All the different layers – acoustic tile, countless layers of flooring – have the effect of diminishing space; they enclose, confine, hide

---

[97] YSKOV, 27–8.
[98] Ibid., 33–4.

from view that which is really important, similar to the excessive self-reflection in which Will feels imprisoned, cut off from participation in the world. 'Less layers' stand for the 'less head' that Will desires, more space in his mind, in his consciousness. Further on in the novel, Will explicitly connects his desire for a consciousness that does not paralyse him to the image of growing spaces, when he says: 'With this my ceiling would have been higher.'[99] These metaphors express a desire for 'openness', spontaneity, the space and ability to move and act.

But how is this desire for a head that is less full, for openness and spontaneity, to be realized? As discussed in Chapter 1, initially Will's attempts are in bad faith, as the only solution he sees is to 'lose' part of his head, for instance, as the result of an accident. His trip around the world with Hand is originally an attempt to escape the tension of existence, too, through speed, using every moment, having the illusion of doing all the things that come on their path. This behaviour, instead of bringing Will back into the world, has the effect, formulated by Hand at a certain point, of Will 'not being there. You're not anywhere.'[100]

But there are also moments during the trip when Will *is* there, when he is more or less free from the paralysing confinement of his head, and is thus 'in' his actions, instead of in his head, reflecting on other options, other things that could or should be done. These moments are often during relatively uncomplicated, physical actions[101] – as in the following passage, in which Will crosses a moat by jumping from rock to rock:

> There was no time to think, which was plenty of time – I had a few fractions of a second in mid-air, between rocks, to calculate the location of the next rock-landing options, the stability of each, the flattest surface among them. My brain and legs and feet all working at top speed, at the height of their respective games – it was thrilling and I was proud for them, for us. I had the thought, while running, without breaking stride, that I would like to be doing this forever.[102]

We can also recognize this in other, comparable passages, for example, when Will and Hand each climb in a tree and jump over to the other's tree. The spontaneity that is achieved in these simple actions seems to be exemplary for the attitude that Will gradually starts to pursue in all his choices and actions. By spontaneity I mean a consciousness that is completely involved *in* the action (has the ability to think and act at the same time: 'brain and legs and feet all working at top speed'). Will realizes – judging by the 'constant debates' described above – that objections can be raised to every possibility (if only because they rule out other options, which raises the question: why not choose one of those?). During his trip he gradually realizes

---

[99] Ibid., 307.

[100] Ibid., 318–19.

[101] Cf. Mae's kayaking in Eggers's *The Circle*, which seems to provide her with a similar calm and focus as Will's rock-jumping. Also see the discussion of the notion of urgency (e.g. running through the rain to return movies to the video store in Eggers's *A Heartbreaking Work of Staggering Genius*) in Chapter 7.

[102] YSKOV, 107–8.

that he cannot do everything, that this amounts to doing nothing. To choose and act without being paralysed by thinking, Will desires a form of reflection that remains in the action, in the world, that is, the spontaneity he feels while rock-jumping and that is how he always wants it to be ('I would like to be doing this forever'). By the end of the novel, it seems as if this has become the stable direction of his striving, as the final scene of the novel describes another jump ('I jumped with my mouth so open, taking it all in'), this time into a swimming pool, at a wedding party, marking the transition to a new stage in Will's life: 'for two more glorious and interminable months I lived! We lived!'[103]

In the example of the demolition work, creating space by removing layers of flooring and ceiling, and also in the image of the round truth, we can see the striving to regain the insight of good faith. Subsequently, Will's simple, physical actions, such as crossing a moat and tree jumping, display what Sartre calls pure reflection, a reflective consciousness that stays in the action that is able to observe itself but at the same time remain present in the action. These instances of pure reflection, in which the pre-reflective awareness of good faith is resumed, show Will what he really wants, that is, he experiences a real, viable alternative to his hyperreflexivity; an alternative that we can call sincerity. Will realizes that he has to be fully engaged in what he does, has to truly choose his actions, instead of wanting to do everything (not choosing and, as a result, not really doing anything). As mentioned, 'jumping' is a recurring image in the novel: the jump (or: leap) expresses the trust in and surrender to the outer world that is embodied by the attitude of sincerity. Moreover, the symbolic jump in the swimming pool with which the novel ends is no longer just an individual, physical action, but one in which Will belongs to a group of people and his commitment is connected to a community (a wedding party, and his mother), expressed through the 'We lived' with which the novel ends. This will be further elaborated in Chapters 7 and 8.

3.4. Sincerity: Don Gately and Hal Incandenza

Don Gately and Hal Incandenza are the two main characters of *Infinite Jest*. It is my contention that both undergo a development from the hyperreflexive irony characterizing drug addiction, to an attitude of sincerity. The novel portrays Hal at the height of his marijuana addiction, his subsequent decision to quit drugs, and the first changes in his behaviour. There is then a gap in Hal's story line and we next find him a year later (in a scene that opens the novel, but chronologically forms the last episode of the entire story line). This requires the reader to fill in what has happened in the meantime. Gately's portrayal starts at the moment that he has been clean for just over a year: as a live-in staff member of Ennet House he counsels new residents during their recovery and, as such, tries to give shape to his new life. In the meantime, Gately's old life as an addict and criminal is portrayed through a series of memories and dreams. Below, I will give a broad outline of Gately's situation. Then, I will analyse Hal's less

[103] Ibid., 371.

clear-cut development in further detail. Although Hal and Gately do not meet during the intervals of the story that the novel explicitly narrates, a meeting between the two characters in the missing intermediate year is suggested by a memory Hal has during the opening scene and a vision Gately has towards the end of the novel, of Hal and Gately digging up the head of Hal's father in a graveyard.[104]

3.4.1. Don Gately

The most important aspect of Gately's development towards sincerity is the role 'Addicts Anonymous' (AA) plays in it. We have already seen that *Infinite Jest* portrays a society in which 'stuff that's really real', real emotions, grief and meaning, are regarded as outdated, as clichés that are to be ignored. AA forms an exception, as a community in which the importance of such clichés, of real things *is* pointed out:

> [I]t has to be the truth to really go over, here. [. . .] And maximally unironic. An ironist in a Boston AA meeting is a witch in church. Irony-free zone. Same with sly disingenuous manipulative pseudo-sincerity. Sincerity with an ulterior motive is something these tough ravaged people know and fear, all of them trained to remember the coyly sincere, ironic, self-presenting fortifications they'd had to construct in order to carry on Out There, under the ceaseless neon bottle.[105]

What AA does is bring fellow-sufferers together, see to it that they open themselves up, that they are honest with others – if only through that one sentence, 'I am an addict' – and, in the course of doing that, learn to be honest with themselves, and as such become selves. For, as we have seen in Part 1, in AA the 'cliché "I don't know who I am" unfortunately turns out to be more than a cliché'.[106]

Openness, sincerity and a stable self are not established instantly; these are things that AA members are encouraged to 'do', in the presence of each other, gradually realizing these qualities. Initially the hyperreflexive, ironic mind of the addict regards AA's insights and guidelines as clichés (just like the 'real stuff' of existence that the addicts have neglected for years and that has to be brought back into sight again by these guidelines). But, as Gately describes, the 'clichéd directives are a lot more deep and hard to actually *do*. To try and live by instead of just say'.[107] The attitude, and the resulting self, that AA strives towards, can only emerge from acts in the world, even though the start of such actions can only be dutiful, at best – AA calls this 'Fake It Till You Make It'. At meetings, every speaker

> starts out saying he's an alcoholic, says it whether he believes it yet or not; then everybody up there says how Grateful he is to be sober today and how great it is to be Active and out on a Commitment with his Group, even if he's not grateful or pleased about it at all. You're encouraged to keep saying stuff like this [. . .] until you start to *want* to go to all these goddamn meetings.[108]

[104] Cf. IJ, 18, 934.
[105] Ibid., 369.
[106] Ibid., 204.
[107] Ibid., 358, 273.
[108] Ibid., 369.

We can connect this to Sartre's assertion that we can never 'believe what we believe'. Good faith means that we have to place trust in phenomena about which we cannot possibly acquire absolute certainty – such as friendship or the fact that AA works – but that we have to trust based on signals that convince us that these things are in fact the case. In AA, this means that a new member can recognize that the program might help him, as it seems to help others, but this does not yet take away his desperation concerning his own fate.

According to Gately, each AA insight or guideline initially incites aversion in the addict because it seems such a cliché.[109] 'Just Do It' and 'Keep Coming' are two of those clichéd guidelines, but everybody is encouraged to keep doing them, to keep coming and ultimately see the real stuff behind the supposed clichés. And then, after about five months, Gately had realized that for several days he had not thought about drugs at all – that he did not feel the constant, compulsive need to get high anymore: he was 'Free', the 'first time he'd been out of this kind of mental cage since he was maybe ten'.[110]

Gately is, as Bell and Dowling formulate it, the evident 'hero' of *Infinite Jest*, because of his 'transformation of character in the months he has been free of his addiction and doing his best to aid other battered souls in their struggle with their own demons'.[111] Gately is the 'knight' (one of his nicknames is 'Sir Osis') who, from a situation of addiction, develops into a stable self, an honest man who tries to form a meaningful life by helping others.

3.4.2. Hal Incandenza

As mentioned earlier, whereas Gately's situation during the novel is quite clear, interpreting Hal's development is anything but simple. In *Infinite Jest*'s opening scene (and, chronologically, the last episode of the story line), Hal, at that moment seen from his own first-person perspective, seems quite normal. However, the admission committee of the University of Arizona perceives him as animal-like, primitive and damaged. This contradiction leaves it up to the reader to decide what kind of state Hal is in, at the end of the story line. Judging by the reactions from the people around him, there is something wrong with Hal; several possible causes are alluded to in the novel: has Hal taken the allegedly very potent drug DMZ? Has he watched the 'lethal entertainment', the movie 'Infinite Jest'? Has he sunk into deep depression, perhaps partly as a result of his marijuana addiction? However, what these tentative suggestions can make us lose sight of is the possibility that Hal is actually on the mend; that, compared to how he is in the rest of the novel, he is getting better. Interpreting Hal's development and final situation depends strongly on how one judges Hal's surroundings, the cultural context described in the novel; for it is this context that determines the perception of Hal as suffering from some sort of fundamental defect.

---

[109] Ibid., 446.
[110] Ibid., 467–8.
[111] Bell and Dowling, *A Reader's Companion to* Infinite Jest, 95–6.

In some ways, Hal is an extraordinary, abnormal character – a prodigy in both sport and academic study – but in many respects Hal is also utterly normal: his addiction, and accompanying hyperreflexivity and endless irony, are, as we have seen in many of the examples already given, typical of the society portrayed in *Infinite Jest*. The first part of Hal's story line contains many descriptions of the gravity of his addiction, and the accompanying state of 'Analysis-Paralysis'.[112]

However, partly because of an upcoming, non-manipulable urine test,[113] Hal decides to quit marijuana and the other drugs he occasionally uses. Not long after this decision, Hal confesses his former drug use to his brother Mario. Hal says that he is afraid of the impendent withdrawal symptoms and asks Mario for help. Mario answers: "'Hal, if I tell you the truth, will you get mad and tell me be a fucking?' 'I trust you. You're smart, Boo.' 'Then Hal?' 'Tell me what I should do.' 'I think you just did it. What you should do. I think you just did.' '. . .' 'Do you see what I mean?'"[114] This confession and call for help indicate an unprecedented open-heartedness on the part of Hal.[115] This might be part of what is described as the 'whole new Hal', who doesn't use drugs anymore and who will go to the next drug test with a 'wide smile' and 'not a secretive thought in his head'.[116]

Shortly after his confession to Mario, Hal starts to narrate from a first-person perspective (and chronologically speaking, keeps on doing so; as mentioned, the novel's opening scene, which is the last episode of the story, is told by Hal in the first-person).[117] Up to that moment Hal's perspective has always been rendered in the third-person, or Hal has been described from the third-person perspective of other characters. We can regard the fact that Hal starts narrating in the first-person, as a sign of the fact that Hal starts to develop a self; the change in perspective marks this development.

However, at the same moment that Hal starts to open up and narrate in the first-person, other characters start asking him whether there is something wrong with him, and Hal has no idea what they are talking about. The first symptom seems to be that others perceive Hal to have a constant 'hilarity face', and either ask why he is crying or why he is laughing, while he thinks he is doing neither.[118] This discrepancy between how others perceive him and how he perceives himself is at its most extreme in the opening scene: Hal, via his first-person perspective, seems normal and thinks: 'I believe I appear neutral, maybe even pleasant.'[119] But when he tries to express what he thinks

---

[112] E.g. IJ, 334; cf. Chapter 1.
[113] Previously, to pass the tests, the drug-taking ETA students submitted urine samples acquired from the youngest students.
[114] IJ, 785.
[115] E.g. right after shifting to the first-person perspective, when Hal strongly hopes that the heavy snowfall will lead to the cancellation of the scheduled tennis matches, he also realizes that he has not really had any active hopes or wishes for a very long time (cf. ibid., 852).
[116] Ibid., 635.
[117] Starting at ibid., 851.
[118] Ibid., 865, 875–6.
[119] By now, Hal knows that he is perceived differently than he feels (cf. ibid., 3, 5, 8, 9).

and feels, the admission committee perceives his facial expression as 'animal-like' and 'contorted', and his voice as a hysterical, terrifying scream.[120]

The novel then describes the build-up to this opening scene. The question 'what happened to / is wrong with Hal?' is one of *Infinite Jest*'s main narrative threads, but the novel offers no explicit answer. Two possible explanations – use of the drug DMZ or having watched the film 'Infinite Jest' – imply that such an event has taken place in the intervening year that the novel does not describe; these explanations are therefore the most mysterious, as well as the most sensationalist (potent drug! fatal film!). As such they are very much in line with the techniques of the commercial, addictive entertainment culture that the novel criticizes, and should therefore perhaps not be taken too seriously. Moreover, the supposed symptoms of what is potentially wrong with Hal have started before this time, before he might have seen the film or used the drug.

Another possibility is that Hal, who is repeatedly described as suffering from anhedonia (characterized as a mild form of depression), has sunk into in a deeper, clinical form of depression.[121] Hal displays several striking similarities to Kate Gompert, a character described as suffering from clinical depression. The following description of her facial expression calls to mind that of Hal's 'hilarity-face': 'She looked either pained or trying somehow to express hilarity.'[122] Another potential similarity is that her depression is connected to withdrawal from marijuana use.[123] She is not just addicted to the marijuana itself, but also to the secrecy surrounding her use of it, just like Hal; Kate says: 'I'm like so obsessed with Do They Know, Can They Tell', and about Hal we read that he likes to secretly get high and that he is just as 'attached to the secrecy as he is to getting high'.[124]

However, there are also unmistakable and crucial differences between Kate's depression and Hal's situation. The uncomprehendedness that Kate describes as connected to depression perhaps calls to mind Hal's uncomprehendedness (for instance, vis-à-vis the admission committee). But Hal's situation, here, is completely opposite to Kate's. Kate is described as completely absorbed by the psychic pain she experiences, and consequently incapable of the empathy that is needed to explain herself to other people. Hal, on the other hand, makes frantic efforts to explain who he is, what he feels and what he deems important, when before the admission committee, for example, he says: 'I am not just a boy who plays tennis. [. . .] I'm not a machine. I feel and believe. I have opinions. [. . .] Please don't think I don't care.'[125]

These statements fit the development, discussed above, in which Hal becomes increasingly aware of his own feelings and starts to open up. This honesty and openness enable Hal's self to take shape, enable him to become a self. At a certain moment Hal looks at the reflection of his face in a window: 'I looked sketchy and faint

---

[120] Cf. ibid., 12.
[121] Ibid., 695.
[122] Ibid., 76.
[123] Ibid., 695.
[124] Ibid., 77, 49.
[125] Ibid., 75, 696, 11, 12.

to myself, tentative and ghostly against all that blazing white.'[126] Hal's 'ghostliness' can be interpreted in two ways: either Hal is starting to *dis*appear, turning 'inside', or he is starting to *appear*: his self, previously empty and invisible, is increasingly taking shape and therefore slowly becoming visible. The second interpretation is in line with Hal's increasing self-expression, and with Hal's own description of the development of his self, further on in the text: 'I felt awakened to a basic dimension I'd neglected. [. . .] I felt more solidly composed [. . .]. I was impossible to knock down.'[127]

Most interpretations of Hal's situation assume that something is wrong with him. But we could also turn the diagnosis around: *Infinite Jest* describes a society in which a lot is clearly amiss, and it is in this society, this culture that Hal has grown up: 'We are shown how to fashion masks of ennui and jaded irony at a young age [. . .] [a]nd then it's stuck there, the weary cynicism that saves us from gooey sentiment and unsophisticated naïveté. Sentiment equals naïveté on this continent.' In his cynical contempt for a self that gives sincere expression to its thoughts and emotions, the old Hal complies perfectly with what is normal within the described culture: 'One of the really American things about Hal, probably, is the way he despises what he is really lonely for: this hideous internal self, incontinent of sentiment and need, that pules and writhes under the hip empty mask, anhedonia.'[128] Hal's disgust is described as an *anxiety* for something that is supposedly childlike and underdeveloped (it is 'incontinent' and 'pules'), and that looks deformed and hideous and 'writhes'; but Hal also realizes that this is in fact an anxiety of being sincere and human:

> [T]hat what passes for hip cynical transcendence of sentiment is really some kind of fear of being really human, since to be really human [. . .] is probably to be unavoidably sentimental and naïve and goo-prone and generally pathetic, is to be in some basic interior way forever infantile, some sort of not-quite-right-looking infant dragging itself anaclitically around the map, with big wet eyes and froggy-soft skin, huge skull, gooey drool.[129]

These descriptions call to mind Mario, who is also described as being hideous, as we can see in the following descriptions: he is 'at 18+ in a range somewhere between elf and jockey', dragging himself along, 'body tilted way forward', and having a '[large but] withered-looking head', 'khaki-colored skin, an odd dead gray-green' that gives him an 'almost uncannily reptilian/dinosaurian look'. In addition, Mario has an 'involuntarily constant smile'; compare this to Hal's hilarity-face and the description of the 'whole

---

126 Ibid., 876.
127 Ibid., 902. This passage is also about Hal saying that he always understood himself as 'vertical', but as a result of his 'horizontality' feels stronger now. We could connect this to the importance of community, of the horizontal connection (transcendence) with others (instead of vertical solitude), discussed in Chapter 8.
128 Ibid., 694, 695.
129 Ibid., 694–5.

new Hal' who does not do drugs anymore and submits his own urine 'with a wide smile'. Mario's sincerity is regarded by the rest of society as a lack of development and sophistication, as some sort of awful handicap. Primitive and hideous, which is also how Hal is perceived in the opening scene of the book: he fills the members of the admission committee with horror; they describe Hal as animal-like, with a contorted face and high-pitched voice.[130]

Accordingly, we could conclude that there is nothing wrong with Hal, but that a change has taken place, from hyperreflexive irony to an openness, to the formation of a self – a change of which the rest of the novel illustrates the desirability – and therefore also conclude that there is something wrong with the society that is horrified by him.[131] The ambiguous descriptions of Hal's situation raise an important question: what is regarded as normal in the society portrayed in the novel, and what does this imply for those who differ from that normality?

Catherine Nichols writes the following about Hal and Gately: 'the trajectory of their transformation is one of restoring personal agency by turning the self inside-out rather than suppressing it beneath deliberate artifice'.[132] Like Will, Gately and Hal gradually turn outside, open themselves up to the world around them, to others, instead of remaining in their initial confinement inside, their addiction to their own heads. In Gately's development, guided by AA, we can recognize the importance of the three elements that are distinguished in Part 2 of this study. For Gately, his AA assisted recovery means that he gets *reality* back in sight (instead of the addicted flight into aesthetic fantasy), and acknowledges that what his hyperreflexive, ironic mind has for years regarded as clichés are clichés exactly because they are so true and real. Furthermore, AA means a *community* for Gately, which is indispensable for gaining insight into and developing the self: it is through listening and confessing to others, through receiving and giving help from and to others, that Gately starts to understand, and to develop a self; compare the remark that many addicts do not know who they are, and that other people can often see an individual better than that individual can himself.[133] Both aspects are made possible by the attitude of *sincerity* that Gately gradually adopts: AA makes him open up and be honest, to others and to himself. This does not happen automatically: it requires a (reflective) decision from the addict to act according to the guidelines, which can be regarded as a reminder of good faith insights. AA brings about a *pure reflection* in Gately: its guidelines, constituting the formation of the self, are taken on by Gately in his actions in AA and in Ennet House; his transformation is based on adopting these insights through a process of reflection.

---

[130] Cf. ibid., 216, 313, 154, 314, 12, 14; also, in this scene Hal calls himself an 'infantophile', a term capturing the negative perception of the desire for sincerity and spontaneity, as felt by the outside world, but at that point not by Hal himself anymore (16).

[131] In Hal's 'self-explanation' to the committee we can read a rejection of the ironic, postmodernist conception of the self, when Hal states that he is not just a 'creātus, manufactured, conditioned, bred for a function' (ibid., 12).

[132] Nichols, 'Dialogizing Postmodern Carnival', 13.

[133] Cf. IJ, 200, 204.

Hal undergoes a similar development, although it seems to be crucial that Gately is part of a community of fellow-sufferers, whereas Hal is alone, facing the ironic community from which he has detached himself. This can also explain the contrast between the clarity of Hal's internal monologue and the complete lack of understanding of his words by the people around him: Hal's development to the attitude of sincerity is connected to a change in language-game(s) – a language-game in which he has become initiated at the time of the opening scene (perhaps via Don Gately and Mario), as a result of which he seems more at ease with his new self than a year earlier, in the scenes at the end of the book. However, the people around him – the members of the committee, Hal's supervisors from the academy – are not familiar with this language-game, and therefore they do not understand him, and get the impression that he is uttering primitive drivel. So it seems as if Hal, in the end, is still or even more deeply confined in himself, but this might be explained by the fact that he has no support network; other people are still missing from what we get to see of Hal's life, but he can be seen to be on the right path, following in the footsteps of Mario and Gately.

From the moment of his confession and call for help to Mario, Hal opens up and acknowledges the importance of the other in judging and becoming who you are. That, from this moment on, Hal starts acting as first-person narrator, that he becomes aware of his thoughts and feelings, and that he feels more 'dense' as a self, indicates that he has become aware of the – in Sartre's terminology – 'transcendent' character of the self: Hal develops his self in an openness, in a casting-towards the world. Hal's transition is prompted by the reflective realization that, for example, Mario's good faith gives him a better understanding of himself, reality and other people. The encounter with Gately, who has after all gained a similar understanding, may also have contributed to that. Hal decides (that is, through a voluntary act) that the intuition he has about what it means to be, as he formulates it himself, 'really human' (open, vulnerable, et cetera) is true and desirable, and he chooses to live according to this insight, and, as such, becomes a *sincere* self.

Conclusion

This chapter has examined the basic attitude of sincerity, as portrayed in the novels of Wallace, Eggers and Foer, in response to the problems of contemporary Western existence that were explored in Part 1. Sincerity has been conceived as the virtue of wanting to form a stable self in the world, and has been further developed in line with Sartre's view of consciousness and self-becoming. Against hyperreflexivity and endless irony (which were shown to be in bad faith), we have seen that 'good faith' is the pre-reflective awareness and acceptance of human-reality, as the need to become a self in connection to the world outside consciousness, by 'existing' the tension between transcendence and facticity. 'Sincerity' consists of resuming this awareness reflectively, through a 'pure reflection', which implies grasping oneself without depriving consciousness of its spontaneity and directedness at the world. The characters Mario Incandenza and Oskar Schell (from Wallace's *Infinite Jest* and Foer's *Extremely Loud & Incredibly Close*, respectively) have been analysed as paragons of good faith, who, through their intuitive awareness of the task of self-becoming, function as exemplary characters demonstrating a life-view that other characters are subsequently shown to arrive at through a more difficult, reflected route. The attitude of sincerity was analysed through the cases of Will Chmielewski, and of Don Gately and Hal Incandenza (from Eggers's *You Shall Know Our Velocity* and Wallace's *Infinite Jest*, respectively). The novels in question show these characters overcoming their reflexive-ironic attitude, by realizing the transcendent character of the self; they show that, to achieve a meaningful existence, consciousness has to be connected to the world outside itself.

In literature, terms like trust and sincerity are often viewed with suspicion, especially when the role of the author is concerned. It is argued that an author of literary texts *cannot* be sincere and reliable because what he describes does not exist, and does not have an unequivocal meaning that can be grasped by the reader. However, in my opinion, the fact that a text can contain many meanings does not mean that it is unreliable. Indeed, to acquire one or more of these meanings, one must have trust in the texts' sincere attempt to convey meaning at all. Wallace's story 'Octet' – which will also be addressed in Chapter 8, in the context of the story's desire to connect to the other, to the reader – suggests that a vulnerable attitude is necessary, if a literary text is to succeed: writer and reader must be convinced that the text, their conversation, has significance, has *meaning*. In that sense, literature is a matter of trust and sincerity. 'The trick to this solution is that you'd have to be 100% honest. Meaning not just sincere but almost naked. Worse than naked – more like unarmed. Defenseless.' And the story ends with the appeal: 'So decide.'[134] These last two words invite the reader to judge whether the text describes something significant, whether it is at all meaningful. In doing so, the story explicitly displays its essential vulnerability.

'So decide' – this formulation connects this chapter to Chapter 7, as further realizing sincerity requires decision, choice. In this respect, Sartre offers an apt description of the honest, reflective attitude he has in mind (and that he 'mislabels' authenticity). He calls it a 'wanting to be'. Thinking that one 'is something' or 'is nothing' is in bad faith (emphasizing, respectively, facticity and transcendence). 'Wanting to be', on the other hand, expresses both the being and not-being that characterizes human consciousness. Sartre writes:

[F]irst of all wanting is not being. And precisely if I want being it is because I am not. Therefore to want to be is both, in one way to be [. . .] and, in another way, not to be [. . .]. To want to be, to will to be is precisely to be in question in his being, to be clear what I am (in the mode of not being it) by means of what I am not (in the mode of having to be it).[135]

---

[134] Wallace, 'Octet', *Brief Interviews with Hideous Men*, 131, 136.
[135] Sartre, *Notebooks*, 477.

Linsenbard explains: 'What Sartre is saying is that the For-itself, in reflectively accepting its contingency and calling itself into question, *decides* its mode of existence.'[136] Linsenbard then refers to a quote from Sartre again, who writes that man (the self), 'conscious of itself as project, that is wanting itself, represents a whole that recaptures itself in the existential dimension of a *choice*'. Sincerity automatically brings forth the matter of 'choice'; for sincerity is 'a willing of what I will'.[137]

---

[136] Linsenbard, *An Investigation of Jean-Paul Sartre's Posthumously Published Notebooks for an Ethics*, 99.
[137] Sartre, *Notebooks*, 480, 479.

7

Reality-Commitment

Introduction

In Chapter 6, we have seen that the notion of sincerity portrayed in the works of Wallace, Eggers and Foer, means a desire for a stable self that is connected to the world and others. Such an attitude of sincerity, if it is to be truly realized (attain substance and meaning), implies the need for choice, for action through which the self connects to reality. In Sartre's formulation: sincerity is 'a willing of what I will', and as such brings forth the matter of choice.[1] The attitude of total negative irony, analysed in Chapter 2, meant an evasion of choice; the aesthetic individual avoids all choice, all action, for they imply a commitment to reality. This absolute, ironic refusal of choice leads, as we have seen, to the gradual disappearance of reality and of the other, and ultimately also of the self, into complete emptiness.

The novels' portrayal of the overcoming of these problems – as a result of the attitude of sincerity, through the realization that action gives meaning to self and world – can best be understood (like the portrayal of the attitude of irony that avoids all choice) in light of Kierkegaard's philosophy, and especially his description of the ethical life-view.

In section 1, I will analyse the novels on the basis of Kierkegaard's contention that the sincere realization (through the acknowledgement of the insufficiency of 'negative freedom', the experience of 'despair', and of 'urgency') of the all-determining importance of choice, of much-needed action, in fact equals that (first) choice that constitutes the transition to the ethical life-view, to the experience of self and world as standing in meaningful connection. In section 2, I will continue by asking: after the realization that one has to choose, how does one come to the choice one has to choose? Kierkegaard says that this requires the individual to relate the past (as his 'gift') and the future (as his 'task') to each other. Finally, in section 3, I will address Kierkegaard's contention that the choice of self-becoming implies 'repetition', which in the novels can be seen to be significant in three ways: first of all, that the responsibility

Unless otherwise indicated, translations are mine.

[1] Sartre, *Notebooks*, 479.

of becoming a self (of relating gift and task) is never done, presents itself over and over again (this regular repetition of choice is also where irony, in a controlled form, has its place in the ethical existence); secondly, repetition versus what the aesthete expects repetition to mean, namely boredom (as in, routine), while the ethical individual welcomes repetition as his responsibility; and thirdly, repetition means that choice is not just dependent on the self, but also always implies a dependence on something that is transcendent to the self, that lies beyond the individual's control. I will regard this transcendence as horizontal – as immanent, this-worldly – contrary to Kierkegaard who regards the transcendence of repetition (of taking on responsibility), in the final instance, as vertical, as religious, as a recurring responsibility before God. However, I regard this limitation of repetition, to stop with the ethical, as justified on the basis of what the novels portray.

1. The realization of choice: Freedom, despair, urgency

In Kierkegaard's philosophy, choice marks the transition from the aesthetic to the ethical life-view. As discussed in Chapter 2, the aesthetic attitude is characterized by not choosing. Endless irony has declared every distinction invalid, immaterial, and thereby denied that there is such a thing as a meaningful choice. The ethical, on the other hand, 'constitutes the choice' and this choice is 'the main concern in life, you can win yourself, gain yourself', as Judge William, also known as the ethicist B, states in Kierkegaard's *Either/Or*. Perhaps, one might want to raise the objection that the ironic-aesthetic life-view is, in fact, a choice as well, the choice to live an aesthetic existence. But the ethicist points out to the aesthete: 'my view of a choice is essentially different from yours, provided that I can speak of such a thing, for the difference in yours is precisely that it prevents a choice'. As said, the ironic-aesthetic attitude is characterized by not choosing. Whereas the aesthete regards each 'Either/ Or' as an expression of the absence of any meaningful choice (a 'dagger' with which to 'assassinate' the 'whole of actuality'), the ethicist claims that in fact 'one *is* faced with a choice, an actual Either/Or'. To which he adds: 'there comes a midnight hour when everyone must unmask'.[2]

In this section, I will discuss three successive insights (each in connection to one of the studied novels): into freedom, despair and urgency, that together constitute the realization (both in the sense of 'awareness' and of 'actualization') of the significance of choice.

1.1. Freedom

In Chapter 2, we have already seen that the aesthete turns irony into a permanent attitude, and wants to retain his negative freedom at all costs, avoiding all obligations and responsibility, while for Kierkegaard negative freedom cannot function as an

---

[2] EO 2, 169, 163, 164, 162 [emphasis added, AdD; cf. EO 1, 527], 160.

end in itself but serves to make freedom possible, as the realization of a self-chosen existence. As the ethicist B in *Either/Or* says to the aesthete A: 'you have not actually chosen at all [. . .] an esthetic choice is no choice. On the whole, to choose is an intrinsic and stringent term for the ethical.'[3]

In *Infinite Jest*, the conversation (briefly referred to in Chapter 2) between wheelchair terrorist Remy Marathe and secret agent Hugh Steeply offers a general discussion of this problem and of the necessity of choice as the only alternative to the dead-end of permanent irony. Marathe says that Americans always talk about freedom, but without knowing what it actually entails. Americans, says Marathe, think of freedom solely in terms of *negative* freedom: 'Your freedom is the freedom-*from*: no one tells your precious individual U.S.A. selves what they must do. It is this meaning only, this freedom from constraint and forced duress. [. . .] But what of the freedom-*to*?' Marathe subsequently connects this positive freedom to the importance of choice: 'How is there freedom to choose if one does not learn how to choose?'[4]

Marathe's remarks sketch out the background of one of the novel's most important themes, namely the addiction to pleasure (stimulants, entertainment): the majority of the characters are solely interested in negative freedom, in the flight into the fantasy world of one's own pleasure, an 'ideality' (a world solely in one's mind) that is disconnected from reality. In the conversation between Marathe and Steeply the ironic-aesthetic misconception of freedom is further illustrated by the example of an experiment in a Canadian psychiatric centre (thereby also illustrating that the dominance of the aesthetic life-view is not just an American but a Western problem). In the experiment the pleasure terminals in a rat's brain are connected to a sort of 'auto-stimulation lever' that the rat can push to subsequently experience pleasure. However, the result is that the rat would continue to press the lever, ignoring basic life necessities, until it dies. Nevertheless, when word of the experiment got out, says Steeply, soon long queues of human volunteers formed in front of the centre, volunteering for 'fatal addiction to the electrical pleasure'.[5]

In the novel, the ultimate symbol of pleasure, the ultimate stimulant, is the film 'Infinite Jest': it offers a fatal pleasure that puts the viewer in a blissful but completely catatonic state of self-neglect. The film is also the reason for the meeting between Marathe and Steeply; have the AFR wheelchair terrorists obtained a copy of the 'lethal entertainment' and are they going to use it for an 'attack' on America? The title of the movie can be read, in this context,[6] as signifying 'endless joke' and thereby referring

---

[3] Ibid., 166.
[4] IJ, 320; cf. the elevator discussion in *The Pale King*: 'Americans are in a way crazy. We infantilize ourselves. We don't think of ourselves as citizens – parts of something larger to which we have profound responsibilities. We think of ourselves as citizens when it comes to our rights and privileges, but not our responsibilities' (130); cf. Boswell, 'Trickle-Down Citizenship: Taxes and Civic Responsibility in *The Pale King*', 217–18; Clare, 'The Politics of Boredom and the Boredom of Politics in *The Pale King*', 198–9.
[5] Ibid., 471–3.
[6] As part of the novel's title, 'infinity' also has a positive meaning, namely the infinity of the story that causes the reader to return to it over and over again, rereading it, finding new meanings. 'Jest', as referring to irony, can then be interpreted as meaning 'controlled' irony, the ethical form of irony discussed further on in the current chapter.

to the endless (total, negative) irony of the aesthetic life-view. And the film's potential societal danger (or, success, for the AFR) is that watching it leads, as it were, to the ideal of that life-view, all choice leading to the 'pleasure of not choosing', Marathe says to Kate ('Katherine') Gompert, one of the resident addicts of Ennet House, after which he offers her the possibility of watching the film, exactly because its consequences are so seductive to an aesthete who wants to avoid every choice and responsibility: 'you would feel more good feeling and pleasure than ever before for you: you would never again feel sorrow or pity or the pain of the chains and cage of never choosing. [. . .] If my claim, it was true, you would say yes, Katherine, no?'[7]

The role of Marathe's remarks in *Infinite Jest* is that they show, via a negative route (that is, by showing what happens when you do not do something), that the sincere acknowledgement of the importance of choice is necessary if self and world are to be experienced meaningfully. His remarks embody the insight that negative freedom (freedom-from, achieved through irony) is not an end in itself but merely a stepping stone towards a positive freedom (freedom-to) that the individual can only realize through choice.

1.2. Despair

The purposeful, fatal flight into the pleasure of the individual fantasy world – purposeful in the sense that the individual knows that it will ultimately lead to his destruction – attests to a hopeless dismay that, in Chapters 3 and 4, we have also seen in the works of Barth and Ellis: Barth's weary fictions, that ask why in fact they are still going on ('I'm as sick of this as you are; there's nothing to say'),[8] and Ellis's character Patrick Bateman who knows that everything he does is of no consequence ('this confession has meant *nothing* . . .').[9] We could, in the words of Kierkegaard's ethicist Judge William, call this attitude '[t]his last life-view', 'despair itself'. Like Sartre, Kierkegaard regards human existence as characterized by an insoluble tension between what one is and what one still has to become;[10] everyone, who does not 'exist' this tension but tries to negate it, is in despair.[11] The ethicist states that 'every esthetic view of life is despair, and that everyone who lives esthetically is in despair, whether he knows it or not', but that the last instance of the aesthetic attitude 'has absorbed [up to a point] the consciousness of the nothingness of such a life-view', and with that it is despair *itself*.[12]

However, whereas the works of Barth and Ellis merely try to show the nothingness of this life-view in ever different ways, the works of Wallace, Eggers and Foer portray the awareness that this nothingness entails the necessity, and possibility, of something

---

[7] IJ, 781–2.
[8] LF, 105.
[9] AP, 362.
[10] Or, in a more Kierkegaardian formulation: both 'gift' and 'task'; I will elaborate these notions further on in this chapter.
[11] Lansink, *Vrijheid en ironie*, 53.
[12] EO 2, 194, 192.

else. The aesthetic life-view 'prevents a choice': as irony declares all distinctions to be immaterial and invalid, it becomes impossible to speak of a preferable alternative – and the worlds that are conjured up within the works of Barth and Ellis stay within the boundaries of this attitude. The awareness of the necessity of an alternative, that is, of a choice, presupposes letting go of irony, and that itself is already a (first) choice or action, through which the individual parts from the aesthetic. Or, as Judge William calls out to the aesthete A: 'What do you have to do, then? [. . .] I have only one answer: Despair, then!' The ethicist writes: 'Choose despair', 'not as a state in which you are to remain, but an act that takes all the power and earnestness and concentration of the soul'.[13] Kierkegaard's *Concluding Unscientific Postscript* looks back to *Either/Or* and describes the difference between the two life-views portrayed therein as follows: the aesthete '*was* despair', while 'The ethicist *has despaired*'. Wanting despair, despairing, means recognizing that something has to change, and that means changing despair from a *state* that one is in (with or without knowing it) to a self-chosen *act*; and with that choice the individual leaves despair behind (for he has thereby taken on the task of becoming). As the ethicist writes: 'in order truly to despair, a person must truly will it; but when he truly wills it, he is truly beyond despair'.[14]

In Foer's *Everything Is Illuminated*, a young girl named Brod (the 'very-great-grandmother' of Jonathan, one of the narrators) initially suffers from an aesthetic aversion to reality; existing things are not good, not beautiful enough for her: '*They were good and fine, but not beautiful. No, not if I'm being honest with myself. They are only the best of what exists.*' Consequently, Brod has come to think that the world 'was not for her, and that for whatever reason, she would never be happy and honest at the same time'. The statement that the world was not meant for Brod, articulates an aesthetic flight into 'ideality', just like the statement that the notions 'happy' and 'honest' exclude each other. Brod thinks that happiness or pleasure have to be created (or better said, fabricated) by oneself and can never be an (honest, real) product of the world. 'So she had to satisfy herself with the *idea* of love – loving the loving of things whose existence she didn't care at all about', as her orientation towards ideality and distance to reality is expressed: it 'was not the world that was the great and saving lie, but her willingness to make it beautiful and fair, to live a once-removed life, in a world once-removed from the one in which everyone else seemed to exist'. These quotations display Brod's passivity: on the one hand a dissatisfaction with the unreality of her existence, but on the other an impotence to do anything about it. Likewise when Brod 'falls in love' with the Kolker, and it could seem as if something has changed, her supposed infatuation takes place completely in ideality: she is in love with the idea of being in love – 'She loved what it felt like.' She longs for that which, in her fantasy, equals love; when the Kolker wants to have a real conversation with her, she cuts him off: 'All she wanted from him was cuddling and high voices'.[15] As we have shown in Part 1, the aesthete regards reality purely as a source of base material for the execution of his fantasies.

---

[13]   Ibid., 164, 207–8, 210.
[14]   CUP 1, 253; EO 2, 213.
[15]   EII, 79–80, 122, 125; cf. Chapter 1.

Nevertheless, at a certain moment a change takes place in Brod's life. When the Kolker wants to give her a present, she tells him that she does not love him (after all, what she had called love up to then was a form of aesthetic self-deceit). After the Kolker walks off in anger, Brod opens the gift-wrapped present: it is a bottle of perfume. At that moment Brod realizes that she has viewed the world in the wrong way, and that another attitude is possible:

> Blue ribbon, blue vellum, box. A bottle of perfume. [. . .] She sprayed a bit on her wrist. It was subtle. Not too pristine. *What?* she said once to herself, and then once aloud, *What?* She felt a total displacement, like a spinning globe brought to a sudden halt by the light touch of a finger. How did she end up here, like this? How could there have been so much – so many moments, so many people and things, so many razors and pillows, timepieces and subtle coffins – without her being aware? How did her life live itself without her?[16]

It is possible that the symbolism of the perfume confronts Brod with the evanescence of her old life-view. Or perhaps the present wakes her up to the Kolker's commitment to her and shows her that love is not an idea but an act. Or maybe the perfume bottle connects her with the factual reality of her past: Brod was born on a wagon that subsequently plunged into a river, after which she floated to the surface amidst the rest of the wagon's contents, which included a bottle of perfume. In any case, Brod realizes that she has not lived in reality, that her consciousness was aimed at something else, while her life continued. Her despair includes the awareness of the necessity and possibility of change that the world has a certain urgency that incites her to act: 'There were so many things to attend to.' Initially the many things that need doing seem to concern the destruction that the Kolker has caused in the kitchen (as the result of an accident at the saw mill, a saw blade has become stuck in the Kolker's skull, and ever since he has suffered from uncontrollable fits of aggression). But it quickly becomes clear that Brod's comments are about *everything* there is to do; there is always something, and this clearly has a positive meaning for Brod:

> Spices were scattered on the floor. Bent silverware on scratched countertops. Unhinged cabinets, dirt, and broken glass. There were so many things to attend to – so much gathering and throwing away; and after gathering and throwing away, saving what was salvageable; and after saving what was salvageable, cleaning; and after cleaning, washing down with soapy water; and after washing down with soapy water, dusting; and after dusting, something else; and after something else, something else. So many little things to do. Hundreds of millions of them. Everything in the universe felt like something to do.[17]

Subsequently, she says to the Kolker: '*I love you* [. . .]. *I do*', after which we read: 'for the first time, if felt precious – not like all of the words that had come to mean nothing, but like the last breath of a drowning victim'.[18] Brod feels a certain urgency in her

---

16   Ibid., 132.
17   Ibid., 132–3.
18   Ibid., 133, 135.

actions – *this* is what has to happen now – and thereby her love has become reality. I will elaborate on the importance of urgency – or, passion, as Kierkegaard calls it – in the next section.[19]

The narrator and character 'Jonathan Safran Foer' seems to have the same aesthetic preference for ideality over reality that we initially saw in Brod.[20] We could say that Jonathan flees into a magical fable about his ancestors, while the other narrator-protagonist, Alexander Perchov – the local guide who helps Jonathan in his search for his forebears in the Ukraine – describes the tragic reality they have discovered on their search.[21] Alex reproaches Jonathan: '*You are a coward for the same explanation that Brod is a coward.* [. . .] *You are all cowards because you live in a world that is "once-removed"* [. . .] *you are all in the proximity of love, and all disavow love*'. Alex, too, connects this with the problem of choice: '*This is about choosing*', and with negative freedom prevailing over positive freedom: '*We all choose things, and we also all choose against things. I want to be the kind of person who chooses for more than chooses against, but* [. . .] *like you, I discover myself choosing this time and the next time* [. . .] *that I will not, instead of that I will*'. This awareness of the importance of choice, of realizing a positive (instead of a merely negative) freedom, means that Alex, as Kierkegaard formulates it, has truly despaired. The closing chapter of the novel contains a note from the grandfather, translated by Alex (indicating the latter has forgiven the former for his morally reprehensible act of betraying his Jewish friend during World War II), in which we read about Alex's decision to kick his alcoholic, abusive father out of the parental home and take responsibility for his own happiness and that of his mother and his little brother Igor. Alex's grandfather also made a decision of his own (the note seems to be a suicide note). His formulation of this decision (which is also the final sentence of the novel) symbolizes the 'illumination' that carries the individual beyond despair: '*it is what I must do, and I will do it. Do you understand me? I will walk without noise, and I will open the door in darkness, and I will* '.[22] With this choice, as Alex does with his decision, the grandfather, who is tormented by the memory of his own moral failure during World War II, aims to take responsibility for his life. This is further emphasized by the repeated use of 'I will', of which the final instance is not followed by a word or punctuation mark, just white space, expressing the openness that the self is – it has to be given shape to, through choice.[23]

---

[19] In Foer's second novel, *Extremely Loud & Incredibly Close*, we can recognize a similar 'waking' to the urgency of reality, of action, to be able to give meaning to existence. Oskar, who has lost his father in 9/11 attacks on the World Trade Center, says, after having been quite withdrawn and introverted for some time: 'I just couldn't be dead any longer'. He goes on a search that, in the end, will help him cope with the death of his father (I will return to this later on in this chapter): 'Even if it was relatively insignificant, it was something, and I needed to do something, like sharks, who die if they don't swim, which I know about' (ELIC, 145, 87).

[20] Perhaps because Jonathan has projected his own problem onto Brod, as he has had to almost completely invent the life-story of his ancestor, and, as a result, has given her some of his own characteristics; e.g. the vegetarianism of Jonathan and Brod (EII, 65, 76).

[21] Collado-Rodriguez, 'Ethics in the Second Degree: Trauma and Dual Narratives in Jonathan Safran Foer's *Everything Is Illuminated*', 56.

[22] EII, 240, 218, 241, 276.

[23] The 'formula' 'I will' recurs throughout the novel, and refers, among other things, to the descriptions of the beginning of Brod's life, of the accident with Trachim B.'s wagon (cf. ibid., 8).

1.3. Urgency

The above has already made clear that, in first instance, it is not about *what* someone chooses, but *that* he despairs and thereby chooses. The ethicist in Kierkegaard's *Either/ Or* writes: 'Therefore, the point is still not that of choosing something; the point is not the reality of that which is chosen but the reality of choosing.'[24] But, as Cyril Lansink explains, 'that does not mean that *what* you choose, *to what* you relate can be something arbitrary or just simply something'.[25] It is after all the choice by which man chooses himself, gives substance to himself. So, one does not just choose an arbitrary option. But what does this reality of choosing look like, then?

Eggers's works are largely dedicated to this reality of choosing and of the accompanying despair (about what one is to do). *A Heartbreaking Work of Staggering Genius* clearly features this true despair, but the resulting meaningful action remains tentative, whereas *You Shall Know Our Velocity* does not just describe the true despair but also portrays more of the salvation of coherent, meaningful action. In both books, characters struggle with the countless possibilities that contemporary Western existence offers them, and the difficulty of choosing from those possibilities; they are struck by the luxury, yet paralysing, problem that everything is possible.

Kierkegaard writes: 'actuality acquires validity through action. But action must not degenerate into a kind of fatuous indefatigableness.'[26] Initially, this is exactly what happens with the characters in Eggers's works. In *You Shall Know Our Velocity* the two main characters, Will and Hand, undertake a trip around the world in eight days, proceeding from the idea of 'unmitigated movement, of serving any or maybe every impulse'.[27] But along the way one setback follows the other – all at the expense of the sparse, precious time that Will and Hand have:

> [Where was teleporting, for fuck's sake?] the one advancement that would finally break us all free of our slow movement from here to there, would zip our big fat slow fleshy bodies around as fast as our minds could will them – which was as fast as they should be going: the speed of thought.[28]

The last remark – that the speed of our movement should be equal to the speed of thought – is an illustration of the hyperreflexive mind that cannot accept the limitations the confrontation with reality imposes on the possibilities the individual has fantasized about. The same problem becomes visible, in *A Heartbreaking Work of Staggering Genius*, when Dave and Meredith talk about their ambitions, about what they want to achieve. The problem, they find, is that everything takes so much time and that this should change: they should be able to realize their projects in a day, instantaneously.[29] This desire for everything to be realized immediately is connected to the desire to instantly continue with something new, pursuing another possibility.

[24] EO 2, 176.
[25] Lansink, *Vrijheid en ironie*, 165.
[26] CI, 329.
[27] YSKOV, 9.
[28] Ibid., 54–5.
[29] AHWOSG, 144.

Further on in *A Heartbreaking Work of Staggering Genius* we read: 'we will not say no to anything, will try to stay awake while everyone is sleeping, will not sleep, will make the shoes with the elves, will breathe deeply all the time'.[30]

In *You Shall Know Our Velocity*, Will is unable to choose and tries to retain all possibilities (and, thereby, his negative freedom): countless life-directions all seem appealing and possible to him.[31] The 'unreality' of the 'possibilities' that Will dreams of – marrying a local African beauty and together vaccinating children, sailing the seas on a boat that he has built himself (after he has learned how to sail), organizing white-water trips in Alaska, and becoming a shark wrangler – emphasize that Will is very much stuck in a fantasized, aesthetic ideality.[32] Similarly, his trip around the world in eight days is inspired by the desperate wish to, at least for a short period of time, be able to do everything (to not have to choose). But that wish, the conviction that everything is important, has an exhausting and numbing effect because Will and Hand have to rush through everything and do not have the opportunity to truly undergo a certain experience or event. That Will ignores the question of what is *really* important to him, results, in fact, in him not really doing anything. It is a flight from choice. Or, as Hand formulates it at a certain moment: 'This whole trip, Will, is about you not being there. You're not anywhere. Where are you? Who are you there for? You're halfway across the world, driving at 100 mph through countries you know next to nothing about.'[33]

The eventual result of Will's trip is true despair: the realization of the necessity of choice. But what to choose? As we have already seen, Will confesses that many times he has hoped for something that would limit his possibilities, that would make the choice for him. But that wish is of course in bad faith, a desire to be determined like a thing.[34] The question is: how does the individual go from what he can do, to what he feels he *has* to do? Kierkegaard writes: '[action] ought to have an apriority in itself, so as not to lose itself in vapid infinity'.[35]

This 'apriority' of action means that the individual realizes that he is both the person who acts *and* who he becomes *through that action*. In Kierkegaard's other works this is described as 'the energy, the earnestness, and the pathos with which one chooses', and of 'venturing the decisive thing [. . .] in utmost subjective *passion* and in full consciousness of an eternal responsibility'; it is an *eternal* responsibility because the individual realizes that, through that choice, he chooses who he is and will be.[36] For Kierkegaard, pathos or passion means an intense commitment to what exists, to

---

[30] Ibid., 433. The idea of 'not sleeping' – a clear instance of the 'fatuous indefatigableness' (CI, 329) that Kierkegaard speaks of – recurs in *You Shall Know Our Velocity*, and there the idea is explicitly criticized. When Will and Hand are six days into their trip around the world, Will is exhausted but does not want to sleep because sleeping means losing time (cf. YSKOV, 252).

[31] Cf. YSKOV, 122–3.

[32] Cf. Lansink, *Vrijheid en ironie*, 173: 'Being ethically inspired contains the paradoxical awareness that you are merely leading one of your possible lives and that yet this is the only life, that many roads were possible that would testify to that inspiration and yet there is only one way.'

[33] YSKOV, 318–19.

[34] Cf. ibid., 323.

[35] CI, 329.

[36] EO 2, 167; CUP 1, 304 [emphasis added, AdD].

the reality that for the individual is of the highest importance. Therefore, passion is not a reflective movement – reflection is actually connected with the preference for ideality, and the ironic-aesthetic distancing from reality.[37] In *Two Ages*, Kierkegaard writes: 'The presence of the crucial either/or depends upon the individual's own impassioned desire directed towards acting decisively', that he can no longer allow 'letting his understanding frustrate him every time he is going to act'.[38] Passion is the realization of the importance of reality that stops reflection and urges one to act. It means, in Lansink's words, that 'the individual identifies with a possibility, makes it his own, after which any further reweighing of this appropriated possibility has to be regarded as an impulsive inclination'.[39] It means that the individual knows himself to be confronted, in his relation to the world, with an *urgency* that demands that he acts, that is, that he moves from possibility to reality.

In Eggers's works, too, characters experience such a realization of urgency. *A Heartbreaking Work of Staggering Genius* describes it as the 'rush of being useful, feeling the justification of one's flesh [. . .], *to feel urgency* – because this part of us craves purpose'. Chapter 6 already remarked on the simple, physical actions that in Eggers's works seem to foreshadow the life-view that is ultimately pursued. This exemplary function of physicality also holds for the experience of passion, or urgency: 'Our bodies love to run in the rain – I subconsciously put off returning movies just so I can run down the street, when it's pouring, before the store closes.' In light of the problems described in the novel, this is an important point; the subsequent passage shows the connected desire for a breach with the ironic-aesthetic existence that lacks all urgency: 'It feels so good, and you do not ever want to go back.'[40] In the book, such experiences tie in with caring for others – the care for Dave's sick parents, the upbringing of his younger brother: 'a place where, I felt, I was needed urgently, where I could lift sandbags, put my finger in the dike, whatever. [. . .] We feel glad that we have a very tangible reason to exist.'[41] The passionate choice means that the individual knows: this is what I have to do – not as an imposed obligation, but as a duty that he himself wants.[42]

2. The reality of the self as gift and task

But how does one, after realizing the necessity of choice – through the insight in one's freedom, followed by despair and the need for urgency – find the urgent choice

---

[37] Cf. 'For Kierkegaard, passion signifies the expression of the individual's existential power, and he opposes it to the impotence of reflection. [. . .] passion unites the qualities of actualization and intensification or inwardness which are essential to the movement of repetition' (Carlisle, 'Kierkegaard's *Repetition*', 528).

[38] Kierkegaard, *Two Ages*, 67.

[39] Lansink, *Vrijheid en ironie*, 38.

[40] AHWOSG, 45–6 [appendix].

[41] Ibid., 46 [appendix].

[42] Cf. 'the person who lives esthetically sees only possibilities everywhere [. . .], whereas the person who lives ethically sees tasks everywhere. [. . .] But in seeing his possibility as his task, the individual expresses precisely his sovereignty over himself' (EO 2, 251); see section 2, on the notion of 'gift' and 'task'.

that one specifically wants to make, thereby realizing a positive freedom and leaving despair behind? The next aspect of Kierkegaard's view of the self, that also plays an important role in the works of Wallace, Eggers and Foer, casts light on this question. As mentioned, Kierkegaard, like Sartre, regards human existence as characterized by the tension between what one is and what one still has to become (as we know, Sartre calls these aspects facticity and transcendence). For Kierkegaard, becoming a self means relating both aspects of human-reality to each other, constantly bringing them into 'synthesis'.[43] He calls these two aspects the gift and task of human existence. I will first elaborate Kierkegaard's conception of these two connected notions, and subsequently apply them to the descriptions offered in the novels in question.

2.1. Kierkegaard on the gift and task of human existence

Kierkegaard writes: 'actuality stands in a twofold relationship to the subject: partly as a gift that refuses to be rejected, partly as a task that wants to be fulfilled'. By reality as a gift, Kierkegaard means 'the individual's relation to a past' (to his facticity). He explains: 'This past will now claim validity for the individual and will not be overlooked or ignored.' Every individual has a certain situation, a history, a factuality that cannot just be denied. But this is what the aesthete tries to do: his negative, ironic freedom is an endless distancing from any connection to reality whatsoever. '[For irony] there really never was a past', writes Kierkegaard, 'it was all of historical actuality that [irony] negated in order to make room for a self-created actuality'. The ironic-aesthetic life-view 'knows it has the power to start all over again if it so pleases; anything that happened before is not binding'. That is why, in *Either/Or*, Judge William writes to the aesthete A: 'the capacity of soul that is actually wanting in you is memory, [. . .] memory of your own life, of what you have experienced in it'.[44]

But, 'the person who chooses himself ethically chooses himself concretely as this specific individual', writes the ethicist in *Either/Or*. Here, 'this specific individual' literally means: *this* individual that is 'specified' (characterized) by *this* facticity, by 'these capacities, these inclinations, these drives, these passions, influenced by this specific social milieu, as this specific product of a specific environment'. To become a self, the individual subsequently has to take 'upon himself responsibility for it all'. He cannot merely accept it as something that is just the way it is (as an immediacy), but he has to take upon himself the given, has to *choose* it, as his. For the individual, his 'actual history' forms the foundation of 'his positive freedom, because therein he possesses his premises'.[45] Man cannot become, develop, from nothing; he always does so on the basis of what he already is. What he is, he takes upon himself as what he becomes, as that *from which* he becomes (which forms the necessary starting point, the premise of self-becoming). If a certain choice is to have relevance for me at all, that choice will have to be related to something that was already there before that choice (something I already have or am); otherwise there would be no reason for this

---

[43] Kierkegaard, *The Concept of Anxiety*, 155.
[44] CI, 276, 277; EO 2, 275, 279, 197.
[45] EO 2, 250–1; CI, 277.

to be *my* choice. When the individual takes his past upon himself in this way, it does not just mean that 'he chooses himself as a product', but he 'can just as well be said to produce himself', states the ethicist in *Either/Or*.[46]

That the individual is not just a product, but also 'produces himself', brings us to reality as a task. For the choice to take one's past upon oneself is a step in the development of the self: it is an act directed to the future, to what the individual wants to become. It is the beginning of the future as a task that will be constantly related by the individual to his gift, to the past that he is, and to which the future is added step by step. Again, the ethicist in *Either/Or*:

> When a person has arrived at an understanding of himself, has had the courage to be willing to see himself, it by no means thereby follows that the story is now past history, for now it begins, now for the first time it gains its real meaning, in that every single experienced moment is led back to this total view.[47]

In *The Concept of Anxiety* Kierkegaard's pseudonym Vigilius Haufniensis speaks of 'the task for every man', to become, out of his freedom, 'whole'.[48] Taking on responsibility for oneself is itself an expression of the individual's freedom, of his task of self-determination towards the future; this to-and-fro between being and becoming characterizes existence. Judge William aptly summarizes: '[my self] is, for if it were not I could not choose it; it is not, for it first comes into existence through my choosing it, and otherwise my choice would be an illusion. But what is it, then, that I choose? [. . .] – it is freedom.'[49]

The aesthete does not realize this task. His reality 'is only possibility', and he wants to keep it that way; everything has to remain possible at all times for the aesthete. The ironic-aesthetic attitude is a flight for the responsibility from the becoming of one's existence: to redeem his task, the individual cannot just remain (non-committal) possibility, but has to freely determine himself, that is, realize himself as a positivity, an actuality.[50]

The self has to have continuity, if it is to exist as a self at all, says Kierkegaard. Continuity, for Kierkegaard, does not simply mean 'staying the same', but signifies the necessity of placing the new in relation to the old, even more so when the new implies a radical change in relation to the old. The transition from the aesthetic to the ethical life-view is itself such a radical change, from a condition of absolute non-committal to a free (continuity-creating) commitment to reality. Kierkegaard writes: 'In order for the acting individual to be able to accomplish his task by fulfilling actuality, he must feel himself integrated in a larger context, must feel the earnestness of responsibility, must feel and respect every reasonable consequence.'[51] Kierkegaard scholar K. Brian

---

[46]   EO 2, 251.
[47]   Ibid., 118.
[48]   Kierkegaard, *The Concept of Anxiety*, 18; cf. 'because [a human being] is a synthesis, he can be in anxiety' (155).
[49]   EO 2, 213–14; cf. Sartre's description of being-for-itself.
[50]   CI, 279.
[51]   Ibid.

Söderquist explains: 'If life is lived without recognizing the limitations of the past, life becomes "hypothetical" and "subjunctive" and one loses a sense of "continuity".' Söderquist adds: 'In order to understand the self, a person must take ownership of the actualized past, which in turn conditions the present and future.'[52] By taking on the past – becoming responsible for who one is – the past, and thereby the self, become actualized, part of the present reality; and that reality, how the person sees his life-up-till-now, forms the situation from which he has to shape his future. As such, the individual realizes a positive freedom, a freedom-to, by becoming himself: 'Now he possesses himself as posited by himself – that is, as chosen by himself, as free.'[53]

Kierkegaard sometimes calls the ethical choice, in which the individual commits to a certain existence, a 'leap'. The term 'leap' expresses the fundamental uncertainty of each commitment to actuality: contrary to aesthetic fantasy, which is fully self-contained, the outcome of the individual's ethical choice is dependent on actuality, and therefore not fully under his control. This is a decisive difference between aesthetic irony and the ethical leap: instead of aesthetically rejecting (a certain) actuality, the ethicist takes responsibility for that actuality (his gift) and tries to reshape it (his task).

2.2. Gift and task in the works of Wallace, Eggers and Foer

This forming of the self that starts from taking up responsibility for the past, plays an important role in the work of Wallace, Eggers and Foer. The main characters in these novels are all involved in such a relating of gift and task. I will address Wallace last, as his work brings together elements we find in the works of the other two, and also prompts most clearly the transition to the next section.

2.2.1. Jonathan Safran Foer

In *Everything Is Illuminated* Brod realizes that she has lived her life in a world 'once-removed', and this insight means that, from that moment on, she attaches great importance to the real world. When the Kolker's health deteriorates, and his fits of aggression become worse, he locks himself in a room; however, Brod, in a sense, stays with him, she takes care of him, from the room next door, talking to him through a hole in the wall. For the first time she is committed to the reality of their marriage (instead of fleeing into fantasy), accepting it for what it is and trying to do whatever she can, within that reality.

Extremely Loud & Incredibly Close describes the mourning process that Oskar goes through after the death of his father. Initially his attempts to cope with the past seem to contain an element of denial. Oskar interprets random things that his father left behind, as clues that Oskar has to decipher, thereby keeping his father 'alive' and present in Oskar's life. But of course the clues are a product of his imagination, and

---

[52] Söderquist, 'Authoring a Self', 157.
[53] EO 2, 223.

lead to nothing (real): 'I could connect them to make almost anything I wanted, which meant I wasn't getting closer to anything.' As a result, Oskar initially contends that '[n]othing is beautiful and true', an echo of Brod contrasting 'happy and honest', and likewise an expression of a certain aesthetic distance to reality.[54]

However, in the final chapter of *Extremely Loud & Incredibly Close*, titled 'Beautiful and True', Oskar comes to accept the truth of the past. Oskar's acceptance takes the shape of him seeing a symbolic 'task' set out for him: he decides to dig up his father's coffin (which was buried empty because there were no bodily remains), together with the man who is renting a room in the house of Oskar's grandmother; at that moment, Oskar does not yet realize that this man is his grandfather, the father of his father. When Oskar tells him about his idea to dig up the coffin, the grandfather asks: '"Why would you want to do that?" I told him, "Because it's the truth, and Dad loved the truth." "What truth?" "That he's dead."' Oskar calls the idea to dig up his father's coffin a 'simple solution to an impossible problem', again employing contrasting terms, but this time it is a real opposition (possible–impossible) that nevertheless has to be 'lived': the impossible problem is the death of Oskar's father, a historical truth for which no solution exists, but that Oskar simply has to take upon himself. At the same time, this truth prompts Oskar to come up with a simple solution, not for his father's death but for his own inability to cope with that death, and accept that reality as the basis for his own actions. When the grandfather asks what they are going to do after they have dug up the coffin, Oskar answers: 'We'll fill it, obviously.' But when the grandfather asks what they will fill it *with*, Oskar does not have an answer. Then the grandfather writes that he has an idea. On the night of the dig, the grandfather brings along two suitcases, containing the countless letters that he wrote to his son (Oskar's father), after leaving him and his mother; he never sent the letters, he just mailed the empty envelopes. When Oskar asks what all the papers are, the grandfather answers: 'Things I wasn't able to tell him. Letters.'[55] Subsequently, Oskar thinks:

> I don't think I figured out that he was my grandpa, not even in the deep parts of my brain. I definitely didn't make the connection between the letters in the suitcases and the envelopes in Grandma's dresser, even if I should have. But I must have understood something, I *must* have, because why else would I have opened my left hand?[56]

For both Oskar and his grandfather digging up the coffin is a way of taking responsibility for the past: both feel shame, Oskar for not picking up the phone when his father called from the World Trade Center, and the grandfather for leaving his family and not sending the letters. Their act opens them up to a future, from which both were cut off by a flight into an imagined, or at least highly reflected past, instead of the reality of the present.[57]

---

[54] ELIC, 9, 43.
[55] Ibid., 315, 321–2.
[56] Ibid., 322.
[57] Some critics are of the opinion that this final chapter of *Extremely Loud & Incredibly Close* ends with a childish, frivolous *denial* of reality, as Oskar finds a series of photos of a body falling from one of the towers of the WTC, which he subsequently lays down in reverse order so that it looks

2.2.2. Dave Eggers

The first part of *A Heartbreaking Work of Staggering Genius* describes episodes from the last months of the life of Dave's terminally ill mother, and returns to that period at the end of the novel, when Dave, while frisbeeing with his little brother Toph, remembers his mother's final moments in the hospital, and how she was 'not ready'. Those final pages describe, like the rest of the novel, the restlessness that Dave feels to make sure that he *is* ready, for everything that comes on his and his little brother's path. In this respect, *A Heartbreaking Work of Staggering Genius* does not describe a complete transition from the aesthetic to an ethical attitude.

However, the book does place the ironic-aesthetic elements of the behaviour of Dave and the rest of the editorial staff of *Might Magazine* in a negative contrast with the impact of 'real', important events: the accident of Shalini, the death of Skye, and, throughout the whole book, Toph's upbringing, leading to the conclusion that, in the end, 'actual life completely overwhelm[s] the endless self-examination that *Might* represented, and the magazine dies, [. . .] and actual things take over, and obliterate our glibness'.[58]

But throughout the work, it remains difficult for Dave to use this ethical awareness to consequently shape his actions, to choose a real commitment; although the end of *Might* – as the result of the ironization of its own, well-intended idealism – near the end of the book, seems to embody a cathartic insight. Perhaps the book can be said to show that ethical self-becoming, as the constant relating of gift and task, is a process that is never finished; the ethical view is not something that one arrives at, after which one is done, and no unclarity and aesthetic confusion remain. The facticity of the past – embodied, above all, by the death of Dave's parents – is constantly present in the book. The past functions as something that gives direction to Dave's future, as a task, in the upbringing of his brother, and in *Might*'s initial good intentions; however, despair is never far away in Eggers's autobiographical novel.

In *You Shall Know Our Velocity*, Hand tells Will about 'The Jumping People', who on the one hand want to carry their entire history around with them, as that which gives weight and wisdom to their souls, and, on the other hand want to fly like birds, which they are not able to do, because of the weight of their souls; so they have to settle for jumping. This story is intended to stand in contrast to Will's own story: Will, who carries his past with him as a burden and feels confined in his endless hyperreflexive rethinking of that past, which actually cuts him off from choice, from

---

as if the person is floating upwards. According to these critics, Foer hereby allows Oskar to spirit away the death of his father (and with that, the death and suffering of many others), and act as if nothing has happened (e.g. Beck, 'Kinderkampf', 94; Munson, 'In the Aftermath', 84; Myers, 'A Bag of Tired Tricks', 119; Siegel, 'Extremely Cloying & Incredibly False'). I do not agree with this critique. Reading the last pages of the novel, we can indeed see Oskar formulating the wish that it all had not happened ('We would have been safe' – but is that such a strange thing to wish for? Moreover: this wish implies that, in fact, it *did* happen), but we can also see that formulating that wish by creating the photo flipbook does not at all deny the reality of his father's death or that of the unknown falling person: Oskar even explicitly states that he does not have enough pictures to let the falling person float all the way back up, back inside. Oskar wishes that the person had not fallen, and that his father had not died, but he accepts that it is in fact the case (ELIC, 325–6).

[58] AHWOSG, 35 [appendix].

'jumping' (compare this to the Kierkegaardian notion of the leap). In the novel, the facticity of the past is embodied by Will's laborious relationship with his mother (in which the memory of Will's alcoholic father seems to play an important role), and, above all, by the recent death of Jack, a childhood friend of Will and Hand. Will's trip around the world in eight days is initially a flight for this facticity and the task it entails. But eventually the trip makes clear that movement and speed (transcendence) do not enable a successful flight from one's past. Will's decision, in the end, to continue (in a different tempo) his journey with his mother (who, before that, functions as the main critic of Will's hurried world trip), changes Will's attitude from flight behaviour to a responsible attempt to relate gift and task. In this respect, it does not matter that Will and his mother die shortly thereafter; in fact, the closing sentence of the novel emphasizes that Will has, in any case, lived in reality during that period: 'for two more glorious and interminable months I lived! We lived.'[59]

2.2.3. *David Foster Wallace*

Regarding the work of David Foster Wallace, I will here focus on the story line of Don Gately and AA in *Infinite Jest*. The development that Gately undergoes, from drug addicted criminal to live-in staffer at a halfway house for recovering drug addicts, resembles in many ways the Kierkegaardian transition from the aesthetic to the ethical life-view. For instance, we can recognize Kierkegaard's contention that true despair leads to choice, in Gately's description of the situation that the addict eventually finds himself in, the 'cliffish nexus of exactly two choices, this miserable road-fork Boston AA calls your Bottom'. Actually, there is only one choice because the other – addiction – comes down to not-choosing (fleeing for one's despair): 'It's all optional; do it or die.' In fact, the term 'Bottom' is not quite right in this respect, says Gately, because it feels more like 'someplace very high and unsupported: you're on the edge of something tall and leaning way out forward' – think back to Kierkegaard's description of the dizziness, the anxiety caused by freedom, discussed in Chapter 2.[60] This anxious despair is the moment of the Kierkegaardian leap, or as Gately formulates it, the 'jumping-off place' for almost every addict's recovery.[61]

Part of AA's 12-step programme is the confrontation with one's past: the addict has to face the facticity of his past, of his addiction as something that he does not completely control, and of the many mistakes he has made as the result of his addiction. The paradox of this is that the historical reality that, at the time, was aesthetically ignored by the addict, is now experienced as an actual presence, 'reexperienc[ing] things that he'd barely even been there to experience, in terms of emotionally, in the first place.'[62]

---

[59] YSKOV, 371.
[60] Cf. Kierkegaard: 'Boredom rests upon the nothing that interlaces existence; its dizziness is infinite, like that which comes from looking down into a bottomless abyss' (EO 1, 291). Also, Sartre: 'First we must acknowledge that Kierkegaard is right; anguish is distinguished from fear in that fear is fear of beings in the world whereas anguish is anguish before myself. Vertigo is anguish to the extent that I am afraid not of falling over the precipice, but of throwing myself over' (BN, 53).
[61] IJ, 347, 349, 357.
[62] Ibid., 446.

Gately's memories of his past, both in his dreams and during the AA meetings when he shares his experiences with other members, form an important part of Gately's story line in *Infinite Jest*: memories of his alcoholic mother, his violent stepfather, Gately's first drug and alcohol use when we was 9 years old, and the further evolution of his addictions, and, linked to all this, his criminal career, with the scene that ends the novel as the horrible high point of his memories: how Gately was forced to look on while his crime partner Gene Fackelmann was tortured to death. In the way he treats his memories, Gately shows that he has assumed responsibility for his past (as gift), and uses it as the basis for his actions in the present (as task). At Ennet House, the halfway facility to which he was once admitted, he helps others who have reached their 'Bottom'. In addition, as customary in AA, Gately speaks at meetings, about his past, his mistakes, about his responsibilities and what he has to do now: speaking at meetings is called '12th-Step work' or 'Giving it away', referring to AA's description of what is at the heart of recovery: 'You give it up to get it back to give it away'. This is Gately's task. AA even literally calls the sobriety that Gately has managed to maintain a 'gift', a 'sort of cosmic loan'. That gift, that loan, functions to subsequently connect the self with the future, because: 'You can't pay the loan back, but you can pay it *forward*', by participating and speaking at AA meetings, thereby helping yourself and others.[63]

I am not suggesting that *Infinite Jest* simply proposes the AA model as *the* integral solution to all of the contemporary problems portrayed in the novel. Rather, I think that the novel emphasizes the importance of certain notions that it attributes to AA and addiction recovery (and that can be found in other parts of the novel as well, for example, in the conversation between Marathe and Steeply), and that are also described by Kierkegaard as crucial to overcoming the ironic-aesthetic attitude and its problems. The leap towards the ethical (towards recovery) is described in *Infinite Jest* as a messy process that has to take place under many of the circumstances that made contemporary existence difficult in the first place. As we have already seen in the discussion of Eggers's *A Heartbreaking Work of Staggering Genius*, this is a process without end. In this case, you are a member of AA for the rest of your life, just like the constant relating of gift and task, of becoming a self, is an endless process, that has to be *repeated* over and over again. This notion of choice as 'repetition' will be further elaborated in the following section.

3. Reality as repetition

Repetition is an important but complex notion within Kierkegaard's philosophy. None of his works unequivocally conceptualize the notion.[64] Niels Nymann Eriksen

---

[63]   Ibid., 344.

[64]   Cf. 'the category of repetition [. . .] remains one of the most obscure elements of the Kierkegaardian corpus. [. . .] The difficulty is not due to the conceptual complexity of this category, but, on the contrary, to an evident lack of conceptuality. [. . .] For repetition is not so much a *philosophical doctrine* as it is a *paradigm of thought*, and as such it is something that cannot be grasped as an object for thought' (Eriksen, *Kierkegaard's Category of Repetition*, 2).

describes repetition as a specific (ethical–religious) 'paradigm of thought', which can be seen as opposed to the aesthetic way of thinking.[65] Repetition is a powerful image that expresses different aspects of the ethical attitude.

Kierkegaard opposes repetition to recollection. For Kierkegaard, the latter term is meant to refer to Western philosophy's longstanding preference for 'ideality', embodied above all by Plato, who regarded acquiring knowledge as a process of recollecting insights that were stored in the soul before birth. So, we should not interpret recollection to mean, for Kierkegaard, the process of recording and recalling actual events in our memory (that is, the ethical memory of one's own life, the acceptance of the historical factuality of the self, discussed in the previous section). Rather it means employing certain ideal images that *precede* those events: these ideal images already lay waiting, as kinds of memories, to which reality consequently should be matched. And it is this *idealized version* of reality that the aesthete regards as *real*, and therefore this is also how he records and recalls it in his mind.[66] In other words, for Kierkegaard, recollection designates the reflective, ironic-aesthetic preference for ideality over reality.

But what then is *repetition*? In Kierkegaard's eponymous work the story of the biblical figure Job functions as an important example: someone who loses everything to ultimately get it all back (and, in that sense, receive a repetition). This might create the mistaken impression that repetition can be adequately defined as a divine gift (or return), as something that is mainly done by God, while the individual perforce remains passive. But for Kierkegaard repetition is, above all, a description of the actions of the individual, of the changed attitude of the self: 'There is but one pregnant repetition, and that is the individuality's own repetition raised to a new power [. . .] being repetition *sensu eminentiori* [in the highest sense] and freedom's deepest interest.'[67] As mentioned earlier, repetition embodies several aspects that signal a departure from the aesthetic sphere.

Now I will discuss three aspects of Kierkegaard's notion of repetition that emerge from the works of Wallace, Eggers and Foer: repetition as responsibility (in his actions, the individual is committed to his choice of what is right), repetition versus boredom (the individual does not flee from reality into aesthetic diversion and distraction), and repetition as transcendence (the individual accepts the uncertain outcome of his actions, that reality is never under his complete control).

---

[65] Ibid.

[66] The young man from Kierkegaard's work *Repetition* offers an example of this aesthetic form of recollection: he uses his beloved as the malleable base material to conjure up a certain ideal image that he holds in relation to love. He 'aestheticizes' his real experiences of the relationship into idealized images that comply with the 'memories' that he already had at his disposal. In *Repetition* the pseudonymous narrator Constantin Constantius writes about the young man's 'love': 'He was deeply and fervently in love, that was clear, and yet a few days later he was able to recollect his love. He was essentially through with the entire relationship. In beginning it, he took such a tremendous step that he leaped over life' (Kierkegaard, *Fear and Trembling/Repetition*, 136). The young man calls to mind, in this respect, the aesthete A, who champions a 'poetic' form of remembering: you should be able to remove from a memory that which you do not like, and embellish that which remains to the maximum that your fantasy can make out of it (EO 1, 293). Also compare what has been remarked about this in Chapter 4, on *American Psycho*.

[67] Kierkegaard, *Fear and Trembling/Repetition*, 295 [Letter to Heiberg].

3.1. Repetition as responsibility through controlled, ethical irony

Choice is always the choice to live in the present.[68] The present is constantly there, forever returning, repeating, and that also means that *choice* has to be repeated, if the present reality of one's actions is to be retained. John W. Elrod writes: 'Time necessitates a continual repetition of the choice in order that the self may retain its eternal validity as a unity (present) of the past (necessity) and future (possibility) through freedom's expression of itself as choice.'[69] So, it is not the case that the individual, by making a choice, is finished, that he will never have to attend to his life-view again. He will have to remain aware of his choice, that he is the one who made it and keeps on making it, for as long as he keeps following it. In other words, he will have to repeat his choice. Choice is never definitive, never finished; otherwise it would become self-evident and could therefore no longer be called a choice.

At this point, we must note that irony is not completely absent from the ethical life. As mentioned in Chapter 2, Kierkegaard's irony critique is not aimed at all forms of irony, but only at the permanent attitude of total negative irony. Now we can see that irony, in a controlled form, has an important (though strictly limited) role in the ethical life. As we have seen, the reality of existence is constantly changing and the resulting paradox is that, precisely because of that change, the individual has to choose his changing existence as *his* existence, as *his* life, over and over again. As Judge William writes in *Either/Or*: 'at the very moment he chooses himself he is in motion. [. . .] he can remain in his freedom only by continually realizing it.'[70] Choice is never definitive, never completed: to be rightly called a choice, that choice cannot become a matter of self-evidence. Kierkegaard calls this process 'controlled irony': the regular resurfacing of the ethical choice so as to properly remain a choice. 'Irony as a controlled element' of the ethical life-view does not signify an endless total negation of actuality, like the irony of the aesthetic life-view, but instead, as Kierkegaard writes, places 'the appropriate emphasis on actuality', by emphasizing the importance of ethical commitment.[71] Richard M. Summers explains: 'Irony in this sense thus plays an essential role in the accomplishment of the human task [. . .]. It is the condition for correctly appraising the dimension of givenness in our situations, and for discerning the shape of the personal task that each of us has to accept.'[72] So, here, irony is not a means to an attitude of utter non-committal, but, quite conversely, a means to responsibility. Through controlled irony, the individual

---

[68] It is important to see this does not amount to (or better said, form the total opposite of) intoxicated absorption in the moment. Through choice the individual relates himself to both past and future, so both are made part of the present. By contrast, the aesthetic flight into ideality *does* imply such an intoxicated timelessness: the aesthete can 'decide' something in his head, after which more or less time goes by, and the aesthete thinks up something else, but, because this never leads to a committed act, the fabrications of the aesthete never attain reality, and the aesthete does not have a real present. The ethicist *does* have a present, and this by definition means that the present is there, over and over again.

[69] Elrod, *Being and Existence*, 139. Quoted in Lansink, *Vrijheid en ironie*, 192.

[70] EO 2, 232.

[71] CI, 328.

[72] Summers, '"Controlled Irony" and the Emergence of the Self in Kierkegaard's Dissertation', 309.

keeps on taking responsibility for his own choices. This way, irony, as a controlled element, is part of the ethical repetition of choice.

Repetition always brings the individual back to the present, as the only moment in which he faces a choice and is able to *make* a choice and thereby realize a responsibility. We have already seen that this desire to be in the act, in the present and in reality, is an important feature of the novels under examination. In two of the novels, this desire even takes on the form of two different notions of repetition that have an effect on the characters in question similar to the intended effect of Kierkegaard's notion of repetition. In Wallace's case, it even seems directly akin to Kierkegaard's notion; therefore, I will address Wallace last.

3.1.1. Dave Eggers

In *You Shall Know Our Velocity*, Hand explains to Will the theory of the 'multiverse', as a possible solution to Will's inability to choose which of the countless 'possible' lives he actually wants to pursue: '[Quantum physics is saying that] everything exists in a bunch of places at once', Hand explains: 'then there's gotta be multiple us's, and multiple worlds, simultaneously'. At first, Hand's multiverse theory, as a multiplication (but in that sense also a repetition) of lives, might seem a far cry from Kierkegaard's notion of repetition. But like the story of Job, the multiverse theory promises a sort of return, albeit a return of possibilities, that Will could still choose in his other lives. The effect of this idea is that it places Will in the present: he understands that he has to commit to choices which have to be made here and now, and that he should not want to keep all life options open; maybe he will choose those in another life, but in this life he has to do what is important now. Initially, Will is lukewarm to the value of the multiverse theory: 'It's useless [. . .], if you don't share any consciousness.' However, from the moment of Hand's exposition of the theory, a gradual shift sets in, in the way Will judges his own actions. He starts to experience reality in a different way. He starts to realize that he misses out on certain things by trying to seize everything, for instance, in Morocco, when they drive along the beach and Will considers spending the day there, playing with the children, looking for crabs – but they continue their trip. Will claims that he was not really convinced by Hand's explanation of the multiverse, but that he did wonder over the possibilities, and: 'for a second I thought that yes something like this was possible'. After not having stopped at the beach, Will and Hand do stop in Marrakesh when they are approached at a traffic light by the people in the car next to them, asking whether they feel like going out: 'It felt good. [. . .] They threw out a line and I felt like I was living a third or fourth life, someone else's life. It felt like regaining, in the morning while slowly waking, the ability to make a fist.'[73] Partly stimulated by the multiverse idea, Will experiences more and more freedom to give shape to himself ('I felt like I was living a third or fourth life'), and thereby *become* a self (symbolized by '[regaining] the ability to make a fist').

[73] YSKOV, 113–14, 188, 320, 236.

3.1.2. David Foster Wallace

Whereas this story element from *You Shall Know Our Velocity* can chiefly be said to describe a similar *effect* to Kierkegaard's notion of repetition, Wallace's *Infinite Jest* contains, in the storyline of Don Gately, a notion of repetition that seems to directly resemble that of Kierkegaard, both in substance and effect. It is displayed most clearly in a conversation between Gately and Joelle van Dyne, a new resident of Ennet House: they talk about the AA insight that getting clean, the choice not to use, only works 'One Day at a Time', by 'Keeping It in the Day'.[74] Here, we can already recognize the importance of the constant repetition of choice, keeping the individual in the present and giving reality to existence, instead of the addict's aesthetic flight from the reality of the present.

With regard to her former attempts at getting clean, Joelle draws the following comparison with motorcycle jumper Evel Knievel:

> I'd throw away the pipe and shake my fist at the sky and say *As God is my fucking witness NEVER AGAIN, as of this minute right here I QUIT FOR ALL TIME.* [. . .] And I'd bunker up all white-knuckled and stay straight. And count the days. I was proud of each day I stayed off. Each day seemed evidence of something, and I counted them. I'd add them up. Line them up end to end. [. . .] And soon it would get . . . improbable. As if each day was a car Knievel had to clear. One car, two cars. By the time I'd get up to say like maybe about 14 cars, it would begin to seem like this staggering number. [. . .] And the rest of the year, looking ahead, hundreds and hundreds of cars, me in the air trying to clear them. [. . .] How did I ever think anyone could do it that way?[75]

Joelle's comparison shows the essence of her former inability to get clean: her hyperreflexive, aesthetic mind kept luring her away from the reality of the present and, as such, precluded a real commitment. Gately recognizes this: 'everything unendurable was in the head, was the head not Abiding in the Present, but hopping the wall and doing a recon and then returning with unendurable views you then somehow believed'.[76]

But now, Gately knows that he could decide not to listen to his 'head'. And Joelle has realized this as well: 'I get to choose how to do it, and they'll help me stick to the choice. I don't think I'd realized before that I could – I can really *do* this. I can do this for one endless day.' Gately assents to this: 'she could as long as she continued to choose to'. Joelle tells him that Pat Montesian, her (and also Gately's former) counsellor, advised her to 'build a wall around each individual 24-hour period and not look over or back'.[77] The only remedy is the continuous repetition of choice in the present. Gately knows this only too well: he experienced

---

[74] Cf. IJ, 858.
[75] Ibid., 859.
[76] Ibid., 860–1.
[77] Ibid., 860, 858.

it firsthand, as the only way to endure the withdrawal symptoms while locked up in a jail cell:

> He had to build a wall around each second just to make it. The whole first two weeks of it are telescoped in his memory down into like one second – less: the space between two heartbeats. A breath and a second, the pause and gather between each cramp. An endless Now stretching its gull-wings out on either side of his heartbeat. And he'd never before or since felt so excruciatingly alive. Living in the Present between pulses.[78]

In time, this radical 'walling in' of each *second* was not necessary anymore ('this inter-beat Present, this sense of endless Now – it had vanished in Revere Holding along with the heaves and chills. He'd returned to himself, moved to sit on the bunk's edge, and ceased to Abide because he no longer had to') – but in fact the same principle holds for *staying* clean as well as for becoming clean, only now Gately has to take it 'One Day at a Time', living 'In the Moment'. Gately, who has been capable of pulling through second by second, was ready for the discipline needed to stay clean, when he was transferred to the halfway house and became a member of AA: a 'whole day at a crack seemed like tit, when he Came In. For he had Abided With The Bird'.[79]

What Gately describes is not just a way to get clean, but a way of life, an attitude that makes life possible; Gately speaks of the 'leap' needed to keep living like that, 'by choice'. This is what AA is aimed at: 'It's a gift, the Now [. . .]: it's no accident they call it *The Present*'.[80] Although, on the face of it, it might seem as if this approach disconnects the present from the flow of time, AA's emphasis on the present actually functions as an anchoring in reality, a protection against the aesthetic flight into ideality. The choice to focus on the present, and therefore on reality, creates a continuity in which the individual acknowledges the facticity of his addiction, and on the basis of that acknowledgement he chooses his actions directed at the future. That choice has to be made again every time, every day, because the person who does not really choose and act is in danger of relapse.[81]

3.2. Repetition versus boredom

Repetition is an ethical category, while boredom is the corresponding aesthetic category. In the eyes of the aesthete, repetition must necessarily amount to boredom.

---

[78]   Ibid., 859–60.
[79]   Ibid., 860.
[80]   Ibid.
[81]   Cf. the following passage from Kierkegaard's *Either/Or*, in relation to the theme of addiction in *Infinite Jest*: 'Imagine a person who has become addicted to gambling. Desire awakens in all its passion; it is as if his life would be at stake if his desire is not satisfied. If he is able to say to himself: At this moment I will not do it; I will not do it for an hour – then he is cured. This hour is the continuity [the unified, stable self – AdD] that saves him' (EO 2, 230).

For him, repetition equals confinement, as it entails a commitment that constantly recurs and that, because of that constant repetition, is not new and interesting, which is what the aesthetic mind wants everything to be.[82] Instead, it is *boring*, and that is what the aesthete fears most. In *Either/Or*, the aesthete A writes: 'Boredom is the root of all evil; it is that which must be held off.'[83]

The aesthete is afraid of being bored, tries fervently to occupy his oversaturated mind with all kinds of distractions, but inevitably ends up being bored. This is what we might call the double nature of boredom: it encompasses both the individual's basic, languid state of apathy, as well as the frenetic attempts that he might make, out of boredom, to distract himself from that state. Kierkegaard thus concludes: 'Boredom is the only continuity the ironist has. Boredom, this eternity devoid of content, this salvation devoid of joy, this superficial profundity, this hungry glut.' The ironic inability to commit to something causes an absolute emptiness. Try as the aesthete might, all his attempts at distraction, at 'poetic' variation, lead back to boredom; 'and behold – you were bored', observes the ethicist in *Either/Or*.[84]

The aesthete A asserts that, '[b]oredom rests upon the nothing that interlaces existence; its dizziness is infinite, like that which comes from looking down into a bottomless abyss'.[85] Boredom is the confrontation with the nothingness of aesthetic existence, and, as such, is connected to what Kierkegaard famously calls anxiety. While fear is always directed at a (supposedly) specific aspect of the world (snakes, heights, the monster under the bed), the object of anxiety is nothingness: it is directed at the undetermined situation of the individual, his freedom to form himself. Anxiety is the realization of the groundlessness of the individual, the realization that he is not automatically himself, but has to *become* a self, as the product of choices for which he is solely responsible.[86] Boredom has the same nothingness as its source, only the bored individual does not yet seem fully pervaded (or 'anxiety-struck') by the existential task that this nothingness represents.[87]

We could perhaps say that in our time, as can be seen in the portrayal of contemporary Western existence in the novels we have looked at, anxiety has been absorbed by boredom. Lars Svendsen observes: 'Boredom simply seems to be a more contemporary phenomenon than anxiety. We no longer suffer as much from anxiety,

---

[82] Kierkegaard writes about this aesthetic 'anxiety' of repetition, and the boredom it is seen to entail: 'for it seems as if [repetition] has a magic power to keep freedom captive once it has tricked it into its power' (quoted in Eriksen, *Kierkegaard's Category of Repetition*, 21).

[83] EO 1, 289.

[84] CI, 285; EO 2, 108.

[85] EO 1, 291.

[86] Cf. 'anxiety does not have a specific object – or, rather: the object of anxiety is nothing'; 'In anxiety it becomes clear that we are not automatically ourselves; we have to become ourselves. [. . .] the task is to become concrete' (Grøn, *The Concept of Anxiety in Søren Kierkegaard*, 5, 12).

[87] The difference between boredom and anxiety lies in the fact that in anxiety, the individual is firmly gripped by the insight into being as endless possibility, staring deeply into the abyss, unable to turn away, while boredom, in the words of Patrick Bigelow, 'recoils from this abyss [of possibility], refus[ing] to recognize it'. I think the term 'anxiety' evokes for us the image of a highly agitated state of being, while boredom is exactly the opposite: it is utter apathy. As Bigelow says: 'It is the despairing insistence that the nothing means nothing, since in the indifference of boredom, nothing matters, not even the nothing'. (Bigelow, 'The Ontology of Boredom', 258, 259–60).

but all the more from boredom.'[88] Whereas the insight into the groundless existence of man once caused deep, existential anxiety, in our time we have come to regard this insight as an insignificant platitude. In other words, a 'cliché', which our aesthetic minds find hard to bear – I will elaborate on this below. As a result, we are no longer anxious, but regard ourselves as 'just' bored, and no longer hear the existential call of the nothingness underlying that boredom.[89] Because the portrayal offered in Wallace's work most clearly prompts the transition to the next section, Wallace will be addressed last.

3.2.1. Dave Eggers and Jonathan Safran Foer

In Eggers's works, restlessness plays an important role. In *You Shall Know Our Velocity*, it is manifested literally, in the desire to constantly keep moving. It is what we already saw Kierkegaard call 'a kind of fatuous indefatigableness'[90] – as a distraction from boredom. Similarly, in *A Heartbreaking Work of Staggering Genius*, Dave says: 'Oh if only something would happen. [. . .] This is all some terrible machine, where only the expected passes through.'[91] In the end, this agitation is replaced by the relative calm of the choice of the stable self.

In Foer's works we can recognize the acceptance (and, thereby, surpassing) of boredom in the acceptance of things that are initially regarded as clichés that eventually turn out to be true. We can see this, among other things, in the afore-mentioned pairs of concepts, 'beautiful and true' and 'simply and impossibly', that are initially used for things that seem to have lost their meaning (and in that sense, have become impossible), but eventually win back their credibility and, exactly because of their simplicity, turn out to be all the more fundamental to the meaningful existence of the characters.

3.2.2. David Foster Wallace

The acceptance and surpassing of boredom, as inextricably connected to the repetition of choice, plays a more prominent, explicit role in Wallace's fiction. Addiction, one of the main themes of *Infinite Jest*, is portrayed as partly a flight (with alcohol, drugs and entertainment as the primary 'routes' or diversions) from boredom, in the above-described sense: that is, a flight from the uncertain and seemingly meaningless existence, from the nothingness that the individual 'is'.[92] In the novel, the acceptance of boredom (of the cliché, of routine, et cetera) plays an important role in attaining a meaningful life, and leaving the situation of addiction

---

88 Svendsen, *A Philosophy of Boredom*, 116.
89 Cf. Prins, *Uit verveling*, 19.
90 CI, 329.
91 AHWOSG, 142.
92 We could say that, in some ways, the addicted flight behaviour of *Infinite Jest*'s Don Gately and Hal represent the two basic aesthetic attitudes: Gately as the immediate flight (comparable to Don Juan, who is described in *Either/Or* as a force of nature; similarly, Gately is described as a muscleman, an enormous physical presence, whose thought and actions, accordingly, have a clear physicality) and Hal as reflected flight (a prodigious intellectual, more like the aesthete A and Johannes the Seducer).

(accompanied by hyperreflexive irony) behind. In Wallace's final, unfinished, posthumously published novel *The Pale King* (2011), this idea of enduring boredom as a route towards the realization of a meaningful life, is in fact the main theme; one of Wallace's notes for the novel reads: 'It turns out that bliss [. . .] lies on the other side of crushing boredom. Pay attention to the most tedious thing you can find [. . .], and, in waves, a boredom like you've never known will wash over you [. . .]. Ride these out, and it's like stepping from black and white into color.'[93] However, I will focus on the portrayal of boredom and repetition in *Infinite Jest*.

The most interesting and prominent manifestation of Kierkegaard's contrast of repetition and boredom in *Infinite Jest* are the so-called clichéd directives of AA. New AA members (with their thought patterns of hyperreflexive irony still largely intact), such as Geoffrey Day, say they are 'bored' by these guidelines; they regard them as 'boring' (stale, unoriginal, and therefore empty and meaningless). Gately knows this, but he also knows that if Geoffrey Day continues based on how things seem to him, 'then he's a dead man for sure'. New members are encouraged to share their exasperation about these clichés, but to keep following them nonetheless. As when Joelle van Dyne tells Gately that she took his advice and shared her complaint about 'One Day at a Time' and 'Keep It in the Day' as 'trite clichés', and says to Gately: 'you were right, they just laughed'. Gately recognizes the feeling. He admits that, initially, the 'idea that AA might actually somehow *work* unnerved him. He suspected some sort of trap'. But, Gately tries to make clear to the new members, 'this grudging move toward maybe acknowledging that this unromantic, unhip, clichéd AA thing – so unlikely and unpromising, so much the inverse of what they'd come too much to love – might really be able to keep the lover's toothy maw at bay'. Gately tells newly admitted residents of Ennet House: 'It starts to turn out that the vapider the AA cliché, the sharper the canines of the real truth it covers.'[94]

The key is realizing that the 'clichéd directives are a lot more deep and hard to actually *do*. To try and live by instead of just say', says Gately. It is about choosing to 'do', to act according to these guidelines, to 'live' them. One does not have to be *absolutely* convinced, to choose to do something – it is perhaps even impossible to be – such absolute assessments only serve to keep the individual locked in endless self-reflection, for there is always an objection to be found. So, instead, AA is

---

[93] Wallace, *The Pale King*, 546. I further elaborate my analysis of boredom and reality-commitment (meaningful existence) in relation to *The Pale King* in my article 'Boredom, Irony, and Anxiety: Wallace and the Kierkegaardian View of the Self'. There, I write: 'What can the ethical dimension of boredom be? The following line from *The Pale King* might point us in the right direction: "*boring* also meant something that drilled in and made a hole" (378). This reference to boredom as "drilling a hole" can be understood in two distinct ways: (1) boredom makes a hole, in the sense that it creates a hole inside of me, emptying me out (this refers to the effect of boredom in the aesthetic life); (2) that drilling, making a hole, has to do with what in other places in *The Pale King* is called "single-point concentration" (293), that is, attending to something and understanding, *penetrating* it. This second interpretation is the starting point of the ethical value of boredom' (56). In the article, I also further explore this connection between boredom and the (ethical) ability to pay attention. For another reading of boredom in *The Pale King*, see Clare, 'The Politics of Boredom and the Boredom of Politics in *The Pale King*'.
[94] IJ, 273, 858, 349–50, 358, 446.

about letting the individual see that 'doing' – in this case, participating in the AA programme – helps. After Gately had expressed his initial doubts about AA and its clichéd guidelines to other members, they told him: 'it didn't matter at this point what he thought or believed or even said. All that mattered was what he *did*.'[95] Gately's counsellor Eugenio Martinez (Gene M.) told him to imagine AA as a

> box of Betty Crocker Cake Mix [. . .] [all Gately had to do was] follow the directions on the side of the fucking box. It didn't matter one fuckola whether Gately *believed* a cake would result, or whether he *understood* the like fucking baking-chemistry of *how* a cake would result: if he just followed the motherfucking directions, and had sense enough to get help from slightly more experienced bakers to keep from fucking the directions up if he got confused somehow, but basically the point was if he just followed the childish directions, a cake would result.[96]

One of AA's clichéd directives is that all AA members have to choose a 'Higher Power', a 'God As You Understand Him', and 'pray' to that entity to ask for assistance in substance recovery, each morning and evening (this regular, repetitive element is an important aspect of the directive). For *Infinite Jest*'s addicted aesthetes, the notion of 'God' is the ultimate boredom, a stale and meaningless concept. They are a perfect example of the situation outlined earlier, that God is 'dead', their existence groundless, but this insight does not disturb them in the least; they are 'just' bored. The passages in *Infinite Jest* about AA's Higher Power have little to do with traditional religiosity, or the supposed need for religion in contemporary Western society. Rather the importance of AA and of accepting a Higher Power lies in moving the addicted individual away from his constant reflection towards realizing the importance of acting, of actually *doing* something (instead of just thinking about it, analysing it while remaining passive). AA's Higher Power is not a matter of believing in some invisible higher order, for the question of belief would only lead the individual back to reflection. It is about experiencing the fact that *doing* it – participating in the AA programme – *works*. Of course, Gately, too, had asked how one is supposed to pray to a God one does not believe in. But he was told 'Just Do It'.[97] And so he did:

> He had nothing in the way of a like God-concept [. . .]; he treated prayer like setting an oven-temp according to a box's direction. [. . .] he always pretended his sneakers were like way under the bed and he had to stay down there a while to find them and get them out, when he prayed, but he did it, [. . .] and after maybe five months Gately [. . .] all of a sudden realized that [. . .] the Desire and Compulsion had been removed.[98]

By a constant, dutiful repetition of the task to pray to his Higher Power, by enduring the boredom inherent in such a task, Gately eventually surpasses the boredom of it;

95 Ibid., 273, 466.
96 Ibid., 467.
97 Ibid., 352, 466, 1002, 350.
98 Ibid., 467.

instead, repetition signals his overcoming of the aesthetic attitude and transition to the ethical life-view. With the role of AA's Higher Power we have arrived at the next and final aspect of repetition: repetition as transcendence.[99]

3.3. Repetition as transcendence

Kierkegaard's ethical pseudonym Constantin Constantius posits: 'repetition is and remains a transcendence'.[100] Repetition, as a return of that which was lost (think back to the story of Job), is a transcendence because it contains an element that goes beyond the self that surpasses the power of the individual. Constantius therefore calls repetition a 'religious movement'.[101] According to Kierkegaard, repetition requires a surrender to a higher, divine force. This element is not present in the works of Wallace, Eggers and Foer, in the same, Christian form as in Kierkegaard. Rather the transcendence that is present in these works should be understood ethically. We have already seen that the role of AA's Higher Power in *Infinite Jest* lies in breaching reflection and shifting the individual's focus to action. Another way to formulate this is that the individual has to surrender to reality over and over again, has to transcend his own consciousness towards the world, for only there does the self truly take shape. This transcendent relation should not be understood as a vertical connection between two unequal 'spheres', a heaven and earth, an 'above' and a 'here'. In *This Is Water*, Wallace states: 'None of this is about morality, or religion, or dogma, or big fancy questions of life after death. The capital-T Truth is about life *before* death'.[102] Here, the repetition of meaningful choice is characterized by a horizontal transcendence: something that does not lie completely within one's control, that transcends the power of the individual, namely, 'the world', has a crucial influence on the formation of the self.

However, we can still understand this ethical repetition from the Kierkegaardian framework. We read: 'it takes courage to will repetition'.[103] Lansink explains that this is the 'courage to live in the present': '[it is about] being able to endure the uncertainty of what is to come, in the consciousness of [dependence]'.[104] The self can only be realized, made actual by acting in the world. For the self, repetition means: getting the world (back), by acting, by surrendering (casting, transcending itself) towards the world and thereby connecting itself to that world.[105] Edward F. Mooney writes: 'repetition

---

[99] In Max's biography we read that Wallace's own AA sponsor simplified the role of the Higher Power as follows: 'All this step says is are you willing to make a decision' (Max, *Every Love Story Is a Ghost Story*, 114).

[100] Kierkegaard, *Fear and Trembling/Repetition*, 186.

[101] Ibid., 187.

[102] Wallace, *This Is Water*, 128–9. For other explorations of Wallace's text and its spiritual implications, see Bolger, 'A Less "Bullshitty" Way To Live: The Pragmatic Spirituality of David Foster Wallace'; and: Timpe, '*This Is Water* and Religious Self-Deception'.

[103] Kierkegaard, *Fear and Trembling/Repetition*, 132.

[104] Lansink, *Vrijheid en ironie*, 194; for the sake of completeness I want to remark that Lansink speaks of 'a religious dependence', but I am of the opinion that this qualification can be left out, on the basis of what I have said and will say in what follows, about the role of religiosity in the studied novels.

[105] I derive this formulation from the title of Edward F. Mooney's article, '*Repetition*: Getting the World Back'.

gives up the idea of self-sufficiency. Realizing that the outcome of our search [. . .] is not under our control may be a necessary condition of [. . .] the satisfaction of the need.' Mooney explains: 'Repetition is based on a need for world, for global value, and completes itself as world or value is transcendentally provided.' To which he adds: 'What is "repeated", restored, is a world infused with objects of sustaining value.'[106]

This return of and to the world is exactly what we have seen earlier, in our discussion of the novels. Listing these elements would therefore largely imply a repetition of the foregoing. It comes down to the fact that choice is a transcendence: it is a connection with something in the world, and this connection has to be taken on over and over again, the relation with the world has to be constantly reaffirmed.

The surrender to the world is also symbolized by the Kierkegaardian image of the leap. The term 'leap' expresses the uncertain character of action: the determination of the outcome does not lie within one's power, the desired outcome cannot be enforced (contrary to aesthetic fantasy, which is completely self-enclosed), but the individual nevertheless wants to act because it is important to him (it feels like his *duty*), and therefore meaningful to undertake the action, uncertain as the outcome may be.

As was noted in Chapter 6, this image of the leap occurs repeatedly in *You Shall Know Our Velocity*. First, there is the rock-jumping, which provides Will with the experience of the spontaneity that he seems to be looking for. Further on in the book, Will and Hand both climb up a tree to subsequently 'jump over' to the other person's tree. The jump with which the novel ends – in a swimming pool, at a wedding party with friends – marks Will's definitive return to reality and thereby his transition to a different life-view: 'I jumped with my mouth so open, taking it all in, and the air was cold and the water was so cold but I jumped all the way in, all at once.'[107] Jumping with an open mouth and taking everything in signals a dedication to the world, the pathos of the leap, and the cold air and water symbolize the uncertainty and unpredictability of the world, that Will takes upon himself, in which he immerses himself, nonetheless.

In *Infinite Jest*, AA is aimed at ending paralysing self-reflection – one of the slogans of AA is 'My Best Thinking Got Me Here', which we can compare with Mooney's claim that, in relation to the meaningful 'repetition' of the affirmation of the world, '[t]oo much theory is a threat'[108] – and instead bringing about the realization that a meaningful life implies a transcendence, a surrender to the world as a constantly repeated choice: 'You give it up to get it back to give it away', goes another AA slogan.[109]

This repeated return to what is real (the constant reminder of what the self is connected and committed to) is the point of the following story, told to Gately by the character Bob Death at an AA meeting: 'This wise old whiskery fish swims up to three young fish and goes, "Morning, boys, how's the water?" and swims away; and the three young fish watch him swim away and look at each other, and go, "What the fuck is water?" and swim away.'[110] In *This Is Water* Wallace refers to this same 'didactic little

---

[106]   Ibid., 290, 301–2.
[107]   YSKOV, 371.
[108]   Cf. IJ, 1026; Mooney, '*Repetition*: Getting the World Back', 302.
[109]   Cf. IJ, 344.
[110]   Ibid., 445.

parable-ish' story, to which he adds: 'The immediate point of the fish story is merely [...] [the] awareness of what is so real and essential, so hidden in plain sight all around us, that we have to keep reminding ourselves over and over: "This is water." "This is water."'[111] It is interesting to note that Eggers has published a very similar story, in which the question what the water feels like to the fishes, is followed by the fishes with the counter-question what the air feels like to humans, challenging them to take a good look at reality and try to describe it.[112]

But repetition as a horizontal transcendence does not just mean a surrender to the uncertainty of the world, but, with that, also to a dependence on other human beings. As Eriksen writes: '[In repetition] a person realizes an openness towards the future that is at the same time an openness towards the other.'[113] The individual is embedded, and becomes a self, in the context of the structures of the communities of which he is part. My self-becoming presupposes a horizon, consisting of others who are transcendent to me.[114] Giving up the desire for autonomy, for complete self-sufficiency, is an openness towards other human beings. The self that thinks that it is 'absolutely its own master', we read in Kierkegaard's *The Sickness unto Death*, 'precisely this is the despair, [...] this absolute ruler is a king without a country, actually ruling over nothing'.[115] Lansink explains: 'Without recognizing an "instance" that is not the human being himself, he cannot escape the doom of the non-committality that sticks to everything he does or abstains from.'[116] Transcendence, the other (who is 'beyond' the individual) is necessary for the individual to realize a meaningful life. I need the other to realize, out of my despair, a meaningful choice; in Kierkegaard's *Concluding Unscientific Postscript*, it is formulated as follows: 'In despairing, I use myself to despair, and therefore I can indeed despair of everything by myself, but if I do this I cannot come back by myself.'[117] For that, I need the other. With this indispensability of the other, we have arrived at the subject of the next and final chapter.

Conclusion

This chapter has offered an analysis of the striving for reality-commitment, portrayed in the novels of Wallace, Eggers and Foer, as following from and giving further substance to the basic attitude of sincerity. This was done by returning to the philosophy of Kierkegaard, in which choice (as the alternative to endless irony, which implies not-choosing) marks the transition from the aesthetic to the ethical life-view. We have

---

[111] Wallace, *This Is Water*, 5, 3–4, 8, 131–3.
[112] Eggers, 'What the Water Feels Like to the Fishes', *Short Short Stories*, 5–6.
[113] Eriksen, *Kierkegaard's Category of Repetition*, 13.
[114] This transcendence does not create a new, vertical opposition, as is the case with some theories of alterity; cf. the fourth type of transcendence of Wessel Stoker's typology of transcendence, 'transcendence as alterity'; Stoker offers the philosophy of Jacques Derrida as an example (Stoker, 'Culture and Transcendence. A Typology', 8).
[115] Kierkegaard, *The Sickness unto Death*, 69.
[116] Lansink, *Vrijheid en ironie*, 123.
[117] CUP 1, 258.

seen how the individual becomes aware (through his experience of freedom, despair and urgency) of the need to connect himself to the world, by choosing. Realizing that one has to choose, subsequently leads to the question of how one comes to the choice one has to choose. We have seen that this requires relating one's factual past (what Kierkegaard calls the self's 'gift') and the freedom of one's future (the self's 'task') to each other. This relating of past and future, of becoming a self, was shown to be a necessarily endless process, which has to be *repeated* over and over again. In turn, this Kierkegaardian notion of repetition, as implied by the ethical life, was shown to have three aspects: repetition as responsibility (to choose is to keep choosing one's choice), repetition versus boredom (committing to choice means desiring its recurrence, and not dreading it out of fear of boredom with 'the same'), and repetition as transcendence (choice implies relying on, committing to something that transcends the individual, that does not lie fully within the individual's control: to something in the world, or to another person).

What has become clear from this chapter, is that one of the desires that connects the works of Wallace, Eggers and Foer is what McLaughlin describes as 'a desire to reconnect language to the social sphere, or, to put it another way, to reenergize literature's social mission, its ability to intervene in the social world, to have an impact on actual people and the actual social institutions in which they live their lives'.[118] As we have seen, postmodernist fiction is unable to forge a meaningful connection to the world we live in: because reality is judged to always unreal, it has to be self-consciously exposed as such when portrayed in literature. Wallace agrees with the postmodernist metafictionists that contemporary Western reality is very diverse and confusing. But according to him, good fiction cannot limit itself to revealing artificiality and unreality because, to Wallace, the conclusion that 'all experience can be deconstructed and reconfigured [. . .] is about as "liberating" as a bad acid trip'.[119] Catherine Nichols describes Wallace's own work as 'attempting to engage the dynamism of reality, rather than professing its fictionality'.[120]

The novels of Wallace, Eggers and Foer have been accused by some commentators of being typically postmodernist in their portrayal of reality, because their novels show us fragmented characters in a confusing world, and because they seem to employ typical 'postmodern hardware',[121] such as footnotes, an abundance of information and characters (who sometimes provide *conflicting* information), self-conscious narrative, and pop references. However, in their rush to reach such conclusions, these commentators pass over the possibility that similar means can

---

[118] To this, McLaughlin adds that the emphasis in the works of these writers 'is less on self-conscious wordplay and the violation of narrative conventions and more on representing the world we all more or less share. Yet in presenting that world, this new fiction nevertheless has to show that it's a world that we know through language and layers of representation: language, narrative, and the processes of representation are the only means we have to experience and know the world, ourselves, and our possibilities for being human' (McLaughlin, 'Post-Postmodern Discontent', 66–7).

[119] EUP, 65.

[120] Nichols, 'Dialogizing Postmodern Carnival', 4.

[121] Kakutani, 'New Wave of Writers Reinvents Literature'.

have a different significance for a different literary generation, and can also be used to different ends. Many aspects of postmodernism have become part of popular postmodern culture and, therefore, part of everyday reality. So, a certain amount of fragmentation, mediation and self-consciousness in a contemporary novel is, in the words of Wallace, 'just plain realistic'. The same goes for pop references, says Wallace: 'the belief that pop images are basically just mimetic devices is one of the attitudes that separates most U.S. fiction writers under c. 40 from the writerly generation that precedes us, reviews us and designs our grad-school curricula'.[122] For these younger writers, who grew up with postmodernism, all these things are part of a reality of which, in their opinion, *certain aspects* have become problematic.[123] But while describing these problems and exploring possible ways to overcome them, a realistic description of the reality that forms the backdrop to these problems, incorporates techniques that were previously deemed subversive, but are no longer considered to be so by this new literary generation.

For example, some of the works of Eggers and Foer use photographs and strange typography, not to expose the *un*reality of the story, but rather as unproblematic depictions of the fictional reality being described. So, all these things are not typical 'postmodern pyrotechnics',[124] but rather, as Nicolas Confessore aptly describes, 'characteristics of a certain generational vernacular, whose sources are widely recognized' – Confessore mentions, among other things, 'six hours of television a day, advertising metastasized to every cranny of life' – 'but whose real purpose is just as widely misunderstood'. This is not a language of 'disengagement', he says, but of 're-engagement'.[125]

To offer another example: *Infinite Jest* is populated by hundreds of characters.[126] In postmodernist metafictional novels the use of an abundance of perspectives, coupled with contradictory information, aims to effect an overload that constantly puts the reader off track, pointing out to her that she is reading something fictional. In *Infinite Jest*, on the contrary, the abundance of information and characters – all portrayed empathetically, and with a caring attention to detail – draws the reader

---

[122] EUP, 43. Also, in an interview, Wallace stated: 'I'm always stumped when critics regard references to popular culture in serious fiction as some sort of avantgarde stratagem. In terms of the world I live in and try to write about, it's inescapable. Avoiding any reference to the pop would mean either being retrograde about what's "permissible" in serious art or else writing about some other world' (McCaffery, 'Interview', 148).

[123] Cf. the fact that Hal (like almost all characters in the novels of Wallace, Eggers and Foer) 'is *already framed* by prevailing cultural thought in the story-world [. . .] [and] is struggling to break out and has to find other, alternative ways of conceptualizing what it means to be human' (Timmer, *'Do You Feel It Too?'*, 30–1).

[124] Kakutani, 'Clever Young Man Raises Sweet Little Brother'.

[125] Confessore, 'Finite Jest', 86; cf. Mary Holland's description of the use of old, postmodernist (or post-structuralist) techniques (in this case, about Wallace and Foer) to new ends: 'self-conscious representation not only to return us to presence and the real, after decades of literature's obsession with the void, but also to remind us of the powerful ways in which acts of reading and writing impact the real world. Thus, these novels enact poststructuralism turned toward the ends of realism and humanism' (Holland, *Succeeding Postmodernism*, 7).

[126] Boswell, *Understanding David Foster Wallace*, 118.

into the story-world, and convinces her of its reality. Wallace's fiction makes clear that what they speak of is real pain, real confusion; they speak about real life.[127]

The desire to engage with lived problems, with what is real, with what is urgent, is clearly an important preoccupation of these novels. They portray plurality and confusion, not as aspects of an unreality that has to be exposed, but as something that already lies in open sight, as the reality of our life-form.[128] This aspect, our being part of a life-form, consisting of other people, directs us towards the subject of the next and final chapter: community.

---

[127] As Frank Louis Cioffi writes about Wallace's fiction: 'actuality and artwork have fully merged [. . .]; the artwork affects [the reader] in the same way as do "real" objects; it has a truth that deeply stirs [her]. It is in fact not art, but life' (Cioffi, 'An Anguish Become Thing', 175).
[128] Cf. Wallace, *This Is Water*, 5, 3–4, 8, 131–3.

8

Community

Introduction

In the final chapter of this book, I will investigate the last requirement, the final antidotal element, that the novels of Wallace, Eggers and Foer portray in response to the problems of contemporary Western existence, in the attempt to overcome hyperreflexivity and endless irony. We have already seen that this presupposes sincerity, as a desire to form a stable self, and that this sincere self acquires meaning and substance by committing itself to reality through choices and actions. In addition, the novels of Wallace, Eggers and Foer convey that meaningful self-becoming presupposes a *community*, an exchange with others. In this chapter, I will analyse this importance of community. With that, we have arrived at the other end of the story of this study: from reflexive-ironic existence, imprisoned in the emptiness of one's supposed self, in solipsism and scepticism, to becoming a self in commitment to the outside world, and most importantly, to the other.[1]

In this chapter, the novels' portrayal of the importance of the other for the individual's self-becoming will be analysed in light of the thought of Albert Camus. His philosophy is in many ways akin to that of Sartre and Kierkegaard. However, while Sartre and Kierkegaard do not seem to attribute an important role to others, Camus regards it as an indispensable part of self-becoming that the individual is part of a community. In that sense, Camus's thought forms a necessary addition to the Sartrean and Kierkegaardian heuristic perspectives used in this study up until this point, and provides, as it were, an existentialist companion piece to the importance of community already emphasized by Wittgenstein in relation to language.

For Camus, the importance of community follows from the two main themes of his philosophy, the 'absurd' and 'rebellion': because the world lacks the meaning that the individual expects of it, the individual rebels to demand meaning, and in this rebellion

---

Unless otherwise indicated, translations are mine.

[1] I am not using the notion of the other in the sense in which, e.g. Derrida and Levinas use it, for whom the other ('Other') brings with it a sort of vertical transcendence (Wessel Stoker calls this 'transcendence as alterity'). By others, I simply mean the other individuals that a person encounters in connecting to the world (Stoker, 'Culture and Transcendence: A Typology', 8).

becomes aware of his connection to the other. Wallace states that the 'great challenge for those of us who want to be decent human beings and citizens' is to see '[t]hat there's probably no absolute right in all situations handed down from God on the stone tablets' and 'that it is our job as responsible decent spiritual human beings to arrive at sets of principles to guide our conduct in order to keep us from hurting ourselves and other people'. Hereupon, Wallace concludes: 'the remedy that I see for it is some very, very mild form of Camus – like existential engagement'.[2] This chapter will argue that the novels under consideration can indeed be seen as embodying a Camusian engagement.

In section 1, I will briefly outline the two main themes of Camus's thought, the absurd and rebellion; in doing so, I will also point out the similarities with relevant aspects of the philosophies of Sartre and Kierkegaard. In section 2, I will further elaborate on the importance of the other resulting from Camus's thought; thereby, I will first briefly indicate that, in comparison to Camus, the importance of the other remains underexposed in Sartre and Kierkegaard. Then, in section 3, I will describe how the connection with the other is 'discovered' by the characters in the novels of Wallace, Eggers and Foer; I will do so by means of the notions of 'attention' (*for* the other) and 'trust' (*in* the other). Finally, in section 4, I will analyse, in light of Camus, the novels' portrayal of the *importance* of this connection to the other for the individual's self-becoming.

1. Absurdity and rebellion: Two main themes of Camus's thought

Camus's philosophy has two main themes: the absurd and rebellion. Camus's notion of the absurd refers to the experience of division, following from the confrontation between, on the one hand, man, who tries to give meaning to his life, and, on the other hand, the world, which lacks this meaning. Rebellion, for Camus, refers to man's protest against the unreasonableness, the meaninglessness of the world – a protest that unites the individual with his fellow man. Camus has developed each of these themes in a philosophical treatise, respectively *The Myth of Sisyphus* (1942) and *The Rebel* (1951). As a result, his philosophy is often divided into two separate periods. It is important, however, not to lose sight of the connection between Camus's treatment of both themes. Hans Achterhuis writes that in Camus's thought we can 'distinguish between an ontological period' – dedicated to the absurd – 'and a period in which he, on the basis of the ontological insights he had gained, tries to construct an ethics' – namely, rebellion as an attitude of solidarity that man adopts in protest against the absurdity of his existence.[3]

---

[2] Karmodi, 'Interview'. As was already mentioned in the Introduction to this study, the 'mildness' that Wallace speaks of, here, probably refers to the fact that Camus's notion of 'rebellion' is quite literal and overtly political, whereas Wallace's version of 'existential engagement' seems to be aimed, above all, at urging individuals from reflective confinement in the self, towards connection with others.

[3] Achterhuis, *Camus*, 10. In advance of the comparison between Camus's and Sartre's views, further on in this chapter, we could say that in this periodization, too, lies a similarity with Sartre; *Being*

I will now further explore these two notions, as the basis of the heuristic perspective that will shed light on the portrayal of community in the works of Wallace, Eggers and Foer. I will also point out the relevant similarities between Camus's notions of absurdity and rebellion, and Sartre's analysis of 'human-reality' and Kierkegaard's irony critique, respectively. These affinities show the implicit coherence of the existentialist heuristic perspectives employed in this study.[4]

1.1. The absurd

The absurd is not a quality of man or of the world, but 'is born of this confrontation between the human need and the unreasonable silence of the world', writes Camus in *The Myth of Sisyphus*.[5] The absurd is the tension, the discrepancy between man asking the world for meaning, for reasons, and the world that does not answer, that stays meaningless, reasonless by itself.

'At any street corner the feeling of absurdity can strike any man in the face', says Camus. Man can live his life unthinkingly: 'Rising, tram, four hours in the office or factory, meal, tram, four hours of work, meal, sleep and Monday, Tuesday, Wednesday, Thursday, Friday and Saturday, according to the same rhythm – this path is easily followed most of the time', writes Camus. Habit is the unconscious explanation of the world, which means that the demand for an actual explanation does not really arise: 'A world that can be explained even with bad reasons is a familiar world.' But, as we read, 'one day the "why" arises and everything begins in that weariness tinged with amazement'. According to Camus this is 'the first sign of absurdity', 'it inaugurates the impulse of consciousness'. From that moment on, man and world are no longer unthinkingly 'one': 'in a universe suddenly divested of illusions and lights, man feels an alien, a stranger. His exile is without remedy since he is deprived of the memory of a lost home or the hope of a promised land', writes Camus, '[t]his divorce between man and his life, the actor and his setting, is properly the feeling of absurdity'.[6]

What Camus describes as the experience of the absurd is man realizing the meaning of his own consciousness, that is, of his freedom. His descriptions of man's 'absurd freedom' are very similar to Sartre's analysis of the intentionality of consciousness, which is always a relation, a distance to the world (as discussed in Chapters 1 and 6); in this context, Sartre, too, speaks of the freedom of human consciousness that does not coincide with anything in the world. *The Myth of Sisyphus* contains a distinction

---

and Nothingness also offers an ontological study, aimed at the analysis of (individual) bad faith, on the basis of which Sartre subsequently tried to formulate an ethics (in the posthumously published *Notebooks for an Ethics*).

[4] Even though there are of course important differences between the mentioned philosophers; furthermore, I am aware of, among other things, Camus's – largely erroneous – critique of the philosophy of Kierkegaard, formulated in *The Myth of Sisyphus*, of the conflict between Camus and Sartre (following the publication of *The Rebel*), and of the fact that Camus did not regard himself as an existentialist; cf. Van Gennep, *Albert Camus*, 131, 125.

[5] MS, 32.

[6] Ibid., 17, 19, 13.

that is comparable to Sartre's distinction between being-in-itself and being-for-itself: 'If I were among the trees, a cat among the animals, this life would have a meaning or rather this problem would not arise, for I should belong to this world. I should *be* this world', Camus describes 'thinglike' being, contrasting it to conscious, human being: '[this world] to which I am now opposed by my whole consciousness and my whole insistence upon familiarity. [. . .] And what constitutes the basis of that conflict, of that break between the world and my mind, but the awareness of it?'[7] From Camus's thought, as from Sartre's, a portrayal emerges of human existence as characterized by the tension between facticity and transcendence; Camus emphasizes on the one hand the physical factuality and on the other hand the free consciousness of man: 'Through the whole of human consciousness runs a fault line; man is double. Due to his body, he also belongs to the world of objects, while as consciousness he is free from this world. It is this division that Camus calls "absurdity"', writes Achterhuis.[8]

Moreover, Camus observes, like Sartre, that man is inclined to try to conceal this absurd division. Achterhuis calls *The Myth of Sisyphus* 'one long description of the struggle between humanity and the wish to escape from it'.[9] Whereas Sartre speaks of bad faith as the desire to cancel out the tension of one's freedom, to 'found' oneself (the 'desire to be God', which 'inevitably results in failure'),[10] Camus speaks of a comparable 'nostalgia for unity', an 'appetite for the absolute' that 'illustrates the essential impulse for the human drama'. Just as Sartre holds that this attempt to flee in the self-deceit of bad faith is tempting and widespread, Camus claims that: 'Everything is ordered in such a way as to bring into being that poisoned peace.' However, Camus also maintains that this desire for 'thoughtlessness' and 'lack of heart' is destined to fail: 'What other truth can I admit without lying, without bringing in a hope I lack, which means nothing within the limits of my condition?'[11]

1.2. Rebellion

From this understanding of human existence as characterized by absurd freedom, Camus subsequently develops his notion of 'rebellion'.[12] 'Man is the only creature who refuses to be what he is', writes Camus at the start of *The Rebel*, in relation to the absurd tension that lies at the heart of human existence.[13] Jeffrey C. Isaac describes the connection between the two main themes of Camus's thought as follows: 'Camus's rebellion refers to the exercise of human freedom, to the fact that humans are agents always capable of surpassing or at least distancing themselves from their existing

---

[7]   Ibid., 51–2.
[8]   Achterhuis, *Camus*, 183.
[9]   Ibid., 76.
[10] BN, 587, 177.
[11] MS, 23, 25, 51.
[12] The theme of rebellion is present in Camus's works prior to *The Rebel*, too, but does not yet take centre stage. In this subsection, I will limit myself to the notion of rebellion as Camus expounds it in *The Rebel*; cf. Achterhuis, *Camus*, 10.
[13] R, 11.

circumstances.'[14] According to Camus 'the real nature of the absurd' is 'that it is an experience to be lived through, a point of departure.'[15] Elsewhere he writes: 'to establish the absurdity of life cannot be an end but only a beginning.'[16] In *The Rebel* we read:

> I proclaim that I believe in nothing and that everything is absurd, but I cannot doubt the validity of my proclamation and I must at least believe in my protest. The first and only evidence that is supplied me, within the terms of the absurdist experience, is rebellion. [. . .] Rebellion is born of the spectacle of irrationality, confronted with an unjust and incomprehensible condition. But its blind impulse is to demand order in the midst of chaos, and unity in the very heart of the ephemeral. It protests, it demands, it insists that the outrage be brought to an end, and that what has up to now been built upon shifting sands should henceforth be founded on rock. Its preoccupation is to transform. But to transform is to act.[17]

Rebellion appears in the world as a protest against the absurd *and* as the confirmation of 'the sudden, dazzling perception that there is something in man with which he can identify himself [. . .]. Therefore he is acting in the name of certain values.'[18] The values that the Camusian rebellion defends is that 'life itself is not the only or exclusive end, but that *meaningful* life, a life worth living, is demanded', explains David Sprintzen.[19] Rebellion is negative in its rejection of the given situation, but also positive in its striving to substitute, through its own actions, the rejected, absurd existence for a new value, a meaningful existence: 'What is a rebel? A man who says no, but whose refusal does not imply a renunciation. He is also a man who says yes, from the moment he makes his first gesture of rebellion', states Camus.[20]

Camus's description of human existence as characterized by absurd freedom does not just connect his philosophy to that of Sartre, but also to that of Kierkegaard. In his view of human existence, Kierkegaard speaks of an unthinking, immediate way of life,[21] and also characterizes the life of the individual who frees himself from this immediacy, as a consciousness of the tension between existence as a gift and task that constantly have to be related to each other. What Camus describes as rebellion, displays interesting similarities with Kierkegaard's description of irony and the importance of choice.

In a similar vein to Kierkegaard valuing ironic negation as a liberation from immediacy, while holding that it does have to be followed by positive choice, Camus writes: 'Great explorers in the realm of absurdity have not been lacking. But, in the last analysis, their greatness is measured by the extent to which they have rejected

---

[14] Isaac, *Arendt, Camus and Modern Rebellion*, 73.
[15] R, 8.
[16] Quoted in Cruickshank, 'Introduction', 15.
[17] R, 10.
[18] Ibid., 14, 16.
[19] Sprintzen, *Camus*, 128.
[20] R, 13.
[21] Kierkegaard calls those who live such a mindless, immediate life '*spidsborger*' (translated as 'philistines'; CI, 304); similarly, Sartre speaks of '*les salauds*' (translated as 'bastards'; e.g. Sartre, *Nausea*, 94; Priest, 'Bad Faith', 205).

the complacencies of absurdism in order to accept its exigencies.'[22] The rejection that irony and rebellion have in common is, as we have seen, not the final goal but just a beginning: 'Therefore, if it was legitimate to take absurdist sensibility into account [. . .], it is nevertheless impossible to see in this sensibility, and in the nihilism it presupposes, anything but a point of departure, [. . .] the equivalent, in the plane of existence, of systematic doubt.' Just as Kierkegaard states that the aesthete wants to retain his negative freedom at any cost, and as a result ends up in non-committality and emptiness, Camus writes that 'nihilistic interpretations isolate [the *no*] in rebellion', but rebellion 'must be faithful to the *yes* that it contains as well.'[23]

The character Caligula, from Camus's eponymous play, in many ways resembles Kierkegaard's Johannes the Seducer, and Patrick Bateman from *American Psycho* (see Chapter 4), as ultimate embodiments of the aesthetic life-view. For Caligula every distinction has become immaterial and fantasy and desire are his only remaining motives. 'Caligula concludes that "everything is permitted"[,] in accord with the logic of an absurd world. Being subject to no higher law, why would he not do "whatever he felt like?"', writes Sprintzen, '[l]etting his desires (or fantasies) become the springs of actions dramatically confronts us with the truth of our world.'[24] Jacob Golomb states: 'the central theme of *Caligula* [is] the difference between "right" and "wrong" freedom' (compare Kierkegaard's distinction between negative and positive freedom).[25] One final similarity that should be mentioned, is that, just as Kierkegaard says that the individual's positive choice, following his ironic liberation, has to be constantly repeated, chosen again, Camus writes that: 'The value that supports [the rebel] is never given to him once and for all; he must fight to uphold it, unceasingly.'[26]

Most importantly, rebellion inevitably directs the individual towards the other: through the experience of the absurd and the value that he derives from it, he discovers himself as inextricably connected to other human beings. I will elaborate this in the following section.

2. The role of the other: Kierkegaard and Sartre versus Camus

Camus's analysis of human existence, outlined earlier, leads him to emphasize the exceptional importance of community, of being part of a group of others, for the individual's meaningful self-becoming; and in this respect, Camus's philosophy differs from that of Kierkegaard and Sartre. Now, I will first briefly sketch out what could be called the neglect of the other by the latter two philosophers, and subsequently turn to Camus's description of community.

---

[22] R, 9; Camus mentions, among others, Nietzsche and Ivan Karamazov as examples of those who do both.
[23] R, 9–10, 285; cf. what Wallace calls the 'bothness' of good fiction, that 'half of fiction's job is to dramatize what makes it tough [to be a real human being]. The other half is to dramatize the fact that we still *are* human beings, now. Or can be' (McCaffery, 'Interview', 131).
[24] Sprintzen, *Camus*, 69–70.
[25] Golomb, *In Search of Authenticity*, 189.
[26] R, 285.

2.1. Kierkegaard and Sartre: The neglect of the other

The reason that the novels of Wallace, Eggers and Foer, and the philosophy of Kierkegaard differ (and the latter loses its applicability as a heuristic perspective) when it comes to the importance of the other, is that, in final instance, Kierkegaard regards self-becoming as an inner process, before God. As Kierkegaard's ethicist Johannes Climacus formulates it in *Concluding Unscientific Postscript*: 'The ethical grips the single individual and requires of him that he abstain from all observing, especially of the world and humankind, because the ethical as the internal cannot be observed by anyone standing outside.' It would be a mistake to speak of Kierkegaard's conception of the self as autonomous. He emphasizes the importance of social context, as the general-ethical: 'In order for the acting individual to be able to accomplish his task by fulfilling actuality, he must feel himself integrated in a larger context, must feel the earnestness of responsibility, must feel and respect every reasonable consequence.'[27] Söderquist even states: 'when Kierkegaard speaks of the individual as a "word" that is integrated into a context of "meaning", [we] could call this context a lifeworld, a semiotic network that always already provides meaning.'[28]

However, Söderquist also writes that Kierkegaard 'is far too suspicious of human culture and human nature to be satisfied with the corrective influence of intersubjectivity.'[29] What is meant, here, by 'corrective influence', is something that binds the individual to reality, and prevents him from fleeing into aesthetic fantasy. According to Kierkegaard, this correction cannot come from others, from the community, but has to come from elsewhere, from a connection through which the individual, in a sense, sidesteps the social: 'It is in this moment of decision that the individual needs divine assistance [. . .] – that is, by being there in passion and inwardness, one indeed becomes aware of the religious', we read in *Concluding Unscientific Postscript*. What is ultimately most important for Kierkegaardian self-becoming is that the 'direction is inward; essentially you have to do only with yourself before God'.[30]

Kierkegaard rightly points out the necessity of a transcendence for regaining the self from despair: the self has to surrender to, or, in less religious language, allow the influence of something that lies beyond its control, the uncertain world, that consists largely of the self's interactions with (transcendent) others. This is necessary to pull the aesthetic self from its reflective ideality (from solipsistic immanence) towards reality. But that transcendent movement does not need to be vertical (see the final section of Chapter 7, on the horizontal transcendence of AA, in Wallace's *Infinite Jest*). Kierkegaard envisioned the obedient, unreflected '*spidsborger*' of his time, and regarded society as the primary source of corrupting roles to which civilians obediently complied – which for Kierkegaard meant that something was needed that went beyond that general, social order. However, in the current Western societal situation the individual has become a highly (hyper)reflexive and ironic being. As a result, the problem has shifted from the

---

[27] CUP 1, 320; CI, 279.
[28] Söderquist, 'Authoring a Self', 158; cf. the late-Wittgensteinian view, outlined in Chapter 5.
[29] Ibid., 163.
[30] CUP 1, 258; Kierkegaard, *Works of Love*, 384.

social corruption of the individual, to a sort of solipsistic corruption of the self: the problem for these individuals is, above all, that from their reflexive-ironic isolation, they cannot possibly attain a meaningful existence. Seen from this situation, the leap towards the other actually resembles, in its liberating return to the real and the other, Kierkegaard's religious leap.

The reason that the perspective offered by Sartre's philosophy does not fit the novels of Wallace, Eggers and Foer, when it comes to the importance of the other, is similar to the mismatch with Kierkegaard's philosophy. Even though Sartre (contrary to the popular perception of his existentialist philosophy) refers quite regularly to the importance of social context and of the possibility of a solidary being-with-others (especially in *The Transcendence of the Ego* and the *Notebooks for an Ethics*), these references are relatively scarce compared to his treatment of other (more individualistic) themes. More importantly, Sartre does not really elaborate his references to the importance of the other in a systematic way. The famous line 'Hell is – other people', from the play *No Exit* (1944), is often mistakenly regarded as an apt summary of Sartre's existentialist view of the other.[31] This seems to be supported by Sartre's equally famous analysis of the look, which dates from about the same period in Sartre's thought. In Chapter 1, we have seen that in the encounter with the other, the individual experiences how this look reduces him into an object: 'If someone looks at me, I am conscious of *being* an object', Sartre writes. This leads Sartre to conclude: 'Conflict is the original meaning of being-for-others.' He explains: 'While I attempt to free myself from the hold of the Other, the Other is trying to free himself from mine; while I seek to enslave the Other, the Other seeks to enslave me.'[32]

However, when reading these descriptions of the individual's relation to other people, we should always be acutely aware of the fact that, as Busch reminds us, '*Being and Nothingness* [. . .] presents a portrait of the attitude of bad faith, and points the way, through a theory of reflection, toward the overcoming of bad faith.'[33] So, the above-quoted description of the look, as well as the famous sentence from *No Exit*, are expressions of, in Sartre's own terms, an 'ontology before conversion'.[34] This means, on the basis of what was discussed in Chapter 6, that through a pure reflection, I can grasp the freedom of the other in a different way, which is not necessarily characterized by conflict (just as I no longer *im*purely objectify my own consciousness, pure reflection implies the same for my treatment of another consciousness – and vice versa). In *Notebooks for an Ethics*, Sartre offers the example of 'extend[ing] my hand to help the person running after the bus to get on board':[35]

> [The person] will grasp my hand as a means/freedom. This object in his world, in the middle of its setting, sixty centimeters away from him, will close around him and pull him toward it as much as he pulls on the object as soon as he snatches it.

---

[31] Sartre, *No Exit*, 45.
[32] BN, 295, 386; cf. 'It is thus the *freedom* of the other people which is an outrage to us, and we try to overcome it by pretending it does not exist' (Warnock, *Existentialist Ethics*, 45).
[33] Busch, *The Power of Consciousness*, 18.
[34] Sartre, *Notebooks*, 6; quoted in Busch, *The Power of Consciousness*, 18.
[35] Ibid., 285.

He does not take it as a mere handhold to pull on in order to increase his speed, but as *also* an active freedom that grasps him and pulls him. At this moment the *human relation of helping* exists.[36]

Linsenbard explains that this 'social outlook' is actually already implied by the conception of the self in *The Transcendence of the Ego*, as constituted 'outside, in the world among others' (a view that in Chapter 5 was described as resembling Wittgenstein's view).[37] She writes: 'If we accept Sartre's view that the ego is a self that exists outside in the world, and that it is a self that is given first for others, we can see how others are indispensable to my perception and understanding of myself and my relation to the world.'[38]

These observations merely serve to make clear that the aspects of Kierkegaard's and Sartre's philosophy employed in other parts of this study, do not form an obstacle for a more social conception of self-becoming, as outlined in this chapter. However, the point remains that both fail to adequately integrate the important role of community, of forming a group with others, into their philosophy. In this respect, the portrayal offered by the novels, regarding the role of the other in contemporary existence, can be seen as complementing or even correcting the views of Kierkegaard and Sartre. Conversely, Camus's philosophy will be shown to offer a perspective that does fit the desire for community that can be found in the novels.

2.2. Camus: Community

As a matter of fact, the emphasis on the importance of the other undergoes a development in Camus's philosophy, as well. In his earlier works – such as *The Myth of Sisyphus*, and the novel *The Stranger* – the striving for an autonomous individuality seems to be the only attitude available in the face of absurdity. We could say, with Achterhuis, that these earlier works necessarily possess a more 'individualistic character' because they offer an ontological analysis of the absurd relation to the world in which the individual finds himself (and at which point the other as yet remains out of view).[39] So it is important to keep in mind that when, for example, Golomb writes that Camus takes on a 'position of strict immanence', and that 'Camus's heroes provide us with this ever-presentness of the spontaneously lived life whose only passionate commitment is the formation of its

---

[36] Ibid., 287
[37] Cf. 'For Sartre each person needs the other in order to be human. [. . .] We need other persons for discovering how we appear in the world; indeed, we need the other for becoming a person, for acquiring our selfhood' (Catalano, *Good Faith*, 20).
[38] Linsenbard, *An Investigation of Jean-Paul Sartre's Posthumously Published Notebooks for an Ethics*, 155–6. Forrest Williams writes, about Sartre's conception of this relating of 'freedoms': 'In tennis, I cannot recognize my status on my side of the net without necessarily acknowledging the other's comparable status on the other side of the net. This is more than logic: my very action (e.g. serving the ball) is such an acknowledgement' (Quoted in ibid., 144–5); cf. the description of tennis by head coach Schtitt in *Infinite Jest*: 'You seek to vanquish and transcend the limited self whose limits make the game possible in the first place' (IJ, 84) – see section 3.3.
[39] Achterhuis, *Camus*, 39.

own unique authenticity', he is referring to Meursault and Sisyphus (the absurd 'heroes' of *The Stranger* and *The Myth of Sisyphus*), and not to the 'heroes' of Camus's later work (Rieux from *The Plague* and, for example, Kaliayev from *The Rebel*). Golomb calls the development from ontology to ethics 'a decided transition from the negative freedom and authenticity of the heroic but lonely individual to the socially conscious humanism of *The Rebel* and *The Plague*'.[40]

In the previous section we have already seen that the rebellious individual acts 'in the name of certain values'. These are values which 'are still indeterminate but which [the individual] feels are common to himself and to all men'. Camus adds that 'an act of rebellion is not, essentially, an egoistic act. Of course, it can have egoistic motives. [. . .] He demands respect for himself, of course, but only in so far as he identifies himself with a [community]'.[41] Here lies for Camus the crucial connection between the experience of the absurd, rebellion and community:

> In absurdist experience, suffering is individual. But from the moment when a movement of rebellion begins, suffering is seen as a collective experience. Therefore the first progressive step for a mind overwhelmed by the strangeness of things is to realize that this feeling of strangeness is shared with all men and that human reality, in its entirety, suffers from the distance which separates it from the rest of the universe.[42]

In rebellion the individual realizes that he shares with others both the experience of the absurd and the value – the right to a meaningful life – on the basis of which he rebels against the absurd. This connection is the first certainty that the rebel can derive from absurdity and that Camus summarizes in a sort of 'intersubjective' cogito: 'I rebel – therefore we exist.'[43]

'We see that the affirmation implicit in every act of rebellion is extended to something that transcends the individual in so far as it withdraws him from his supposed solitude and provides him with a reason to act', writes Camus.[44] Community as first certainty has two important implications: first of all, it ends the individual's loneliness; secondly, it forms the basis of meaningful individual action. Sprintzen elucidates the first implication as follows: '[Cut-off from others] we are anguished and spiritually impoverished. If the movement from the absurd to revolt means anything, it refers to our need for others in the face of the metaphysical solitude.' And the second: '[the precondition of constructive human action] is an essentially communal base to living.'[45] These two aspects form the basis of the discussion in section 4. However, we first have to see how the bridge towards the other is spanned in the novels, before we can describe the necessity of this connection for the meaningful self-becoming of the individual. Above all, the applicability of the perspective of Camus's philosophy for

---

[40] Golomb, *In Search of Authenticity*, 168, 21, 187.
[41] R, 16 [original: 'natural community', AdD].
[42] Ibid., 22.
[43] Ibid.
[44] Ibid., 16.
[45] Sprintzen, *Camus*, 126–7, 104.

the novels of Wallace, Eggers and Foer, lies in the way it outlines these two important implications of community; these are what makes community indispensable to overcoming the portrayed problems of contemporary existence.

3. Discovering the other: Wallace, Eggers and Foer

Before we can go into these two aspects of the importance of the other for the self, we first have to see how the self-confined characters from the works of Wallace, Eggers and Foer come to connect to the other in the first place. The previous section outlined Camus's description of how solitary absurdity leads to rebellious community. Despite the relevance of this description for the interpretation of the significance of community, Camus says relatively little about the actual course of the transition; he seems to regard it as a radical turn from one thing to another. For Wallace, Eggers and Foer establishing the connection with the other is a cautious and vacillating process, whereas Camus does not really elaborate on it. To rectify this gap, I will first briefly describe Camus's concept of the self as transcendent, which ties in with the views of the self discussed earlier in this study. As I will explain, these views can be seen to imply the notions of 'attention' and 'trust' that are portrayed in the works of Wallace, Eggers and Foer as the key elements of establishing the connection with the other.

3.1. The transcendent self

The self is, in Sartre's formulation, transcendent: it comes into being 'in the world'. Camus emphasizes that this world is always a world *with others*. The sincere self attains substance, meaning (becomes a stable self), by connecting consciousness, through choices and actions, to the world, and thus to others. So, the development of the self is partly a transcending of one's own consciousness towards the other.

Camus speaks of the absurd, 'divided existence that we represent', pointing out the transcendent working of our consciousness, and says that rebellion, through the transcendent self-surpassing of the individual's consciousness, subsequently realizes an 'identification with another individual'. He adds: 'When he rebels, a man identifies himself with other men and so surpasses himself.'[46] And Isaac writes: 'To rebel, to resist or revalue one's condition, is to move beyond oneself.'[47] According to Camus, 'rebellion, [. . .] though it springs from everything that is most strictly individualistic in man, questions the very idea of the individual'. He emphasizes: 'Rebellion is in no way the demand for total freedom. On the contrary, rebellion puts total freedom up for trial' (compare this to Kierkegaard's critique of the permanent, negative freedom of total irony).[48]

---

[46] R, 251, 16, 17.
[47] Isaac, *Arendt, Camus and Modern Rebellion*, 121.
[48] R, 15, 284.

Camus's play *Caligula* is an expression of this critique of autonomous individuality; it offers 'an illustration of the failure of lonely authenticity', writes Golomb, '[in the play] Camus rejects the view of radical individualistic authenticity as invariably leading to destructive nihilism'.[49] The novel *The Plague* expresses a similar critique, but aimed at a more common form of autonomous individualism. '[Having cut themselves off] from one another, the citizens of Oran have succeeded in reducing passion and spirit to the habitualized pursuit of material success and physical satisfaction', writes Sprintzen about the inhabitants of the city struck by the plague. He continues: 'Care and concern for others, for the quality of public life, or for the possibilities of human excellence, have simply been lost in the shuffle'.[50] In *The Fall* the protagonist Clamence tries to '[escape] from his own loneliness, by means of a truly human encounter with "the other" who hears his confession'. Achterhuis writes: 'When in the end [Clamence] turns out to be unable to be solidary both men fall back into the prison of their own I. [. . .] Only if the own ego could have been forgotten before the other, would the exile have been lifted'.[51]

However, this view of the self transcending itself towards the other implies two notions (that have already been implied and mentioned in Chapters 5, 6 and 7) that are an important part of the portrayal offered in the novels of Wallace, Eggers and Foer, but that Camus does not explicitly analyse in his philosophical works. These notions are attention and trust.

Attention, here, means attending to the world; that is, the outward-directedness of consciousness, *out* of itself. Thus, attention signifies the opposite of introspection (as a form of self-attention); it is outer- and thus also other-directed. Iris Murdoch offers the following definition (indebted to Simone Weil): 'The direction of attention is, contrary to nature, away from the self which reduces all to a false unity, towards the great surprising variety of the world, and the ability so to direct attention is love'.[52] Attention thus implies a willingness to open up the self to the outside, which was discussed in Chapter 6, in relation to the notion of sincerity; attention means an acceptance of vulnerability and uncertainty.

This willingness or acceptance presupposes trust or faith ('good faith' as the basis of sincerity). We already saw in Chapter 5 that Wittgenstein emphasizes this point as well, when he writes: 'I really want to say that a language-game is only possible if one trusts something (I did not say "can trust something")'; this means 'trusting some*one*', as it implies the other as part of a shared form of life: 'When we mean something, it's like going up to someone, it's not having a dead picture of any kind.[53] We can clearly see, here, the reciprocity between the notions of attention and trust, that in the case of the

[49] Golomb, *In Search of Authenticity*, 186.
[50] Sprintzen, *Camus*, 90.
[51] Achterhuis, *Camus*, 65.
[52] Iris Murdoch, 'On "God" and "Good"', 354; in light of the 'existentialist' perspective of this study, it is perhaps relevant to note that Murdoch was very critical of existentialism ('[existentialism] is (it seems to me) an unrealistic and over-optimistic doctrine and the purveyor of certain false values' [ibid., 337]), but in my opinion largely because of issues addressed or obviated in this study, by employing different perspectives for different issues.
[53] Wittgenstein, *On Certainty*, 66ᵉ [§509]; PI, 112ᵉ [§455]; cf. Timmer, *'Do You Feel It Too?'*, 368.

novels by Wallace, Eggers and Foer seems to start from an initially wavering attention for the other, and develops into trust, which in turn allows for a further intensification of attention and further growth of trust, et cetera.

Even though Camus does not explicate these notions in his philosophical works, they are strongly connected to his social view of meaningful existence (compare the significance of attention and caring for the other in *The Plague*, and in *The Fall* the need for trust in the other if the confession is to succeed). I will now analyse, in separate subsections, the portrayal of both notions in the works of Wallace, Eggers and Foer leading up to the importance of dialogue and community, which will be discussed in section 4.

3.2. Attention

Chapter 7 was devoted to choice, as a commitment to reality. We could say that choice always presupposes attention: choosing implies attending to that which one relates oneself to. We could even say that the experience of urgency, of passion, which was discussed in Chapter 7, is the result of truly paying attention to something to the point at which connection is no longer a choice, in the sense of being optional: it has become a commitment.[54] Attention can thus be seen as the effort or energy underlying choice and commitment.

This includes connecting to the other. The desire for the connection to others that the works of Wallace, Eggers and Foer describe, 'could possibly counter the feeling of entrapment in an empty self', writes Timmer.[55] This confinement in the self is the result of the attitude of hyperreflexive irony, of 'an ideology that celebrates an autonomous, independent subject', as N. Katherine Hayles writes. We have seen this conception of the self to be a widespread illusion with far-reaching consequences. Therefore, 'nothing less than a reconceptualization of subjectivity can offer a solution', Hayles writes.[56]

3.2.1. David Foster Wallace

This exposure of the illusion of autonomy and subsequent reconceptualization of individuality is performed above all in Wallace's work. In *This Is Water*, Wallace writes: 'The really important kind of freedom involves attention and awareness [. . .][,] being able truly to care about other people.' Wallace states: 'It's a matter of my choosing to do the work of somehow altering or getting free of my natural, hard-wired default setting which is to be deeply and literally self-centered and to see and

---

[54] Cf. 'If we ignore the prior work of attention and notice only the emptiness of the moment of choice we are likely to identify freedom with the outward movement since there is nothing else to identify it with. But if we consider what the work of attention is like, how continuously it goes on, and how imperceptibly it builds up structures of value round about us, we shall not be surprised that at crucial moments of choice most of the business of choosing is already over' (Murdoch, 'The Idea of Perfection', 329).

[55] Timmer, '*Do You Feel It Too?*', 313.

[56] Hayles, 'The Illusion of Autonomy and the Fact of Recursivity', 692–3.

interpret everything through this lens of self.'[57] We could call this ability to attend to others the starting point of the realization of the importance of community.[58]

As Zadie Smith writes, '[Wallace] invested much in this idea [the way out of solipsism into communality]. He was always trying to place "relationships between persons" as the light at the end of his narrative dark tunnels'. Smith's characterization of Wallace's view clearly resembles the above-discussed notion of the transcendent self. She writes that Wallace's 'particular creed' with regard to 'awareness' is that it should be '*extrorse*' – which literally means 'facing outward': 'awareness must move always in an outward direction, away from the self'. Smith adds that, as a result, Wallace's works always describe '[t]he struggle with ego, the struggle with the self, the struggle to allow other people to exist in their genuine "otherness"', and she summarizes the answer supplied in his works as follows: '*You may have to give up your attachment to the "self"*.'[59] Elizabeth Freudenthal calls the conception of identity expressed in *Infinite Jest* 'anti-interiority',[60] a term that puts a similar emphasis on the outward-directedness of consciousness as we saw earlier in Murdoch's definition of attention, in Wallace's own description of the importance of attention, and in Smith's formulation of the 'extrorseness' of consciousness.

As we have seen in Chapter 6, *Infinite Jest*'s Mario Incandenza seems to base his existence on the intuitive awareness that the self, the meaning of what he feels and thinks, is something that comes into being outside him. Expanding our analysis of Mario, we should note that he is honest and empathetic, likes to be in the company of others and listens to them (even when they are sad or depressed), is sensitive to their problems and needs, and dedicated to their well-being. He is described as a 'born listener', as someone whose 'ears are extremely sensitive'.[61] These and other characterizations, already given in Chapter 6, emphasize that the 'success' of Mario's life-view lies in its focus on social interaction, beginning with attention for the other.

---

[57] Wallace, *This Is Water*, 120, 44.

[58] It is important to see the enormous difference between this 'ethical' ability to pay attention, and the aesthete's constant self-reflective absorption. The problem with the latter – and why it cannot possibly be called 'attending to something' – is that it has no object, except for itself; e.g. the self-reflecting aesthete is solely interested in his own self-reflective processes, absorbed by the endless associations produced by the ideality of his own mind. Cf. the remark made in *The Pale King* by the character Chris Fogle: 'awareness is different from thinking' (Wallace, *The Pale King*, 190). Paying attention implies exactly the opposite of hyperreflexivity: it means that consciousness is completely 'in' the world, unaware of itself, fully attending to the object of attention. We can see this in *The Pale King*'s Shane Drinion, whose instances of full attention are accompanied by levitation: 'Drinion is actually levitating slightly, which is what happens when he is completely immersed; [. . .] Drinion himself [is] unaware of the levitating thing by definition, since it is only when his attention is completely on something else that the levitation happens' (Wallace, *The Pale King*, 485).

[59] Smith, 'Brief Interviews with Hideous Men', 283–4, 268, 291.

[60] Freudenthal describes it as 'a mode of identity founded in the material world of both objects and biological bodies and divested from an essentialist notion of inner emotional, psychological, and spiritual life' (Freudenthal, 'Anti-Interiority', 192).

[61] IJ, 80, 756 (in the latter quotation the sensitivity of Mario's hearing is meant literally, in first instance, as head coach Gerhardt Schtitt is playing an unspecified opera record at full volume, but in the context of Mario's character the qualification has a strong symbolic meaning).

Mario's brother Hal remembers, from when they were young, Mario hanging around for games 'in which he had no interest other than proximity to his brother'. And their mother, Avril, remembers 'Mario still wanting Hal to help him with bathing and dressing at thirteen – [. . .] and wanting the help for Hal's sake, not his own'.[62] But the story that best expresses Mario's attention for others, is the anecdote about Barry Loach, who wants to prove to his older brother, a disillusioned Jesuit, that 'basic human nature wasn't as unempathetic and necrotic as the brother's present depressed condition was leading him to think'. The brother then challenges Barry to make himself look homeless, and

> to stand out in front of the Park Street T-station on the edge of the Boston Common, right alongside the rest of the downtown community's lumpen dregs, who all usually stood there outside the T-station stemming change, and for Barry Loach to hold out his unclean hand and instead of stemming change simply ask passersby to touch him. Just to touch him. Viz. extend some basic human warmth and contact. And this Barry does. And does. Days go by. His own spiritually upbeat constitution starts taking blows to the solar plexus [. . .] when along toward the end of the ninth month of the Challenge, his appeal – and actually also the appeals of the other dozen or so cynical stem-artists right alongside Loach [. . .] were taken literally and responded to with a warm handshake [by ETA's own Mario Incandenza].[63]

In this anecdote, Mario is the ministering angel in a world full of cynics. The story symbolizes Mario's role in the novel: he demonstrates intuitively that the connection with others is indispensable for a meaningful existence.

In *Infinite Jest*, the significance of the other is further elaborated in the story line of Don Gately and Addicts Anonymous. AA, as we will see further on in this chapter, functions as a Camusian community. This starts, however, with the importance of simple attention for the other during AA meetings: new members are encouraged to sit up front, 'where they can see the pores in the speaker's nose and try to Identify'. And: '[e]verybody in the audience is aiming for total empathy with the speaker [. . .]. Empathy, in Boston AA, is called Identification'[64] – we can also recognize here the identification that Camus speaks of: the recognition of one's absurd suffering in others.

3.2.2. Dave Eggers

In Eggers's works we can see that, for their narrating main characters, attention for the other is indispensable for developing a self. In *You Shall Know Our Velocity* the attention for the other (or the initial lack of it) is frequently symbolized by the use of the simple image of 'eyes'. In the novel, this image refers above all to man as an (overly) reflective being, regarding the world but not participating in it: the person who limits

---

[62] Ibid., 316–17.
[63] Ibid., 969–71.
[64] Ibid., 345.

himself to his eyes applies a separation, places himself at a distance from the world and others. 'It was a choice between the world or your eyes', as main character Will expresses this separation.[65]

Although not the cause, an important catalyst of Will's solipsism – his feeling of being confined in his own head – seems to have been a fight (which, in itself, is an understandable explanation for a certain amount of subsequent distrust of the other). When Will comes to, after having been beaten up, we read: 'There were only my eyes. They felt as if they'd been removed, dipped in acid and then fastened to me with pins. [. . .] [My skull was] cracking from within, a constant chopping of the inner walls of the cranium, by pickaxes. To see things hurt my eyes. I closed them.' Will is solely a distrustful look (hateful even, 'dipped in acid'), the hyperreflexive chaos in his head is in full motion, and in the end, by closing his eyes, he shuts out the world completely.[66]

In the novel, characters are frequently described as closing or shielding their eyes. Perhaps the most telling image, in this context, is that especially Will and Hand are constantly described as 'rolling their eyes', in ironic disapproval of what the other says: they literally turn their eyes inside – a self-reflective movement of sorts – and thereby distance and enclose themselves from the other.

Eventually, Will has an insight that this is not the way he wants it to be: 'I don't want it be just my eyes, do I, Jack?' Will says, in his head, to his dead, childhood friend Jack: if 'it was just us, ghosts, irrelevant and unbound, not people but only eyes, then there was something wrong. Something would feel wrong. [. . .] at different times of my life I've wanted to be eyes only but I don't want to be eyes only.' The four people that approach Will and Hand at a traffic light in Marrakech, and with whom they end up going to a discotheque, are also described as 'eyes'. In this case, it turns out to be a different sort of look, namely one of connection to the other: '*Why should people look over at you? Why would they care?* But these people do. They threw out a line.' This is the connection, the love that Eggers's narrators look for, in response to what Camus calls the absurdity of existence: 'Love is implicit in every connection', Will says: 'Thus when absent it makes us insane. It breaks our equilibrium and we have to flounder for reasons.'[67] In *A Heartbreaking Work of Staggering Genius*, we can recognize this type of connection in the important motive of the care for others: for Dave's terminally ill parents, for Shalini, and in the upbringing of Dave's younger brother Toph.

3.2.3. Jonathan Safran Foer

In Foer's work we can also see the indispensability of the attention of and for the other, that the self can only attain substance through this transcendent movement, through this connection with outside. In *Extremely Loud & Incredibly Close* this becomes clear from the countless small story elements and descriptions, together illustrating the importance of the other. For instance, Oskar's grandmother says,

---

[65] YSKOV, 319.
[66] Ibid., 91–2, 152.
[67] Ibid., 324, 235, 236, 287.

about the attention that her future husband – Oskar's grandfather – the sculptor Thomas, once paid to her, when using her as a model: 'His attention filled the hole in the middle of me.' Conversely, we see that the self can become an emptiness when it closes itself off, for example, in the case of Oskar who carries a secret with him – that his father had called from the World Trade Center and left a message on the answering machine: 'That secret was a hole in the middle of me that every happy thing fell into.' For a while, Oskar's grandfather goes to the airport each morning and evening, not because he expects someone there, but because he likes to watch people being reunited, coming together again. 'I like to see people reunited [. . .] I like the hugging, the bringing together, the end of missing someone. [. . .] Being here fills my heart with so much joy, even if the joy isn't mine.' The title *Extremely Loud & Incredibly Close* can be understood, among other things, as a reference to Oskar's (at times even somewhat intrusive) attention to the people he meets on his search: he comes very close to these people, often literally – coming in close physical vicinity to them. Oskar also meets an older man, Mr Black, whose hearing is impaired and has consciously left his hearing aid switched off for years – a symbol of a self-chosen disconnection from the world, from communication with others. Mr Black speaks 'extremely loudly', just as Oskar is, in a figurative sense, a loud, unremitting speaker; Oskar offers to switch on Mr Black's hearing aid and the two become friends.[68]

In *Everything Is Illuminated* we can see the attention for the other in how the two narrating characters attend to each other's stories. Together Alex and Jonathan construct the story of the book: '*We are talking now, Jonathan, together, and not apart.*' They comment on and correct each other's narratives. For instance, Alex writes to Jonathan: '*I do not have any homage for anyone in your family, [. . .] because you are all in the proximity of love, and all disavow love. [. . .] Of course, I understand, in some manners, what you are attempting to perform. There is such a thing as love that cannot be, for certain.*'[69] Here, Alex remarks that the attention for, the commitment to the other – called, here, a form of love (compare, in this respect, the description given by Murdoch) – brings with it a certain vulnerability, and therefore, the need to trust the other, which Jonathan – and his portrayed relatives – initially seems to disavow. I will elaborate this in the next subsection.

What should strike us in these passages is the deep contrast with the (almost) complete absence of the other, in any meaningful role whatsoever, in the fiction of Barth and Ellis. What I mean by saying that the novels of Wallace, Eggers and Foer are characterized by the effort of attention is that they display (through their narrators and characters) an orientation towards the other, realizing the importance of the other for one's existence. The above-quoted examples all offer situations of characters slowly breaking out of loneliness and starting to connect to other people (for example, Mario's solidary empathy, Will's desire not to be eyes, and Jonathan and Alex's co-writing). As such, attention is the first stage of this final part of the antidote for the problems of contemporary existence: it is the onset of the definitive movement out of the solipsism and scepticism resulting from hyperreflexivity and endless irony.

[68] ELIC, 83, 71, 109, 97, 152.
[69] EII, 214, 240–1.

3.3. Trust

We have already shown that attention *for* the other brings with it an openness *towards* the other. The willingness to be vulnerable and to endure the uncertainty that accompanies an exchange with the other (as this exchange, by definition, is not fully controlled by the individual), presupposes trust, a certain amount of faith. Such trust in the exchange with the other, as part of the process of meaningful self-becoming, is the next step in the realization of (the importance of) community. I will start with Foer, so as to continue from the preceding subsection 3.2.3. Then I will move on to Eggers and Wallace, in whose work explicitly invoking the reader is an important part of the formulation of the need for trust.

3.3.1. Jonathan Safran Foer

In *Everything Is Illuminated*, the two narrating characters, as we have seen, comment and correct each other's narratives. The identity of both characters takes shape precisely as the result of this dependency of one story line on the other (and, thus, does not have the destabilizing effect that such techniques are used for in so-called postmodernist texts).[70] Alex states: '*With our writing, we are reminding each other of things.*'[71] What we can subsequently see in the novel, is 'the emergence of the frail textual "we"', says Katrin Amian: from the exchange between both narrators gradually a 'we' arises, from which both of them give meaning to themselves. Such interdependence requires trust, faith. Amian writes that the novel 'frames this "new" sense of correspondence as a question of "*feel*[ing]", or rather, as a question of being able to "*also feel it*", to "share" a "sense" of involvement in "*the same story*" without ever articulating or even knowing for sure wherein this "sameness" actually lies'.[72] She refers to a passage in which Alex writes to Jonathan:

> *We are with each other, working on the same story, and I am certain that you can also feel it. Do you know that I am the Gypsy girl and you are Safran, and that I am Kolker and you are Brod, and that I am your grandmother and you are Grandfather, and that I am Alex and you are you, and that I am you and you are me? Do you not comprehend that we can bring each other safety and peace? When we were under the stars in Trachimbrod, did you not feel it then?*[73]

Note the emphasis that Alex places on 'feeling' the 'safety and peace' that they have created between them. Both narrating characters describe things about themselves on the basis of how this feeling is shared by the other; from this emerging 'we' they formulate their individual identity. '*Everything Is Illuminated* thus eventually ties the "sense of urgency" it carefully builds to the vague potential of a frail, affective connection', writes Amian.[74]

---

[70] Amian, *Rethinking Postmodernism(s)*, 175.
[71] EII, 144.
[72] Amian, *Rethinking Postmodernism(s)*, 182.
[73] EII, 214.
[74] Amian, *Rethinking Postmodernism(s)*, 182.

3.3.2. Dave Eggers

In Eggers's work this 'demand for trust' and the resulting 'waking up this dormant "we",
this potential structure of intersubjectivity',[75] as Timmer describes it, can be recognized
too. In *You Shall Know Our Velocity* we can see it in the spontaneity that Will longs for,
and the decision of Will and Hand not to remain 'just eyes' when they are approached
in Marrakech; they trust in the connection they have made, they surrender to the
uncertainty of it. In *A Heartbreaking Work of Staggering Genius*, the importance or,
in this case, the enjoyment of trust is illustrated by an experiment – one of Dave's
attempts at making contact with others – in which he gives away the artwork for his
cartoon in *SF Weekly*: he would leave the trunk of his car unlocked, and if readers
would see the car, they could take a drawing and sign a register: 'In a few weeks, all
the artwork was gone, and everyone had signed their names.' The idea – of 'trust' and
'community' – worked: 'The point is that trust is usually rewarded, even though trust is
sometimes violated. [. . .] It is fun to risk what you can reasonably risk – like, your car,
or your reputation – on the trust of people.'[76]

However, in *A Heartbreaking Work of Staggering Genius*, the most important,
structural form of this wish to establish a mutual trust and ensuing exchange with the
other can be found in the way the entire narrative is presented by the protagonist (and
first-person narrator) Dave. The passages concerning the artwork in the boot of the
car are in fact examples of how the narrator wants his entire story to work, namely:
in an exchange with the other, the reader, a 'you' who is regularly 'invoked', and with
whom the narrator hopes to have a certain kinship, in the form of shared feelings and
experiences, on the basis of which a 'we' can take shape. '[The often extensive use of
the addressee form ("you")] works as a way to reach out', writes Timmer, 'as a way to
hypothesize a potential structure of a "we" which revolves around the possibility of
sharing feelings'.[77] The use of the addressee form can be seen, for instance, in the motto
of the book: 'I am tired. I am true of heart! And also: You are tired. You are true of
heart!'[78]

According to Timmer '[w]e should not underestimate the awkwardness that goes
with [. . .] raising this possibility of a "we" and with "sharing feelings", especially
for such solipsistic minds as depicted in the [novels].'[79] We have already seen this
awkwardness, for example, in Dave singing unashamedly in his living room until he
suddenly feels the look of the other upon him (see Chapter 1). This suspicion of one-
directional vulnerability can even cause frustration and anger: 'Don't you know that
I'm connected to you? Don't you know that [. . .] this is for you, that I hate you people,
so many of you motherfuckers.'[80] In the appendix we read the following explanation of
this anxiety: 'while writing the original text, I had in my head [. . .] the Mean/Jaded/

---

[75] Timmer, *'Do You Feel It Too?'*, 346.
[76] AHWOSG, 11–12 [appendix].
[77] Timmer, *'Do You Feel It Too?'*, 47.
[78] AHWOSG, v; also cf. 34 [appendix].
[79] Timmer, *'Do You Feel It Too?'*, 47.
[80] AHWOSG, 436.

Skimming Reader – the person I had been for many years. [. . .] But a weird thing happened: People were kind.'[81]

3.3.3. David Foster Wallace

In Wallace's work, a similar invocation of the assumed reader, as the other to whom the narrator surrenders and places trust in, finds its clearest expression in the short story 'Octet'.[82] In the story, the narrator describes how, at a certain moment, he comes to the realization that he can simply ask the reader ('Because now it occurs to you that you could simply ask her. The reader') whether the reader thinks the story succeeds in expressing what the narrator wants to express (that is, whether the reader feels or thinks something like that – 'ask her straight out whether she's feeling anything like what you feel'). What the narrator wants to express is the very question as to whether others share his 'fundamental intuitions about urgency and sameness', and 'whether people deep inside experience things in anything like the same way you do'.[83]

This gives the story a complex, multilayered structure, which is at the same time quite simple, as it leads to a simple question. What the narrator wants to express is the desire for connection with the other, for shared feelings. The story actually expresses these things by *asking whether and how* it can connect to the reader and express (convey, share) a certain feeling. In the end, the narrator concludes that the story can only do this by connecting with the reader (by addressing the reader) about *this* feeling (the desire for the other, for shared feeling) and sharing it (asking whether the other feels 'it' like 'this' as well – that is, whether the other shares the feeling).

In this way, the story is an exploration of the vulnerability, the awkwardness and the fear of being misunderstood that accompany the attempted connection and openness towards the other: '"This thing I feel, I can't name it straight out but it seems important, do you feel it too?" – this sort of direct question is not for the squeamish. For one thing, it's perilously close to "*Do you like me? Please like me.*"'[84] Timmer states: 'What this comes down to is a tentative construction of some form of *trust*, based on parallel experiences.' Because the reader, too, is undoubtedly familiar with these anxious feelings implied in social exchange. 'The narrator is inviting "you" to feel *with* the narrator', writes Timmer, and this feeling 'in effect becomes a possible index of a relationship, and it seems that only if "you" feel "it" too, *as the narrator*, [can] this feeling somehow be legitimized'.[85] The story thus makes itself dependent on the reader – for as the narrator declares: 'You'll have to ask the reader straight out whether she feels it, too, this queer nameless ambient urgent interhuman sameness.'

---

[81] Ibid., 20 [appendix].
[82] Cf. Holland describes 'Octet' as 'sculpting through fiction a powerful human presence whose insistent engagement with the reader makes her feel, in her own life, less alone'. Holland also signals the similarity between the above-described elements from Foer's *Everything Is Illuminated* and this short story by Wallace (Holland, *Succeeding Postmodernism*, 179, 180–90).
[83] Wallace, 'Octet', *Brief Interviews with Hideous Men*, 130, 131, 136.
[84] Ibid., 131.
[85] Timmer, '*Do You Feel It Too?*', 114–15.

This dependence receives its ultimate expression in the last sentence of the story, in which it surrenders itself as it were, leaving the assessment to the reader; it asks the reader whether the reader feels it too: 'So decide'.[86]

With this appeal 'Octet' is not just a surrender to the reader but at the same time (or perhaps above all) a call upon the reader to surrender, to trust in the story – or, preferably: to be aware of the fact that the reader's willingness to place trust in the story, is all-decisive. The reader can also decide to see 'Octet' as an annoying, contrived, insincere story; such a reader does not believe that the story really does surrender itself to the reader, and therefore, in turn, the reader decides not to surrender himself to the story. Although 'Octet' explicitly concerns the surrender of the story to the reader, implicitly, if the text is to succeed, it is just as much about the surrender of the reader to the story, about having to trust it.[87]

'Octet' expresses a conception of the self that has already been attributed to Wallace's works in general, at the start of this section. The story speaks of 'fundamental intuitions' that the narrator wants to share, namely, the fact that there is 'some sort of weird ambient *sameness* in different kinds of human relationships, some nameless but inescapable "*price*" that all human beings are faced with having to pay at some point if they ever truly want "to be with" another person'.[88] That price is being able to give up the self, as Smith states, or, somewhat summarizing Wallace's formulation from *This Is Water*: 'altering or getting free of my self-centered setting'.[89]

Wallace's work contains multiple characters and stories that display such giving-up, a giving-up which presupposes trust or *faith*. Prayer, faith and God are different expressions of the importance of surrender, of *transcendence* in Wallace's work. As mentioned in Chapter 7, the notions of transcendence in these works do not refer to a surpassing of 'mundane reality',[90] to a vertical distinction between heaven and earth.[91] *Infinite Jest* and other writings by Wallace outline a form of transcendence that takes place within a horizontal order: the forms of beyond are all part of the here and now (the horizontality) of this world. 'Horizontal' transcendence implies not just one level without an absolute above; it also means that the individual is always part of a horizon, embedded within the structures of a community consisting of others that are transcendent to him.[92] In the existentialist view expressed in Wallace's work, the

---

[86] Wallace, 'Octet', *Brief Interviews with Hideous Men*, 132, 136; cf. Timmer, '*Do You Feel It Too?*', 349.
[87] Cf. '[W]hat he's really asking is for you to have faith in something he cannot possibly ever finally determine in language: "the agenda of the consciousness behind the text". His urgency, his sincerity, his apparent desperation to "connect" with his reader in a genuine way – these are things you either believe in or don't' (Smith, 'Brief Interviews with Hideous Men', 290).
[88] Ibid.
[89] Wallace, *This Is Water*, 44.
[90] Stoker, 'Culture and Transcendence: A Typology', 6.
[91] One cannot speak, here of 'religious' transcendence, of a (vertical) relation between two spheres, in the sense of the types 'radical transcendence' and 'immanent transcendence'. Instead, the transcendence portrayed in *Infinite Jest* can be described, from the perspective of Stoker's typology, as 'radical immanence' or 'horizontal transcendence', to use Harry Kunneman's term (Kunneman, *Voorbij het dikke-ik*, 64). Stoker's 'radical immanence' does not, to be sure, imply a complete neglect or absence of transcendence. Such an absence is characteristic of the semi-solipsism that is criticized in *Infinite Jest* (Stoker, 'Culture and Transcendence. A Typology', 6–9).
[92] Cf. Wittgenstein's notion of 'forms of life'.

self is regarded as transcendent, as emerging outside itself, outside consciousness, in its actions and commitment to that outside (this view is opposed to the idea of the individual having some sort of privileged access to the self). We can see this view of the self as transcendent expressed, in *Infinite Jest*, in Mario and in the workings of AA.[93]

According to Smith, we can best label these different instances of other-directed surrender in Wallace's work, a form of prayer: 'It's true that this is prayer unmoored, without its usual object, God, but it is still focused, self-forgetful, and moving in an outward direction.'[94] Murdoch's description of prayer, as attention directed towards making the right choice, is strikingly similar to what Smith describes and what we find in Wallace. Murdoch speaks of 'the purification and reorientation of an energy which is naturally selfish'. She says that prayer 'is properly not petition, but simply an attention to God which is a form of love'. In a secular sense, it means 'being able to focus [one's] thought upon something which is a source of energy'. Murdoch adds: '[It is a psychological fact], that we can all receive moral help by focusing our attention upon things which are valuable: virtuous people, great art.'[95] Compare this to the need, formulated by Wallace, to get free from one's self-centred setting, in order to become a real human being. In *This Is Water*, Wallace states: 'The only choice we get is *what* to worship'; as we already saw in Chapter 7, for Wallace, '[n]one of this is about morality, or religion, or dogma, or big fancy questions of life after death', and has 'everything to do with simple awareness', which he explains as 'being able to care about other people and to sacrifice for them, over and over, in myriad petty little unsexy ways, every day'.[96]

We can regard prayer as unifying the elements of attention and trust. Attention is the directedness at something that is not the self, to what is outside consciousness. Trust is the surrender to that other, trusting in the validity of that connection, to which you have committed yourself. Prayer is attention, a movement out of oneself and out of distrust, resulting in a commitment that is trust, which is what connects the self to the world, to the other. Thereby, the individual is brought to the brink of leaving solipsism and scepticism behind.

4. Towards a dialogic community of meaning

In the previous section, attention and trust were described as aspects of the movement from the lonely, solipsistic self, towards the other. These notions form a bridge, as it were, between Camus's notions of solitary absurdity and rebellious community.

---

[93] This does not present a new form of verticality, in which the other becomes the new 'above', as is the case in what Stoker calls 'transcendence as alterity', which, through the notion of 'alterity', reintroduces a vertical relation towards 'otherness'; Stoker sees this type of transcendence in Derrida (Stoker, 'Culture and Transcendence. A Typology', 8).

[94] Smith, 'Brief Interviews with Hideous Men', 298.

[95] Murdoch, 'On "God" and "Good"', 344–5; cf. literary works functioning as sources of paradigmatic cases for the foundation our complex, moral (human) concepts, as outlined in Chapter 5.

[96] Wallace, *This Is Water*, 101, 128, 130, 120; cf. what the character Marathe says in *Infinite Jest* about the need for principles (what he calls 'our temple') in order to shape our freedom through choice (cf. IJ, 107; also see Chapter 7 of this study).

Below, the Camusian perspective will be taken up again for the analysis of the two main effects of the rebellion against absurdity, as they are portrayed in the works of Wallace, Eggers and Foer: first of all, eradicating the solipsistic loneliness of the individual and replacing it with a connection to others, and secondly, establishing a dialogical process of meaning-acquisition between the connected individuals, which replaces scepticism.

4.1. An end to solitude: 'The solidarity of chains'

The Camusian community ensues from rebellion, from the protest against the meaninglessness of existence. What the members of the community have in common is the absurdity of their individual existence. Their community is a 'solidarity of chains', as Camus famously formulates it in the following passage from *The Rebel*: 'rebellion defined a primary value. It put in the first rank of its frame of reference an obvious complicity among men, a common texture, the solidarity of chains, a communication between human being and human being which makes men both similar and united.'[97]

The absurd fate condemns man to loneliness: it tears man and world apart, as it were. However, this pain of solitude and meaninglessness strikes every individual: they '[infringe] on something in him which does not belong to him alone, but which is common ground [of] all men', writes Camus; the individual is part of a 'community of victims'.[98] The person who realizes this is in rebellion. Rebellion is the realization of communality. And that communality is the first value, the first meaning that human beings find in response to the lonely meaninglessness of absurd existence.[99]

4.1.1. David Foster Wallace

What in Camus's *The Plague* is described as the insight, in this case of the plague-stricken people of Oran, that 'everybody's in the same boat',[100] is in fact the only thing that can remedy the situation of the addicted, hyperreflexive characters in *Infinite Jest*. For instance, the students of the Enfield Tennis Academy, whose sport seems by all accounts to be a very individualistic activity and whose education is at risk of being exclusively self-focused (focused on their individual qualities, potential, development), are exposed to exhausting training days that are aimed at establishing community: the students are all in the 'same boat', share their pain and loneliness, and in that way move out of their individual 'I' to a 'we', as Hal explains the point of these training sessions to a group of younger students:

> [W]e'd all just spent three hours playing challenges against each other in scrotum-tightening cold. [. . .] We're all on each other's food chain. All of us. It's an individual

---

[97]   R, 281.
[98]   Ibid., 16n2.
[99]   Cf. '[Cut-off from others] we are anguished and spiritually impoverished. If the movement from the absurd to revolt means anything, it refers to our need for others in the face of the metaphysical solitude' (Sprintzen, *Camus*, 126–7).
[100] Camus, *The Plague*, 28.

sport. Welcome to the meaning of *individual*. We're each deeply alone here. It's what we all have in common, this aloneness. [. . .] So how can we also be together? [. . .] how can we keep from being 136 deeply alone people all jammed together? [. . .] then so notice the instant group-cohesion that formed itself around all the pissing and moaning down there [. . .]. The suffering *unites* us.[101]

The students form a Camusian 'community of victims'. Subsequently, Hal even formulates an alternative version of Camus's rebellious, communal cogito, on the basis of the suffering inflicted on the students during training: '*I* may despise K. B. Freer, or [. . .] Evan Ingersoll, or Jennie Bash', says Hal, listing fellow students, 'But *we* despise Schtitt's men, the double matches on top of runs, the insensitivity of exams, the repetition, the stress. The loneliness. But we get together and bitch, all of a sudden we're giving something group expression. A community voice. Community.' Hal speaks of the 'need for a *we* here'.[102]

In the novel, the situation of the students, and their need for community, are clearly mirrored by the situation of those who are truly at the bottom of existential suffering, namely the addicts in halfway facility Ennet House and AA. Boswell's description of this group of characters as a 'community of sufferers'[103] calls to mind Camus's notion of rebellion. We could say that Camus's notion receives a striking literary portrayal in Wallace's description of the rebellion of these characters against their addiction, a rebellion that in many ways is a fight against the emptiness and loneliness of their absurd existence. They all share the hope of liberating themselves from addiction:

> [S]o this unites them, nervously, this tentative assemblage of possible glimmers of something like hope, this grudging move toward maybe acknowledging that this unromantic, unhip, clichéd AA thing – so unlikely and unpromising, so much the inverse of what they'd come too much to love – might really be able to keep the lover's toothy maw at bay.[104]

The importance of attending AA meetings is that new members realize they are not unique. All of them initially regard their own individual situation as hopeless. Think of the solipsistic illusion, discussed earlier on in this book, of everyone thinking that their suffering is unique. But it is the very fact that this perception is mistaken, that this despair is shared by all that breeds hope: 'this initial hopelessness unites every soul in this broad cold salad-bar'd hall. [. . .] Every meeting is a reunion, once you've been in for a while.'[105]

Through this experience of communal suffering, AA seems to do something that Wallace also regards as one of the main purposes of 'serious fiction', namely: 'giv[ing] access to other selves'. Wallace states: 'Since an ineluctable part of being a human self is suffering, part of what we humans come to art for is [a sort of "generalization" of

---

[101] IJ, 112–13.
[102] Ibid., 114.
[103] Boswell, *Understanding David Foster Wallace*, 145.
[104] IJ, 350.
[105] Ibid., 349.

suffering]. [. . .] This is nourishing, redemptive; we become less alone inside.'[106] At that point, we can say, in the words of Camus, that '[we have] conquered solitude'.[107]

4.1.2. Dave Eggers

In Eggers's works the Camusian 'solidarity of chains' is a clear, explicit theme. In *You Shall Know Our Velocity*, Will formulates the absurd disconnection between himself and others, especially the people that he and Hand pass by on their world trip: 'There wasn't one thread connecting us to anyone and we had to start threading, I guess, or else it would be just us, without any trail or web [. . .], ghosts, irrelevant and unbound, not people but only eyes' – and in the rest of the novel he commits himself to this 'threading', making connections.[108] The last scene of the novel, with Will jumping (leaping) into a swimming pool at a wedding party, has been repeatedly referred to in this study, but the scene also has significance in light of the theme of this chapter. There, Will is finally at ease, connected to others, and with a plan for the future in which others (symbolized by his mother, who, at first, embodied the hostile, questioning other) play an indispensable role. In the novel's final sentence Will summarizes the realization of these connections, of a community with others, just as Camus does in his rebellious cogito ('I rebel – therefore we exist'),[109] by stating the inevitable connection between 'I' and 'we': 'I jumped with my mouth so open, taking it all in, [. . .] and for two more glorious and interminable months I lived! We lived.'[110]

In *A Heartbreaking Work of Staggering Genius* the desire for community in response to the absurdity of existence plays an even more prominent role. As I have explained, the book describes how, in a short period of time, both of Dave's parents die of cancer, after which Dave becomes responsible for the upbringing of his younger brother Toph. Dave summarizes his situation as follows: 'rootless, ripped from all foundations, an orphan raising an orphan'. Setting up *Might Magazine* has its origins in this experience of 'rootlessness' and the desire to somehow counterbalance it.[111] Even though the later cynicism of *Might* is sharply criticized in the book (partly because of its evident *exclusionary* effect), *Might*'s initial, underlying desire for community is not.[112] In the appendix we read that the editors 'honestly did want people banding together' that what was 'important first was the alliance'.[113] Sharing and (thereby 'diluting') pain is even mentioned as one of the aims of the narrative: 'it makes us feel un-alone'.[114]

---

[106] McCaffery, 'Interview', 127.
[107] R, 281.
[108] YSKOV, 323–4.
[109] R, 22.
[110] YSKOV, 371.
[111] Cf. AHWOSG, 236–7, 144–8.
[112] Cf. the discussion of liberating irony in Chapter 2. Also: '[H]owever much the narrator ridicules their narcissistic quasi-activism, the "hope" with which *Might* was started is not completely ridiculed and debunked in the text. [. . .] They are strengthened by others who, like them, want to start creating their world [. . .]. Ultimately, it is this "connection" which appears to be the sole purpose of their actions, their magazine' (Timmer, 'Do You Feel It Too?', 231).
[113] AHWOSG, 29 [appendix].
[114] Ibid., 10.

As part of this dilution of suffering, Dave introduces his notion of the 'lattice', a frame, a community of people supporting each other:

> The lattice is the connective tissue. The lattice is everyone else, [. . .] each one of us responsible to one another, because no one else is. [. . .] and if we can bring everyone to grab a part of the other, like an arm at the socket [. . .] and if we can get everyone to, instead of ripping this arm from the socket, instead hold to it, tight, and thus strengthening [. . .] the connections between people, [. . .] become a sort of lattice.[115]

The connection of the members of the lattice results from the fact that they are marked by the same loneliness and meaninglessness, and from there, by the desire to form a solidary community. It is based on the decision to want to form a community, to care for each other, not on the basis of some external principle, but 'because no one else is'.[116]

4.1.3. Jonathan Safran Foer

In the previous section, we have already described that the two narrating main characters from Foer's *Everything Is Illuminated* both try to come to grips with their family histories. We could say that Jonathan tries to derive the meaning of his existence from that history, and when he finds nothing – not the meaning he had perhaps hoped for – he loses himself in a largely fantasized version of the past. Alex, by contrast, finds meaning in the exchange with Jonathan, who helps him formulate his identity and acknowledge his struggle with his aggressive, alcoholic father and his grandfather's distant but questionable past. That the parts narrated by Alex are part of the larger narrative, which actually is Jonathan's story of his search for his heritage, implies that Jonathan has decided to incorporate Alex's parts; this means that Jonathan, too, has now come to realize that the true value of the story lies in the connection between him and Alex.

Extremely Loud & Incredibly Close contains many small references to community born out of a shared resistance against loneliness, meaninglessness and suffering. As Oskar's grandmother says about her relationship with her husband: 'We were always trying to help each other. But not because we were helpless. He needed to get things for me, just as I needed to get things for him. It gave us purpose. Sometimes I would ask him for something that I didn't even want, just to let him get it for me.'[117] The two desperately try to come up with things that can give meaning to the life of the other; and thereby, they implicitly give meaning to their own lives. The old, hearing impaired Mr Black tells Oskar about a group of Russian artists, who had been exiled to a distant, desolate village, which they had then completely decorated with paintings. Mr Black, a journalist at the time, wanted to write about this, but when he arrived at the village, Stalin had ordered the arms of the artists to be broken: 'They couldn't feed themselves, because they couldn't get their hands to their mouths! So [t]hey fed each

---

[115]   Ibid., 211–12.
[116]   Ibid., 211.
[117]   ELIC, 175–6.

other! That's the difference between heaven and hell! In hell we starve! In heaven we feed each other!'[118]

The novel takes place against the background of different instances of great communal loss and suffering: the attacks on the World Trade Center, the bombardment of Dresden, implying, on a more individual level, the loss of loved ones; in all these instances, the question is whether the victims help (feed, heal) each other, or choose to turn inside and wither away.

4.2. The start of meaning: 'If we are not, then I am not'

'[Camus] has made clear the need for the establishment of a shared consciousness of our common condition as the precondition for the development of a human community', writes Sprintzen.[119] The first, temporary value that rebellion creates is communality, the insight that the loneliness of absurd existence is a fate that all human beings share, an insight that puts an end to this loneliness. However, in itself, the end of loneliness does not seem to imply the end of the *meaninglessness* of absurd existence. The significance of the insight into the communality of absurdity is that the resulting cohesion serves as the foundation for the formulation of meaning for the individual's existence.

Camus writes: 'the "We are" paradoxically defines a new form of individualism. [. . .] I have need of others who have need of me and of each other. Every collective action, every form of society, supposes a discipline, and the individual, without this discipline, is only a stranger.'[120] Concerning the implications of Camus's conception of rebellion and (resulting) community, Sprintzen explains: 'Since we are bound together in fact, what is called for is a strategy that transforms this factual commonality into a mutually sustaining recognition of value. This is the promise to which revolt bears witness – and the source of the value to which it makes claim.'[121] Camus concludes: 'Therefore the individual is not, in himself alone, the embodiment of the values he wishes to defend. It needs all humanity, at least, to comprise them.' Based on this, Camus formulates the indispensability of others in a reverse version of his rebellious cogito: 'If we are not, then I am not.'[122] Sprintzen explains: 'others are essential to me; they are constituents of my experience and of the possibility of a dignified happiness. I cannot live, I cannot even conceive of myself, without them. But as they are essential to me and share the same conditions as I do, so I am essential to them.'[123]

I do not just need the other to acknowledge my independently formulated identity, but to discover and be able to formulate that identity, in reciprocity with the other. The other thus has an active role in the individual's self-conception. For Camus, it is 'on this basis alone that the individual can achieve the felt intersubjective meaning by opening out to others in the conjoint endeavors that constitute the moment of community', in 'a

---

[118] Ibid., 164.
[119] Sprintzen, *Camus*, 104.
[120] R, 297.
[121] Sprintzen, *Camus*, 244.
[122] R, 17, 282.
[123] Sprintzen, *Camus*, 244.

developing experience in which, at least for the moment, meaning is felt as sufficient', writes Sprintzen.[124]

More recently, Charles Taylor has formulated a view similar to that of Camus. Taylor writes: '[w]e become full human agents, capable of understanding ourselves, and hence defining an identity, through our acquisition of rich human languages of expression' – a view which is clearly connected to that of the later Wittgenstein ('No one acquires the languages needed for self-definition on their own', writes Taylor). I need others – whose situation and circumstances make them part of a community to which I also belong – to be able, at all, to give meaning and identity to myself. However, there is an important difference between Taylor's view of the self and the view underlying the novels of Wallace, Eggers and Foer. According to Taylor, the description that I give of myself always draws on the horizons of meaning that I share with others. That description can be acknowledged by others, or not. In that sense, my identity is dependent on others: my description of myself presupposes that it is subject to the judgment of others, whether it is meaningful or not. But, in line with the notion of authenticity that he retains, Taylor speaks of an 'inwardly derived, personal, original identity' that '[doesn't enjoy] recognition a priori' but 'has to win it through exchange'.[125] In the works of Wallace, Eggers and Foer (as well as in the existentialist philosophies utilized in this study) there is no such original identity.

4.2.1. David Foster Wallace

In one of the passages in *Infinite Jest* concerning Ennet House, we read that one of the many new facts that one acquires when spending time at such a facility – which some of the characters, but of course also the readers of the novel, in a sense, do – is that the 'cliché "I don't know who I am" unfortunately turns out to be more than a cliché'. The many addicted characters in *Infinite Jest* do not have a self. The novel shows how some addicts, among them Don Gately, try to form a stable self, on the basis of their insight into another truism about addiction, namely that other people can often 'see things about you that you yourself cannot see, even if those people are stupid'.[126] The metaphor of addiction makes the idea of the self as something non-private more acceptable; in this context, it is quite clear that others *are* often in a much better position to establish that something is wrong with a person, that she is in terrible mental pain, while that person herself is still in deep denial about this. So, characters like Gately try to form a stable self in a connection with the world and others. In the novel, Gately is the most prominent and, in this study most extensively analysed, example of this. He tries to create a meaningful life by helping others, as part of the staff of Ennet House, and as a member of AA.

What we see in *Infinite Jest* is empty, anhedonic individuals who, in a constant to-and-fro of communal meaning processes, again give substance to the self. They cannot acquire meaning alone, but need constant interaction with others. This dynamic

[124] Ibid., 268.
[125] Taylor, *The Ethics of Authenticity*, 33, 38–9, 48.
[126] IJ, 200, 204.

of meaning is expressed, above all, by the workings of AA, in which individuals try to regain a self through communal processes: it is through the observations of others and in dialogue with the (recognizable) stories that these other people tell about themselves, that individuals are better able to understand themselves and give meaning to their existence.

It is also symbolized by Gately's exchange with a wraith (the ghost of James Incandenza, the father of Hal and Mario) who appears to Gately after the latter has been shot and is in the hospital, where (because of his addiction) he refuses every form of pain suppression. That is why Gately concludes that his apparent interactions with the wraith are probably a fever-dream, a delusion; but at the same time he also has to 'admit he'd kind of liked it. The dialogue. The give-and-take. The way the wraith could seem to get inside him.'[127] Gately and the wraith have a sort of direct communication: the wraith seems to be inside Gately's consciousness. Even though the wraith discusses all kinds of things that Gately knows or understands little about, Gately still has the idea that he understands the urgency of what is told to him (and it might be that this urges him to meet Hal and help him with his self-problems – see Chapter 6): so, we could say that meaning comes into being both inside and outside of Gately.

Similarly, in Hal's confession to Mario, about his drug addiction, and in their ensuing conversation, the realization of a meaningful life is portrayed as necessarily taking place via a dialogue with the other. The same holds for the advice and stories offered to Gately by his counsellors (Gene M. and Pat Montesian), and in turn for Gately, in his attempts to help Joelle van Dyne overcome her addiction.

4.2.2. Dave Eggers

After Dave, in *A Heartbreaking Work of Staggering Genius*, has called himself 'rootless, ripped from all foundations', and has thereby described the absurdity of (his) existence, he adds to this description the desire for meaning: 'I need community, I need feedback, I need love, connection, give-and-take.' The community, the 'lattice' that Dave desires, is meant as an antidote to the loneliness of contemporary existence *and* as a source of meaning; this process of meaning is, as discussed, a dialogical process, that runs between community members via feedback. Dave seems to want nothing more than to be the initiator of such a community.[128] 'Dave partly wants to be the unique spokesman of this community of peers and partly, rather desperately, needs feedback from someone else to be able to authorize his own life story', writes Timmer, 'Dave turns himself inside out in an attempt to get a better grasp of what he feels and who he is.'[129] At the end of the book, Dave says, to the frequently addressed 'you': 'There is nowhere I stop and you begin'[130] – and thereby expresses that self-becoming is a process of constant reciprocity between individual and other(s).[131]

---

[127] Ibid., 923.
[128] Cf. AHWOSG, 237.
[129] Timmer, *'Do You Feel It Too?'*, 188–9, 342.
[130] AHWOSG, 436.
[131] *The Circle*, too, takes up this theme of community, which runs through all of Eggers's work. The novel also addresses the dangers of what one could call 'pseudo-community': professing the

4.2.3. Jonathan Safran Foer

We have already seen that the main narrating characters in *Everything Is Illuminated* derive meaning and self-understanding from their communal acts of telling. Amian states that their 'epistolary negotiations are revealed to create [a] frail sense of inter-subjectivity' and that an '[intricate tie] is forged between "meaning" and intersubjective exchange'.[132] Furthermore, we have seen that the attention for the other is an important theme in *Extremely Loud & Incredibly Close*. This attention saves characters from their loneliness, and they arrive at meaning in an exchange with each other. For instance, together, Oskar and his grandfather make digging up the father's coffin and filling it with letters from the grandfather, a meaningful act that forms a milestone in their coping with the loss of their father/son, and the shame they feel towards him. Earlier in the book, the grandfather formulates the insight that you can only understand yourself via the other: 'She said, "There's nothing wrong with not understanding yourself", she saw through the shell of me into the center of me [. . .]. She went home with her father, the center of me followed her, but I was left with the shell of me, I needed to see her again, I couldn't explain my need to myself.'[133]

These descriptions illustrate the dialogical process of meaning-making portrayed in all of the novels we have looked at: 'Sense-making from such a perspective takes place neither "inside" the self (as autonomous and private endeavor) nor "outside" the self', writes Timmer, 'but instead involves exactly the kind of "give and take" that for example the narrator in [*A Heartbreaking Work of Staggering Genius*] craves for, a feedback process between a self and an other'.[134] Here, Timmer connects this with Eggers's debut, but it holds for Foer's and Wallace's works as well (Gately, too, as we have just seen, speaks of 'give and take', in this context). According to Hayles, *Infinite Jest* offers a 'reconceptualization of subjectivity', amounting to the following: 'to shed the illusion of autonomous selfhood and accept citizenship in a world in which actions have consequences that rebound to the self because everything is connected with everything else'.[135] *Infinite Jest* and Wallace's other fiction show, as Boswell formulates it, 'that in fact this process of human-making is a reciprocal arrangement: we acquire our sacred rights as humans only granting those rights to others'.[136] In Foer's novels, we have also seen such a dialogical process of meaning: '[a] move toward a frail, dialogic textual "*we*" that engages characters and readers alike in a dynamic process of exchange resonates with novels like Wallace's *Infinite Jest* [. . .] and Dave Eggers's *A Heartbreaking Work of Staggering Genius*', writes Amian.[137] In all these works, 'through a kind of feedback loop', as Timmer formulates it, characters 'come to grips with what

---

importance of community without giving any substance, any reality to so-called connections to others. In the novel, one of the slogans of internet company 'The Circle' is '*Community First*'; however, the company understands community in purely quantitative and reductive terms ('like', 'dislike', 'smile', 'frown'), and in fact contributes to the breakdown of real attention (see section 3.2) and communication – to 'social autism', as one character calls it (Eggers, *The Circle*, 47, 132, 260).

[132] Amian, *Rethinking Postmodernism(s)*, 182.
[133] ELIC, 113–14.
[134] Timmer, '*Do You Feel It Too?*', 349.
[135] Hayles, 'The Illusion of Autonomy and the Fact of Recursivity', 693.
[136] Boswell, *Understanding David Foster Wallace*, 196.
[137] Amian, *Rethinking Postmodernism(s)*, 185.

they are feeling, a feedback loop that runs via a "you", and that ultimately allows them to make some sense of who they are.'[138]

Conclusion

In Chapters 6 and 7, we have seen that sincerity can be regarded as the basic attitude in the attempt to overcome the problems described in Part 1, and that this attitude receives further substance by committing to reality through choice. In this final chapter, we have analysed the subsequent, final virtue portrayed in the works of Wallace, Eggers and Foer: forming a community with other human beings, as to achieve a meaningful existence. This striving for community was analysed in light of Camus's philosophy of the rebellion against the absurd, as the previously employed perspectives of Sartre and Kierkegaard were shown to insufficiently address the role of other human beings in meaningful self-becoming or attach the same importance to it as the works of Wallace, Eggers and Foer do. For Camus, the connection with the other follows from the communality of the rebellion against the absurd. Although in the works a similar connection to the other is eventually realized, this is the result of a somewhat more tentative movement: we have seen that the works emphasize attention (as the outer-directedness of consciousness, as attending to another human being) and trust (as having faith in the validity – or desirability – of the openness, the vulnerability towards the other, who turns out to be an indispensable part of self-becoming). Finally, we have seen that the importance of the resulting interhuman connection lies in the ending of (reflexive-ironic) solitude in the solidary community, and, the subsequent start of meaning, which is brought about by the dialogue with others.

As for fiction itself: the works of Wallace, Eggers and Foer all treat fiction as a dialogue between writer and reader. Kevin Mattson writes about *A Heartbreaking Work of Staggering Genius*: 'Crack open a copy of [the book] and early on you get a sense of how this young writer is struggling to bring readers into a two-way, communicative relationship.' To this, Mattson adds: 'Some might think these examples nothing more than gimmicks. Nonetheless, they represent Eggers's hope to draw the reader into the act of communication.'[139]

In Foer's *Everything Is Illuminated* we read: '*With our writing, we are reminding each other of things. We are making one story, yes?*' And: '*We are talking now, Jonathan, together, and not apart. We are with each other, working on the same story, and I am certain that you can also feel it.*'[140] These passages belong to letters written by one narrating character to another, but they also seem to address the reader.[141] Art is

---

[138] Timmer, '*Do You Feel It Too?*', 333.
[139] Mattson, 'Is Dave Eggers a Genius?', 76.
[140] EII, 144, 214.
[141] Cf. Collado-Rodriguez, who writes that 'the novel's use of two narrators serves to evaluate the power of fiction as an ethical instrument [. . .] to fix the meaning of his book and urge an ethical reading of it through a dual narrative structure [. . .] to bridle the free play of cultural relativism' (Collado-Rodriguez, 'Ethics in the Second Degree: Trauma and Dual Narratives in Jonathan Safran Foer's *Everything Is Illuminated*', 54–5).

described (in the novels in question, and by Foer himself) as a communal activity, as something that can only acquire meaning through exchange. For example, in the short story collection *The Unabridged Pocketbook of Lightning*: 'as if writing weren't something that one person does, but an ongoing communal project, expressed, at different moments, from different people.'[142] Foer speaks of 'collective creation' to describe, as Amian explains, 'the larger cultural, political, and societal processes of (self-)reflection and creative invention to which he sees his novels contribute and respond.'[143] In an interview, Foer has stated: 'I write because I want to end my loneliness. Books make people less alone. That, before and after everything else, is what books do. They show us that conversations are possible across distances.'[144]

According to Wallace:

> [A] piece of fiction is a conversation. There's a relationship set up between the reader and the writer [...]. Somebody at least for a moment feels about something or sees something the way that I do. [...] I feel human and unalone and that I'm in a deep, significant conversation with another consciousness.[145]

This aspect of Wallace's writing should of course be seen in the light of Wittgenstein's philosophy. Wallace assentingly refers to Wittgenstein by writing 'that for language even to be possible, it must always be a function of relationships between persons [...] dependent on human community'. The model of 'Addicts Anonymous', portrayed in *Infinite Jest*, can be regarded as an example of how fiction should work, as forging community. For Wallace, the purpose of fiction is to 'reaffirm the idea of art being a living transaction between humans', to establish 'a relationship between the writer's consciousness and [the reader's], and [...] in order for it to be anything like a real full human relationship, [the reader]'s going to have to put in her share of the linguistic work'.[146] As we have seen during the course of this study, *Infinite Jest* forces the reader to 'put in work' in many ways – the abundance of information, the countless characters who all have to be processed and aligned, resulting in a story-world that for the reader becomes all the more credible because of its comprehensiveness. Boswell writes that in doing that linguistic work, writer and reader 'become a community where meaning is made'.[147]

Perhaps we could say that the works of Wallace, Eggers and Foer affirm that a novel is at heart a language-game: it is a dialogue between writer and reader, grounded in the communal structures of the life-form. And by showing this, these fictions supply complex, human concepts, virtues such as sincerity, reality-commitment and community with meaning.

---

142   Foer, 'Author's Note', in *The Unabridged Pocketbook of Lightning*, vii.
143   Amian, *Rethinking Postmodernism(s)*, 189.
144   Solomon, 'The Rescue Artist'.
145   Miller, 'Interview'.
146   McCaffery, 'Interview', 143, 138, 142.
147   Boswell, *Understanding David Foster Wallace*, 121.

Concluding Remarks

This study set out to analyse the shared philosophical dimension of the literary works of David Foster Wallace, Dave Eggers and Jonathan Safran Foer, in their portrayal of the situation of the contemporary Western individual. The study has shown that these novels are indeed connected through their shared preoccupation with similar themes, portraying similar problems and solutions, and that the most important formal aspect of these novels is their reaffirmation of the possibility of connecting fictional stories to the real world, thereby setting them apart from certain preceding trends in American literary fiction. As such, we have established that these works form a new literary trend and that what unifies these novels, what forms their common 'aesthetic', is their shared thematic preoccupation through which they engage themselves with the reality of contemporary Western existence.

But analysing this shared philosophical dimension also implies a claim about what these literary works are, what they do, namely: that they are partly philosophical, not in the limited and subsidiary sense that they could be used to illustrate certain philosophical views, but in the sense that these literary works themselves provide philosophical insights. Throughout this study, these insights have been further explored and analysed by viewing them in light of relevant heuristic perspectives derived from different philosophers. Now that we have reached the end of this study, we are able to reflect on the productivity of this interdisciplinary approach to literature and philosophy. I will also remark upon the existentialist connection between the literary and philosophical works, and on the realization of the attitude, portrayed in the novels, in the contemporary Western world.

1. Literature and philosophy

The relation between literature and philosophy, and whether the former can contribute something to the latter, is the subject of a longstanding and ongoing debate. Most of the arguments in this debate refer to a number of supposedly fundamental differences between philosophy and literature; one's position then depends on whether one judges those differences to be either conducive to or incompatible with philosophical insight. Oft-mentioned distinctions are the generality that most philosophy aspires to versus the particularity of literary descriptions; also, the form: most philosophy has an argumentative structure, while literary texts are predominately structured as a narrative;[1] and, on a related

---

[1] At least, all the literary texts (novels) analysed in this study have a narrative structure. But of course, literature in general also includes lyrical poetry.

point: philosophy is characterized as wanting to avoid all ambiguity whereas literature frequently intentionally invites ambiguity.[2] Several thinkers have argued that literature, precisely because of these alleged fundamental differences, constitutes an alternative source of (or route to) philosophical insight and, as such, offers a valuable or even indispensable supplement to 'regular' philosophy.[3]

However, in my opinion, sharp distinctions between literature and philosophy, such as the ones offered above, amount to distortive generalizations. I am not suggesting that the characterizations lack all validity, but as they tend to emphasize the differences between literature and philosophy, such descriptions result in isolating the two from each other, which then makes it difficult to bring their connections into view. At first glance, all the contrasts mentioned in the preceding paragraph might seem like truisms. But one only has to look at the thinkers employed throughout this study – Kierkegaard, Sartre, Wittgenstein and Camus – to realize that such clear-cut distinctions need to be refuted: these thinkers are all regarded as 'literary' philosophers, in whose works general philosophical argumentation and particular, ambiguous literary narrative are closely intertwined.

Thus, merely emphasizing the differences between literature and philosophy hinders our understanding of the relations between them, and how literature might bring forth philosophical insight. I think that adopting an interdisciplinary approach will prove to be much more productive, and make visible where and how literature and philosophy actually come together and overlap. I hope to have contributed to this by means of this study, and, below, I will reflect on what insights can be drawn from the specific cooperation between literature and philosophy offered in it.

First of all, we can conclude that, throughout the preceding chapters, the constant interplay between the literary portrayals and philosophical perspectives proved to be very fruitful: both served to illustrate and clarify aspects that were problematic, unclear or absent in the other. For example, Kierkegaard's notion of aesthetic irony allowed us to understand the irony critique formulated in Wallace's and Eggers's novels, but on the other hand, it was only through these literary works that we were able to properly see that such an existential attitude of endless irony forms a truly fundamental problem of contemporary Western existence. Similarly, the Sartrean view of consciousness served to clarify the role of sincerity in the works of Wallace, Eggers and Foer, while at the same time these works served to point out and correct both Sartre's own as well as the more general philosophical misconception of the phenomenon of sincerity.

Furthermore, we should remember (in contrast to what might seem to follow from the traditional distinction between philosophy as offering general, structured insight, and literature as offering specific illustrations of particularities) that the overall (philosophical) structure and substance of the explorations in this study was largely determined, not by the philosophical sources, but by the portrayals depicted in the novels of Wallace, Eggers and Foer. The novels dictated the overall structure, the philosophical route taken and its component themes (the hermeneutic keys).

---

[2]   Cf. Lamarque, *The Philosophy of Literature*, 253–4.
[3]   In contemporary philosophy, one could think of, among others, Iris Murdoch, Martha Nussbaum and Paul Ricoeur as putting forth such theses; cf. Lamarque, *The Philosophy of Literature*, 220–54.

Subsequently, specific aspects of different philosophies (but not one, singular, imposed, coherent philosophical framework) were employed (as heuristic perspectives) to further explicate the different elements encountered on this philosophical route.

In my opinion, the philosophical subject matter analysed in this study requires this trajectory via literature. It is from the descriptions offered by the novels, that, for example, hyperreflexivity and endless irony can most convincingly be seen as contemporary problems. I know of no contemporary philosophical texts that offer equally encompassing descriptions of the different aspects of these problems. This could of course be due to a lack of acquaintance with such texts on my part. However, there might be a more fundamental explanation, namely: that a proper investigation of these problems simply cannot do without the kind of detailed descriptions provided by the novels.

It is important to note that the issues at stake, here, are existential issues, the problems and solutions for attaining a meaningful life, as experienced by the individual as part of the reality of his existence. It requires elaborate descriptions to be able to truly grasp such experiences. For example: what is it for the self to be confined in self-reflection? How should I understand the apparently contradictory assertion, made by many philosophers, but convincingly described in the novels, that a constant focus on the self leads to a loss of self? And while we are at it: what exactly does 'losing' one's self mean? Another example: what does it mean to be unable to choose and how does the overcoming of this inability take shape? The novels give access to the experience and consciousness of these complicated, many-sided and contradictory processes, which to me seems to be a requirement for understanding these existential phenomena.

But the fact that the novels give access to experience and consciousness (perhaps a quality of literature in general) could still be interpreted as a subsidiary, mainly illustrative function. However, when confronted by such a consideration, we should realize the wider scope of the issues at hand, and think not just in terms of how they are investigated in philosophy and how literature might 'assist' in that investigation. We should remember that we are talking about existential issues, about 'what it is to be a fucking *human being*' – as Wallace puts it[4] –, and wonder how in life itself (and not just in philosophy, as an activity brought forth by that experience) we are able to understand our existence as a 'human' reality. We do so by means of a whole range of complex, moral concepts. How are we able to understand, store and pass on the meaning of such concepts, so that they can play a crucial role in our descriptions of existence? Does this not always require the elaborate depictions that, for instance, literature provides? Our meaningful use of such complex concepts presupposes paradigmatic cases, portrayals embodying a concept, that are common knowledge within a life-form, and that function as a standard of meaning for the use of that concept within a given group of people. As we already saw in Chapter 5, and without wanting to repeat the argument described there: literary works can be regarded as an important source of such paradigmatic cases.

---

[4] McCaffery, 'Interview', 131.

Concerning the study's subject matter: what makes the novels of Wallace, Eggers and Foer stand out, makes them important, is that they actively re-assume this function of literature, as offering meaningful, foundational portrayals of reality; a function that was discredited by the postmodernist view, which sees language and fiction as cut off from reality. For example, the works of Wallace, Eggers and Foer offer portrayals that give new meaning to the concept of sincerity, a notion that had been discounted (not perceived as meaningful) for quite some time. This shows the indispensability of the novels for the philosophical analysis offered in this study (and thus of the interdisciplinary, cooperative approach to literature and philosophy employed therein): the novels offer elaborate portrayals of contemporary Western existence, and thereby breathe meaning into concepts signifying the problems and possible virtues of that existence. As such, they form the foundation of a (philosophical) understanding of the world that was further explicated and analysed in the foregoing.

I do not think that there is, nor do we need to find or formulate, a decisive quality or set of qualities that distinguishes all philosophical and literary texts from each other. I regard philosophy and literature as consisting of many widely varying, but diversely interconnected language-games; and, even though we are quite capable of drawing rough distinctions between both collections of language-games, when we approach these roughly drawn borderlines, we will find many cross bonds, and cases that take part in both collections. Most of the literary and philosophical texts employed in this study are characterized – though in varying degrees and arrangements – by such a 'hybridity', which in the preceding chapters has been proven to provide fertile ground for insight. In my opinion, there is no need to 'purify' the divide between literature and philosophy; for what else would this mean other than wanting to 'enforce' the divide?

2. Existentialist engagement

At the start of this study, we noted that the portrayal of the problems and virtues concerning the realization of meaningful existence in the contemporary Western world, offered in the novels of Wallace, Eggers and Foer, seems to have strong connections to existentialist thought. To further explicate and analyse this shared philosophical dimension, the novels were viewed in light of relevant heuristic perspectives derived from different existentialist philosophers, namely: Kierkegaard, Sartre, Wittgenstein and Camus. The resulting investigation has made clear that the works of Wallace, Eggers and Foer indeed offer profoundly existentialist portrayals of contemporary existence, and that the literary trend that these works represent, could thus, as the title of this study suggests, be rightly labelled as existentialist. However, these works should not be understood as simply returning to and adopting the ideas formulated by the philosophers referred to. We have seen that in certain aspects, the novels can be seen to update and correct the views of these thinkers. Whereas these existentialist philosophers can sometimes be seen to waver between a view of the self as transcendent, as coming into being 'in the world', among others, and a latent desire for autonomy, leading to a neglect of the other, the novels provide a harrowing portrayal of individuals who have become encaged in themselves and make clear that there is only one direction for meaningful existence: out of the self, towards the world and the other.

Furthermore, we could say that the affinity with existentialism lies in the attitude of engagement that the novels of Wallace, Eggers and Foer express. By taking on these themes they address the problematic condition of contemporary Western existence, acknowledge it as a situation that needs to be overcome, and embody an attempt to formulate such an overcoming. They portray characters who are involved in such engaged attempts, and as these portrayals clearly concern actual contemporary existence, the novels themselves are also expressions of such engagement. One could perhaps say that all literary trends are a critical response to something (to preceding literary trends, or societal developments in general). But in the works of Wallace, Eggers and Foer, the centrality of contemporary problems and possible solutions constitutes a distinctive engagement that can also be said to be a defining characteristic of works of existentialism.[5]

The engagement with both existential problems and possible solutions, offered in the works of Wallace, Eggers and Foer, reflects what, according to Wallace, all fiction should do, namely 'both to depict [the time's darkness] *and* to illuminate the possibilities for being alive and human in it', applying 'CPR to those elements of what's human and magical that still live and glow despite the times' darkness'.[6] This is also how we could understand Wallace's term '*both*ness':[7] the works portray the problems of contemporary existence, including the enormous difficulty of escaping the grip of these problems, but they also address the avenues that are still available to somehow try to realize a meaningful, human life.[8] This dynamic might also be an expression of what Wallace calls the oft-contested compatibility of 'cynicism and naïveté', an issue that appears in several of his works, and as such functions as a leitmotif in his writing.[9] More specifically: the works in question describe difficult aspects of contemporary existence ('cynicism'), but also offer a portrayal of a possible solution, a commitment (and thus a vulnerability) to a 'positivity', to something that is valued or affirmed again ('naïveté').

In doing so, the works of Wallace, Eggers and Foer constitute a literary execution of Sartre's notion of 'pure reflection' (connecting themselves to the world we live in, resuming the recognition of the irresolvable tension lying at the heart of human existence) and of what Kierkegaard calls the 'leap' (from the recognition of that fundamental tension, venturing to formulate such ethically motivated fiction,

---

[5]   Cf. Van Stralen, *Beschreven keuzes*, 40, 229–30.
[6]   McCaffery, 'Interview', 131.
[7]   Cf. Chapter 2, section 4.3.
[8]   Wallace, 'David Lynch Keeps His Head', 211.
[9]   Wallace, 'Westward', *Girl with Curious Hair*, 304; cf. IJ, 694; EUP, 63; 'Wallace's work, in its attempt to prove that cynicism and naïveté are mutually compatible' (Boswell, *Understanding David Foster Wallace*, 17).

committing to meaning, instead of endlessly retreating from it, as in postmodernist fiction), and thereby establish what Wittgenstein and Camus describe as a community of meaning (by offering, in dialogue with the reader, insightful portrayals into contemporary problems and virtues required in response to those problems).

The contrast between this engagement and the problematic life-view it responds to is aptly summarized by the two different denotations of the title of Wallace's *Infinite Jest*. On the one hand, *in* the novel, there is a film called 'Infinite Jest', which symbolizes the problematic reflexive-ironic attitude: the film sets off in its viewers an infinite, self-obsessed desire for entertainment, non-committal pleasure, that ignores the world completely, and thus, in the end, proves to be fatal. On the other hand, there is the novel *Infinite Jest*, which is expressive of a completely different 'infinity': not excessive reflexivity and endless irony leading to solipsism and scepticism, but a novel that facilitates endless re-engagement, as an ethical choice that is constantly taken up again.

Also, in this context of engagement and commitment in and through literature, I would like to remark upon the state of consciousness that reading literary works in general (or at least, most of them – see below) and the analysed novels in particular, can be said to bring forth: a state of consciousness that constitutes a realization of the view of the (engaged, committed) self outlined in this study. To me, this state of consciousness while reading seems to be one of the grounds on which we base our broad, intuitive distinction between most novels and most philosophical texts, and, therefore, also tells us something about what the former might add to the latter. I follow Ger Groot and Patricia de Martelaere in their suggestion that an important part of reading literature is not so much forgetting the unreality of the story (the so-called willing suspension of disbelief) but forgetting the self; that is, truly attending to something outside the self, consciousness directed towards the world as it is portrayed in the story. It might be for this very reason that our engagement with fiction is so real and deep.[10] The forgetting facilitated by fiction should not be interpreted as a form of blissful escapism. On the contrary, as the words of the text demand to be given meaning, the self can no longer (self-reflectively) immunize or insulate itself, as it does so often in daily life (when watching the news, when stuck in traffic, when standing in line in the supermarket),[11] but has to commit to realizing the meaning of the reality brought on by the words.

So, reading a novel might in some ways be regarded as a model for the realization of engagement: in the situation described above, the novel represents a possible source of meaning, something worth thinking about, worth the reader's attention and trust, whereupon the reader indeed commits to the novel in such a way, so as to realize the exchange of meaning. As we have already seen throughout this study, these virtues – sincerity, reality-commitment and community (attention, trust) – are part of what happens *in* the story-worlds of the works of Wallace, Eggers and Foer, but they are also qualities *of* these novels themselves, aspects of what they do, as texts. The novels

---

[10]   De Martelaere, 'Echter dan werkelijk', 141–2; Groot, *Vergeten te bestaan*, 24–5.
[11]   Cf. Wallace, *This Is Water*, 68–73.

represent something worth trusting in, committing to, and are aimed at achieving meaning through a dialogue with the reader. Establishing this engagement with the novel is what Wallace describes as the reader 'putting in work', and thereby realizing that he is in a 'deep, significant conversation with another consciousness'.[12] Compare this to postmodernist metafiction and minimalism that, both in their own way, frustrate this very process of commitment to meaning: Barth's metafiction by pushing the reader back into self-consciousness and Ellis's minimalism by leaving the reader with no meaning or value at all. By contrast, the works of Wallace, Eggers and Foer are explicitly aimed at realizing such an engaged consciousness.

Having outlined this engaged, virtuous form of fiction, an objection or uneasiness might rear itself: have I not tried to describe a sort of 'end of literature'? It might seem as if I am suggesting that the 'right' form of literature has now been realized, in the works of Wallace, Eggers and Foer, that all is well now and that no further literary development is necessary or perhaps even possible. In reply to this suggestion I would like to emphasize that the literary works of Wallace, Eggers and Foer should be seen in relation to the problems of our time, as an attempt to address these problems and suggest ways to alleviate or even overcome them. This is also how these works have been analysed in this study. I do not claim that they embody the best, most perfectly literary and philosophical literature ever written; indeed, I do not think that it would make sense to suggest of any literary corpus that it constitutes such a final form. However, I do think, as I have stated in the Foreword, that these works constitute a view of contemporary Western existence and of overcoming the problems therein, that I find convincing. These fictions strongly emphasize certain existential and literary virtues (some of which can be said to be qualities of almost all literature; see the above-described engaged consciousness), because these seem to have been lost in the shuffle of preceding trends.

Does this mean there is no place for 'darker' works in my view of literature? I would like to emphasize that the works of Wallace, Eggers and Foer are in certain respects very dark: for example, the descriptions offered, in Wallace's *Infinite Jest*, of the suffering of some of the addicted characters, are gruesome. Many aspects of contemporary Western reality are undeniably dark and horrible, and therefore feature unabatedly as such in the works of Wallace, Eggers and Foer. My critique of Bret Easton Ellis's *American Psycho* is not aimed at the fact that the novel is dark, that Patrick Bateman is a disturbing character or that his descriptions of torture, rape and murder are absolutely horrifying, but at the fact that all of this functions as part of a novel that can only be seen, in the end, to echo its main character's contention that there is no meaning and value to be found or formulated in this world.

As stated above, I have analysed the works of Wallace, Eggers and Foer from the perspective of what these novels say about the problems and possible solutions for meaningful existence in the contemporary Western world. In my opinion, the current time stands in need of the virtues expressed by those works: sincerity, reality-commitment and community. I can very well imagine that there will come a time that

[12] Cf. McCaffery, 'Interview', 142; Miller, 'Interview'.

deeply mistrustful or introspective literature is again very much needed, but then it will be in answer to societal developments that are diametrically opposed to the ones from which these novels arose.

3. Love me till my heart stops?

So what about the actual realization of the view portrayed in the novels, of overcoming the problems of contemporary existence and finding new sources of meaning? I have suggested that the fact that complex, moral concepts acquire new, different meanings, that a notion like sincerity is increasingly perceived as meaningful again, through paradigmatic cases such as the ones offered in the works of Wallace, Eggers and Foer, signifies a transformation of our life-form.

I think we can conclude that the 'negative' concepts employed in this study, 'hyperreflexivity' and 'endless irony' – although these concepts undoubtedly do not constitute the only way of looking at the contemporary phenomena of self-reflection and irony – offer an illuminating perspective on our experience of contemporary Western existence. As such, they might even be considered as ringing true (as describing something that indeed 'has been the case' over the past decades).

Of course, the actual realization of the virtues of sincerity, reality-commitment and community intended to address these problems, has a more tentative status: these processes are still on their way. The outlined elements of engagement have the status of describing a *possible* overcoming of the problematic contemporary situation, as this situation and its problems are still largely in place. The culture-wide crystallization of this possible overcoming has come into motion but is still in full progress. The renewed emphasis on the notions arising from the works of Wallace, Eggers and Foer, as possible components of our self-becoming, will have to solidify itself as part of this cultural transformation.

It has been my contention that the portrayal of these notions offers a meaningful perspective, from which to understand and further shape contemporary Western existence, and that I have therefore tried to explicate and analyse in this study. However, whether the offered (philosophical explorations of the) literary portrayals will indeed be able to function as influential paradigmatic cases – that is, as widely shared standards within our life-form –, is up to the readers, of the novels, and, to a lesser extent, of this study.

As Wallace's short story 'Octet' concludes: So decide.

Acknowledgements

This study would not have been realized without the guidance and support of a great number of people. It is because of their help that I have been able to prepare, conduct and complete a wide-ranging academic study on a subject that I regard as existentially urgent and relevant. For this, I am immensely grateful.

First and foremost, I would like to express my deepest gratitude to my supervisors: Wessel Stoker, Dick Schram and Mariëtte Willemsen. Their collaborative supervision has been dedicated purely to helping me find the right (interdisciplinary) approaches that the subject matter required, and, as such, complete this study to the best of my ability. Moreover, in addition to being helpful and constructive, discussing my work with my supervisors has always been a great joy.

I am very grateful for the generosity of the three novelists who form the main focus of this study, David Foster Wallace, Dave Eggers and Jonathan Safran Foer, in allowing me to interview them about their work.

I would like to thank the Prins Bernhard Cultuurfonds and two smaller funds (which prefer not to be mentioned by name) for the scholarships awarded. These grants enabled me to travel to the United States to interview (among others) the above-mentioned authors and perform preliminary research, and to subsequently begin my project. I am also grateful for the support of the Van Coeverden Adriani Stichting, a publication fund related to the VU University Amsterdam. For their support in these initial stages of my research, I am indebted to Antoon de Baets, Maarten Doorman, Stine Jensen, Ann Rigney, Henk Woldring and René van Woudenberg.

For their comments on drafts of different chapters of this study (or papers derived from these chapters), inspiring discussions and other helpful contributions to my research project, I would like to thank: Robert Bolger, Hannah Bonjer, Marshall Boswell, Loes Derksen, Yra van Dijk, Johan Goud, Ger Groot, Sébastian Hüsch, Henry Jansen, Adam Kelly, Scott Korb, Edwin Koster, Anthony Leaker, Willie van der Merwe, Suzanne Metselaar, Gerben Meynen, Bert Musschenga, Haaris Naqvi, Diederik Oostdijk, Ellen Rutten, Thomas Vaessens, Jacco Verburgt and Job Zinkstok.

I want to thank my parents for their undying support.

And finally, Yvette: love me till my heart stops.

Works Cited

Editions of David Foster Wallace's works

Literary works

Wallace, David Foster. *Brief Interviews with Hideous Men*. Boston: Little, Brown & Company, 1999.

—. *The Broom of the System*. London: Penguin Books, 2004.

—. *Girl with Curious Hair: Stories*. New York: W.W. Norton & Company, 1989.

—. *Infinite Jest: A Novel*. Boston: Little, Brown & Company, 1996. [abbreviated as IJ]

—. *Oblivion*. London: Abacus, 2005.

—. *The Pale King: An Unfinished Novel*. New York: Little, Brown & Company, 2011.

Non-literary works

Wallace, David Foster. 'David Lynch Keeps His Head'. In *A Supposedly Fun Thing I'll Never Do Again. Essays and Arguments*, 146–212. London: Abacus, 2002.

—. 'E Unibus Pluram: Television and US Fiction'. In *A Supposedly Fun Thing I'll Never Do Again. Essays and Arguments*, 21–82. London: Abacus, 2002. [abbreviated as EUP]

—. 'The Empty Plenum: David Markson's *Wittgenstein's Mistress*'. *The Review of Contemporary Fiction* 10, no. 2 (1990): 217–39.

—. *Everything and More. A Compact History of Infinity*. New York: W.W. Norton & Company, 2003.

—. *Fate, Time and Language: An Essay on Free Will*. Edited by Steven M. Cahn and Maureen Eckert. New York: Columbia University Press, 2011.

—. 'Fictional Futures and the Conspicuously Young'. *The Review of Contemporary Fiction* 8, no. 3 (1988): 36–45.

—. 'Introduction: Deciderization 2007 – a Special Report'. In *The Best American Essays 2007*, xii–vviv. New York: Houghton Mifflin Company, 2007.

—. 'Joseph Frank's Dostoevsky'. In *Consider the Lobster, and Other Essays*, 255–74. New York: Little, Brown & Company, 2005.

—. 'Some Remarks on Kafka's Funniness from Which Probably Not Enough Has Been Removed'. In *Consider the Lobster, and Other Essays*, 60–5. New York: Little, Brown & Company, 2005.

—. 'Tense Present: Democracy, English, and the Wars over Usage'. *Harper's Magazine*, April 2001, 38–59.

—. *This Is Water. Some Thoughts, Delivered on a Significant Occasion, about Living a Compassionate Life*. New York: Little, Brown & Company, 2009.

Editions of Dave Eggers's works

Literary works

Eggers, Dave. *The Circle*. New York/San Francisco: Alfred A. Knopf/McSweeney's
    Books, 2013.
—. *A Heartbreaking Work of Staggering Genius*. London: Picador, 2000.
—. *A Heartbreaking Work of Staggering Genius*. London: Picador, 2001 [includes
    appendix *Mistakes We Knew We Were Making*]. [abbreviated as AHWOSG]
—. *A Hologram for the King*. San Francisco: McSweeney's Books, 2012.
—. *How We Are Hungry*. San Francisco: McSweeney's Books, 2004.
—. *Short Short Stories*. London: Penguin Books, 2005.
—. *What Is the What. The Autobiography of Valentino Achak Deng: A Novel*. San
    Francisco: McSweeney's Books, 2006.
—. *You Shall Know Our Velocity*. San Francisco: McSweeney's Books, 2002. [abbreviated
    as YSKOV]
—. *Zeitoun*. San Francisco: McSweeney's Books, 2009.

Non-literary works

Eggers, Dave. Foreword to *Infinite Jest*, by David Foster Wallace, xi–xvi. New York: Back
    Bay, 2006.
—. 'Interview with David Foster Wallace'. *The Believer* 1, no. 8 (2003): 85–92.

Editions of Jonathan Safran Foer's works

Literary works

Foer, Jonathan Safran. *Everything Is Illuminated*. London: Hamish Hamilton, 2002.
    [abbreviated as EII]
—. *Extremely Loud & Incredibly Close*. New York: Houghton Mifflin Company, 2005.
    [abbreviated as ELIC]
—. *Tree of Codes*. London: Visual Editions, 2010.
—. *The Unabridged Pocketbook of Lightning*. London: Penguin Books, 2005.

Non-literary works

Foer, Jonathan Safran. *Eating Animals*. New York: Little, Brown & Company, 2009.

Editions of Jean-Paul Sartre's works

Sartre, Jean-Paul. *Being and Nothingness. An Essay on Phenomenological Ontology*. Translated by Hazel E. Barnes. London: Routledge, 2010. [abbreviated as BN]

—. Foreword to *Reason and Violence: A Decade of Sartre's Philosophy*, by R. D. Laing and David Cooper, 7. London: Tavistock, 1964.

—. *Notebooks for an Ethics*. Translated by David Pellauer. Chicago: University of Chicago Press, 1992.

—. *The Transcendence of the Ego. A Sketch for a Phenomenological Description*. Translated by Andrew Brown. London: Routledge, 2004. [abbreviated as TE]

Literary works

Sartre, Jean-Paul. *Nausea*. Translated by Lloyd Alexander. New York: New Directions, 2007.

—. *No Exit, and Three Other Plays*. Translated by S. Gilbert and I. Abel. New York: Vintage Books, 1976.

Editions of Søren Kierkegaard's works

Kierkegaard, Søren. *The Concept of Anxiety. A Simple Psychologically Orienting Deliberation on the Dogmatic Issue of Hereditary Sin*. Translated by Reidar Thomte and Albert B. Anderson. Princeton, NJ: Princeton University Press, 1989.

—. *The Concept of Irony: With Continual Reference to Socrates; Together with Notes of Schelling's Berlin Lectures*. Translated by Howard V. Hong and Edna H. Hong. Princeton, NJ: Princeton University Press, 1989. [abbreviated as CI]

—. *Concluding Unscientific Postscript to Philosophical Fragments*, 2 vols, trans. Howard V. Hong and Edna H. Hong. Princeton, NJ: Princeton University Press, 1992. [abbreviated as CUP]

—. *Either/Or*. 2 vols. Translated by Howard V. Hong and Edna H. Hong. Princeton, NJ: Princeton University Press, 1987. [abbreviated as EO]

—. *Fear and Trembling / Repetition*. Translated by Howard V. Hong and Edna H. Hong. Princeton, NJ: Princeton University Press, 1983.

—. *The Sickness unto Death. A Christian Psychological Exposition for Upbuilding and Awakening*. Translated by Howard V. Hong and Edna H. Hong. Princeton, NJ: Princeton University Press, 1980.

—. *Two Ages. The Age of Revolution and the Present Age: A Literary Review*. Translated by Howard V. Hong and Edna H. Hong. Princeton, NJ: Princeton University Press, 1978.

—. *Works of Love*. Translated by Howard V. Hong and Edna H. Hong. Princeton, NJ: Princeton University Press, 1995.

Editions of Ludwig Wittgenstein's works

Ludwig Wittgenstein. *The Blue and Brown Books*. Oxford: Blackwell, 1998.
—. *Culture and Value. A Selection from the Posthumous Remains*. Translated by Peter Winch. Oxford: Blackwell, 2006.
—. *Last Writings on the Philosophy of Psychology. Volume 1: Preliminary Studies for Part II of 'Philosophical Investigations'*. Edited by Heikki Nyman and G. H. Von Wright. Oxford: Blackwell, 1982.
—. *On Certainty*. Translated by Denis Paul and G. E. M. Anscombe. Oxford: Blackwell, 2004.
—. *Philosophical Investigations. The German Text, with a Revised English Translation*. Translated by G. E. M. Anscombe. Oxford: Blackwell, 2001. [abbreviated as PI]
—. *Zettel*. Translated by G. E. M. Anscombe. Berkeley, CA: University of California Press, 2007.

Editions of Albert Camus's works

Camus, Albert. *The Myth of Sisyphus: An Essay on the Absurd*. Translated by Justin O'Brien. London: Penguin Books, 2000. [abbreviated as MS]
—. *The Rebel: An Essay on Man in Revolt*. Translated by Anthony Bower. New York: Vintage Books, 1991. [abbreviated as R]

Literary works

Camus, Albert. *The Collected Plays of Albert Camus: Caligula, Cross Purpose, The Just, The Possessed*. Translated by Stuart Gilbert, Henry Jones and Justin O'Brien. London: Hamish Hamilton, 1965.
—. *The Plague*. Translated by Stuart Gilbert. New York: Vintage Books, 1991.

Editions of John Barth's works

Literary works

Barth, John. *Lost in the Funhouse: Fiction for Print, Tape, Live Voice*. New York: Anchor Books/Doubleday, 1988. [abbreviated as LF]

Non-literary works

Barth, John. 'The Literature of Exhaustion'. In *The Friday Book. Essays and Other Nonfiction*, 62–76. Baltimore: Johns Hopkins University Press, 1984.

—. 'The Literature of Replenishment'. In *The Friday Book. Essays and Other Nonfiction*, 193–206. Baltimore: Johns Hopkins University Press, 1984.

—. 'Muse, Spare Me'. In *The Friday Book. Essays and Other Nonfiction*, 55–9. Baltimore: Johns Hopkins University Press, 1984.

Editions of Bret Easton Ellis's works

Literary works

Ellis, Bret Easton. *American Psycho*. London: Picador, 1991. [abbreviated as AP]

—. *Less than Zero*. London: Picador, 1986.

Other works

Achterhuis, Hans. *Camus: De moed om mens te zijn*. Utrecht: Ambo, 1969.

Allison, David B. 'Derrida and Wittgenstein: Playing the Game'. *Research in Phenomenology* 8, no. 1 (1978): 93–109.

Altieri, Charles. *Act & Quality. A Theory of Literary Meaning and Humanistic Understanding*. Brighton: Harvester Press, 1981.

—. 'Wittgenstein on Consciousness and Language: A Challenge to Derridean Literary Theory'. *MLN* 91, no. 6 (1976): 1397–1423.

Amian, Katrin. *Rethinking Postmodernism(s). Charles S. Peirce and the Pragmatist Negotiations of Thomas Pynchon, Toni Morrison, and Jonathan Safran Foer*. Amsterdam/New York: Rodopi, 2008.

Annesley, James. *Blank Fictions. Consumerism, Culture and the Contemporary American Novel*. London: Pluto Press, 1998.

—. 'Review Essay: David Foster Wallace'. *Journal of American Studies* 43, no. 1 (2009): 131–4.

Aubry, Timothy Richard. *Literature As Self-Help: Post-war United States Fiction and the Middle-Class Hunger for Trouble – John Cheever, Erica Jong, David Foster Wallace*. PhD diss., Princeton University, 2003.

Baelo Allué, Sonia. 'Serial Murder, Serial Consumerism: Bret Easton Ellis's *American Psycho*'. *Miscélanea: A Journal of English and American Studies*, 26 (2002): 71–90.

Baker, G. P. and P. M. S. Hacker. *Wittgenstein: An Analytical Commentary on the 'Philosophical Investigations'*, vol. 1, *Understanding and Meaning*. Oxford: Blackwell, 1980.

—. *Wittgenstein: An Analytical Commentary on the 'Philosophical Investigations'*, vol. 2, *Rules, Grammar and Necessity*. Oxford: Blackwell, 1985.

Barnes, Hazel E. 'Sartre's Concept of the Self'. In *Jean-Paul Sartre*, edited by Harold Bloom, 65–92. New York: Chelsea House, 2001.

Baskin, Jon. 'Death Is Not the End: David Foster Wallace – His Legacy and His Critics', *The Point* 1, 2009, http://www.thepointmag.com/2009/essays/death-is-not-the-end.

Beck, Stefan. 'Kinderkampf. Review of *Extremely Loud & Incredibly Close* by Jonathan Safran Foer', *The New Criterion*, June 2005, 92–5.

Bell, Robert H. and William Dowling. *A Reader's Companion to 'Infinite Jest'*. Bloomington: Xlibris, 2005.

Bennett, Jane. 'Franz Kafka'. In *Dictionary of Existentialism*, edited by Haim Gordon, 235–9. Westport, CT: Greenwood Press, 1999.

Bigelow, Patrick. 'The Ontology of Boredom'. *Man & World* 16, no. 3 (1983): 251–65.

Birkerts, Sven. 'The Alchemist's Retort. A multi-layered postmodern saga of damnation and salvation', *The Atlantic Monthly* 2, 1996, http://www.theatlantic.com/ past/docs/issues/96feb/alchem/alchem.htm.

Blazer, Alex E. 'Chasms of Reality, Aberrations of Identity: Defining the Postmodern through Bret Easton Ellis's *American Psycho*'. *Americana: The Journal of American Popular Culture* 1, no. 2 (2002). http://www.americanpopularculture.com/journal/articles/fall_2002/blazer.htm.

Bolger, Robert K. 'A Less "Bullshitty" Way To Live: The Pragmatic Spirituality of David Foster Wallace'. In *Gesturing toward Reality: David Foster Wallace and Philosophy*, edited by Robert K. Bolger and Scott Korb, 31–51. New York: Bloomsbury, 2014.

Boomkens, René. *De angstmachine. Over geweld in films, literatuur en popmuziek*. Amsterdam: Uitgeverij De Balie, 1996.

Boswell, Marshall. '"The Constant Monologue Inside Your Head": *Oblivion* and the Nightmare of Consciousness'. In *A Companion to David Foster Wallace Studies*, edited by Marshall Boswell and Stephen J. Burn, 151–70. New York: Palgrave Macmillan, 2013.

—. 'Trickle-Down Citizenship: Taxes and Civic Responsibility in *The Pale King*'. In *David Foster Wallace and 'The Long Thing': New Essays on the Novels*, edited by Marshall Boswell, 209–25. New York: Bloomsbury, 2014.

—. *Understanding David Foster Wallace*. Columbia, SC: University of South Carolina Press, 2003.

Brill, Susan B. *Wittgenstein and Critical Theory. Beyond Postmodern Criticism and Toward Descriptive Investigations*. Athens, OH: Ohio University Press, 1995.

Burn, Gordon. 'The Believers', *The Guardian*, 27 March 2004, http://www.guardian.co.uk/books/2004/mar/27/fiction.zadiesmith.

Burn, Stephen. *'Infinite Jest': A Reader's Guide*. New York: Continuum Books, 2003.

—. 'Some Weird Bunch of Anti-Rebels and Millennial Fictions', *The London Times Literary Supplement*, 4 February 2007, http://infinitejest.wallacewiki.com/david-foster-wallace/index.php?title=Infinite_Jest_-_The_Times_Literary_Supplement.

Busch, Thomas W. *The Power of Consciousness and the Force of Circumstances in Sartre's Philosophy*. Bloomington, IN: Indiana University Press, 1990.

Carlisle, Clare. 'Kierkegaard's *Repetition*: The Possibility of Motion'. *British Journal for the History of Philosophy* 13, no. 3 (2005): 521–41.

Carlisle, Greg. *Elegant Complexity: A Study of David Foster Wallace's 'Infinite Jest'*. Los Angeles/Austin, TX: SSMG Press, 2007.

Catalano, Joseph S. *A Commentary on Jean-Paul Sartre's 'Being and Nothingness'*. Chicago: University of Chicago Press, 1985.

—. *Good Faith and Other Essays. Perspectives on a Sartrean Ethics*. Lanham, MD: Rowman & Littlefield Publishers, 1996.

Cioffi, Frank Louis. '"An Anguish Become Thing": Narrative as Performance in David Foster Wallace's *Infinite Jest*'. *Narrative* 8, no. 2 (2000): 161–81.

Claassen, Eefje. *The Author's Footprint in the Garden of Fiction. Readers' Generation of Author Inferences in Literary Reading*. PhD diss., VU University Amsterdam, 2009.

Clare. 'The Politics of Boredom and the Boredom of Politics in *The Pale King*'. In *David Foster Wallace and 'The Long Thing': New Essays on the Novels*, edited by Marshall Boswell, 187–207. New York: Bloomsbury, 2014.

Collado-Rodriguez, Francisco. 'Ethics in the Second Degree: Trauma and Dual Narratives in Jonathan Safran Foer's *Everything Is Illuminated*'. *Journal of Modern Literature* 32, no. 1 (2008): 54–68.

Comte-Sponville, André. *A Short Treatise on the Great Virtues. The Uses of Philosophy in Everyday Life*. Translated by Catherine Temerson. London: Vintage, 2003.

Confessore, Nicolas. 'Finite Jest', *The American Prospect*, 19 June 2000, 86–8.

Cross, Andrew. 'Neither Either Nor Or: The Perils of Reflexive Irony'. In *The Cambridge Companion to Kierkegaard*, edited by Alastair Hannay and G. D. Marino, 125–53. Cambridge: Cambridge University Press, 1998.

Cruickshank, John. Introduction to *Caligula, Cross Purpose, The Just, The Possessed*, by Albert Camus, 7–32. Harmondsworth: Penguin Books, 1984.

Culler, Jonathan. *On Deconstruction*. London: Routledge, 2007.

Dante Alighieri. *De goddelijke komedie* [*Divina Commedia*], vol. 2. Amsterdam: Athenaeum, Polak & Van Gennep, 2000.

Derrida, Jacques. 'Envoi [Sending: On Representation]'. In *Psyche. Inventions of the Other: Volume 1*, edited by Peggy Kamuf and Elizabeth Rottenberg, translated by Peter Caws and Mary Anne Caws, 94–128. Stanford: Stanford University Press, 2007.

—. 'Force of Law: The "Mystical Foundation of Authority"'. In: *Deconstruction and the Possibility of Justice*, edited by Drucilla Cornell, Michael Rosenfeld and David Gray Carlson, translated by Mary Quaintance, 3–67. New York: Routledge, 1992.

—. *Limited Inc*. Translated by Samuel Weber, Jeffrey Mehlman and Alan Bass. Evanston, IL: Northwestern University Press, 1988.

—. *Margins of Philosophy*. Translated by Alan Bass. Brighton: Harvester Press, 1982.

—. *Of Grammatology*. Translated by Gayatri Chakravorty Spivak. Baltimore: Johns Hopkins University Press, 1997.

—. *Positions*. Translated by Alan Bass. Chicago: University of Chicago Press, 1981.

—. 'Response to Mulhall'. *Ratio* 13, no. 4 (2000): 415–18.

—. *Writing and Difference*. Translated by Alan Bass. London: Routledge, 2001.

Dewey, Bradley R. 'The Erotic-Demonic in Kierkegaard's "Diary of the Seducer"'. *Scandinavica. An International Journal of Scandinavian Studies* 10, no. 1 (1971): 1–24.

—. 'Seven Seducers. A Typology of Interpretations of the Aesthetic Stage in Kierkegaard's "The Seducer's Diary"'. In *International Kierkegaard Commentary*, vol. 3, *'Either/Or' Part 1*, edited by Robert L. Perkins, 159–99. Macon, GA: Mercer University Press, 1995.

—. 'Søren Kierkegaard's *Diary of the Seducer*: A History of Its Use and Abuse in International Print"'. *Fund og Forskning* 20 (1973): 137–57.

Diez, Georg. 'Der Klang der Gedanken. Ein Gespräch mit David Foster Wallace', *Die Zeit*, 25 January 2007, http://www.zeit.de/2007/05/L-Interview.

Doedens, Udo. *Het eenvoudige leven volgens Søren Kierkegaard*. Baarn: Ten Have, 1999.

Doorman, Maarten. *De romantische orde*. Amsterdam: Uitgeverij Bert Bakker, 2004.

Douthat, Ross G., 'After Tragedy. Review of *Extremely Loud & Incredibly Close* by Jonathan Safran Foer', *National Review*, 20 June 2005, 48–50.

Drury, M. O'C. 'Conversations with Wittgenstein'. In *Recollections of Wittgenstein*, edited by Rush Rhees, 97–171. Oxford: Oxford University Press, 1984.

Dulk, Allard den. 'American Literature: A New Aesthetic of Sincerity, Reality and Community'. In *Reconsidering the Postmodern. European Literature Beyond Relativism*, edited by Thomas Vaessens and Yra van Dijk, 225–41. Amsterdam: AUP, 2011.

—. 'Beyond Endless "Aesthetic" Irony: A Comparison of the Irony Critique of Søren Kierkegaard and David Foster Wallace's *Infinite Jest*'. *Studies in the Novel* 44, no. 3 (2012): 325–45.

—. 'Boredom, Irony, and Anxiety: Wallace and the Kierkegaardian View of the Self'. In *David Foster Wallace and 'The Long Thing': New Essays on the Novels*, edited by Marshall Boswell, 43–60. New York: Bloomsbury, 2014.

—. 'Een juweel op dun ijs. Het engagement van *Eternal Sunshine of the Spotless Mind* bezien vanuit het denken van Søren Kierkegaard'. *Tijdschrift voor Humanistiek* 37 (2009): 6–16.

—. 'Good Faith and Sincerity: Sartrean Virtues of Self-Becoming in David Foster Wallace's *Infinite Jest*'. In *Gesturing Toward Reality: David Foster Wallace and Philosophy*, edited by Robert K. Bolger and Scott Korb, 205–27. New York: Bloomsbury, 2014.

—. 'The Transcendence of a Meaningful Life: The Portrayal of the Contemporary Self in David Foster Wallace's *Infinite Jest*'. In *Looking Beyond? Shifting Views of Transcendence in Philosophy, Theology, Art, and Politics*, edited by Wessel Stoker and W. L. van der Merwe, 413–29. Amsterdam/New York: Rodopi, 2012.

—. 'Voorbij de doelloze ironie. De werken van Dave Eggers en David Foster Wallace vergeleken met het denken van Søren Kierkegaard'. *Het postmodernisme voorbij?*, edited by L. Derksen, E. Koster and J. van der Stoep, 83–98. Amsterdam: VU University Press, 2008.

—. 'Wallace and Wittgenstein: Literature As Dialogue Concerning the Real World'. In *Philosophy and Literature and the Crisis of Metaphysics*, edited by Sébastian Hüsch, 343–58. Würzburg: Verlag Königshausen & Neumann, 2011.

Dwyer, Philip. 'Freedom and Rule-Following in Wittgenstein and Sartre'. *Philosophy and Phenomenological Research* 1, no. 1 (1989): 49–68.

Elrod, John W. *Being and Existence in Kierkegaard's Pseudonymous Works*. Princeton, NJ: Princeton University Press, 1975.

'Endnotes: David Foster Wallace', *Sunday Feature*, BBC Radio 3, broadcast on 6 February 2011. http://www.bbc.co.uk/programmes/b00y6ggl.

Eriksen, Niels Nymann. *Kierkegaard's Category of Repetition. A Reconstruction*. Berlin: Walter de Gruyter, 2000.

Erkelens, Rob van. 'Patrick B.', *De Groene Amsterdammer*, 31 July 1996, 16.

Evink, Eddo. *Transcendentie en inscriptie: Jacques Derrida en de hubris van de metafysica*. Delft: Eburon, 2002.

Federman, Raymond. 'Self-reflexive Fiction'. In *Columbia Literary History of the United States*, edited by Emory Elliott, 1142–57. New York: Columbia University Press, 1988.

Fogel, Stan and Gordon Slethaug. *Understanding John Barth*. Columbia, SC: University of South Carolina Press, 1990.

Fowler, Alastair. *Kinds of Literature. An Introduction to the Theory of Genres and Modes*. Oxford: Clarendon Press, 1982.

Franzen, Jonathan. 'Why Bother?' In *How to Be Alone. Essays*, 55–97. London: Fourth Estate, 2002.

Freccero, Carla. 'Historical Violence, Censorship and the Serial Killer: The Case of *American Psycho*'. *Diacritics* 27, no. 2 (1997): 44–58.

Fretz, Leo. 'Individuality in Sartre's Philosophy'. In *The Cambridge Companion to Sartre*, edited by Christina Howells, 67–99. Cambridge: Cambridge University Press, 1994.

—. 'Inleiding', Introduction to *Het Ik is een Ding: schets ener fenomenologische beschrijving*, by Jean-Paul Sartre, 7–34. Meppel: Boom, 1978.

Freudenthal, Elizabeth. 'Anti-Interiority: Compulsiveness, Objectification, and Identity in *Infinite Jest*'. *New Literary History* 41, no. 1 (2010): 191–211.

Garver, Newton and Seung-Chong Lee. *Derrida and Wittgenstein*. Philadelphia: Temple University Press, 1995.

Gaut, Berys. 'Fiction'. In *The Cambridge Dictionary of Philosophy*, edited by Robert Audi, 309. Cambridge: Cambridge University Press, 1999.

Gennep, F. O. van. *Albert Camus. Een studie van zijn ethische denken*. Amsterdam: Polak & Van Gennep, 1962.

Gibson, John. *Fiction and the Weave of Life.* Oxford: Oxford University Press, 2007.

—. 'Reading for Life'. In *The Literary Wittgenstein*, edited by John Gibson and Wolfgang Huemer, 109–24. London: Routledge, 2004.

Giddens, Anthony. *Modernity and Self-Identity: Self and Society in the Late Modern Age.* Cambridge: Polity Press, 2004.

Gier, Nicholas. 'Wittgenstein and Deconstruction'. *Review of Contemporary Philosophy* 6 (2007): 174–96.

—. *Wittgenstein and Phenomenology. A Comparative Study of the Later Wittgenstein, Husserl, Heidegger, and Merleau-Ponty.* Albany, NY: State University of New York Press, 1981.

Goerlandt, Iannis. '"Put the Book Down and Slowly Walk Away": Irony and David Foster Wallace's *Infinite Jest*'. *Critique: Studies in Contemporary Fiction* 47, no. 3 (2006): 309–28.

Golomb, Jacob. *In Search of Authenticity. From Kierkegaard to Camus.* New York: Routledge, 1995.

Gornick, Vivian. 'About a Boy. Review of *Extremely Loud & Incredibly Close* by Jonathan Safran Foer', *The Nation*, 25 April 2005, 29–32.

Grassian, Daniel. *Hybrid Fictions. American Literature and Generation X.* Jefferson, NC: McFarland & Company, 2003.

Grene, Marjorie. 'Life, Death and Language: Some Thoughts on Wittgenstein and Derrida'. *Partisan Review* 43 (1976): 265–79.

Greve, Wilfried. 'Künstler versus Bürger. Kierkegaards Schrift "Entweder/Oder"'. In '*Entweder/Oder'. Herausgefordert durch Kierkegaard*, edited by Jörg Splett and Herbert Frohnhofen, 38–62. Frankfurt am Main: Knecht, 1988.

Grimshaw, Mike. 'Cultural Pessimism and Rock Criticism: Bret Easton Ellis' Writing (as) Hell', *CTheory*, 25 September 2002, http://www.ctheory.net/articles.aspx?id=346.

Grøn, Arne. *The Concept of Anxiety in Søren Kierkegaard.* Translated by Jeanette B. L. Knox. Macon, GA: Mercer University Press, 2008.

Groot, Ger. 'Inleiding', Introduction to *Marges van de filosofie*, by Jacques Derrida, 7–24. Hilversum: Uitgeverij Gooi en Sticht, 1989.

—. *Vergeten te bestaan. Echte fictie en het fictieve ik.* Nijmegen: Uitgeverij Vantilt, 2010.

Gross, Beverly. 'The Anti-Novels of John Barth'. In *Critical Essays on John Barth*, edited by Joseph J. Waldmeir, 30–42. Boston: G.K. Hall & Co., 1980.

Guignon, Charles. *On Being Authentic.* London: Routledge, 2008.

Gutman, H. 'Rousseau's Confessions: A Technology of the Self'. In *Technologies of the Self: A Seminar with Michel Foucault*, edited by L. H. Martin, H. Gutman and P. H. Hutton, 99–120. Amherst, MA: University of Massachusetts Press, 1988.

Hacker, P. M. S. *Wittgenstein: An Analytical Commentary on the 'Philosophical Investigations'*, vol. 3, *Meaning and Mind.* Oxford: Blackwell, 1990.

—. *Wittgenstein: An Analytical Commentary on the 'Philosophical Investigations'*, vol. 4, *Mind and Will.* Oxford: Blackwell, 1996.

Hannay, Alastair. *Kierkegaard: A Biography*. Cambridge: Cambridge University Press, 2001.

Harris, Charles B. *Passionate Virtuosity: The Fiction of John Barth*. Urbana, IL: University of Illinois Press, 1983.

Harris, Elise. 'Infinite Jest', *The Nation*, 20 March 2000, http://www.thenation.com/article/infinite-jest.

Harrison, Bernard. 'Imagined Worlds and the Real One. Plato, Wittgenstein, and Mimesis'. In *The Literary Wittgenstein*, edited by John Gibson and Wolfgang Huemer, 92–108. London: Routledge, 2004.

Hayles, N. Katherine. 'The Illusion of Autonomy and the Fact of Recursivity: Virtual Ecologies, Entertainment, and *Infinite Jest*'. *New Literary History* 30, no. 3 (1999): 675–97.

Higgins, Dick. *A Dialectic of Centuries: Notes Toward a Theory of the New Arts*. New York: Printed Editions, 1978.

Holland, Mary K. '"The Art's Heart's Purpose": Braving the Narcissistic Loop of David Foster Wallace's *Infinite Jest*'. *Critique: Studies in Contemporary Fiction* 47, no. 3 (2006): 218–42.

—. *Succeeding Postmodernism. Language and Humanism in Contemporary American Literature*. New York: Bloomsbury, 2013.

Huemer, Wolfgang. 'Introduction: Wittgenstein, Language and Philosophy of Literature'. In *The Literary Wittgenstein*, edited by John Gibson and Wolfgang Huemer, 1–13. London: Routledge, 2004.

Hultkrans, Andrew. 'Books – *A Supposedly Fun Thing I'll Never Do Again* by David Foster Wallace'. *Artforum* 35, no. 10 (1997): 15–22.

Hutcheon, Linda. *Irony's Edge: The Theory and Politics of Irony*. London: Routledge, 1995.

—. *A Poetics of Postmodernism: History, Theory, Fiction*. New York: Routledge, 1988.

Hyde, Lewis. 'Alcohol and Poetry: John Berryman and the Booze Talking'. In *The Pushcart Prize: Best of the Small Presses*, edited by Bill Henderson, 71–94. Yonkers, NY: Pushcart Book Press, 1976.

Ibsch, Elrud. 'The Conventions of Interpretation'. In *The Search for a New Alphabet: Literary Studies in a Changing World. In Honor of Douwe Fokkema*, edited by Harald Hendrix, Joost Kloek, Sophie Levie and Will van Peer, 111–17. Amsterdam/Philadelphia: John Benjamins, 1996.

—. 'Die Interpretation und kein Ende. Oder: warum wir auch nach der Jahrtausendwende noch interpretieren'. In *Interpretation 2000: Positionen und Kontroversen. Festschrift zum 65. Geburtstag von Horst Steinmetz*, edited by Henk de Berg and Matthias Prangel, 15–29. Heidelberg: Universitätsverlag C. Winter, 1999.

Isaac, Jeffrey C. *Arendt, Camus and Modern Rebellion*. New Haven, CT: Yale University Press, 1992.

Jacobs, Timothy. 'The Brothers Incandenza: Translating Ideology in Fyodor Dostoevsky's *The Brothers Karamazov* and David Foster Wallace's *Infinite Jest*'. *Texas Studies in Literature and Language: A Journal of the Humanities* 49 (2007): 265–92.

Kakutani, Michiko. 'Clever Young Man Raises Sweet Little Brother', *The New York Times*, 1 February 2000, http://www.nytimes.com/2000/02/01/books/books-of-the-times-clever-young-man-raises-sweet-little-brother.html.

—. 'Critic's Notebook: New Wave of Writers Reinvents Literature', *The New York Times*, 22 April 2000, http://www.nytimes.com/2000/04/22/books/critic-s-notebook-new-wave-of-writers-reinvents-literature.html.

Karmodi, Ostap. 'Interview with David Foster Wallace'. *Radio Svoboda*, September 2006. Transcript: http://ostap.livejournal.com/799511.html.

Kelly, Adam. 'David Foster Wallace and the New Sincerity in American Fiction'. In *Consider David Foster Wallace. Critical Essays*, edited by David Hering, 131–46. Los Angeles/Austin, TX: SSMG Press, 2010.

Kiernan, Robert F. 'John Barth's Artist in the Fun House'. *Studies in Short Fiction* 10, no. 4 (1973): 373–80.

Kirsch, Adam. 'The Importance of Being Earnest', *The New Republic*, 18 August 2011, http://www.tnr.com/article/books/magazine/92794/david-lipsky-foster-wallace-pale-king.

Korthals Altes, Liesbeth. *'Blessedly post-ironic'? Enkele tendensen in de hedendaagse literatuur en literatuurwetenschap*. Inaugural Oration, Rijksuniversiteit Groningen, 2001.

—. 'Sincerity, Reliability and Other Ironies – Notes on Dave Eggers' *A Heartbreaking Work of Staggering Genius*'. In *Narrative Unreliability in the Twentieth-Century First-Person Novel*, edited by Elke D'hoker and Gunther Martens, 107–28. Berlin: Walter de Gruyter, 2008.

Kunneman, Harry. *Voorbij het dikke-ik. Bouwstenen voor een kritisch humanisme – Deel 1*. Amsterdam: Uitgeverij SWP, 2009.

LaCapra, Dominick. *A Preface to Sartre*. London: Methuen, 1979.

Lamarque, Peter. *The Philosophy of Literature*. Malden, MA: Blackwell, 2008.

Lansink. *Vrijheid en ironie. Kierkegaards ethiek van de zelfwording*. Leuven: Peeters, 1997.

Leclair, Tom. 'The Prodigious Fiction of Richard Powers, William Vollmann and David Foster Wallace'. *Critique: Studies in Contemporary Fiction* 38, no. 1 (1996): 12–37.

—. 'Two Cheers. Review of *Extremely Loud & Incredibly Close* by Jonathan Safran Foer', *American Review* (July/August 2005), 19.

Lindholm, Charles. *Culture and Authenticity*. Malden, MA: Blackwell, 2008.

Linsenbard, Gail Evelyn. *An Investigation of Jean-Paul Sartre's Posthumously Published 'Notebooks for an Ethics'*. Lewiston, NY: Edwin Mellen Press, 2000.

Lipsky, David. *Although Of Course You End Up Becoming Yourself. A Road Trip with David Foster Wallace*. New York: Broadway Books, 2010.

Little, Michael. *Novel Affirmations: Defending Literary Culture in the Fiction of David Foster Wallace, Jonathan Franzen, and Richard Powers*. PhD diss., Texas A&M University, 2004.

Longuenesse, Béatrice. 'Self-Consciousness and Self-Reference: Sartre and Wittgenstein'. *European Journal of Philosophy* 16, no. 1 (2008): 1–21.

Love, Robert. 'Psycho Analysis', *Rolling Stone* 601 (4 April 1991), 45–9.

McCaffery, Larry. 'An Interview with David Foster Wallace'. *Review of Contemporary Fiction* 13, no. 2 (1993): 127–50.

McConnell, Frank D. *Four Postwar American Novelists. Bellow, Mailer, Barth, and Pynchon*. Chicago: University of Chicago Press, 1977.

McDonald, Henry. 'Crossroads of Skepticism: Wittgenstein, Derrida, and Ostensive Definition'. *The Philosophical Forum* 21, no. 3 (1990): 261–76.

McGinn, Marie. *Wittgenstein and the Philosophical Investigations*. London: Routledge, 1997.

McHale, Brian. *Postmodernist Fiction*. New York: Methuen, 1987.

McInerney, Jay. 'The Year of the Whopper', *The New York Times*, 3 March 1996, http://www.nytimes.com/1996/03/03/books/the-year-of-the-whopper.html.

McLaughlin, Robert L. 'Post-Postmodern Discontent: Contemporary Fiction and the Social World'. *Symploke* 12, nos 1–2 (2004): 53–68.

Marino, Gordon. 'Introduction'. In *Basic Writings of Existentialism*, edited by Gordon Marino, ix–xvi. New York: The Modern Library, 2004.

Martelaere, Patricia de. 'Echter dan werkelijk'. In *Een verlangen naar ontroostbaarheid. Over leven, kunst en dood*, 137–48. Amsterdam: Meulenhoff, 1993. http://www.dbnl. org/titels/titel.php?id=mart003verl01.

—. 'Wittgenstein en Derrida: taalspel en deconstructie'. *De Brakke Hond* 9, no. 34 (1992): 95–113.

Mattson, Kevin. 'Is Dave Eggers a Genius? Rebelling and Writing in an Age of Postmodern Mass Culture'. *Radical Society* 29, no. 3 (2002): 75–83.

Max, D. T. *Every Love Story Is a Ghost Story. A Life of David Foster Wallace*. New York: Viking, 2012.

—. 'The Unfinished', *The New Yorker*, 9 March 2009, 48–61.

Messud. 'Crushed by a Killing Joke', *The Times*, 6 July 1996.

Miller, Laura. 'Interview with David Foster Wallace', *Salon*, 9 March 1996, http://www.badgerinternet.com/~bobkat/jest11.html.

Mooney, Edward F. 'Repetition: Getting the World Back'. In *The Cambridge Companion to Kierkegaard*, edited by Alastair Hannay and G. D. Marino, 282–307. Cambridge: Cambridge University Press, 1998.

Moore, Steven, Dave Eggers, Kathleen Fitzpatrick et al. 'In Memoriam David Foster Wallace'. *Modernism/modernity* 16, no. 1 (2009): 1–24.

Moyaert, Paul. 'Jacques Derrida en de filosofie van de differentie'. In *Jacques Derrida: een inleiding in zijn denken*, edited by Samuel IJsseling, 28–89. Baarn: Ambo, 1986.

Mullins, Matthew. 'Boroughs and Neighbors: Traumatic Solidarity in Jonathan Safran Foer's *Extremely Loud & Incredibly Close*'. *Papers on Language & Literature* 45, no. 3 (2009): 298–324.

Munson, Sam. 'In the Aftermath. Review of *Saturday* by Ian McEwan and *Extremely Loud & Incredibly Close* by Jonathan Safran Foer', *Commentary* (May 2005), 80–5.

Murdoch, Iris. 'The Idea of Perfection'. In *Existentialists and Mystics. Writings on Philosophy and Literature*, 299–336. London: Chatto & Windus, 1997.

—. 'On "God" and "Good"'. In *Existentialists and Mystics. Writings on Philosophy and Literature*, 337–62. London: Chatto & Windus, 1997.

Murphet, Julian. *'American Psycho'. A Reader's Guide*. New York: Continuum Books, 2002.

Myers, B. R. 'A Bag of Tired Tricks', *The Atlantic Monthly* 5 (2005), 115–20.

Nichols, Catherine. 'Dialogizing Postmodern Carnival: David Foster Wallace's *Infinite Jest*'. *Critique: Studies in Contemporary Fiction* 43, no. 1 (2001): 3–16.

Nicol, Bran. *The Cambridge Introduction to Postmodern Fiction*. Cambridge: Cambridge University Press, 2009.

Orbán, Jolán. 'Die Herausforderung von Wittgenstein durch Derrida'. *Neohelicon* 21, no. 1 (1994): 95–115.

Perkins, David. *Is Literary History Possible?* Baltimore: Johns Hopkins University Press, 1992.

Priest, Stephen. 'Bad Faith'. In *Jean-Paul Sartre: Basic Writings*, edited by Stephen Prince, 204–6. London: Routledge, 2001.

—. *The Subject in Question: Sartre's Critique of Husserl in the Transcendence of the Ego*. New York: Routledge, 2000.

Prins, Awee. *Uit verveling*. Kampen: Klement, 2007.

Pulmer, Karin. *Die dementierte Alternative. Gesellschaft und Geschichte in der ästhetischen Konstruktion von Kierkegaards 'Entweder-Oder'*. Frankfurt am Main/ Bern: Peter Lang Verlag, 1982.

Raynova, Yvanka B. 'Jean-Paul Sartre, a Profound Revision of Husserlian Phenomenology'. In *Phenomenology World-Wide. Foundations, Expanding Dynamics, Life-Engagements: A Guide for Research and Study*, edited by Anna-Teresa Tymeniecka, 323–35. Norwell, MA: Kluwer, 2002.

Rehm, Walter. *Kierkegaard und der Verführer*. Munich: Hermann Rinn, 1949.

Rousseau, Jean-Jacques. *The Confessions of Jean-Jacques Rousseau*. Translated by J. M. Cohen. Harmondsworth: Penguin Books, 1953.

Rutten, Ellen. 'Russian Literature: Reviving Sincerity in the Post-Soviet World'. In *Reconsidering the Postmodern. European Literature Beyond Relativism*, edited by Thomas Vaessens and Yra van Dijk, 27–40. Amsterdam: AUP, 2011.

Ryerson. 'Introduction: A Head That Throbbed Heartlike'. In *Fate Time, and Language: An Essay on Free Will*, by David Foster Wallace, edited by Steven M. Cahn and Maureen Eckert, 1–33. New York: Columbia University Press, 2011.

Santoni, Ronald E. *Bad Faith, Good Faith, and Authenticity in Sartre's Early Philosophy*. Philadelphia: Temple University Press, 1995.

Sass, Louis A. *Madness and Modernism. Insanity in the Light of Modern Art, Literature, and Thought*. New York: BasicBooks, 1992.

—. *The Paradoxes of Delusion. Wittgenstein, Schreber, and the Schizophrenic Mind.* Ithaca, NY: Cornell University Press, 1994.

—. 'Self and World in Schizophrenia: Three Classic Approaches in Phenomenological Psychiatry'. *Philosophy, Psychiatry, and Psychology* 8, no. 4 (2001): 251–70.

Sass, Louis A. and Josef Parnas. 'Schizophrenia, Consciousness, and the Self'. *Schizophrenia Bulletin* 29, no. 3 (2003): 427–44.

Schalkwyk, David. 'Fiction as "Grammatical" Investigation: A Wittgensteinian Account'. *The Journal of Aesthetics and Art Criticism* 53 (1995): 287–98.

Scholtens, Wim R. 'Inleiding', Introduction to *Over het begrip ironie*, by Søren Kierkegaard, 7–31. Amsterdam: Boom, 1995.

Scott, A. O. 'The Panic of Influence – Review of *Brief Interviews with Hideous Men*', *The New York Review of Books* 47, no. 2 (2000), 39–43.

Shain, Ralph. 'Derrida's References to Wittgenstein'. *International Studies in Philosophy* 37, no. 4 (2005): 71–104.

Shakespeare, William. *The Complete Works of William Shakespeare*. Project Gutenberg. http://www.gutenberg.org/ebooks/100

Siegel, Harry. 'Extremely Cloying & Incredibly False', *New York Press*, 13 April 2005.

Sijde, Nico van der. *De visie op literatuur van Jacques Derrida*. PhD diss., Rijksuniversiteit Groningen, 1997.

Silverblatt, Michael. 'Interview with David Foster Wallace', *Bookworm*, KCRW, broadcast on 11 April 1996. Transcript: http://web.archive.org/web/20040606041906/www.andbutso.com/~mark/bookworm96/.

Smith, Zadie. 'Brief Interviews with Hideous Men: The Difficult Gifts of David Foster Wallace'. In *Changing My Mind: Occasional Essays*, 257–300. London: Hamish Hamilton, 2009.

Smoot, William. 'The Concept of Authenticity in Sartre'. *Man and World* 7, no. 2 (1994): 135–48.

Söderquist, K. Brian. 'Authoring a Self'. In *Kierkegaard Studies Yearbook 2009: Kierkegaard's Concept of Irony*, edited by Niels Jorgen Cappelørn, Hermann Deuser and K. Brian Söderquist, 153–66. Berlin: Walter de Gruyter, 2009.

Solomon, Deborah. 'The Rescue Artist', *The New York Times*, 27 February 2005, http://www.nytimes.com/2005/02/27/magazine/27FOER.html.

Sprintzen, David. *Camus. A Critical Examination*. Philadelphia: Temple University Press, 1988.

Stack, George J. *Kierkegaard's Existential Ethics*. Tuscaloosa, AL: University of Alabama Press, 1977.

Star, Alexander. 'Being and Knowingness. Review of *A Heartbreaking Work of Staggering Genius* by Dave Eggers', *The New Republic*, 14 September 2000, 37–40.

Staten, Henry. *Wittgenstein and Derrida*. Oxford: Blackwell, 1985.

Stoker, Wessel. 'Culture and Transcendence. A Typology'. In *Looking Beyond? Shifting Views of Transcendence in Philosophy, Theology, Art, and Politics*, edited by Wessel Stoker and W. L. van der Merwe, 5–28. Amsterdam/New York: Rodopi, 2012.

Stone, Martin. 'On the Old Saw, "Every Reading of a Text Is an Interpretation". Some Remarks'. In *The Literary Wittgenstein*, edited by John Gibson and Wolfgang Huemer, 186–208. London: Routledge, 2004.

Stralen, Hans van. *Beschreven keuzes. Een inleiding in het literaire existentialisme.* Leuven/Apeldoorn: Garant, 1996.

Suglia, Joseph. 'Bret Easton Ellis: Escape from Utopia', *Youth Quake Magazine*, 27 May 2004, http://www.youthquakemagazine.com/author_articles/breteastonellis.htm.

Summers, Richard M. '"Controlled Irony" and the Emergence of the Self in Kierkegaard's Dissertation'. In *International Kierkegaard Commentary*, vol. 2, *The Concept of Irony*, edited by Robert L. Perkins, 289–316. Macon, GA: Mercer University Press, 2001.

Svendsen, Lars. *A Philosophy of Boredom*. London: Reaktion Books, 2005.

Taels, Johan. *Søren Kierkegaard als filosoof. De weg terug naar het subject.* Leuven: Universitaire Pers Leuven, 1991.

Taylor, Charles. *The Ethics of Authenticity*. Cambridge, MA: Harvard University Press, 1991.

Theuwis, Toon. *The Quest for Infinite Jest: An Inquiry into the Encyclopedic and Postmodernist Nature of David Foster Wallace's 'Infinite Jest'.* PhD diss., Ghent University, 1999. http://www.thehowlingfantods.com/toon.html.

Timmer, Nicoline. *'Do You Feel It Too?' The Post-Postmodern Syndrome in American Fiction at the Turn of the Millennium.* PhD diss., University Utrecht, 2008.

Timpe, Kevin. *'This Is Water* and Religious Self-Deception'. In *Gesturing Toward Reality: David Foster Wallace and Philosophy*, edited by Robert K. Bolger and Scott Korb, 53–69. New York: Bloomsbury, 2014.

Trilling, Lionel. *Sincerity and Authenticity*. Cambridge, MA: Harvard University Press, 1973.

Truong Rootham, Mireille M. 'Wittgenstein's Metaphysical Use and Derrida's Metaphysical Appurtenance'. *Philosophy & Social Criticism* 22 (1996): 27–46.

Uytterschout, Sien. 'An Extremely Loud Tin Drum. A Comparative Study of Jonathan Safran Foer's *Extremely Loud and Incredibly Close* and Gunter Grass's *The Tin Drum'. Comparative Literature Studies* 47, no. 2 (2010): 185–99.

Uytterschout, Sien and Kristiaan Versluys. 'Melancholy and Mourning in Jonathan Safran Foer's *Extremely Loud and Incredibly Close'. Orbis Litterarum* 63, no. 3 (2008): 216–36.

Vaessens, Thomas and Yra van Dijk. 'Introduction: European Writers Reconsidering the Postmodern Heritage'. In *Reconsidering the Postmodern. European Literature Beyond Relativism*, edited by Thomas Vaessens and Yra van Dijk, 7–23. Amsterdam: AUP, 2011.

Verstrynge, Karl. 'De autonomie van de esthetiek in Kierkegaards *Enten/Eller*. Over ledigheid en verveling'. *Algemeen Nederlands Tijdschrift voor Wijsbegeerte* 92, no. 4 (2000): 293–305.

Waldmeir, Joseph J. 'Introduction'. In *Critical Essays on John Barth*, edited by Joseph J. Waldmeir, i–xi. Boston: G.K. Hall & Co., 1980.

Warnock, Mary. *Existentialist Ethics*. London: MacMillan, 1967.

Waugh, Patricia. *Metafiction: The Theory and Practice of Self-Conscious Fiction*. London: Methuen, 1984.

Weber, Bruce. 'David Foster Wallace, Influential Writer, Dies at 46', *The New York Times*, 14 September 2008, http://www.nytimes.com/2008/09/15/books/15wallace.html.

Weldon, Fay. 'An Honest American Psycho', *The Guardian*, 25 April 1991, http://www.guardian.co.uk/books/1991/apr/25/fiction.breteastonellis.

Wheeler, Samuel C. 'Wittgenstein as Conservative Deconstructor'. *New Literary History* 19, no. 2 (1988): 239–59.

Wider, Kathleen. 'Hell and the Private Language Argument: Sartre and Wittgenstein on Self-Consciousness, the Body, and Others'. *Journal of the British Society for Phenomenology* 18, no. 2 (1987): 120–32.

—. 'A Nothing about Which Something Can Be Said: Sartre and Wittgenstein on the Self'. In *Sartre Alive*, edited by Ronald Aronson and Adrian van den Hoven, 324–39. Detroit: Wayne State University Press, 1991.

Wiley, David. 'Interview with David Foster Wallace', *The Minnesota Daily*, 27 February 1997, http://www.badgerinternet.com/~bobkat/jestwiley2.html.

Willemsen, Mariëtte F. 'Friedrich Nietzsches getuigenis: de waarachtigheid van een immoralist'. In *'Levensecht en bescheiden': essays over authenticiteit*, edited by Atie Th. Brüggemann-Kruijff, Henk G. Geertsema and Mariëtte F. Willemsen, 139–55. Kampen: Kok Agora, 1998.

Winch, Peter. 'Introduction: The Unity of Wittgenstein's Philosophy'. In *Studies in the Philosophy of Wittgenstein*, edited by Peter Winch, 1–19. London: Routledge & Kegan Paul, 1969.

Worthington, Marjorie. 'Done with Mirrors: Restoring the Authority Lost in John Barth's Funhouse'. *Twentieth-Century Literature* 47, no. 1 (2001): 114–36.

Young, Elizabeth. 'The Beast in the Jungle, the Figure in the Carpet'. In *Shopping in Space. Essays on America's Blank Generation Fiction*, edited by Elizabeth Young and Graham Caveney, 85–122. New York: Atlantic Monthly Press, 1993.

—. 'Children of the Revolution'. In *Shopping in Space. Essays on America's Blank Generation Fiction*, edited by Elizabeth Young and Graham Caveney, 1–20. New York: Atlantic Monthly Press, 1993.

—. 'Vacant Possession'. In *Shopping in Space. Essays on America's Blank Generation Fiction*, edited by Elizabeth Young and Graham Caveney, 21–42. New York: Atlantic Monthly Press, 1993.

Young, Elizabeth and Graham Caveney. 'Introduction'. In *Shopping in Space. Essays on America's Blank Generation Fiction*, edited by Elizabeth Young and Graham Caveney, i–iv. New York: Atlantic Monthly Press, 1993.

Index